Half a Century
of Scottish Deer Stalking

Half a Century
of Scottish Deer Stalking

G. Kenneth Whitehead

SWAN·HILL
PRESS

Copyright © 1996 G. Kenneth Whitehead

First published in the UK in 1996
by Swan Hill Press, an imprint of Airlife Publishing Ltd

British Library Cataloguing in Publication Data
  A catalogue record for this book
  is available from the British Library

ISBN 1 85310 731 X

Typeset by Litho Link Ltd, Welshpool, Powys, Wales.
Printed in England by Butler & Tanner Ltd, Frome and London.

Swan Hill Press
an imprint of Airlife Publishing Ltd
101 Longden Road, Shrewsbury, SY3 9EB England.

CONTENTS

ACKNOWLEDGEMENTS

But for the generosity and hospitality of numerous deer forest owners in Scotland who, during the past half century or so, have provided me with so many memorable days on their forest this book could never have been written. Although I have had the good fortune to meet many of the owners on their forest, there were others who, knowing my intense interest in deer and stalking, kindly made arrangements for me to have a day or two on the hill accompanied by their stalker. And there were also some who, due to shortage of staff, were prepared to allow me to venture, unaccompanied, on to the hill and when successful, return the following morning with a ponyman to collect the carcase. Hard work at times, but in those days I was young and fit.

Although my father, who was a good game shot and excellent with the rifle on the target, never had the slightest interest in deer, and it was my uncle, Sydney, who first introduced me to deerstalking. It happened in this way. I was staying with him for a week's grouse shooting at Skipness Castle on the Mull of Kintyre. There were, in addition to a good stock of grouse and blackgame, a number of sika and roe deer on the estate, and on the 27 August 1930, my uncle arranged for me to go out with Cameron, the head gamekeeper, to try for a stag. Eventually we spotted a good 8-point stag couched down in a patch of thick bracken, and as soon as it stood up, using Cameron's shoulder as a rifle rest, I hurriedly took a shot – the range being only about 80 yards. Unfortunately, the bullet struck its right antler breaking it off just above the brow tine. After rushing off some 50 yards until clear of the bracken the stag stopped, thus enabling me to take a second shot which proved more successful. I had now shot my first deer – the forerunner to several hundred more in Scotland, not to mention those taken elsewhere in the World.

Two years later, coincidently on the same date 27 August, I had my second success at Skipness, but on this occasion, owing to shortage of staff, I was sent out completely on my own. Late that evening an elated and somewhat bloodstained young stalker was able to report to his uncle that *two* carcases had been left out on the hill and would have to be collected the following morning.

This report, I am afraid, received a rather mixed reception for not only had my late arrival back somewhat delayed a dinner party, but plans for a grouse shoot on the following morning would now have to be modified so as to allow time for the carcases to be recovered. Nevertheless, I am sure he was proud of his nephew who had now been made a stalker for life.

It is said that on occasions, 'good' comes out of 'evil' and there is no doubt that but for the War, myself and many other keen amateur stalkers would not have had the opportunity to stalk on a number of forests which, in the absence of the professional staff on military service, were only too prepared to allow a reliable 'shot' to assist in their deer cull. Stalking during the War years was purely a culling operation, and since numbers of carcases in the larder were of more importance than a trophy for the wall, one did not have much time to be too selective on what was shot, particularly when, on occasions, five or six carcases were required in the larder that evening. Fortunately, since most of my army service was spent in Britain, this allowed me to spend my autumn and winter leaves stalking somewhere in Scotland, the most enjoyable and successful two separate weeks being spent at *Forest Lodge* Blair Atholl in 1942 and 1943, when 14 and 23 stags respectively were shot, the stalkers on these visits being McLeod and Macdonald in 1942 and Macdonald and Stewart the following year.

For a number of years prior to his tragic death as a result of a shooting accident at Endsleigh, Devon, in 1953, I regularly used to spend a few days, each October, at *Cairnsmore*, in Galloway, as a guest of Hastings, Duke of Bedford. Although keen on bird shooting, the Duke, who was a great naturalist, would never shoot at a deer as he considered himself not sufficiently accurate with a rifle to do it humanely. Nevertheless, he enjoyed his days on the hill, and would often accompany me and Nicholson, his stalker, being very selective – in fact too selective, at times – on what was allowed to be shot!

About this period, for a number of years, I was fortunate enough to be invited to stalk at *Strathconon*

(Ross-shire), as a guest of Peter Combe, and although, unfortunately, he was by then confined to his bed, on my return to the lodge each evening from a day on the hill, after a bath and suitable liquid refreshment, we always had an interesting hour or two discussing the day's events, and when I got home to Lancashire, we were able to maintain our mutual interest in deer and stalking by frequent correspondence.

Two other once active stalkers who, alas, had to spend their final days confined to bed were David and Penelope Bowlby, and I am eternally grateful to both for the many days between 1961 and 1976 spent at *Inverinate*, stalking the stags in the steep corries of *West Benula*. Alas, following their once active life, their final days in the world could not have been more tragic – Pen dying of multiple sclerosis, whilst David, as a result of an unsuccessful eye operation, becoming totally blind. Worse, however, was to follow, for within a few years he also had to have both legs amputated from about the knee.

For a number of years between 1958 and 1961, I was a guest each season of Leslie and Bunty Hunt, the one-time owners of the *Invergarry Hotel*, Fort Augustus, who rented five or six forests in order to provide stalking for guests staying in their hotel, and this gave me the opportunity to stalk on a number of new forests, accompanied by different stalkers, in the hills around Loch Ness. The Hunts were delightful and kind hosts, and being a keen stalker herself, Bunty knew exactly what her guests required when they returned wet and hungry from the hill.

One of the forests rented by this Hotel was nearby *Culachy*, which was then owned by N.J.W. Usher, and who subsequently sold the estate to Ian Biggs. Both Ian and his wife, Audrey, are keen stalkers and during the last twenty years I have enjoyed many happy days on the hill in their company.

Between 1968 and 1990 – many visits were made to *Glencarron* (Ross-shire) – first as a guest of Toby Sladen, and more recently of his son Angus – and I have many happy memories of stalking on this delightful forest, particularly on the *Glenuig* beat.

During this period, by way of contrast to the steep terrain of the west coast, I enjoyed many happy days stalking at *Dunbeath* (Caithness) as the guest of Hi and Hellie Blythe – two delightful visitors from California, who rented this forest for a number of years before it was eventually sold to R. Stanton-Avery. Hellie was a keen and efficient stalker, which was in contrast to her husband who seemed to prefer ranching in California to crawling after deer in Caithness! Whilst staying at *Dunbeath* I received a number of invitations to stalk on the neighbouring forests of *Braemore* and *Langwell*, and it was always an enjoyable experience to stalk on these two Portland Estate forests.

Other forest owners to whom I owe a special debt of gratitude for some wonderful days on their forests include Anne (Nancy) Duchess of Westminster (*Gobernuisgach* and *Lochmore* 1981, '83, '90), H.C. Birkbeck (*Kinloch Hourn* 1988), Anthony Hignett (*Kildermorie* 1969, '83, '93), Count Adam Knuth (*Ben Loyal* 1993), Lord Leverhulme (*Badanloch* 1985), Lt.-Colonel Douglas Moncrieff (*Kinloch* and *Strathmore* 1948, '49, 53), Viscount Mountgarrett (*Wyvis* 1974), Major R. Pilkington (*Dalnacardoch* 1961, '63, '65, '66, '67), E.M.W. Robson (*Erchless* 1990), James Teacher (*Fealar* 1995), George Wood (*Badanloch* 1949) and J.M. Wotherspoon (*Affaric* 1955).

Irrespective of whether the visits have been frequent, long or short, all have been equally rewarding, and to one and all of these kind hosts – some of whom, alas, are no longer with us – I can only repeat my sincere thanks for having enabled me to have such an enjoyable *Half a Century of Scottish Deer Stalking* at its best.

G. Kenneth WHITEHEAD

The author with an 11-pointer shot on *Fealar*, Perthshire (1995)

INTRODUCTION

I t was in 1930 that I was first introduced to deerstalking, and since then deer and deerstalking, both with rifle and camera, have been my main interest in life. During these sixty years or so I have witnessed many changes, both in deer management and the manner in which the modern stalker goes about his business.

Compared to pre-War, mechanisation has undoubtedly brought about the biggest change in Scottish stalking, for in those early days stalkers had to rely on the pony (garron) not only to carry them to the hill but also to act as transport for the carcase to be conveyed back to the larder in the evening. Unless, therefore, a carcase was left out on the hill for collection the following morning, this strictly limited the number of deer that could be shot in a day. Today, with suitable transport, up to half-a-dozen deer carcases can be retrieved in a day on suitable terrain even though a double journey may sometimes be required.

Pre-War the majority of deer carcases reaching the larder had to be skinned, resulting in staff having to work well into the night. Today, only those carcases required for the house or gifts to guests etc. will be skinned, and entire unskinned carcases, complete with 'pluck' but minus head and feet, will be collected daily by a game dealer's van.

Before the War, on some of the larger forests and even astride a pony, it was impossible regularly to reach some of the more distant corries and, as a result, there were many areas in the highlands that were seldom stalked and which, as a consequence,

became sanctuaries, allowing many a stag to reach maturity before perhaps wandering on to hostile territory and paying the price.

With mechanical transport these 'safe areas' have virtually disappeared and, even if the deer have not been disturbed by stalkers, they probably will have been by hikers, climbers and bikers. There are, therefore, no 'safe areas' and, as a consequence, fewer stags are now able to reach maturity.

Prior to the War, and before many of the larger estates had been broken up into smaller units, one owner was able to take a personal interest and control over a large area, deciding what deer were to be shot and, more important still, what stags were to be left on the forest for breeding. In a large forest a spared stag was less likely to run into trouble than on the same area now split up into smaller units, where it is continually crossing marches and putting its life at risk.

Today, stalking over much of Scotland is being organised by sporting agencies whose dual and difficult interests are to satisfy both owners and clients – the two not necessarily being in agreement over the class of stag to be shot.

Owing to constant inflation, stalking costs, stretching over half a century, are more difficult to compare. In 1950 a day's stalking from a hotel would have cost about £25. In 1994 a number of estates were offering stalking at £200 per stag plus VAT. Because of inflation these figures are only comparable when converted and, according to a letter (9/11/94) from Barclays Bank, '£50 today would have been worth £865.62 in 1950 and

£387.53 in 1970.' At the above rate of conversion a £25 stag in 1950 would be equivalent to £433 in today's currency value, so on this basis the cost of a £200 stag today is cheaper.

Prior to the War few stalking rifles were equipped with a telescope sight, and indeed a number of the older generation considered their use to be a 'trifle unsporting'. Today the 'scope is the norm and many modern stalking rifles are no longer equipped with an open sight, with the result that crawls in approaching deer are shorter and shots longer.

There has also been a change in clothing, and whilst woollen tweeds and leather boots are still much favoured by the older generation these are gradually being replaced by waterproofed fabrics and rubber boots.

By 1945 I had begun to realize how badly deer were being treated in this country, with no close-season, poaching widespread and any method or weapon justified to bring about their demise.

This ill-treatment of deer then became a major concern of mine, and in numerous articles to the press I made repeated proposals as to how their status could be improved. One of my early recommendations was to stress the urgency of legalised close-seasons, and an early article on this subject appeared in *Country Life* (7/4/50). Nevertheless, we still had to wait another twelve years before the Deer Scotland Act 1959 was eventually passed, the close-season clause of which did not become effective until 21 October 1962. Since then – unless considered marauders – stags have enjoyed a close-season from 21 October to 30 June, and hinds from 16 February to 20 October, as compared with my original suggested dates of 15 October–30 June (stags) and 1 March–31 October (hinds).

Close-seasons for deer were not, however the cure to all ills, and in an article to *Oryx* – the

Journal of the Fauna Preservation Society – entitled '*The Problems of a Close season for Deer*' (1953), further suggestions included:

1 Formation of Deer Control Associations (D.C.A.) in every county in which deer are present.
2 Each D.C.A. should institute an annual census in its county.
3 Deer carcases should be tagged.
4 Venison retailers must be licensed to deal *only* with tagged carcases.
5 Grading of deer carcases should be considered.

Forty years on – apart from the vexed question of carcase-tagging (*see* Chapter 21) – it would appear that most of my proposals, in some form or another, have now been adopted. Instead of D.C.A.s we have D.M.G.s (Deer Management Groups), the majority of which do undertake an annual census. And venison dealers are licensed.

Not surprisingly, I derive considerable satisfaction from the knowledge that most of my views and proposals expressed over the years have now been largely adopted, and it would seem that the main problem for the future will undoubtedly have to be a more enlightened attitude to population and sex ratio control.

Note: This book is a compilation of the author's annual reviews on the Scottish deer stalking seasons since 1948, and of other relevant articles that have appeared in the following sporting journals: *Country Life, The Field, Shooting Times and Country Magazine*, and *Stalking Magazine* (*see* Bibliography).

Individual reports have been submitted annually by owners and/or tenants on a standard questionnaire form (*see* next page) which was distributed during September of each year.

ERRATA

REVIEW OF DEER STALKING SEASON OF 19....

1. Name of Forest...
2. Name and address of Owner ....
   ....
   ....
3. Name and address of tenant (if applicable)..
   ....
   ....
4. Name of Head Stalker ....
5. Total number of stags killed..
6. Average weight .... stone .... lb., (with OR without heart and liver)
7. Weight of two heaviest stags: .... stone .... lb., ... stone .... lb.
8. Measurement of any heads worth recording:

Number of Points		Length		Beam*		Inside Span †	Shot by	Remarks (if any)
Left	Right	Left	Right	Left	Right			
i.								
ii.								
iii.								
iv.								

* The beam should be measured at the **smallest** circumference between the bay and tray, or between brow and tray if bay point is missing.

† Measured at widest distance **between** the two antlers - **not** overall spread.

9. Rut. A few general remarks on date it commenced, etc.
   ....
   ....
   ....
10. Condition of Deer.
   ....
   ....
   ....
11. Weather conditions.
   ....
   ....
   ....
12. Number of hummels on ground or seen during season...
    Number of hummels shot ....
13. Number of hinds killed during last season ....
14. General Remarks - Any general remarks with regard to natural history, unusual incidents etc. Any good photographs would be welcome.
   ....
   ....
   ....
   ....
   ....
   ....
   ....

Signature...

When complete please return as soon as possible to **G. Kenneth Whitehead**,
The Old House, Withnell Fold, Nr. Chorley, Lancs PR6 8AZ. Tel. 01254 830444

PART I:
STALKING – GENERAL

CHAPTER 1

Be Prepared

Each autumn an increasing number of sportsmen and women from both the UK and overseas – and in particular from the USA – travel to Scotland for a day or two after the stag, and for many it will be their first introduction to an exciting and exacting sport that is unique to the Scottish highlands. Yet it is surprising how few of them bother to take any target practice, and I am sure that if they did, better shooting would result. Some may only have the chance to fire at three or four stags per season – some even fewer – and this small number of shots in a year is unlikely to keep anyone in the best of form. Target practice is not only to familiarise the shooter with his weapon, recoil, trigger pressure etc., but also to assure him that the rifle and scope are properly zeroed, so that should any miss occur, the fault will be with the shooter and not the rifle. Accidents do happen, and even though the rifle may have been shooting 'spot on' at the end of the previous season, the 'scope *may* have received a jolt during the journey to or from Scotland. So it is always prudent to make sure at the beginning of the holiday, rather than have it spoilt by poor marksmanship.

Target Practice

Among the earlier writers on the sport, opinions differed as to the merits of target practice for a deer stalker. W. Scrope, for instance, who by his writings probably did more than anyone else to popularise deerstalking, thought that target practice was a waste of time. In *The Art of Deerstalking* (1839) he states, 'having once become a fair shot at the target, I would advise no-one to continue the practice. It is apt to make one slow and indecisive.' Patrick R. Chalmers, in *Deerstalking* (1935), thought it a good thing to have 'half a dozen shots at a target on the morning of the first day of a season', whilst Lady Breadalbane, in *The High Tops of Black Mount* (1907), stated that 'during all the years I have been deerstalking, throughout the whole season I have gone regularly to the target, holding that no amount of trouble is too great which may help to fewer wounded stags, fewer misses and fewer disappointments to the stalkers and oneself.' I endorse every word of that.

Personally, I always like to fire a number of shots at a target, before both the roe-stalking season in May and the stags in autumn. The reason for this is that, although the same rifle is used for both animals, the position from which the shot has to be taken often differs considerably. For instance, in roe stalking, a shot from a sitting or standing position has generally to be taken, whilst for the stag in Scotland it is usually a prone shot.

Although good grouping on the target will not necessarily ensure similar results on deer, it will at least satisfy you that should a miss occur, it is not due to any fault of the rifle but the man behind it! Indeed, the fact that someone is a first-class target shot does not necessarily mean that he will be a first-class deer shot, and I have known a Bisley winner take about ten attempts to kill his first deer in Scotland. The reason for such a poor performance at the live target is that distressing complaint known as 'stag-fever', which is brought on purely by the shooter being over-anxious to succeed. No one seems to be immune from it, but doubtless at Bisley, with an inanimate target, it is of a less virulent type.

Assuming that the rifle and 'scope have been correctly zeroed *by yourself*, there are a number of things that can be done to improve one's shooting.

Rifle Support

First of all, don't be ashamed of using a rest, which could be a peat hag, telescope or binocular case, a rolled-up rifle cover or even your companion's backside. Should it be a rock or hard surface, be sure to have a hand between the rifle and this, and hold the rifle *firmly* – don't just lay the weapon on your hand for, when firing, the recoil will throw the barrel up and a high shot will result. Some people, whenever possible, will grasp with the supporting hand a clump of growing grass or heather along with the barrel, and this helps to reduce any upward flip of the barrel.

Apropos 'rifle flip', I once went stalking with an American who had only one arm. When firing the rifle, a fork stick was used as support and, provided targets within about 110 yards (100 m) were selected, results were extremely good. One day I myself tried his rifle on the target and found that, with normal aim, all my shots were low due to the fact that my grip with the left hand was exerting some control on the 'flip' of the rifle. It will be realised, therefore, that a rifle carefully zeroed by one person will not necessarily, due to difference in grip, be 'spot on' for anyone else. So it is *essential* that everyone should sight-in his or her own rifle, and never rely on this being done by someone else.

Some sportsmen – mostly from overseas – use a small portable and adjustable support on which to rest the rifle, and this can be useful when shooting over long heather or grass etc. In my opinion, however, gadgets of this sort are probably unnecessary for, as mentioned above, one can generally find something else to use as a rest. Not only do these contraptions take time to get into position, but they constitute another piece of equipment to carry and possibly lose on the hill. A binocular case, for instance, measuring perhaps $7 \times 8 \times 3$ in ($18 \times 20 \times 8$ cm) does provide one with a variation in height support to choose from, whilst a conventional telescope case will give up to about 11 in (28 cm) of firm support. On one occasion a stalker was not amused when a visitor from Germany asked him to carry on to the hill a collapsible canvas seat from which he normally shot his deer in Germany.

In most firing positions, particularly in a high wind, the use of a sling will be found invaluable in helping to hold the rifle steady. Assuming a shot is to be taken from the right shoulder, the left arm will be placed from outside in between the rifle and sling and then, with the sling running from the elbow over the forearm to the wrist, and with the left hand grasping the rifle in the normal way, the sling, provided it has been adjusted to the correct length to suit the man using it, will be found to give an excellent support to both the elbow and wrist. Positions, of course, are reversed if shooting from the left shoulder.

For accurate shooting it is, of course, essential that the rifle is held perfectly upright, and when using a telescope sight beware of being influenced by horizons in relation to the horizontal reticule. When firing, gently squeeze rather than pull or jerk the trigger and, when doing so, take a deep breath and hold it until the shot is fired.

The cheek plays an important part in helping to hold the rifle steady and, when using open sights, the stock will – or should – fit comfortably against the cheek. When a telescope sight is fitted above the open sight, unless the head is raised about 1–1½ in (3 cm), it will be impossible to see through the 'scope at all. The stock is, therefore, no longer a good fit with the cheek and, in consequence, one has great difficulty in holding the rifle really steady. This is one of the reasons why good shots with the open sight are sometimes indifferent performers with the telescope sight.

The Germans have long appreciated this, and some of their rifles are provided with a rising cheek-piece which jumps into position on pressing a button, thus providing a good support for the shooter's cheek. I, personally, have made a small wooden attachment about 8½ in (22 cm) long which raises the cheek level by about 1¼ in (3 cm). This attachment is held in place by means of two split pins which enable it to be quickly clamped in position. The overall length of this attachment is really governed by the amount of room required to remove the rifle bolt, for it mustn't foul this mechanism. Unless one removes this attachment one cannot, of course, use the open sight, as the head will be too high. The detachable cheek-piece has to be carefully planed down to suit the user's cheek, for few cheeks have a standard profile.

Telescope Sight

The 'scope should be mounted low on the rifle so that the line of sight is as near as possible to the line of bore, and on most rifles it should be possible to do this to within about 1¼ in (3 cm). With a very low mounting, however, no provision can be made to use the open sight with the 'scope *in situ*, as is possible with the 'scope mounted on stilts.

Trigger Pressure

There is no doubt that trigger pressure plays an important part in shooting, and is mainly responsible for indifferent shooting by an established good shot when using a strange weapon. Generally speaking it can be said that the lighter the pressure the easier it is to shoot accurately, the ultimate being the set-trigger – often referred to as the hair-trigger. Whilst a set-trigger is best for shooting from a high seat, it cannot be considered safe for stalking deer under Scottish conditions, which involve a considerable amount of crawling. Unless the user of the rifle is *completely* familiar with the workings of a 'set-trigger' and how to make it safe once set, accidental discharge can easily occur.

Set-trigger (hair-trigger)

The set-trigger, which is a small lever similar in appearance to the normal trigger, is fitted to some continental rifles, being situated either immediately before or after the normal trigger, requiring a forward or backward pressure to activate the firing mechanism. Once set, only a feather-light pressure is required to fire the rifle.

The set-trigger is much favoured by European sportsmen, being particularly useful when firing from a high seat, or for long-range shooting as when after chamois. Owing to the chance, however, of accidental discharge once the trigger has been set, it is a dangerous mechanism for any shooting that involves crawling, as in Scottish stalking.

During the 1987 stalking season on *Glenshee* forest (Perthshire), Ronnie Hepburn, the stalker, had a lucky escape, for during a stalk, in an attempt to stop a stag from walking away and thus give the *Rifle* a chance to shoot at a stationary target, he gave a vocal roar which not only startled the stag but also the *Rifle*, causing him to touch the trigger which had already been set, and so discharge the rifle. The result was, of course, a complete miss, but the incident highlighted the dangers of this sort of mechanism for hill stalking in Scotland.

I am of the opinion, therefore, that a conventional firing mechanism with a trigger pressure of not more than 3½ lb (1.5 kg) is probably ideal for all deer shooting in Britain, and I would not object if the set-trigger mechanism, on safety grounds alone, was made illegal for stalking in Scotland.

Many new rifles, when supplied, may have a trigger set at 6 to 7 lb (2.7 to 3 kg) so when taking over a new weapon one of the first tests before sighting-in should be to have the trigger pressure tested and adjusted to your choice.

Most sporting rifles are fitted with a standard trigger which is somewhat straighter in design than the 'match-shoot' trigger. The amount of digital pressure required will vary in accordance with which part of the trigger the pressure is being applied to. For instance, far less pressure is required if it is applied to the trigger at its tip rather than near the base. With the deeper, curving match-trigger, its shape helps to ensure that digital pressure, whether in summer or begloved in winter, is always applied at the same point, which is not always the case with the straighter trigger. I have, therefore, had match-triggers fitted to all my rifles, and, since having also standardised on 3½ lb (1.5 kg) pressure, results have been very rewarding.

Zeroing the Rifle

Zeroing a rifle means just that, and when the last shot at the target has been made *that* shot *must* be in the target area. Otherwise, further shooting at the target will be necessary. It is not sufficient to go to the hill in the knowledge that your rifle is shooting, say, 3 in (7.6 cm) high or low, left or right at 100 metres, for although some allowance in aim can be made, unless you are expert in judging range, the allowance for distances over 100 metres will have to be increased proportionally.

Having decided upon the type of ammunition – manufacturer, weight, soft-nosed, hollow-nosed or silver-tipped etc. – that suits your requirements, *stick* to it and whenever a fresh supply is received, check the batch number.

Should it be different to the previous batch, then it is a wise precaution to test it on the range, for mass-produced factory supplies can vary slightly from time to time. This is particularly important when the fresh batch comes from a different manufacturer.

It is essential that any sighting-in should be carried out with the *actual* cartridge and bullet to be used on the hill. It is useless to sight-in with a cartridge that has a different bullet weight or different muzzle velocity.

People who are unfamiliar with ballistics do not realise the extent to which a bullet will fall once it has passed the 100-metre mark, which is the ideal range at which to shoot a deer. A hundred metres is the range at which a rifle is generally zeroed and is also the range at which a newcomer to the hill will probably be tested out before being allowed to shoot at a stag.

Before the War, in the pre-telescope sight days, anyone getting a good group with open or iron sights on the 100-yard (90 m) range target, would probably perform equally well on the hill, for there was not the same temptation to shoot at longer ranges, when the distinctive features of a deer would be barely discernible at, say, 200 yards (182 m) or greater. Now, however, with the telescope sight, and in particular one of the varipower models, the crosswires look as clear behind the shoulder of a stag at about 250 metres as at half this range, and the *Rifle* is, therefore, tempted to shoot, not realising that by the time the bullet reaches the target it may well have dropped 10–12 in (25-30 cm) below the point of aim. The result, hopefully, will be a miss, but more than likely a stag with a broken foreleg will be seen to limp away.

For woodland stalking, sighting-in at about 90 metres is probably the ideal range, for few shots will be taken beyond this. Indeed, the majority will be nearer 70 metres, when the difference between point of aim and strike is less than about 1.5 cm. For the open hill, however, 200 metres is the best range for sighting-in. Even when a shot has to be taken at half this distance, the line of flight of a bullet weighing 150 grain or less will not be more than about 2½ in (6.3 cm) higher, and this would certainly account for the deer.

Even if you are in practice, should you ever have to borrow a strange rifle it is essential that a few rounds should be fired at a target before proceeding to the hill. It is also prudent to take too many rather than too few cartridges to the hill, for one can easily empty the magazine should, unhappily, a wounded beast have to be followed up, when every opportunity *within reason and range* will have to be taken to ensure its demise.

Cartridges

As to the number of cartridges one should take, this will obviously depend on the number of deer you expect to kill in the day. On a large forest the stalking party may take to the hill with, perhaps, a Snowcat vehicle or four ponies, and with reasonable luck and straight shooting may be back in the larder that evening with four deer carcases. Anyone, therefore, having the opportunity to shoot four stags – or hinds for that matter – in the day would be well advised to take about twenty rounds of ammunition. For a lesser number of deer, about ten should be ample. This does not mean that one expects to expend five rounds on every beast shot. One should normally use only one or two, but accidents do sometimes happen and it is always comforting to have a few spare rounds available, especially when – God forbid – a beast with a broken leg has to be dealt with and which may entail one or two 'running' shots. To deal with such an unfortunate event, David James, M.P. – the father of the present owner of *Glenforsa* forest, Isle of Mull – always took twenty-seven rounds with him on to the hill: not, he stated, because he believed 'in the magic power of the cube of three,' but because he liked to put 'five rounds into the magazine, three into each of his four waistcoat pockets, where they could not rattle and their weight would be evenly distributed, and a spare box of ten in the lunch bag'.

As to the number of rounds in the magazine, unless one is expecting to have more than one shot following a stalk, such as when shooting hinds, I prefer to have four rather than five in a five-round magazine, as this will avoid having the spring under constant near-maximum tension.

Should you at any time be reduced to your last cartridge, *never* fire it at a fresh beast, for should it be wounded, you will be powerless to prevent it escaping.

'Scope Reticle

Telescope sights are supplied with a variety of reticles, ranging from broad posts and aiming spots, to a fine hair-line cross which may only be visible in good light. My own preference is for a combination of fine crosswires for precision shooting in good light, and stout posts to assist in shooting during the failing light of dawn and dusk. Some manufacturers refer to this arrangement as the No. 4 reticle.

The No. 4 reticle is also useful as a range finder. For instance, with a $4 \times$ power 'scope – which is the recommended maximum magnification for all deer stalking in the British Isles – if the body of a highland stag, standing about 42 in (106 cm), fills

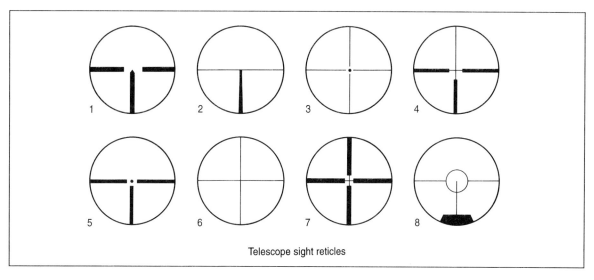

Telescope sight reticles

the space between the two lateral pillars, then the range is probably not further than about 125 yards (114 m). But should the body of the deer only fill the space between one lateral pillar and the fine vertical line, then the range will not be less than 250 yards (228 m). So, if the latter is the picture you see through the 'scope, think twice about taking an agitated stalker's plea to "take him now"!

Much of deerstalking is really common sense and this can only be gained from experience in the field – in other words, trial and error is the best tutor.

Moreover, particularly in woodland stalking, one must always be mindful of the fact that the last chance of a shot before the light fails in an evening is also the best chance to lose a wounded animal. So, if there is any doubt, don't take it. The fact that it may be your last chance that day does not, in any way, mitigate the circumstances, for no shot should ever be taken unless the outcome is as certain as it can be. Remember, there is always a tomorrow – or even the day following should the next one be a Sunday.

The Boy Scout motto – 'Be prepared' – should also be that of the deer stalker, for preparation and attention to detail – which includes not only constant zeroing and the restraint not to take chances, but also one's own physical condition – is the key to success.

Safety with Firearms

One cannot be too careful with firearms. Once the shot has been taken and stalking finished for the day, the magazine *must* be emptied before the rifle is returned to its cover.

On some forests the rifle may only be in the hands of a guest when the actual shot is being taken, the rifle having been passed to him by the stalker on arrival at the firing point. If the shot has been successful, and no further stalking that day is contemplated, then the chamber and magazine must be completely emptied before the rifle is returned to its cover.

To show how easily an accident can happen, I remember one incident which happened a few years ago whilst staying as a guest on one of the larger deer forests. On this forest, where it was possible to send out two or three rifles each day, on the return to the lodge after stalking it was the general practice for guests to leave their rifles on the hall table for collection by one of the staff, to be taken to the gunroom for cleaning. On this particular occasion the stalking parties were gathered around the sitting-room fire, for a drink and talk about events of the day, before proceeding upstairs for a bath and change, when a loud bang was heard coming from the hall. Apparently a live round had been left in the breech of one of the guest rifles which, whilst being lifted off the table, had been discharged. Fortunately the rifle barrel was pointing upwards and the only damage was a hole in the ceiling, but the result could easily have been a fatal accident. I do not know whether the guest responsible for the accident was invited to stalk there again!

Apropos cleaning rifles; this is a chore which I insist on doing myself, for I am then certain that it has been done to my satisfaction and the 'scope setting not interfered with. Quite apart from a rifle and 'scope being accidently knocked or dropped, it is not unknown, I fear, for an inquisitive – or malicious – individual to play about with the reticle setting on a 'scope, and so upset its accuracy.

CLOSE SEASON DATES FOR DEER
all dates inclusive

	Scotland (1)	England & Wales (2)
RED DEER		
stags	21 Oct.–30 June	1 May–31 July
hinds	16 Feb.–20 Oct.	1 March–31 Oct.
SIKA DEER		
stags	21 Oct. 30 June (3)	1 May–31 July
hinds	16 Feb.–20 Oct.	1 March–31 Oct.
RED/SIKA HYBRID		
stags	21 Oct.–30 June (3)	1 May–31 July
hinds	16 Feb.–20 Oct.	1 March–31 Oct.
FALLOW DEER		
bucks	1 May–31 July (3)	1 May–31 July
does	16 Feb.–20 Oct.	1 March–31 Oct.
ROE DEER		
bucks	21 Oct.–31 March (3)	1 Nov–31 March
does	1 Apr–20 Oct. (3)	1 March–31 Oct.
MUNTJAC		
bucks } does	No legal close season. Recommended both sexes should have close season 1 March–31 Oct.	
CHINESE WATER-DEER		
bucks } does	No legal close season. Recommended both sexes should have close season 1 March–31 Oct.	

1. Under the *Deer (Scotland)* Act 1959
2. Under the *Deer Act* 1991
3. Under the *Deer (Close Seasons) (Scotland)* Order 1984

Note: A deer may only be killed during the close season by the occupier of the land or an *authorised* person if it can be shown that serious damage was, or would be, caused to crops, growing timber, etc.

CHAPTER 2

Hit or Miss

There is an old hunter's saying that 'a good stag deserves a good shot' - an opinion that is true for every living creature, which should never become a target until the rifle has been correctly zeroed. Even when the rifle has been zeroed, a little target practice is certainly not a waste of time or cartridge for, apart from anything else, it does enable one to become familiar with the trigger pressure - so essential for accurate shooting.

Sixty years ago, on the comparatively few occasions when a deer forest owner decided to let his forest, he did so only on a long-term tenancy spread over a number of years. Today this situation has largely changed and many owners, anxious to obtain some revenue from their estate, are now prepared to let stalking on short-term tenancies, varying in period from perhaps a month to a week, or even a day or two. Many of these short-term tenancies are handled by one of the sporting agencies. In many cases some of these short-term tenants are out on the forest to shoot their first stag and will probably have to hire or borrow a rifle. Not unnaturally, due to unfamiliarity with the weapon, 'stag fever' or just poor physical condition to face the Scottish mountains, the shooting – and in some cases the tenant's behaviour on the hill – can sometimes leave a lot to be desired, as reported in some of the seasonal returns received in some years.

In the majority of lettings, before embarking on a stalk, the client is required to fire a few rounds at a target. Good results on the target do not, unfortunately, always guarantee similar results on the hill, and misses or – worse still – a wounded stag have been the result. In fact the return I received from one forest read rather like a War Office casualty memo, with separate figures given for beasts killed as well as those wounded and lost. The following is but one example of what occurred on a well-known northern forest.

Missed Shots and Wounded Deer

Two tenants from England had taken three days stalking during which, by sharing the same stalker, each could shoot one stag per day. It was not their first experience of deerstalking in Scotland and both acquitted themselves well on the target.

On the first day, after two misses, one of the *Rifles* shot a calf by mistake, and then proceeded to empty his magazine on the retreating stag, fortunately without contact.

The second day was even more disastrous, resulting in three wounded stags, two of which, fortunately, were eventually accounted for. The first beast was shot in the chest, the bullet passing between the shoulder blade and ribs. After the shot the stag ran off, but after travelling a short distance was seen to lie down, so a fresh stalk was made, the *Rifle* insisting that he himself should give it the final shot. Unfortunately, at only a few yards range, the shot went high, breaking off an antler and causing the stag to bolt off, and when last seen it had crossed over on to the neighbouring forest.

The next stalk resulted in a stag running off with a broken jaw, but on this occasion a re-stalk was possible and the beast accounted for by the stalker. There was still time for another stalk, but once again a wounded beast was the result, the stag escaping with a stomach wound on to the neighbouring forest. It was not surprising, therefore, that the clients were refused their third day's stalking, the stalkers having to go out to search for the two wounded beasts. Fortunately the one with the shoulder injury was accounted for, but the other was not seen again, in all probability having succumbed during the night from its injury.

With the modern precision rifle it is seldom that a beast is able to survive more than two or three attempts on its life, but on a Sutherland forest in the early 1950s there was a one-antlered stag with a misplaced pedicle that was missed on no less than twenty-two occasions and, by the end of the 1951 season, had still managed to survive. What the eventual fate of this stag was I never heard, but by then he should surely have qualified for a reprieve – or maybe he was like the 'phantom stag' that required a silver bullet (*see* page 58).

In 1964 a young *Rifle*, during his one and only day's stalking, had four complete misses before making contact on his fifth target, but even so a further nine shots were required before the unfortunate stag was eventually accounted for.

On another forest a guest had four misses on consecutive days before, on his fifth day on the hill, a stag was wounded and had to be finally finished off by the stalker. On this particular forest the owner estimated that, but for the misses, a further fifteen carcasses would have reached the larder (1964).

In the following year two *Rifles* shared a beat on *Killiechonate* forest (Inverness-shire), and when eventually a stag was spotted, one of the *Rifles*, accompanied by the head stalker, began a stalk, whilst the other *Rifle* remained behind with the under-stalker. In due course the stalking party got within range of the stag and a shot was taken which resulted in a miss, whereupon the stag ran off in the direction of the other *Rifle* who killed it. It was not this stag's lucky day!

During the same season a stalking party had successfully approached a stag on *Glenlochsie* (Perthshire), and a shot was about to be taken when the animal suddenly collapsed. It had, apparently, been wounded on a neighbouring forest and had wandered over the march before dying on *Glenlochsie*.

During the 1971 season a young guest, using a borrowed rifle that was fitted only with an open sight, had already proved his marksmanship by killing three stags with successive shots on his first day out. Alas, this accuracy was not to last, for on the following day no less than ten shots hit the dust without drawing blood. On this occasion one stag was obliging enough to allow five shots to be fired at it before moving on. It did not travel far and a further stalk was made, ending in similar fashion to the first with five shots again missing the target. Unfortunately for the stag, however, he played his luck too long, for an accompanying *Rifle* brought about his downfall. For the remainder of the week the young guest was able to borrow an estate rifle that was fitted with a telescope sight, and no further misses occurred.

During the 1978 season one particular stag was stalked on five separate occasions within a fortnight, during which time it was shot at four times before being accounted for. On the first occasion there was a clean miss. A day or so later it was unfortunately wounded by a guest, but not too badly, and managed to get away. A week later the same stag was seen holding hinds and, apart from a slight limp, appeared little the worse. On this occasion, owing to intervening hinds, it was not possible to get a clear shot before it moved off. Two days later the stag was missed again but did not travel far, and after a further stalk was eventually shot. On examination, the stag was found to be suffering from little worse than a flesh wound at the top of the off side foreleg, and so had not been seriously incapacitated.

On the subject of misses, since the introduction of the telescopic sight to Scottish stalking, there is little doubt that longer shots are now being taken than was the practice pre-War with the old iron or open sight, and although a good shot can regularly kill his stag at ranges up to 200 yards (180 m), this is beyond the capabilities – although often attempted – of the beginner. Furthermore, the telescopic sight is a delicate instrument which can so easily be knocked out of zero, and even the best rifle shot in the world may not be aware of this until a shot has been fired – and should a miss or wounded beast result, it is not really due to any bad shooting but faulty equipment. All rifles fitted with a telescopic sight should, therefore, be *frequently* zeroed at a target, and it is surprising – and worrying at times – how often some slight adjustment will have to be made.

Occasionally in the press one reads reports of someone boasting of having killed a stag at 500 yards (457 m). He may well have done so but it was a fluke and not good shooting, for there is no definite point of aim at this distance unless the rifle has been zeroed for such extreme ranges and it is, therefore, pure guesswork on the amount required to aim above the beast for the bullet to hit the target area.

Fines for Missing and Wounding

In some parts of eastern Europe the fine for wounding a trophy deer that is not recovered is often based on half the assumed monetary figure the trophy was expected to achieve – a figure which could well run into £1,000 or more.

In Scotland a penalty fine is levied by the Forestry Commission in some areas, for both a missed shot and one that results in a wounded deer that is not recovered. There is, however, not a great deal of difference in the fine for either event – the fine for a complete miss being £20, which will be increased to £25 if the deer has been hit but subsequently lost. In England, whilst the penalty for a complete miss remains the same, the fine for a wounded deer that is not recovered will be £50.

Regarding wounded deer, the following instructions apply: A deer is slightly wounded and, although there is evidence of a hit by the presence of hair, there is no blood trail to follow, so it will be assumed that the injury is only light and the deer will recover. On the other hand, if from evidence of a strong blood trail the deer would appear to have been severely wounded and a follow-up is essential, any time spent over and above the standard three-hour outing time will be added to the £25 penalty charge, at the rate of £15 per hour.

'John Macnab'

During 1985 two letters appeared in *The Field* (14 September) and the *Shooting Times* (5 September) from David Bishop, describing how his 15-year-old son had managed to obtain the prestigious 'John Macnab' – a salmon, grouse and stag all in one day. Whilst young Jeremy should be congratulated on his achievement, I question the wisdom of allowing anyone – young or old – who 'had never stalked before' to go out 'late in the afternoon' to try for his first stag. Surely a few practice shots with the actual weapon to be used for the stalk on a life-size 'iron stag' or large, paper cut-out target would have been preferable to having the point of aim shown to him on a picture of a stag in the lodge! Fortunately the story ended happily, and within about two hours a 14-stone 9-pointer stag was shot at a range of 150 yards, (137 m) which for a *complete* beginner is bordering on the extreme. Had the last chapter ended differently, with a wounded beast left out on the hill in the dark, I doubt if the incident would have received the same publicity – but it should, if only to warn others from attempting to do likewise.

On 12 August the same year, Alec Bond, who is a paraplegic, achieved a well deserved 'John Macnab'. Starting at 8.30 a.m. on the Tay, a salmon was caught, followed shortly afterwards by a brace of grouse, and the mission was then completed, some twelve hours later, with a stag in Aberdeenshire (*The Field* 31/8/85).

For those anxious to achieve a 'John Macnab', while the salmon is undoubtedly the hardest of all three to bag, the stag, due to problems which may be caused by a misplaced shot, should perhaps be the first one to try for, starting as early in the day as possible so as to have it hanging in the larder before midday. This will then allow the rest of the day for the salmon and grouse, in that order. If, however, following a spate, conditions on the river are ideal, then the day should start with the salmon which, hopefully, will be on the bank by mid-morning.

In 1985 a modified version of a 'John Macnab' was achieved by a guest staying at *Glenkinglass* (Argyllshire) when, having shot a roe buck at dawn, he then proceeded to the river for a salmon, following which he shot his first grouse.

During 1975 Captain A. A. C. Farquharson advertised, through a store in Texas, U.S.A., an invitation to Americans to come to his forest of *Invercauld*, near Braemar, Aberdeenshire, and try for a 'John Macnab' at a cost of £2,400, which included a four-day stay at the Castle. On my enquiring from Derek Petrie, who was then factor

for the Invercauld Estate, he was unable to recall there being any application from any visitor to stay at Invercauld House in order to achieve a 'Macnab'. He stated that, by August 12 – which would have been the first date on which a grouse could legally be shot – the best fishing on the Dee would have been long past, and during the first few weeks of the grouse season – provided there was a satisfactory stock of birds – little or no stalking would be taking place, since this does not usually start until September.

Irresponsible Shooting

During 1960 there were reports that guests on the *Balnagown* Estate, which included the forests of *Benmore Assynt* and *Invercassley* in Sutherland, and *Attadale*, *Braelangwell* and *Deanich* in Ross-shire, were being permitted to go out after stags with an array of most unsuitable weapons ranging from a 6-foot (1.8 m) fibreglass bow and arrow to a 12-bore shotgun loaded with lethal ball – a missile of limited range, but frequently used in Europe for shooting running boar during a *battue*. One guest claimed to have shot a stag at 'over 500 yards (457 m)' with an H.V. .22, and considered himself well qualified for doing so because he was 'mercifully gifted with good eyesight . . . and the shot was downhill!'

What assistance a downhill shot will do to improve accuracy I fail to see, and 500 yards is certainly a range that should not be attempted, unless to a kill a wounded animal. At that date, of course, there were no legal restrictions on calibre and ammunition for deer in Scotland (*see* page 19 for legal weapons for deer in Scotland).

In reply to considerable criticism in the press on the availability of this form of 'stunt stalking' being available on the 300,000-acre (121,404 ha) *Balnagown* Estate, William Hunter, the Estate Sporting Manager, wrote as follows (*Shooting Times* 27/1/61):

> At 25 yards [23 m] the modern glass fibre long bow has sufficient power to drive an arrow-head clean through a stag and drop it stone-dead in its tracks. At 30 yards [27 m] there can be few more lethal sporting weapons than a 12-bore shotgun with a single ball load. A ball weighing 450 grains still has a velocity of 1,300 ft per sec. at 30 yards – and there is a second barrel available.

At 30 yards the modern .44 and .38 hand guns (pistols and revolvers) with muzzle velocities in the region of 1,400 ft per sec. and muzzle energies of 1000 ft/lb and over are equally as lethal and as accurate as the majority of sporting rifles used on deer.

The use of these unorthodox weapons means, he continues, that the deer

must be stalked into 25 to 30 yards before a shot can be taken [and as such demands] a minutely planned stalk over the last 130 yards [119 m] or so . . . rarely is the last 100 yards covered in less than two hours.

He concludes his letter by saying,

The satisfaction to both the stalker and his guest when, from 30 yards, the final and simplest part of the operation is completed is very real . . . and should any doubts on this score still remain, an excursion to Balnagown Estates, where the opportunity exists to try it, would very soon dispel them.

Range, of course, is the most important factor when using these unorthodox weapons for deer stalking, and since 30 yards (27 m) would appear to be the most accurate lethal range for a handgun, why was 'the crack revolver shot' allowed to take his shot at 50 yards (45 m), as one report claims? With even the most proficient rifle shot a second shot is sometimes necessary in order to finish off a wounded beast and, if the first shot with a rifle has been taken at, say, 100 to 150 yards (114 m), one still has several hundred yards of accurate range within the capabilities of the rifle in order to complete the job. On the other hand, a wounded stag resulting from a misplaced pistol or revolver shot is *very soon* out of lethal range for a second and finishing shot, i.e. within a distance of perhaps only 10 to 15 yards of the place from where the original shot was taken.

Furthermore, as many stalkers will have learnt to their sorrow, a wounded stag is far more wary to approach than a fresh animal, and if the stalker is seen – as indeed he most likely will be when the range for the second shot also has to be around 30 yards instead of 100 – then the wretched animal will summon up all its strength to escape and, once on its feet, will not stop until sheer fatigue or loss of blood makes it have to. By that time it is probably over the march and lost for ever.

Fortunately, since 1985 The Deer (Firearms etc.) (Scotland) Order has made it illegal to use these unorthodox weapons on deer, so if there is a demand for this type of 'close-in' stalking, why not take a photograph? There is always a shortage of good photographs of wild deer in the highlands, but no shortage of wounded deer. A photograph is ample proof that your object has been achieved. Having taken the photograph, the deer can still be killed, if required, with a modern rifle.

Being a good target shot does not necessarily guarantee the same standard of marksmanship on a deer, where the point of aim is not so clearly defined.

Not infrequently one can hear the bullet strike the beast, particularly when hit in the shoulder or stomach region. A similar sound may also be heard when a missed shot strikes a peat hag.

Quite often, also, when a stag is standing amongst peat hags or against a bank, a missed shot can be seen striking the ground, thus giving some indication as to whether the shot has been high or low.

Two Stags Shot in Error

I shall never forget one occasion, when out with a stalker who seldom failed to remark 'high' or 'low' to any shot that failed to find its mark. On this particular day I myself was not shooting, but was accompanying the stalker and a young guest who was anxious to get his first stag of the season, though he had shot one or two in previous years. A good 8-pointer in company with two other stags was seen but, by the time we had approached within range, only his two companions were visible – one a 6-pointer and the other a 7-pointer. Just as my friend was about to shoot the latter, I happened to see the 8-pointer standing near a peat hag some 70 yards (64 m) to the right of the other two, all three animals being within 100 yards (91 m) of us. I pointed the 8-pointer out to the stalker who immediately said to my friend, without taking his glass off the 8-pointer, 'Take him'. At the sound of the first shot he at once said 'high', and again 'still high' when the second shot rang out. By this time the 8-pointer had taken the hint and disappeared over the skyline – the stalker, however, hadn't noticed that the other two stags would never follow him, for my young friend had shot both of them stone dead! I think the stalker felt a little shamefaced when he discovered that he had been giving a running commentary on the wrong target!

A complete miss – apart from damage to one's ego and an empty hook in the larder – is not all that serious, except that it interferes with the cull programme, but when a wounded deer has to be left on the hill, an unnecessary suffering has been inflicted on a wild creature, and a sleepless night for the stalker if he is a caring type. To reduce the risk of either, the answer is simple – don't wait for a missed shot or wounded beast to remind you that it is time to go to the range and check the zero of your rifle.

A 'Royal' Shot in Error

Many stalkers today like to spare the good and promising heads, but on occasions mistakes are made and a good head pays the price. One such event occurred in 1971 on *Killilan* (Ross-shire), where John F. Ormiston was stalking. Describing the events which led up to the shooting of a 'royal', Mr Ormiston writes,

> Going back to 1928, I have never shot – or wanted to shoot – a good head. One day, when we were drenched and I had left my glass and binoculars with the stalker, I crawled forward after a stag which had gone down a steep, narrow corrie. After a long time – I was in full view of hinds – in dark mist 'he' appeared and was shot. I then found, on approaching the beast, that the stag I had been stalking had gone, and the one shot turned out to be a Royal – not a super one, but it cost me a bottle of whisky and having it set up! So I paid the price after all these years. It sounds pretty stupid for someone with a certain amount of experience . . . it never occurred to me that there would be two of them!

I suppose the only lesson to be learnt from such an occasion is *never* to leave your glass or binoculars behind when making a stalk, for even if the right beast is shot at, one or other of these optical aids – particularly the latter in really wet weather when a telescope is often useless – is invaluable should the movements of a wounded beast have to be followed.

Introducing a Beginner to Stalking

On the question of introducing the young entry to deerstalking, I question the wisdom of allowing a junior to kill a good trophy – and in particular a 'royal' – as a first stag, for it may well encourage him to become a trophy hunter, despising the less well-adorned 'monarchs' which should be the main concern of every keen and reliable stalker. There is no greater thrill in stalking than the occasion of that first stag and whether the stag is switch or 'royal' it will be the same. So why shoot the latter? Far better that this landmark in a stalking careeer should be a pleasure deferred, thus providing a chance to recapture, perhaps, in later life something of that 'first stag' thrill.

Apropos priorities for a beginner to stalking, a great friend of mine in Austria introduced his son to stalking on the following progressive routine: at about the age of 15, he was allowed to shoot his first deer – a roe doe. During the next holiday, provided he had worked hard at school and passed his examinations, he would be allowed to shoot his first roe buck. In subsequent holidays, if the school report continued to be satisfactory, he could graduate from roe buck to chamois – then to red deer hind and finally, when all final exams had been passed, he could tackle a red deer stag – but needless to say, only one of very moderate trophy value (C.I.C. points score).

First Stags and some Coincidences

In 1961 there was a letter in *The Field* (5/10/61) from Harold T. Morton of *Glenfiddich*, Banffshire, describing how his son-in-law Lieut-Commander Peter Seed, 'on his first day's stalking shot an Imperial stag (14 points) weighing 18 st 3 lb (115.6 kg) gralloched', and enquired whether anyone else had 'ever done better than this on their first stalk?'

In my opinion 'records' of this sort mean nothing, for it is all a question of opportunity. My reply was, therefore.

> if one is fortunate enough to be invited to have one's first stalk on a well-managed, first-class forest and be taken up to such a stag by an experienced stalker, then the feat is probably far less difficult than a first stalk after a switch on sheep ground with probably the local shepherd as one's only assistant. [In conclusion I wrote], Whether it is, in fact, a 'record', I cannot say, for such events are seldom recorded. About four years ago I was informed by a proud parent that his 13-year-old son had killed a 13-pointer as his first stag on 13 September. This I would prefer to call a coincidence and not a 'record'. (*The Field* 2/11/61)

In a follow-up to my letter E. de P. Bainbridge wrote that in 1958 his 'father killed a 13-pointer (not his first stag) on September 13 at one o'clock, being the thirteenth hour of the day. We also took 13 bullets to the hill' (*The Field* 16/11/61).

Beginners' Luck

It is sometimes said that beginners often have all the luck, but W. Eberstadt – a septuagenarian from the U.S.A. – was certainly a 'lucky novice' for in 1991, whilst stalking at *Dalnaspidal* (Perthshire), on his very first day on the hill, he not only shot a good 10-pointer stag but, with a weight of 17 st 7 lb (111.1 kg), it turned out to be the heaviest stag that had been shot on the forest during the previous fifteen years.

Record Number of Stags Killed by Stalkers

In 1955 Macpherson's, the sporting stores in Inverness, received a 10-pointer stag from *Glenquoich* forest (Inverness-shire) for mounting. Although there was nothing very spectacular about this particular trophy, it happened to be the 3,111th stag shot by Charles Williams, M.P. – the owner of the forest – shortly before his death in that year.

Records of this sort do not necessarily mean very much, for it is all a question of opportunity. I do not know at what age Mr Williams started his stalking career but, as he served in the Royal Navy during the First World War, it is unlikely that he was able to stalk regularly for more than fifty seasons during his life, if as many. It would appear, therefore, that he probably averaged about sixty-two stags per season throughout his life.

Whilst more hinds have doubtless been shot by professional stalkers during a lifetime on the Scottish hills, Charles Williams' total of 3,111 must be a record number of stags killed by an individual in Scotland during this century. During the last century, however, A. I. McConnochie (1923) records that, 'for the total number of stags killed in one's lifetime, the Duke of Fife (1849–1912) held the record with about four thousand' – the majority being shot on his forest of *Mar* (Aberdeenshire). Large as these numbers are, both fall into insignificance when compared to the

43,649 red deer accredited to the Elector John George of Saxony (1656–80) in Europe, the majority of which would doubtless have been shot during a *battue*.

More recently, by the time of his death in 1940, Captain Christian Combe had shot 1,575 stags on his forest of *Strathconon* (Ross-shire), whilst by 1934, among the 1,400 stags shot at *Langwell* (Caithness) by the 6th Duke of Portland, were ninety 'royals'. The Duke shot his 1,000th stag on 23 September 1921.

Lady Stalkers

There are a number of very keen lady deer stalkers, who each year kill a large number of deer, but I don't know what the record bag of Scottish stags for any lady stalker may happen to be.

The first stag killed on *Blackmount* forest (Argyllshire) at the start of the 1968 season was Mrs P. Fleming's 600th stag, and before the season ended she had added another twenty-three to her total. By the time her stalking days had finished, Mrs Fleming, who is the mother of Robin Fleming, the owner of *Blackmount*, had shot 930 stags, the last being shot on 25 September 1985, when she was 84 years old.

Other lady stalkers who were still killing stags in their eighties were the late Mrs Jessie Tyser of *Gordonbush* (Sutherland), who died in 1978 at the age of 85, and Mrs Arthur Strutt who in 1992, at the age of 84, shot ten stags on *Glensanda* (Argyllshire), which included two 'right-and-lefts', all shot through the neck. By 1968 500 stags had already fallen to this lady's rifle.

The record for the highest number of stags shot in Europe by a lady would seem to belong to a French lady – Anne, Duchess d'Uzès, who died in 1933 at the age of 86. During her life she killed over 2,000 stags.

On the merits of 'scopes, I remember meeting, while staying at *Glencarron* Lodge in the early 1970s, Irene, Marquesa de Torrehermosa, who owned *Achanalt* forest some 15 miles (24 km) away to the east in Strathbran. She was a keen stalker, but at the time was suffering from one of those spells which happen to all stalkers, when the bullet wasn't quite following the path intended. Like many pre-War stalkers, she had always used a rifle equipped with open or iron sights, believing a 'scope was quite unnecessary – if not unsporting – for deerstalking.

In those days 'scopes were generally detachable, and as often as not carried in a special leather 'scope-case and, if the weather was wet, was only clipped on to the rifle just prior to the shot, attachment being a two-pronged bayonet clamp and catch. Attachment and removal was, therefore, a simple operation that could be achieved in seconds. Needless to say, constant removal and replacement of the 'scope eventually caused some slight wear on the attachment lugs, which necessitated frequent re-zeroing.

Armed with her 'scope-fitted rifle, the accuracy of the Marquesa did not, unfortunately, return and when, after missing one or two good chances, the next stag ran off quite unscathed, she quickly whipped off the 'scope sight, and took a parting shot at well over 500 yards (457 m) killing it stone dead with a bullet in the neck. Needless to say, this only increased her conviction that a telescope sight was really unnecessary for stalking!

The Marquesa was a small lady who used to drive around Scotland in a large pre-War Alvis car and all of her that was visible to an approaching motorist was her tiny nose and forehead peering over a large steering-wheel that was being tightly gripped with her fingers. Indeed, she looked in all the world like the wartime character cartoon of 'Wot no . . . Mr Chad'!

A 'Royal' Hand – Three 'Royals' on Successive Days

Lord Reidhaven, during three days stalking on *Kinveachy* (Inverness-shire) in 1959, shot a 'royal' and a 9-pointer on 29 September, repeated the performance on the following day, and on 2 October shot a 'royal' and a 13-pointer, to give him a total of three 'royals', two 9-pointers and a 13-pointer for his three days on the hill, 1 October being a Sunday. The measurements of the best 'royal' and 13-pointer were as follows:

	Length	Beam	Inside span
'Royal'	33 in	4½ in	24 in
	83.8 cm	11.4 cm	61 cm
13-pointer	30½ in	4½ in	28 in
	77.5 cm	11.4 cm	71.1 cm

Three 'royals' in three successive days was also achieved by C. Dalgetty in 1971, whilst stalking at

Glencannich (Inverness-shire), the best of which had a length of 31¼ in (79.4 cm) and an inside span of 25⅝ in (65 cm).

In contrast, a 'royal' shot by Lord Macpherson on *Dalnacardoch* forest (Perthshire) was his first after twenty-five years of stalking.

A Veteran Stalker

During the 1959 stalking season D. Mackay, who was stalking on one of the forests owned by the *Balnagown* estate (Sutherland) (*see* page 12), shot a good 10-pointer in his 86th year.

Royalty at Balmoral and Elsewhere

On 2 October 1943 H.R.H. Princess Elizabeth – now Her Majesty the Queen – shot a 'royal' on *Abergeldie* forest (Aberdeenshire), which adjoins *Balmoral* to the east and has been on lease to H.M. the Queen from the Gordon family for very many years, with the following measurements: length 32¼ in (82 cm), beam 5½ in (14 cm) and inside span of 31¼ in (79.4 cm).

Three years later on 2 October 1946, whilst stalking as a guest of Lord Elphinstone at *Glenmazeran* (Inverness-shire), the Princess shot a much better 'royal': length 37 in (94 cm), beam 4½ in (11.4 cm) and inside span 31½ in (80 cm).

After succeeding her father, George VI, to the throne in 1952, Her Majesty continued to regularly stalk at Balmoral, and in 1958 she shot an 11-pointer with the following measurements: length 35 in (89 cm), beam 4¾ in (12 cm) and inside span 30½ in (77.5 cm).

During the following season Her Majesty shot a rather indifferent 'royal' at *Balmoral*, with bent-down brows and some damage to the crown points: length (left) 27¹³⁄₁₆ in (71 cm), (right) 27 in (68.6 cm); beam 4½ in (11.4 cm); inside span 25¾ in (65.4 cm).

Alas, their Days on the Hill are Over

Sadly, there are some who have had their last stalk, and fortunate are those who are able to remain active to the end. During the 1971 season C. H. Charrington was taken ill whilst stalking at

Moidart (Inverness-shire) and died ten days later at the early age of 47.

Major Philip Fleming, the father of Robin Fleming, the present owner of *Blackmount* forest (Argyllshire), died on 13 October 1971 just after he had returned south at the end of the stalking season, whilst in August of that year Peter Fleming had collapsed and died on the hill having just achieved a 'right and left' at 'walked-up' grouse – a sad year, indeed, for *Blackmount*.

Another stalker who died that year at the age of 71 was Willie Macdonald, the stalker at *Aberchalder* (Inverness-shire). He collapsed and died whilst about to gralloch a stag that had just been shot by a guest *Rifle*.

Dying on the Hill

On 13 August, during the 1988 season, John Chalmers, the stalker on *Bolfracks* (Perthshire), collapsed and died while out on the hill – John Chalmers had been at *Bolfracks* for over thirty years and really did care for his deer and grouse.

Stalkers Drowned

During the 1964 season two stalkers on the *Glenkinglass* ground of *Blackmount* (Argyllshire) were drowned on Loch Etive towards the end of September.

During October 1995 David Mayer, an 18-year-old student from Chester, who was acting as a ghillie on the *Loch Carron* estate, in Wester Ross, was returning alone from the hill during appalling weather conditions, when, whilst crossing a rope bridge over the River Damh, his rucksack became entangled and he was drowned.

CHAPTER 3
Weapons and After the Shot

General

In the early 1950s, when there was no legislation concerning the use and calibre of firearms on deer in Scotland, there were a number of people using a .222 rifle and, not surprisingly, there were many reports of wounded deer, and not in every case had a poacher or farmer been responsible.

As I said in my report in 1953 (*The Field* 8/4/54),

> There are, it seems, many mistaken ideas about the potential killing power of certain types of 'special' H.V. .22 ammunition. Nothing, however, can alter the size of the bullet, no matter how hard it hits, so unless the marksman can guarantee to put his bullet exactly where he wants it every time, then when he fails to do so a wounded beast will generally result.

As a result of the Deer (Firearms etc) (Scotland) Order 1985, the .222 rifle is now a legal weapon for roe deer *only* in Scotland, but not in England, and no one can deny the fact that this calibre, in the *right hands*, is certainly an excellent weapon for the smaller species of deer such as roe, muntjac and Chinese water-deer. There are, unfortunately, a number of people in Britain, including members of both the British Association for Shooting and Conservation (B.A.S.C.) and the British Deer Society (B.D.S.), who favour that the .22 centre-fire rifle should now be made a legal weapon for the above three-mentioned species of deer in England as well.

Stalking conditions, however, in England are not comparable to Scotland, for there are six different species of deer in some areas leading a feral existence, and a situation could well arise when, during a single morning, a stalker could be confronted with several different species of deer ranging from a 20-stone-plus (127 kg) red deer stag to a 30–40 pound (13–18 kg) muntjac or Chinese water-deer. Unless, therefore, like a golfer, he was carrying his two rifles in a golf bag so as to be able to select the correct weapon for the target in view, he would be sorely tempted to try his luck with the .222 should the opportunity of bagging a larger species present itself. Far better, therefore, to avoid any such possible temptation and continue, as at present, with the only legal rifle for *all* deer species in England – namely one having a calibre of not less than .240 inches or a muzzle energy of not less than 2,305 joules (1,700 foot pounds) – (Deer Act 1991).

I shot my first deer – a Japanese sika deer – on the Mull of Kintyre on 27 August 1930, with a .256 Mannlicher Schoenauer rifle which I had borrowed from my uncle, and I continued to use this rifle on sika deer until 1934 when I purchased a second-hand .275 Mauser, which was later exchanged for a new .275 Rigby after the War. For the next thirty years or so I continued to have excellent results on all British species of deer, as well as chamois in Austria, using the Rigby 'special 140-grain soft-nosed bullet' which was packed in cartons labelled 'ideal for red and similar deer'. Following a fresh supply of ammunition from the manufacturers in the early 1980s, although I found it quite excellent on roe, I had some disappointing results on red deer, and when the matter was referred to the suppliers I was informed that their latest bullet, although of identical weight, was intended for roe deer only, and a label to that effect replaced the existing red deer label on the carton.

For 'red and similar deer' a special 140-grain Nosler Partition bullet was then produced, and once more my confidence in the rifle and ammunition was restored. It was not possible, however, to continue using the 'roe only' cartridge along with the Nosler cartridge without re-zeroing, for at 100 yards (90 m) there was a difference of about 2 in (5 cm) in bullet strike.

Since red, roe and sika all frequent the areas in which I now regularly stalk, for the last ten years I have generally used a Parker Hale .30–06 rifle firing the 150-grain Norma bullet, and results have

been highly satisfactory. Provided one's shooting is accurate then, with the 150-grain bullet, there is remarkably little damage on a roe carcase but, if not spot on, then a reasonable blood trail will result, which is essential when stalking unaccompanied by a dog, though one should always be available when required. No matter how good a shot a stalker may be, he cannot, in poor light, avoid a possible deflection of the bullet by a twig *en route* to its target, and with, say, the .222 there will generally be less blood trail to follow than from a misplaced shot from a larger-calibre rifle. It is, therefore, wiser to be over rather than under-gunned. Sika deer are notoriously able to withstand severe punishment, and I understand that erstwhile devotees of the .243 are now getting better results with something heavier.

For use of the hair or set-trigger for Scottish stalking *see* page 5.

Legal Weapons for Deer in Scotland

Legal calibres for shooting deer in Scotland are governed by The Deer (Firearms etc) (Scotland) Order 1985, the main difference from the law in England and Wales being that no mention is made in the Order of a minimum calibre, but only to the performance of the bullet which must be soft nosed. Bullet performances are therefore defined, and relate to those of the 50-grain (3.24 g) .222 Remington load for roe *only*, and the 100-grain (6.48 g) .243 Winchester for any species of deer.

The minimum permitted under the Order are, therefore:

	Bullet Weight grain (grams)	Muzzle Velocity feet per second (metres per second)	Muzzle energy foot pounds (joules)
Any species of deer	100 (6.48)	2,450 (746,76)	1,750 (2,373)
Roe deer only	50 (3.24)	2,450 (746.76)	1,000 (1,356)

Shotguns

Only in order to prevent serious damage to crops, pasture or trees etc. is it legal for the occupier of such land to use a shotgun, whose gauge must be of not less than 12-bore, against deer. It must be loaded with the following lawful ammunition:

All species of deer.
Either a single, rifled, non-spherical projectile weighing not less than 380 grains (24.62 g) or a cartridge containing pellets of not less than size SSG.
Roe deer only.
A cartridge containing pellets of not less than size AAA.

Recovering Carcases

Before the War, and until the late 1940s, the highland garron or pony was the more general method of extracting deer carcases from the forest to the larder, but the early 1950s saw the dawn of mechanisation and some forests were using a sledge drawn by a farm tractor.

> Thanks to our tractor [wrote one forest owner] we are now able to shoot stags where we have never shot them before. We are now able to kill more and get the carcases home earlier, particularly if the *Rifle* didn't mind riding a bit rough on the sledge along with the carcase. One day we were able to collect, with the tractor, three stags within forty minutes – an operation that, with a pony, would have taken four hours.

Apropos killing surplus deer, Lt.-Colonel G. Hornung of *Dalnaspidal* (Perthshire) wrote to me in 1968, saying,

> Mechanisation in lieu of ponies facilitates the killing of many more stags and hinds. If only more people would switch over to mechanisation, more deer – particularly hinds – could be killed, and the quality of stags, both as regards weight and heads, improved. At the moment there are far too many of both.

Sadly the pony has steadily disappeared from the stalking scene as mechanical aids for carcase extraction have gradually been developed. Among the larger forests, *Braulen* (Inverness-shire) was one of the first to give up the garron in 1966. Ponies, however, are still used on *Lochmore* (Sutherland) by Anne, Duchess of Westminster – the owner of Grand National winner Arkle, which was named after the highest mountain on her forest.

A number of years ago I understand the Norwegian Haflinger pony was given a trial on *Lochmore* and, although an excellent little animal for the hill, was a trifle on the small side for carrying a large highland stag.

I personally dislike riding, much preferring 'shanks's' pony to any journey on the back of a garron, but I must confess that on one occasion in 1990, during a long and sometimes steep walk out to our stalking area, with a rope wrapped round my waist, I certainly enjoyed having a tow up some of the steeper gradients before reaching our first spying-point.

One of the earliest vehicles used on the deer forest was the Haflinger – so named after the Norwegian horse – which was extremely useful in extracting carcases over boggy ground. Frequently used, however, on terrain for which it had not been designed, and with spares hard to obtain, it gradually disappeared from the stalking scene in the face of more robust and improved equipment.

By the 1970s many forests were using a small vehicle called a Gnat which, on reasonable terrain, was an ideal vehicle for the single-handed stalker, but quite unsuitable for rocky ground. Another one-carcase pick-up vehicle was the Snow-tric which, like the Gnat, was best suited for heathery rather than rocky terrain. The 'Rolls-Royce' of early recovery vehicles was – and still is – undoubtedly the Snow-trac which was capable of retrieving half a dozen carcases at a time, with heated and covered accommodation for the stalking party. But it must not be abused, otherwise the tracks will give trouble.

On forests that are divided by a loch, in order to save time in taking a pony around the shore, a boat was formerly essential. Today, however, a number of amphibious vehicles are available, one of the most versatile being the Argocat. For larger loads the Glencoe and Glenalmond are possibly the best type.

For the single-handed stalker, the four-wheel Kawasaki and Honda have also proved their worth, particularly when culling hinds, for two carcases can easily be transported at a time. On reasonably flat terrain, a sledge can be towed in order to transport further carcases.

Another small vehicle of the early 1960s was the 'Weasel' which was useful in retrieving carcases from flat, boggy ground, such as at *Big House* (Sutherland), which is primarily a grouse moor, with the highest point under 800 feet (244 m) above sea level.

Mechanical transport is good when it is new and is being well serviced, but by the early 1980s many forests, with their aging recovery vehicles constantly breaking down and spares sometimes difficult to obtain, were beginning to wonder whether it would not be wise to bring back the garron for at least part of the recovery work.

One of the drawbacks in using ponies is that extra staff are required, and apart from difficulty in loading up a large stag without male assistance, I have seen excellent work with garrons done by girls, who seem to have a closer relationship with their charge than men. Certainly, two male university students employed at *Strathconon* (Ross-shire) for a vacation job could hardly have been less satisfactory. On one occasion in 1950, whilst stalking there as a guest, I was taken to the East Big Hills beat, and since it was our intention to shoot three stags, we were accompanied by three ponies in the charge of the two students. Eventually, having spotted some deer and decided that the stag was shootable, we set off on a stalk, leaving the ponies and students in a deep burn out of sight of the deer, and with full instructions not to move until we returned, even if a shot was heard, for we might have launched out on a further stalk. Eventually, after about an hour and half, the beast was shot, but when we returned to the burn, there were the two students busily engrossed in their homework, with no sign of the ponies, who by then had started the journey home on their own. So that, unfortunately, was the end of stalking for that day, for by the time one of the ponies had been caught and returned to collect the carcase it was too late to venture on any further stalks.

Signalling with the use of 'walkie-talkies'

The 'walkie-talkie' has undoubtedly saved many a wasted walk for the ponyman for, if a stalk has been successful, he can be summoned to the spot or, if unsuccessful, can be sent home without having to wait for the return of the stalking party.

Most forests have fixed waiting points from which the ponyman can move, at a prearranged hour, to the next 'bus stop' if no message has been received from the stalking party that a stag has been shot.

Occasionally the ponyman may be signalled to the carcase with a smoke signal but, in dry weather, care must be taken not to start a conflagration, as once happened to me whilst stalking near Garve in 1946. A stag had been shot on Little Wyvis, and we lit a small fire to summon the ponyman. Unfortunately the wind strengthened, and by the time the pony arrived the fire had spread to large patches of dry grass and heather. Despite our efforts to extinguish the flames, by midnight much of the western face of Little Wyvis was well alight and continued to smoulder throughout the following day.

During a stalk, if the ponyman or 'ghillie' with the transport, has a 'walkie-talkie', and from his waiting point can maintain a watch on the deer being stalked, useful instructions can be given to the stalking party who, in broken ground, may well be stalking an unseen target. When no 'walkie-talkie' is available, provided the distance is not too great, useful instructions can also be conveyed by hand signals, such as holding both hands clasped on top of the head to indicate that the deer are well settled and resting. An arm held out to the left or right would indicate the direction in which the deer were moving, whilst a gesture of walking away down the hill would indicate that the deer had disappeared and the stalk should be abandoned.

Buck-toter

I once saw a mobile type of stretcher, called a Buck-toter, which was being used on *Kintail* forest (Ross-shire) during the early 1960s. Consisting of a conventional wooden stretcher with carrying handles at each end, it was supported centrally by two large wheels and, provided the terrain was reasonably smooth and free of rocks, carcases could be wheeled around in barrow-fashion, thus avoiding a tiresome drag. A single wheel version had an all-metal bicycle type frame.

Manhandling Carcases

No matter how the carcase will eventually be conveyed from the hill to the larder, there is a good chance that initially it may have to be manually dragged to a place where it can be loaded on to a pony or mechanised transport, so a suitable drag-rope should always be available.

The rope, equipped with a loop at one end, should be about 13 to 14 feet (4 to 5 m) in length and must not be too thin, otherwise it will chafe the shoulder or dig into the hands during the drag. To attach the rope to a stag's head, the looped end should be passed round the coronets and, after the other end has been threaded through the loop, the rope pulled tight. A half hitch should then be taken round the nose – or better still, round the upper jaw behind the canines, or through an insertion cut through the nostril, as this will prevent the rope slipping off the nose. When manhandling a carcase down a steep gradient, if accompanied by a companion, a second rope should be attached to a hind foot, so that speed of descent can be checked.

Swollen burns and lochs, lashed by gale-force winds, can sometimes make the recovery of a carcase not only difficult, but at times extremely dangerous. On one occasion during 1967 a beast on *Inversanda* (Argyllshire) was only recovered by floating the carcase down a swollen river, tailed by two drag ropes, for a distance of about a mile (1.6 km) from where it could then be transported back to the lodge by pony.

A somewhat similar operation was attempted on *Ledgowan* (Ross-shire), also in 1967, which, though equally successful, could easily have ended in tragedy. On 7 October Mr Ruggles Brise, accompanied by a shepherd, shot a 16½ stone (105 kg) stag on the far beat and, in order to save a long drag back of about two miles (3 km) to the Land Rover, an attempt was made to float the carcase down a burn that was in full spate. At one point the shepherd – a non-swimmer – lost his footing in a deep hole but, although temporarily swept under, he was fortunately able to regain his feet and clamber ashore. Eventually they reached the lodge about 8 p.m., both very wet and somewhat shaken.

Use of Helicopter

Although the helicopter is widely used by the Red Deer Commission in their census work and has, on occasions, been used for the extraction of deer carcases, thankfully, owing to the expense involved, I hope this noisome creature will never become part of the highland scene. On the question of its use for recovering deer carcases, there was a letter in the *Shooting Times and Country Magazine* (24–30/12/81) from Captain B. F. Bamber, a helicopter pilot, which stated

I have yet to see any type of terrain that I cannot successfully hover over, lower a lifting strap (of varying length) to be attached to the deer and in the space of a few minutes fly the beast back to a suitable road access point.

Although costs may seem initially high (£150–£200 per flying hour) this has to be balanced against time and man-hours saved. Whilst I have assisted in extracting a deer traditionally, I was told by the stalker of my last job that I had done, in ten minutes, what would have otherwise occupied an entire day.

In New Zealand the helicopter is widely used for shooting deer from with tranquiliser darts, subsequently capturing them.

During June 1995 it was announced that Sir Hector Munro, M.P., the Scottish Agriculture Minister, would legislate on a number of proposals submitted by the R.D.C., which would include the use of vehicles and aircraft to drive deer during 'essential culling work'.

As I wrote in my article '*Seize the chance for deer changes*' (*Shooting Times* 22–28 June 1995) nothing could be more unselective and cause greater disturbance to deer than a low, buzzing helicopter. In reply to this comment, Patrick Gordon-Duff-Pennington, the Chairman of the R.D.C., stated that there was 'no intention to amend existing provisions which made it illegal to kill deer from aircraft' (*Shooting Times* 20–26 July 1995).

If the movement of deer by aircraft – not with the intention of shooting from the air, but driving them to rifles posted on the ground – is to be permitted, the result will be the same – disturbance of the deer not only on the estate in question, but also to adjacent forests, and should not be considered.

When does stalking cease to be a sport and become 'essential culling work'? If, suppose, by about 10 October an estate, due to bad weather, poor marksmanship and out-of-condition guest *Rifles* is well below the target cull, it could be argued that some very 'essential culling' would have to be done if the target was to be achieved by 21 October, Under such circumstances authorisation for the use of aircraft should never be considered – and, indeed, should this particular proposal ever become legislation, then I would suggest that it should only be granted for use over a *clearly defined* area and during a *specified* period, none of which should take place before 1 November, thereby reducing disturbance to all estates in the area to a minimum

Perquisites and Tips

I have never been happy about the question of so-called 'stalkers perks', which seem to increase in number as the years go by and a fresh use is found for some item of a deer's carcase which previously was discarded as being useless.

At one time the recognised stalker's perk was the *poca-bhuide* – which literally means yellow bag – and is the first compartment of the stomach, i.e. the rumen or tripe. Other items have gradually been listed and by 1975 the following were being claimed by some stalkers: tushes (canine teeth), hearts, livers, antlers, skins etc. All these items, which together at that date were probably worth about £4 to £5 to the stalker, had really come into their own since the War. More recently, other items such as antlers in velvet, testicles, leg sinews, tails etc. have all found a market in the Far East, and for the past twenty years New Zealand has been actively interested in the market. By 1975 even a deer's bladder had its use, and a Midlands firm was then paying a stalker in Scotland 40 pence each for them plus postage. They were being used, I understand, in a preparation with which compost heaps could be treated. At that date I understood that supplies from just one forest were sufficient for the needs for this particular firm. I then estimated that if the bladders of all stags being shot each year in Scotland were retained for this purpose, their value might bring in about £5,000 to £6,000 per annum, which was then being left on the hill.

During 1976 testicles were fetching anything from 50 pence to £2 a pair, depending on whether the sale was to a game dealer or direct to the representative of the Chinese firm interested in making these purchases for the aphrodisiac market. At that date tails were fetching about 25 pence each. Altogether, therefore, if the stalker had time to shop around, each stag brought into the larder would be worth anything from £6 to £10 in perks.

Another rather odious practice which crept in during the mid-1970s was the demand by one or two unscrupulous stalkers for a client to purchase, in addition to the fee already paid for the day's stalking, the antlers of the stag he had shot, should he wish to take them away. Such was the experience of a friend of mine whilst stalking in Perthshire in 1975, for when he suggested that he wished to take away two of the heads he had shot during the week, the stalker demanded something like £16 from him – the charge being based on £1 per point. To avoid any unpleasantness he paid the sum demanded, but subsequently complained by letter to the factor about this extra charge. Quite rightly his money was refunded, but if he had been an overseas visitor the stalker would probably have got away with it.

If heads are to be priced in accordance with the number of points they carry, then any extra trophy fee belongs to the estate and not to the stalker, for whom the *Rifle*'s tip should be adequate.

Whether or not it was as a result of my adverse comments on stalkers' perks in *The Field* 19/2/76 and elsewhere, the whole question of stalker's perquisites was later considered that year by the Deer Committee of the Federation of Scottish Landowners and the following views were expressed:

> Particularly in the case of Continental tenants, the trophy, in the form of heads complete with horns and teeth, is the more important consideration and where stalkers regard antlers and teeth as their perquisite by right, difficulties arise. It is particularly unfortunate when the question arises on the ground in dispute between a tenant paying a particularly high rent and a stalker.

Continuing, it states

> The Deer Committee has been in consultation with letting agents and representative stalkers on the question, and finds there is no single uniform method to recommend as a solution for all cases, as situations and views are strongly varied. Large highly organised estates operate differently from small estates, and letting to Continental tenants introduces features which do not arise on estates letting to home-based tenants working on traditional lines, and there is the question of greater direct tax liability for stalkers in one method from another.

As a result, the Deer Committee made the following recommendations to forest owners and their letting agents:

1. The items which will affect gratuities for stalkers and the disposition of trophies (heads), which would normally be treated as stalker's perquisites, should be agreed between the

prospective tenant and the forest owner at the time the let is being agreed. The stalker should be informed of the arrangements that affect him so that no dispute will arise on the ground.

2. The current gratuity for stalkers is from £4 to £7 per day, and for ghillies £2 to £3 per day. These figures include the cost of preparing heads. In the event of the gratuity being inadequate, the proprietor shall be prepared to make it up in some form of perquisite or payment.

In my opinion the head (antlers) has never been – and must never be – considered a stalker's perk. The head belongs to the owner of the forest and it is for him to decide whether his guest or paying tenant should have claims to it. If neither wants it, then it *may* be offered to the stalker – but it should not be his *right* to claim it automatically.

With reference to the practice of some stalkers making a charge to the client who wished to take away the antlers, I was informed in 1991 by a European sportsman that he had been required by the stalker 'to sign a paper *before* going out on the hill', to the effect that, in addition to the sum of £260 already paid for the day's stalking, a sum of £20 would be paid to the stalker for each stag shot. Whilst a tip of £20 is certainly not excessive for a day's stalking, successful or otherwise, it does seem outrageous that a demand of this type should be made by any stalker in this fashion.

On a previous occasion it would appear that the stalker in question, on receiving a tip for collecting two stags in his Argocat, had considered the amount was insufficient and had informed the client that in future he would not collect any further beasts for him, 'as that sort of money was not worth the time spent'. Not knowing the amount involved, one can only assume that the stalker had expected at least £40 and had received less.

Whether this was an individual case is not known but, to avoid this sort of unpleasantness in future, it would be helpful if sporting agencies would fully brief their clients as to the scale of tip currently being given to stalkers and ghillies in Scotland for the service expected of them during a day's stalking.

Canines or Tushes (grandelns)

The tushes or canine teeth of red deer – referred to by Europeans as *grandelns* – are much valued by sportsmen from Europe, and it was not long before stalkers in Scotland realised their commercial value and included them in the stalkers' perk. During the 1960s a good pair of dark-coloured stag tushes were worth about £3, with those of a hind fetching about a third of this value. Not surprisingly, many carcases were reaching the larder with the tushes missing. Indeed, during this period I more than once saw the stalker remove the tushes from a stag just shot before even commencing on the gralloch!

The only individual, unfortunately, who from 1975 onwards was unable to look forward to a stalker's perquisite at the end of a successful day was Sandy, my faithful labrador, who generally accompanied me to the hill. For whereas formerly he had been able to look forward to an evening meal of deer's heart, this in future, had to be included in the 'pluck' (heart, lungs and liver) and accompany each carcase to the game dealer's larder for veterinary inspection (*see* page 206).

As a postscript to perks, on the 15 October 1988 a poacher was caught red-handed on *Abernethy* forest (Inverness-shire) whilst in the act of gralloching a stag, and made off through the forest carrying his rifle. The incident was immediately reported to the police but apparently no prosecution followed. In his haste to leave the scene, however, the poacher had left behind his gold watch and knife – but whether these were considered stalkers' perks is not recorded.

CHAPTER 4
Injured and Wounded Deer

Nature is ever cruel and unless a stalker or poacher has been responsible, when tragedy happens on the hill there is seldom, if ever, anyone present to help out until too late. Some tragedies, such as winter mortality and accidental falls, are not entirely man's responsibility, but he can do much to reduce the former by a better control of the population and sex ratio, and keep the forest clear of man-made hazards such as discarded wire.

Following up Wounded Deer

One must never assume, if a deer runs off apparently uninjured after a shot, that contact has not, in fact, been made. This applies particularly to a shot through the ribcage area. The bullet may have passed through the body without hitting a rib bone that would have caused the bullet to break up, thus increasing the damage and enlarging the exit hole. After every shot, therefore, it is imperative to remain concealed and watch the actions of the deer until it is out of sight, or perhaps has lain down, when a fresh stalk can be made. The spot where the deer was standing when the shot was taken, as well as the path taken during its retreat, should be carefully examined for signs of hair (pins), blood or stomach contents, remembering that the last two may not become evident until a hundred yards or more of ground have been covered by the retreating animal.

Such an incident had doubtless occurred on a Ross-shire deer forest in 1991, when the owner came across a dead stag that had obviously come off an adjoining forest. It was still warm, and had been shot through the stomach.

On such occasions no reasonable owner would object if a neighbour crossed the march in order to finish off a wounded beast that was still in sight. Otherwise the incident should be reported immediately on the return to the lodge, so that the neighbour's stalker could be alerted and look for it on the following day, or maybe permission granted for the party concerned to make a more thorough search on their neighbour's ground, even though it might cause some interference to the next day's stalking. The main object, however, must be to recover the deer as soon as possible and, if still alive, shoot it and end any further suffering.

Leg Injuries

It is amazing what severe injuries a deer can survive and still manage to lead a more or less normal life.

In 1967 on *Leckmelm* (Ross) there was an old stag which had, two or three seasons previously, suffered a shattered hock, resulting in the leg, when healed, being an inch or two (3-5 cm) shorter than the other. It was shot in company with hinds, its slight deformity being no handicap when it came to defending its harem against local opposition.

In 1975 a stag was shot on *Kinlochluichart* (Ross-shire) that had lost a hoof, resulting in the whole shoulder being very emaciated, whilst the antler on the same side was weak.

Three-legged Stags

In 1973 a stag with three legs, described as being in very good condition, was seen about five times during the season on *Dalnamein* (Perthshire) by Lord Allerton. But it eluded all attempts to be stalked and shot.

During the 1974 season a stag was shot on *Ederline* (Argyll-shire) with only three legs but, despite its incapacity, it was in good condition and able to hold a dozen hinds. On the same forest another stag was shot with a festering wound which appeared to have been the result of an injury caused by a .22 bullet.

In 1976, on *Kinlochewe* (Ross-shire), a three-legged stag was shot, the stump of the missing leg being well healed, but with no apparent reason for the deficiency. On this occasion the antler on the opposite side was deformed.

Broken Leg and Jaw Injury

On *Ben Loyal* (Sutherland) during the 1992 season Count Adam W. J. Knuth, the owner, had just shot a stag and, whilst walking towards the carcase, came across another beast which, although still on its feet, appeared to be badly wounded, so it was shot. When the carcase reached the larder it was found to have suffered not only a broken leg and damaged jaw, but also several puncture-holes in the ribcage, presumably the result of a recent and savage fight, possibly with the stag just previously shot by the Count.

Shattered Jawbone

On *Achentoul* (Sutherland) a stag was shot during the 1992 season with a shattered jawbone – presumably the result of a bullet wound. Estimated to be only four years of age, it was, as to be expected, in very poor condition and weighed only 8½ stone (54 kg).

Injured Stag Dispatched with Knife

Apropos being reduced to your last cartridge (*see* page 7). A disturbing incident occurred on *Glenkinglass* (Argyllshire) on 13 October 1989 after Mrs Helen Whitbread had shot a large 8-pointer stag that, on reaching the larder, weighed out at 18½ stone (117 kg). Not intending to shoot any more stags that day, whilst the beast was being gralloched, Mrs Whitbread, accompanied by her daughter, decided to walk back down the glen, taking the rifle and telescope with them so as to reduce the weight to be carried by the stalker and ghillie, who would subsequently have to drag the stag down.

Having completed the gralloch, the men started to drag the beast down the hill when they came across an injured stag which appeared to be in a very bad way. They now, of course, had no rifle with them, for it was well down the hill with the ladies, so their only weapon was the gralloching knife. However, by careful stalking up to the injured beast, one of the men was able to seize it by the antlers whilst the other successfully killed it with the knife. This second stag – which later weighed in at 16st 4lb (103.4 kg) – had been badly injured in a fight, with one of its antlers completely broken off at the pedicle.

Long Chase after Wounded Deer

In 1971 a strenuous chase took place after a hummel that had been wounded on the home beat of *Ledgowan* forest (Ross-shire). After swimming across Loch Rosque – a distance of about 760 yards (700 m) – it was seen to cross the Achnasheen–Kinlochewe road and go on to *Lochrosque* forest. It was followed up by the shepherd who that day was acting as stalker, but it was not until the hummel had passed right through the *Lochrosque* ground and on to *Kinlochewe* forest that it was finally killed. A great show of persistence by the stalker.

During the same season another wounded beast, which gave a long chase before being finally dispatched, was first seen on *Tulchan (Caenlochan)* forest (Angus) on 11 September carrying a broken hindleg. On the following day a *Rifle* went out with Bob Campbell, the head stalker, and although the injured stag was seen, the shot unfortunately missed. During the next ten days the injured stag was seen on several occasions and a number of stalks attempted, but without success. Finally it was shot on 23 September, by which date it had lost a lot of condition. When shot, its hindleg was found to have been broken right through and was just attached by skin. How and where the original injury occurred was never discovered.

Also in 1971, for the fourth year in succession, a stag was seen with the lower part of one hind limb completely missing from the knee joint, whilst the other hindleg was also broken at about the same point. Despite its obvious immobility, all efforts to get a shot at it failed.

One Accident Leading to Another

An unusual accident befell a reasonably good 'royal' on *Glenmuick* forest (Aberdeenshire) during the 1986 season. Describing the incident, Sir Peter Walker-Okeover, the owner of the forest, writes,

> It was knocked off its feet when a stag standing alongside to it was shot and, whilst falling down a steep hill, apparently broke a shoulder on a rock before hobbling away on three legs. An hour later it was seen with hinds, driving off two young stags before being shot. As there was only one bullet hole in the carcase, the reason for its initial fall remains a mystery.

Self-inflicted Injury

On *Cluanie* (Ross-shire), during the 1965 season a 15-pointer was found dead, having apparently succumbed to a self-inflicted wound sustained while in combat with another stag. This particular stag had a strong rear tine extending from the left antler, and during the fight it would appear that this rear tine had penetrated its own stomach. The measurements of this head were: length 35 in (88.9 cm), beam 5 in (12.7 cm) and inside span 25½ in (64.7 cm).

Hoof Caught in Pelvic Bone

During the 1969 season Ian Biggs shot a stag on his forest of *Culachy* (Inverness-shire), with one of its feet firmly wedged in a pelvic bone which it had doubtless picked up whilst nosing around a skeleton found lying on the hill.

Falling Casualties

In 1966 a dead hind, still warm, was found on *Glencarron* (Ross-shire) with a broken neck, having apparently fallen down a rock face. It was not known what had caused her fall, but disturbance by an eagle was suggested as a possible reason.

On *Inversanda* (Argyllshire) a hind was found dead during the 1968 season with a dislocated shoulder, presumably the result of a fall.

In 1968 a stag was found dead in the snow on *Glencally* (Angus). Describing this discovery, Major J. P. O. Gibb writes,

> The stag was lying dead at the bottom of a steep slope with rocks and heather on it. It appeared to have been dead only about 24–36 hours, and had no signs of any bullet wound or shot on it when skinned. It was lying with its head underneath with a horn stuck into the ground. My only guess is that it had missed its footing during a stormy night whilst fighting with another stag and, falling over backwards, had got stuck.

In 1987 the stalking party on *Kylestrome* (Sutherland), while walking along the steep side of a corrie, heard a noise coming from above and, looking up, saw a large rock followed by a stag crashing down the hillside, the stag rolling and cartwheeling over and over in its descent before finally coming to rest some 200 yards (180 m) away. There was no sign of any bullet wound on the stag, so it was assumed that the unfortunate animal had lost its footing after having been hit by the falling rock.

During the 1984 season a good 10-pointer slipped, presumably whilst feeding along the edge of a rocky gulley on *Knoydart* (Inverness-shire), and in falling its antlers became wedged between the roots of two small trees, from which the wretched animal hung suspended until death put an end to its suffering.

A somewhat comparable incident occurred on 16 October on *Glencarron* (Ross-shire), and I can do no better than quote the account sent to me by Rory Collins, a guest, who was stalking the Glenuig beat that day.

> We were traversing the middle slopes of Creagh Dubh Mohr when, coming over the brow into one of the many small runners, we saw, some 500 yards [450 m] ahead of us, a young stag who appeared to have been wounded. He was facing downhill, his hind legs beneath him, and vainly struggling to pull himself up by his front legs. As we got nearer it became clear that he was caught fast in the rocks by his haunches. Approaching the stag carefully from behind, Brian Watson, the stalker, succeeded, after considerable effort, in pulling the stag free from the rocks, but it was unable to stand, having apparently dislocated a hip or broken its back, so had to be finished off with a shot through the neck. It was the opinion of the stalker that the stag had earlier fallen whilst running down hill, or perhaps had fallen whilst serving a hind.

By a strange coincidence, on the following day, whilst driving up to *Glenuig*, the stalking party came across another wounded animal lying by the side of the track close to the *Achnashellach* march. It had not been there for more than about twenty minutes, as the Achnashellach party had only just passed that way. The stag was losing strength fast, having apparently received a fatal blow during a fight with another stag, and so had to be shot.

Perils of Bone-chewing

On *Invermark* forest (Angus) in 1989 a hind was found dead with the skull of a five-month-old calf firmly wedged in her mouth, thus preventing her from eating. Whether this was a case of cannibalism is not clear, but there are several reports of stags eating dead rabbits, and even the report, in a park, of a Rusa deer stag (*Cervus timorensis*) killing and partially eating a ten-day-old calf.

On *Kinrara* (Inverness-shire) a stag was shot in 1977 which had a stick of wood, about 11 in (25 cm) in length and of pencil thickness, wedged below its tongue and apparently down the throat. When shot, the stag had a full stomach, but its coat was in poor condition. In 1995 a stag was shot on *Balmacaan* (Inverness-shire) which had a six inch (15 cm) piece of antler inside its stomach, one end of which had penetrated the stomach wall. Nevertheless it was in fair condition.

In 1991, on *Ben Loyal* (Sutherland), a hind in very poor condition was seen with part of a sheep's skull firmly wedged on to its lower jaw. Unfortunately the day happened to be the Sabbath and no *rifle* was at hand but, despite a search for it during the following week, it was never seen again.

In 1982 a stag was shot on *Loch Choire* (Sutherland) with a sheep's pelvic bone firmly attached to its lower jaw, having apparently been there for about a week.

Antler-chewing

Whilst stalking on *Cluanie* forest (Inverness-shire) during the rut of 1968, Miss E. A. Robertson saw a hind chewing at the antlers of a resting stag, which appeared to be enjoying the attention she was giving him.

Highland deer – particularly hinds – are fond of chewing cast antlers and any bone found lying about, but it is unusual to see one having a go at the living article. Not infrequently this appetite for bone has had serious consequences (*see* above).

Fighting Casualties

In 1965 a good stag was being stalked on *Ledgowan* (Ross-shire), when it was attacked by another beast – an 8-pointer – of about similar size. Shortly after the attack it was seen to be standing in a very distressed manner, with its head down and obviously very sick. The stag then lay down, shortly after which it was shot by G. E. Ruggles-Brise. When skinned out it was found to have suffered, in addition to a broken rib, a punctured lung and liver. A sequel to this incident was that two days later the same 8-pointer was shot by the same stalker. In the larder it weighed out at 16 st 8 lb (105.2 kg).

On *Reay* forest (Sutherland) there was a casualty, in 1968, to one of the Warnham park (Sussex) stags which Anne, Duchess of Westminster, had introduced to the forest as fresh blood in the early 1960s. Following the rut, two stags – one a 17-pointer and the other a 15-pointer – returned to the stalker's house from the hill on 3 November, a date much earlier than usual, and during the night a fight ensued resulting in the death of the 17-pointer, which carried an excellent head: length 36 in (91.4 cm), beam 5 in (12.7 cm) and inside span 31½ in (80 cm).

On *Auchnafree* (Perthshire) a stag was shot during the 1969 season by P. Maddocks, shortly after it had been ousted in a fierce fight with another stag. On inspection it was found that not only was one of the antlers broken off, but there was also a broken piece of antler firmly embedded in the neck.

During the 1971 rut, which occurred slightly earlier than in previous years, more fights than usual were reported, but this was undoubtedly due to an exceptionally fine spell of weather in most areas, thus inviting stalkers to spend more time spying than plodding blindly on in mist and rain hoping that something shootable would come their way. I myself, whilst stalking on *Glencarron* (Ross-shire), saw one of the most savage encounters I have ever witnessed between two well-matched opponents, and when the battle eventually ended one of the contenders could barely limp away – doubtless a sorrier, if not wiser, stag!

During that same season a 9-pointer stag was killed in a fight on *Strone* (Ross-shire), whilst the carcase of a 'royal' that had been killed during a fight, was found on *Glenartney* forest (Perthshire).

Whilst the 1971 rut could have been described as an aggressive one, that which followed was quite the reverse, and a number of stalkers commented on the paucity of fights seen that year, and I myself recorded seeing only one – a very passive affair.

A particularly savage fight between two stags, however, was witnessed on *Killilan* (Ross-shire) by John Ormiston in 1972. Describing the event he wrote,

> On 10th October we were some 300 yards [274 m] from three roaring stags which were on ground slightly above us. Suddenly two of them started a real fight. Being evenly matched, this

continued for three to four minutes when, without seeing exactly how it happened, one of the stags was lying on its back kicking its legs furiously in the air, but was still fighting with its horns. The standing stag showed no mercy and things looked extremely gruesome. After, perhaps, thirty seconds, the lying stag was able to regain its feet, but we then saw it had a broken foreleg and was shot. It seemed a miracle that the vanquished animal, while lying on its back, had been able to defend itself without suffering further injury.

On 19 October 1981 the stalking party on *Gaick* (Inverness-shire) came across a young stag lying on its back, having apparently been killed recently during a fight. Both antlers had been broken off at the base of the pedicles, resulting in part of the brain being exposed and hanging out. Two years previously a similar incident had occurred on the same ground.

Also in 1981, an 8-pointer was found dead on *Strone* (Ross-shire) with a pierced flank and one antler torn completely out of its skull.

On *Hunthill* (Angus) in 1983, a stag was shot with the forked top of a broken antler firmly embedded in its ear – presumably the result of an encounter with another stag.

In 1986 the stalking party on *Glencarron* (Ross-shire) came across the still-warm carcase of a stag that had recently been killed in a fight, the probable opponent having been a large switch which was to be seen holding hinds nearby.

During the same season another fighting casualty was a strong-beamed 13-pointer which was shot on *Torosay* (Isle of Mull), for not only had it severe lacerations on hind leg and muzzle, but also a damaged eye which was half-closed in consequence.

Despite a rather passive rut in 1988, a number of fierce encounters were witnessed, at least two of which ended fatally. On *Camusrory*, which is part of the former *Knoydart* estate (Inverness-shire), a stag was killed by an old 6-pointer which itself was badly mauled in the process. On *Glenfeshie* (Inverness-shire), following a fierce encounter, one of the contestants was shot and found to have had one of its eyes gouged out during the fight.

On 10 October 1988 a fight between two stags on *Mamore* (Inverness-shire), which lasted fully ten minutes, ended with the death of the smaller stag – an old 10-pointer – which subsequently weighed in at 14 st 8 lb (92.4 kg). The victor – an old 8-pointer – was then stalked and subsequently shot. On reaching the larder it weighed some 2 stone (12.6 kg) heavier than the vanquished. It had a left brow of 9 in (23 cm) in length, and it was assumed that this tine must have inflicted most of the damage received by its opponent.

During the 1995 season, the stalking party on *Braeroy* (Inverness-shire) were watching two stags fighting on the edge of a small cliff when one of them disappeared from view, having, apparently, been pushed over the edge. After the other stag and attendant hinds had moved off, the stalkers went over to investigate what had happened, and duly spied the injured beast, obviously in distress and unable to rise, so was shot. On close inspection it was found to have a broken back, caused by the fall. But for the exceptional circumstances of the stalking party being at the right place and having witnessed the incident, the unfortunate stag was thus spared a long a painful death.

In 1988 two dead stags, with their antlers interlocked, were found at the bottom of a cliff on *Rhum* (Inverness-shire), presumably having fallen whilst fighting on the top.

During the 1972 season a stag was shot on *Hunthill* (Angus) which was blind in one eye that had apparently been pierced only recently, presumably during a fight. On *Remony* (Perthshire) during the same season, a particularly fierce fight was witnessed by the stalking party, resulting in one of the contestants being severely wounded. It happened close to the march with *Bolfracks* and, whilst having lunch, the stalking party observed two evenly matched stags fighting about 500 yards (450 m) away. After several minutes of particularly fierce in-fighting, both stags fell but were soon on their feet again, when one of the stags broke off the fight and ran away, but didn't travel far before collapsing again. Believing it to be severely damaged, Angus Hogg, the stalker, had no difficulty in approaching to within a few yards and, as the animal was gasping heavily, it was shot. On gralloching the beast it appeared that, during the fight, it had suffered two broken ribs, one of which, when falling, had punctured the liver.

During the 1990 season one of the best fights between two well-matched stags that had been seen for years was witnessed on *Boreland* (Perthshire), and lasted fully ten minutes before the contestants called it a day. At one stage of the scrap, with antlers firmly locked together, both stags lost their balance and finished up lying on their backs.

Hind Killed by Stag

During the 1973 season a stag was stalked on *Caenlochan* forest (Angus) because it appeared to be acting in a most unusual manner. On closer inspection, it was discovered that he was standing near a dead hind, and whenever any other beast approached he saw it off in no uncertain manner. Finally the stag was shot, and when the hind was examined it was found that the carcase had been badly mutilated, the injuries obviously having been caused by a stag's antlers. Although no indication as to the age of the stag was given, I suspect that the 'murderer' was probably a young beast, and since this event took place in mid-October, this particular stag had probably, until then, been deprived of rutting by the presence of older stags. Having already been covered, the hind had doubtless refused to stand for the young stag who, as a consequence, became so incensed that he had tried to butt her into submission, with fatal results. Hastings, the late Duke of Bedford, once told me that this sort of behaviour occasionally happened among his Père David deer at Woburn.

Stag's Aggression towards a Sheep

Apropos the petulant nature of stags at rutting time, H. T. Wills witnessed, during the 1961 rut, a most unusual introduction to a fight on *Coulin* (Ross-shire). The heavier of the two stags – which proved to be the eventual winner – was so enraged before the bout had even commenced that he approached a lamb which was standing in his way and tossed it aside for a good 10 yards (9 m).

Stag Tracking Stalkers

During the 1961 season an enraged stag on *Eilanreach* (Inverness-shire) was seen to follow, like a labrador dog, along the tracks of the stalking party and, when it had reached the spot where the stalkers had sat down to spy, proceeded furiously to tear up the ground with its antlers.

Blind Deer

A 12-pointer was killed on *Glenshee* (Perthshire) during the 1965 season. It was found to be completely blind in the left eye, presumably as a result of an injury sustained during a fight. It proved to be the heaviest stag – 15 st 12 lbs (100.7 kg) – shot on the forest that season, so it would appear that the injury had not caused it much inconvenience.

During the same season, on nearby *Chesthill* (Perthshire), a completely blind stag was shot. When first seen, the beast was stumbling about among some rocks with little sense of direction, but as soon as it reached a green patch it became more assured and was able to graze normally. The stag, which turned out to be a *monorchid* (*see* page 88), was in good condition.

During 1974 a stag was shot on *Glencarron* (Ross-shire) which was blind in one eye, the other having been damaged, apparently by an antler prod from another stag.

In 1981 two 8-pointer stags – each blind in one eye – were shot on *Fairburn* and *Strone* (Ross-shire) respectively, both presumbly blinded by fighting.

A stag, completely blind in both eyes, was shot on *Mar* forest (Aberdeenshire) during the 1986 season, whilst during the same year a blind calf had to be killed on *Fairburn* (Ross-shire). The latter was first spotted whilst lying in some bracken and, when roused, appeared to have great difficulty in moving off in any direct line but continued to move in small circles, twisting its head continuously. When killed, in addition to being blind it was found to be suffering from louping-ill – a viral disease which causes inflammation of the brain and spinal cord. It is transmitted by bites of the castor-bean tick (*Ixodes ricinus*). Deer and other animals, including man, are susceptible (*The New Encyclopedia Britannica*, vol. 7, 1986) but, according to A. McDiarmid (*in lit* 1987), no clinical louping-ill had up to that date occurred in free-living wild deer, and possibly only once in a farmed deer due, probably, to stress in transit.

During the last week of the 1994 stalking season a young calf was seen on *Camusericht* (Perthshire), behaving in similar fashion to the *Fairburn* calf, and was shot by George Macdonald, the estate stalker. On examination it was found to have no eyeballs, with only narrow slits to mark the location of the 'eye'. The calf, nevertheless, was in good condition and weighed out at 48 lb (21.8 kg) in the larder.

On Eignaig – a beat of *Ardtornish* forest (Argyllshire) – a narrow 12-pointer (7+5) was shot on 15 October 1993 that was not only completely blind in one eye, but the other had also been badly damaged. The wretched animal appeared to be in some pain and was continually to be seen lying down with its head and neck resting flat on the ground.

Gut-shooting

In my report for 1961 I was able to comment favourably on what had been achieved on *Rhum* by the Nature Conservancy, by their blitz on all rubbish and their stock reduction (*see* page 75). The following season I had no bouquets to hand out to them but rather a censure, for I was horrified to learn that on occasions the stalkers there were resorting to 'gut-shooting', so that a wounded deer could be moved out of rough terrain on to more favourable ground before being finally dispatched with another shot. This practice was brought to my notice by an Austrian friend, who had spent a few days on *Rhum* during the season in order to see how the culling was being managed and whether it would be applicable to his mountainous estate in the Tyrol.

Believing that he must surely have been mistaken, or misinterpreted what he had witnessed, I made enquiries from P. Lowe of the Nature Conservancy, who at the time was in charge of the culling operations on Rhum. To my astonishment, he confirmed that 'gut-shooting' was, in fact, resorted to when shooting any deer on the Benan Stac face, which

is so steep that if a beast is shot dead on it, the carcase is not worth collecting, since every bone in its body will be broken by the fall and the meat is always hopelessly bruised . . . If all the stags are on this face, they cannot be driven off it without being *lost* into Harris Valley or into Alt-na-ba

where they cannot be stalked on the same day. The actual number shot in this way does not *normally* exceed half-a-dozen in a season and these beasts are always killed as soon as they settle on a flat surface, normally within a very few minutes [italics mine].

If an unwounded animal can be easily *lost* in Alt-na-ba, which is within half a mile (0.8 km) of Ben an Stac, surely the same would apply to a gut-shot beast? *Rhum* may be an island, but its mountainous terrain can provide innumerable holes in which a wounded deer can take refuge.

Whatever the reason may be for the gut shot, in my opinion any policy whereby an animal is purposely wounded so that a second shot can subsequently be taken on more favourable ground is quite inexcusable and completely unsportsmanlike – indeed, hardly good propaganda for any visitor invited from Europe to see how deer were being managed by a national institution in Scotland!

Shotgun Injuries

Stags in the *Dochfour* district (Inverness-shire) weigh extremely heavy for they have access to both woods and crops. M. E. V. Baillie (subsequently Lord Burton) writes,

doing much damage to crops and lying in the woods all day. They are very difficult to get as the ground is wooded with much bracken, and the stags never roar by day and little even through the night. One of the few hopes of getting them is to hear a roar before daylight in the morning, and then try to get as near as possible for a shot at first light . . . In this very late year (1958) it is remarkable that the first two big stags which did roar a little should have started as early as the 6th September, and had, of course, been feeding on crops all winter and, as a result, were full of shot. The big one – 25 st 2 lb (159.6 kg) in particular had a considerable amount of very big pellets in him and the 21 stone (133 kg) stag had pellets in the skull. He also had a broken foreleg which had, however, mended, two broken ribs and carried shotgun pellets of all sizes. It was not surprising that neither had a particularly good head.

Drowning Casualties

On 25 September 1967 a stag, one morning at around 7 a.m., was seen swimming across Loch

Gowan towards the road on *Ledgowan* forest (Ross-shire). It never reached the road, however, for it would appear that before doing so, it was headed off by a car and turned back. Subsequently that same day it was found drowned, and when the carcase was recovered it was found to have a broken jaw that had been shattered by a bullet – apparently some two or three days previously. It was an old stag with a wide head of seven points, but only weighed 12 st 2 lb (76.5 kg). Where it had come from was never discovered, but it seems that its long swim had obviously proved too much for it.

In 1977 a young stag was found drowned in a burn on *Ben Armine* (Sutherland), having been caught up in the lines attached to a parachute (*see* page 35).

Trapped in Wallow

An unusual incident happened on *Glenkinglass* forest in (Argyllshire) in 1967. During a stalk after another beast a young stag was seen struggling on its back in a wallow, apparently trapped by its antlers which were embedded in the mud. After completing the stalk the party returned to the spot where the young stag had previously been seen struggling, with the intention of either attempting to free it or shoot it. However, as they were approaching, the trapped stag, with an extra effort, managed to extricate itself and ran off. It would appear that it had been embedded in the wallow for at least three quarters of an hour.

A somewhat similar incident occurred on *Boreland* (Perthshire) in 1992 when, during a grouse shoot, a stag was found buried in a deep peat-hole some 8 feet (2½ m) below the surrounding ground-surface. After the shooting party had scraped some of the peat away in order to reduce the gradient, the stag eventually succeeded in getting its front legs up on to the bank and, with assistance from a member of the party who seized an antler, managed to scramble out. Although rather weak, it otherwise appeared none the worse for its experience and was able to trot away.

Killed by Lightning

During July of 1976 ten stags were discovered dead near the north summit of Ben a Bhuird, on *Glenavon* forest (Banffshire), having been killed by lightning. There was a deep furrow about 18 in (46 cm) long in the ground and the corpses all lay with their mouths wide open.

Killed by Avalanche

So far as I am aware, apart from the occasional death of a deer being buried in a snowdrift or slipping to its death on snow or ice, there have been no multiple deaths in this country, during this century, as a result of avalanches. Fifteen deer, however, were killed by an avalanche on *Glenfiddich* forest (Banffshire), and a similar number overwhelmed on *Gaick* forest (Inverness-shire) in 1889.

Telephone and Fencing Wire Casualties

Stags will frequently rub their antlers against any strange objects found lying about and this is particularly common at the onset of the rut. Not infrequently such encounters may end in a fatality and the importance of removing old fencing-wire from the hill cannot be overstressed.

Caenlochan (Angus)

A good stag was shot in 1974 with about 50 yards (45 m) of telephone wire entangled around its antlers which gave it the appearance of a Christmas tree.

Hunthill (Angus)

A young stag was shot in 1977 with a coil of fencing wire entangled around its antlers.

Strathconon (Ross-shire)

A near tragedy – but fortunately with a happy result – occurred in 1982 when one of the feeder stags, which carried a good 'royal' head, got so badly caught up in some wire fencing that a vet had to be summoned in order to tranquilise the beast before it was disentangled. After release the stag recovered and was able to rejoin the hinds.

Knoydart (Inverness-shire)

Two stags were shot during the 1993 season, both of which had wire entangled about their antlers and head.

Park (Isle of Lewis)

During the 1988 season a number of stags were seen with strands of wire wrapped around their antlers, which had been picked up on the beach.

Rhum, Isle of (Inverness-shire)

During the 1983 season two stags were shot, each carrying a considerable length of fish netting, which had been picked up on the beach, entwined around their antlers.

Ardtalla (Islay)

A 13-stone (82 kg) stag was shot in 1992 with about 20 feet (6 m) of wire wrapped around a front leg and antler.

Coulin (Ross-shire)

A stag was shot in 1992 which had a length of green garden-wire around and firmly embedded into the flesh of a hind leg.

Glenbanchor (Inverness-shire)

During the 1990 season a three-legged hind was frequently seen on the ground with the lower part of a rear leg missing.

An injury of this type is generally caused by the deer's failure to clear a wire fence, resulting in a hind limb becoming trapped between the two upper strands of wire, leaving the deer suspended by a leg. Ensnared in this fashion, the deer will generally starve to death but on occasions, provided that its front feet are in contact with the ground, this will enable the deer to feed. Eventually, after a few days, due to the tourniquet effect of the wires having prevented any blood supply from reaching the lower limb, this will separate from the upper limb, and so permit the deer to escape. Provided, therefore, there has been no dislocation to the hip joint during the deer's struggle to escape, the deer should recover.

During the past fifteen years or so I have shot about half a dozen wild sika deer in the north of England injured in this fashion. Even on three legs the deer, when running, has been able to keep up with its companions, and it is only when confronted with a fence or other obstacle that an alternative route will be selected.

Two stags bound together with fencing-wire

Lea MacNally (1982) recalls the finding by a shepherd of two large stags bound together by a strand of stout fencing-wire which was tightly wrapped around their antlers.

Nylon Netting Casualty

Wire in fencing is not the only cause of accidents. A number of years ago nylon netting was loudly acclaimed as a suitable and cheap method of fencing for gardens and plantations, and for a time was extensively used by the Forestry Commission and others. It was not long, however, before this type of fencing proved to be little more than a legal snare, for not only deer but also sheep. Fortunately it is no longer used by the Forestry Commission, and indeed has largely disappeared from the countryside. Occasionally, however, one comes across lengths of it that have escaped removal, and a few years ago I found a young red deer stag, that had recently shed its antlers, lying dead in a pool of water. Tightly wound around its head was about 20 yards (18 m) of nylon netting which had become entangled in a low branch, supporting the stag's head in a lifelike position even when death had finally ended its terror. Had I been a few hours earlier, I would probably have found it alive and *might* have been able to cut it loose.

Roebucks in hard antler, as well as horned sheep, were the usual victims and on one occasion I found a roebuck and two Blackfaced sheep entangled within about 200 yards (182 m) of each other. I was able to cut loose one of the latter but the others were dead.

Antlers Entangled in Weather Balloon Rigging Lines

Ben Armine (Sutherland)

During the 1977 season a young stag was found drowned in a burn, its antlers having become entangled in the rigging lines of a small parachute used for meteorological work. The lines were attached by a long cord to a metal cylinder weighing about 2 to 3 lb (1 to 1½ kg) and this, apparently, had got caught up behind a rock whilst being dragged along the side of the burn by the entangled stag. In its struggle to free itself, the stag had broken a leg and eventually fallen into the burn where it drowned.

Cluanie (Ross-shire)

In 1970 a young 10-pointer, with a weather balloon entangled on its antlers, was seen roaming the forest for a full fortnight before it was able to discard it.

Stag Eating a Fairground Balloon

Kinveachy

Whilst gralloching a stag shot during the 1995 season, a fairground balloon was found in its stomach.

Antlers Entangled in Climbers' Rucksack

Achdalieu (Inverness-shire)

A young stag was shot in 1986 that had a climber's alloy-framed rucksack firmly entangled around its head. Since its nose was pushed through the frame, with the nylon cords firmly twisted around its antlers, it had obviously experienced considerable difficulty in feeding.

Antlers Entangled in Sheep's Fleece

Affaric (Inverness-shire)

During the 1971 season an unusual episode occurred when a stag managed to get its antlers entangled in a discarded sheep's fleece. Describing the incident Duncan MacLennan, the head stalker, wrote,

> While out stalking on the 20th September, on a fine sunny day, we were spying from a high ridge into a corrie where there were over 200 hinds lying among the peat hags. Suddenly the hinds jumped up and came rushing across towards us until catching our wind. They retraced their footsteps, but avoided the area from which they had originally come. On spying the hillside for a possible hiker, a white object was seen to be running down the steep slope about half a mile distant, which was subsequently identified as a stag which had something white hanging over its face and antlers. The stag was very restless and kept tossing his head about. After a stalk, the stag was eventually shot and it was found that he had a complete sheep's fleece well and truly entangled on its antlers, and this is what had frightened the hinds.

Hind's Head Trapped in Old Bucket

Shortly after the First World War a hind was shot on *Badanloch* (Sutherland) with a bottomless, rusty, old metal bucket firmly implanted around its neck. Apart from some inconvenience it did not seem to interfere with feeding, and when shot the hind was in good condition.

Stag's Antlers Caught in Tree

During the 1994 season a large 10-pointer stag was found dead on *Alladale* (Ross-shire) with its antlers trapped among the twisted branches of a silver birch tree, the scrapings in the bank below the tree being evidence of the stag's frantic efforts to escape.

A similar accident occurred on *Knoydart* (Inverness-shire) in 1984 (*see* page 28).

CHAPTER 5

Disease, Parasitical Infection and Physical Disabilities

Angleberry

On *Auchlyne* (Perthshire) a young stag, which was in poor condition, was shot during the 1986 season with an Angleberry growth about the size of a football on the inside of its left thigh. The Angleberry, which is a wart-like tumour of the skin, is of frequent occurrence in cattle but less common in deer. Nevertheless, during the last twenty years or so several cases have occurred among Scottish deer.

Bloat

Whilst fermentation is taking place in the rumen, large quantities of gas, principally carbon monoxide and methane, are formed which are removed by a complex and efficient mechanism. If for any reason the removal mechanism breaks down 'the gases build up rapidly causing great distension of the abdomen and making the skin taut like a drum' (Chapman, 1975). This is referred to as bloat.

A dead deer will also rapidly become 'bloated', the reason being that fermentation and the production of gas will continue for a while after death, but the eructation mechanism will no longer be operating.

On September 27 1974 I shot a 6-pointer stag on *Glencarron* (Ross-shire) that was suffering from bloat. Estimated to be about fourteen years old, the antlers were still in velvet. Its weight was only 9 st 9 lb (61.2 kg).

Foot-and-Mouth Disease

During the winter of 1967–68 an outbreak of foot-and-mouth disease among cattle temporarily put a stop to hind killing, resulting in a number of estates failing to meet their planned hind cull (*see* page 205). Although deer and other free-living ruminants are susceptible to the disease, which on occasions appears enzootically, deer seem to have played little or no part in the general epidemiology of this condition. There is, however, always the risk of mechanical transfer of the disease virus on the cloven feet of deer as well as sheep and cattle, and for this reason their movement during an outbreak is prohibited.

Jaundice

During the 1995 stalking season a young stag was seen on *Glenshee* (Perthshire) which appeared to be in some distress but by the time the stalking party had reached it, it had died. The carcase was examined by a vet who reported that the cause of death was jaundice.

Tuberculosis

During the 1991 stalking season a stag was killed on *Glenfeshie* (Inverness-shire) which was found to be affected with T.B. It was sent to the Scottish Veterinary Investigation Service in Inverness for examination and the infection was diagnosed as avian (*Mycobacterium avium*) rather than bovine T.B. (*M. bovis*). In almost fifty years of reporting the Scottish stalking scene, this is the first time there has been any mention of T.B. in a report.

There is a statutory requirement under the Tuberculosis (Deer) Order 1989 that any carcase suspected of having tuberculosis should be reported to the appropriate Divisional Veterinary Officer (D.V.O.) and the carcase retained until it has been examined.

Liver Fluke (*Fasciola hepatica*)

Liver fluke is one of the most important helminths among deer in the United Kingdom, particularly *F. hepatica*. The surface of the infected liver may appear mottled, and the flukes can be detected in the bile ducts. Roe deer suffer the worst, particularly in the west of Scotland.

During 1965 a number of beasts killed on *Ardgour* (Argyllshire) had their livers affected with fluke.

The liver of one stag killed in *Glenavon* (Banffshire) was covered with hard white spots identified as calcified parasitic cysts caused by a tape worm (cestode). A liver in such condition had never been seen before on this forest.

During the 1977 season eight stags shot on *Kinloch* (Isle of Skye) were diagnosed as being affected by liver fluke.

Prolapse

This is any displacement of an organ from its usual place. In 1972 the writer shot a 6-pointer stag on *West Benula* (Ross-shire) with a rectal prolapse.

Hairball (*Tricho bezoar*)

On *Fairburn* (Ross-shire) a hind was shot during the 1990 hind culling with what appeared to be a ball of string about the size of a shinty ball inside her rumen. It was probably a *Tricho bezoar* or hairball, which is a ball about 2–3 in (5–7.7 cm) in diameter consisting of densely matted hair covered with a leathery veneer. It is formed from hair swallowed by the animal as it licks itself. Although hairballs are frequently found in the rumen of cattle, their occurrence in deer appears to be rare. Hairballs are sometimes referred to as *Bezoars* or '*madstones*'.

Stomach Wound

Quite distinct from a hairball, a stag was shot on *Borrobol* (Sutherland) with what appeared to be a ball of fat, about the size of a cricket ball and covered in hair, suspended from the lower part of its stomach. The cause of this growth was presumed to have been an old stomach wound, probably the result of a shot low in the stomach which had subsequently healed over.

Cleg (*Haematopota*)

There are a number of clegs, the most common of which in Scotland is *H. pluvialis*, particularly in the Western Highlands. This cleg, which is a blood-sucking fly, emerges during the latter half of June and will remain active until the latter part of August. Clegs are most active in bright sunshine when the weather is hot and sultry. They are silent in flight, and the bite is often felt before their presence has been noted. Only the females suck blood, and clegs are inactive during the hours of darkness.

Deer-biting Louse (*Trichodectes cervi*)

According to Cameron (1932) this parasite is found most abundantly on Scottish red deer during the winter months, the numbers gradually decreasing with the advance of summer. Nevertheless, despite an intensive search of a number of deer skins between October and January, during which hairs were examined with a magnifying glass and skins washed, Darling (1937) was unable to find any lice whatsoever, so he assumed that the deer in Wester Ross, anyway, were not seriously affected by the deer-biting louse.

Deer Ked (*Lipoptena cervi*)

According to Darling (1937) the deer ked is winged in the early imaginal state, and there appears to be only one generation each year. Winged keds are most commonly found near the deer wallows in the autumn, and by middle of October winged keds will have disappeared, having mated and found a host. As soon as the keds are in the deer's coat they lose their wings and begin blood-sucking. On beasts shot or found dead during the winter, Darling 'found hundreds and even thousands of these parasites'.

Flies

Flies play an important role in the behaviour and movement of red deer, not only causing them individual distress by irritation, but at times causing near panic among herding animals such as red deer and reindeer.

The most important of the blood-sucking flies include Cleg (*Haematopota*) and Midge (*Culicoides*).

Warble Fly (*Hypoderma diana*)

The short-lived adult fly is on the wing in late spring and early summer, laying its eggs in the hair of its host. When hatched, the grubs migrate to a resting site in the spinal canal before their final journey to the subcutaneous tissue along the back, which they reach sometime about the new year. Once the back is reached they remain static, encased inside a gradually enlarging cyst, from which they will emerge in the spring and drop to the ground.

The emergence of warbles must cause considerable irritation to the deer and may be one of the reasons for red deer wallowing in the spring.

Warble fly can severely damage the skins of red deer, thereby reducing their value.

Nasal or Bot Fly (*Cephenemyia auribarbis*)

According to McDiarmid (1977) although the botfly probably occurs throughout Britain, it is the red deer in the north of Scotland which are mainly affected.

The adult flies are on the wing from late May until July, the female darting close to the deer's muzzle and ejecting larvae into the nostrils. After about twelve months' development they pass out through the nostrils on to the ground, helped, perhaps, by the sneezing of their host.

According to Darling (1937), this fly is probably more common in some parts of the Highlands than others, but so far as Wester Ross was concerned there were comparatively few.

When a beast has been attacked by the nasal fly, the so-called 'false gid' may be produced, and this has sometimes been confused with 'staggers' which is caused by tapeworm infection.

Midge (*Culicoides*)

1972 was one of the driest stalking seasons of the past half century, and not surprisingly the fine, hot weather brought out the midges which, on some forests, remained extremely active throughout the whole season, making life for both deer and stalker decidedly unpleasant at times.

Although midges (*Culicoides pulicaris*) start to emerge in comparatively small numbers towards the end of May, it is not until the months of July, August and September, when they emerge in countless numbers, that they start to be really troublesome to deer, concentrating their attention on the eyelids, ears, udder, anus and vulva. Antlers in velvet are particularly attractive to these insects and the stags, in consequence, keep clear of low, altitudes on a midgey evening or morning (Darling 1937).

By October, which may coincide with the first frosts of coming winter, one doesn't normally expect much trouble from midges, but October 1989 was an exception and it was prudent in Wester Ross, and doubtless in many areas elsewhere, to take some insect repellent with you, for even at 2,000 feet (610 m), in the middle of the month, without some protection, any lengthy spy or wait for deer to shift during a stalk soon became unbearable. In that particular year the deer on *Park* forest (Isle of Lewis), instead of frequenting the tops, preferred to keep to lower altitudes, and for most of the season remained low down along the coastline.

The rut throughout much of Scotland in 1989 was a late and rather passive one – the deer, no doubt like the stalkers, had other matters to think about!

Ticks (*Ixodes ricinus*)

The sheep tick, which, in spite of its name, will feed on any available mammal or bird, is ubiquitous on wild deer. Describing this arthropod Dunn (1986) writes,

> The life cycle takes three years to complete. The adult female feeds for about two weeks, and when fully engorged she drops off, lays her eggs on the ground and dies. The eggs do not hatch until the following year, and the larvae which emerge feed on a host for about a week, drop to the ground and moult to the nymphal stage which, in the following year, finds a host and feeds for about a week before dropping to the ground. In the third year the nymph moults to the adult stage which finds a further host, engorges and lays eggs. In the three years of the cycle the total time spent on animals is a maximum of four weeks.

The spring invasion of ticks is believed to be one of the reasons for the spring wallowing of deer – as is also the attention of the warble fly (*Hypoderma diana*).

This obnoxious parasite appears to have a rather patchy existence in Scotland, and its presence has received scant notice in the annual reports received from deer forests.

During the immediate post-War years, in the interest of grouse, efforts were being made to reduce the red deer population on *Glen Dye* forest (Kincardineshire), for it was considered that the deer were acting as hosts to the tick which was causing the death of many young grouse chicks.

To digress slightly from red deer in Scotland, there is little doubt that the sheep tick in parts of north-west England – and doubtless elsewhere– has become a very serious threat to many other species of wild life, particularly in Cumbria, where I have been regularly stalking roe for over sixty years. Up to the mid-1950s, roding woodcock and the crepuscular flight of the nightjar were always a delight to watch during early summer evenings, as I sat waiting in my high seat for the arrival of a buck. But that, alas, is all a memory of the past, and during recent years an evening would often pass without a roding woodcock to be seen, whilst it must be at least fifteen years since the unique churring sound of the nightjar was last heard.

In former days, both myself and labrador could spend hours in the woods without collecting a tick, but today that has all changed and a careful body examination and change of clothes is always advisable to locate *Ixodes ricinus* before it gets properly 'stuck-in'.

A number of years ago, there was some correspondence in the sporting press concerning suitable remedies for warding off the sheep tick, and one enlightened correspondent wrote to say that having tried most of the advertised brand remedies, the best one in his experience was to be accompanied by an attractive young girl whenever he went into the woods, for her presence attracted the ticks, leaving him unmolested. Furthermore, this provided an additional bonus, for on returning home he was able to enjoy a further half hour or so in stalking ticks on his fair companion.

Overgrown Hooves

On *Ardtalla* (Islay) a stag was shot on 20 October 1992 with front hooves grown to about 11 in (28 cm) in length. It was limping badly but had no other sign of injury. A malformation of this kind is often a result of old age for, with increasing years, the animal will become more static and the hooves, in consequence, are not subjected to the same amount of natural paring off by contact with hard surfaces as formerly. Once the hoof has reached a certain length the fibres begin to bend over and the animal is forced to walk on the side of the hoof, which rapidly assumes a deformed appearance. At

times, however, overgrown hooves would appear to be a definite malady quite unconnected with lack of mobility or age. This deformity is sometimes referred to as 'Aladdin's slippers'.

Twisted Maxillae

During the 1987 season there were three reports of stags with twisted nasal bones or *maxillae*, which are often the result of poor nutrition. One beast – estimated to be eleven or twelve years old – was shot on *Glencarron* (Ross-shire) and, in addition to a deformed skull, had the right antler suspended only by gristle hanging down over its right eye. Shot on 17 October, with both antlers still in velvet and in winter coat, it barely weighed 11 stone (70 kg). The other two beasts with twisted *maxillae* came from Sutherland and were shot on adjacent forests – one on *Achentoul* (9 October) and the other on *Badanloch* (8 October). Weighing 14 st 6 lbs (92 kg) and 15 st 10 lb (99.8 kg) respectively, both beasts were in good condition but were not holding hinds.

In 1991 two stags with twisted *Maxillae* were shot on *Dalness* (Argyllshire), and although in one case this may have been the result of some injury, it was apparent that the other stag had been deformed since birth.

Jaw – Overshot and Undershot

A mismatch of the incisor teeth to the dental pad may also be caused by poor nutrition, resulting in either an overshot or undershot jaw – the former occurring when the mandible (lower jaw) overshoots the upper jaw and protrudes beyond it. Undershot jaw – known as *Brachygnathia* – is of more common occurrence, particularly among the feral sika deer (*Cervus nippon*) of the Bowland valley, north Lancashire – a possible cause may be inbreeding.

During the 1995 season a stag was shot on *Glencarron* (Ross-shire) with 'the underjaw some 3 in (7.6 cm) shorter than the upper'.

Deformed Limbs

During the last weeks of the 1987 stalking season a small stag, about the size of a young hind, was found dead on *Affaric* (Inverness-shire), having died perhaps two days previously. Both antlers, about 6 in (15 cm) and 12 in (30 cm) in length, were still in velvet, with the latter growing down the side of its face. Although the right front leg was normal, the hoof from below the ankle joint was missing on the remaining three legs, each of which terminated in a bulbous stump. Due to the disparity in length of limbs, the stag had apparently had to use its right front knee when either walking or feeding, with the result that the claws of the hoof had become considerably overgrown. From its teeth, Duncan MacLennan, the head stalker, estimated the stag appeared to be 'at least three years old' and had the curly coat of an older beast. There was no sign of any injury likely to have caused death.

A possible cause for the loss of three hooves was suggested to Duncan MacLennan by a local vet, who informed him that during one January, in very frosty weather, before a cow had been able to lick clean its new-born calf, the hooves and ears of the calf were so badly frostbitten that they eventually fell off.

Scottish red deer calves are not, of course, born in January, but if the deer described by Duncan MacLennan as being 'at least three years old' had, in fact, been four years old, then it would have been born in 1983 – and probably in early June. Is it not more than a coincidence, therefore, that during the period from 30 May to 14 June, when the calf might have been born, the weather at *Affaric* was extremely cold, with snow lying well down the hill? So this, therefore, could well be the explanation for the deformed limbs.

'Dwarf' Deer on *Braeroy*

During August 1949 a 'dwarf' deer, thought to be a malformed calf, appeared on *Braeroy*

(Inverness-shire). It was described by Brigadier R. B. R. Colvin, the owner of the forest, as being,

> very short in the leg, long in the body, out at the elbows in front, and with its hocks 'tied-in'. It had the appearance of a Corgi dog or perhaps a bob-tailed fox. It seemed unable to run uphill.

During the third week of November 1950 this freak deer was rounded up by a shepherd's dogs in a burn, and as its off-hind leg was broken, it was killed by the shepherd. According to the shepherd, who, I understand, was knowledgeable in these matters,

> the beast was no calf at all but a freak stag with a five to six-year-old mouth, antlers 2 in [5 cm] long, growing from a full-sized head, but with an extraordinary square muzzle and very short mouth. The tail was large, feet full-sized but legs only about 14 in [36 cm] long.

Following the shepherd's report Brigadier Colvin's comment was,

> The interesting part is that when I saw the beast on 18 August 1949, it was definitely being looked after by a hind. When it was next seen in February 1950, it was running with a number of young stags, and a fortnight later was seen just above the lodge taking severe punishment from another stag.

Shortly after the War, in Woburn park (Bedfordshire), the Formosan sika deer (*Cervus nippon taiouanus*) occasionally produced a calf with abnormally short legs – especially the hindlegs – and although these 'Dachshund' type calves were generally treated as freaks and shot, the odd one which was allowed to survive any length of time, did not appear to be any weaker than the other young deer.

CHAPTER 6

Winter Mortality and Other Factors

On the Continent, snow and avalanches take a regular toll in the mountains of Austria and elsewhere, but it is seldom that avalanches have caused any casualties in Scotland. During the last century two such incidents were recorded by McConnochie (1923), when fifteen deer were killed by an avalanche on *Glenfiddich* forest (Banffshire) and a similar number were overwhelmed on *Gaick* forest (Inverness-shire), in 1884.

Gaick has also suffered two other such incidents. In 1921 eleven stags were buried under an avalanche, whilst in about 1800 the old Gaick lodge was destroyed by an avalanche, and with it perished five stalkers who had taken shelter in it whilst hind stalking.

Apart from these incidents, little other information is available concerning winter mortality during the last century, but I think it can be assumed that they were considerably less than has occurred recently in Scotland for two main reasons: first, the deer population was less, and second, they had access to large areas of favourable wintering ground which, due to afforestation and submersion in connection with the development of hydro-electric schemes, is now denied them.

Those who live in the south and whose contact, therefore, with the north of Scotland is confined only to the stalking season have little appreciation of the hardship and privation that face both deer and professional stalker should the winter be long and severe, as it has been on numerous occasions during the past fifty years.

The following is a description of the mortality which has followed some of the worst winters during that period.

1939–49

During the War years the blizzards of 1940–41 caused a big loss of deer – particularly hinds – on *Kinlochluichart* (Ross-shire), whilst hundreds perished on *Rhidorroch* (Ross-shire), despite the fact that this forest is low lying with some 400 acres (162 ha) of woodland available for shelter. On *Badanloch* (Sutherland) it was estimated that winter casualties that year depleted the deer population by about 50 per cent.

The winter of 1942–3 was also a bitter one, and several hundred deer were found dead on *Kinlochewe* (Ross-shire).

In 1947 severe blizzards over the whole country caused many casualties among the deer, ranging from Galloway in the south-west to *Mudale* in Sutherland, resulting, on the latter forest, in no hinds being shot for four years.

1950–51

Following the atrocious weather of the 1950 stalking season (*see* page 219), and the severe winter and cold spring that followed, literally thousands of deer perished during the spring and summer of 1951. It was difficult to estimate just how many deer had perished but there was no doubt that thousands died during the winter, and many more reached the spring of 1951 in such weak condition that some had difficulty in walking. Donald Stewart, who had formerly been a stalker on *Dalnacardoch* (Perthshire), said that when they were attempting, in the spring, to herd the deer back from arable land to Glen Tilt with sheep dogs, some of the previous season's calves – particularly the young males – were so weak that they were unable to travel far without having to lie down for breath. The older beasts and hind calves, however, were in better shape.

In Perthshire, where the full fury of the 1950–51 winter storms seem to have vented itself on the high ground to the west of Loch Ericht, it was reported that some 400 carcases were found during the spring on the hill behind *Ardverikie* House (Inverness-shire). In Aberdeenshire, *Mar* forest lost over 650 stags and about a similar number had to be buried on nearby *Balmoral* forest.

On *Affaric* (Inverness-shire) it was estimated that the loss of hinds alone was over 300. 'It was nothing unusual', reported Duncan MacLennan, the head stalker, 'to find seven or eight deer lying in heaps in the shelter of knolls and clumps of trees, where the snow had drifted over them. Most of the deer were found lying with their heads across their shoulders.

Reports from other forests that year were similar, but some did escape lightly. On *Achdalieu* (Inverness-shire), for instance, which has some excellent low ground with woods running right down to the loch side, the deer had every chance to escape the worst of the blizzards, whilst on *Coignafearn* (Inverness-shire) most of the deer left the ground entirely during the storms and sought shelter elsewhere on lower ground.

Undoubtedly the most serious loss was not so much in the number of carcases found in the spring but in the paucity of calves, evident everywhere, during the summer of 1951 (*see* page 219).

Unfortunately the 1951 calves arrived just when their dams most needed nourishment, and because of the lack of it many calves died for want of milk.

1954–55

The cold, wet winter and dry spring caused heavy mortality among the older stags in some of the west-coast forests. On *Ardlussa* (Jura) 'over 200 head of deer, mostly stags, were lost', whilst on *Ben More* (Mull), 'many of the stags died'.

Following the severe snowstorms of the 1954–55 winter, a number of forests reported very heavy casualties, particularly among calves, yearling hinds and old stags. On *Affaric* (Inverness-shire) it was estimated that about 300 deer perished, their carcases being found in groups of six to eight along the loch side where they had evidently gathered for shelter. On *Kinlochewe* (Ross-shire) 167 carcases were counted, and on one of the *Atholl* (Perthshire) beats at least 150 deer perished. Not every carcase is found, of course.

Langwell (Caithness), *Loch Choire* (Sutherland), *Inverinate* (Ross-shire), *Atholl* (Perthshire) and *Inveraray* (Argyllshire), to mention but five forests in counties widely separated, all reported heavy losses, which showed how widespread the damage to deer stock must have been. Some of the west-coast mainland and island forests escaped more lightly, but on *Rhum* the loss in hinds, yearlings and older stags was considerable.

Other species of deer also suffered, and on *Corrievarkie* (Perthshire), for instance, the roe population was practically exterminated by the prolonged frosts, while on *Achanalt* (Ross-shire) the sika deer also had high losses.

Even more disturbing was the very poor crop of calves in 1955, and a number of those that were seen were either undersized or had been calved late. On *Glenquoich* (Inverness-shire) a hind calved during the first week of October. Late calves start any winter at a disadvantage, and had the 1955–56 winter been another severe one, with a poor spring and summer to follow, the deer population would have suffered badly. Already, by January 1956, it was estimated in some quarters that the greater part of one year's breeding stock had been lost. Fortunately, 1956 was a very good year for the deer, and not only was the mortality in the spring and early summer one of the lowest for years, but the hinds also calved well. A number, however, were born extremely late, which was only to be expected after the late rut of 1955.

1961–62

The winter of 1961 was one of the most severe and prolonged for many years over much of Scotland, and many forests had deep snow from mid-November until March or April, whilst frost was continuous on some of the more central forests for about six months on end. On *Inverinate* (Ross-shire), for instance, the snow started in late October and there were many falls all the way through the winter until well into May, so the hills were never wholly free – indeed, there was still quite a depth here and there on the tops at the end of May. The winter frosts were also much more severe than one normally expects in Wester Ross. From other western forests, such as *Knoydart, Mamore, Killiechonate, Glenshero* (all Inverness-shire), *Ben More* (Isle of Mull) and *Blackmount* (Argyllshire), the winter weather was similar.

On *Ben More* there was early snow followed by cold north and east winds and, in consequence, there was no hill grass before the middle of May. Thus, coupled with the fact that the heather had failed to recover from the violent hurricanes of the previous September, the death rate among the deer had been very heavy, and those that had survived were said to be in a very emaciated condition.

On the forests of *Mamore, Glenshero* and *Killiechonate* (Inverness-shire) heavy snow, which subsequently froze, made feeding conditions very difficult for the deer, and there was a considerable loss by death due to sheer starvation – the main casualties being among calves and young hinds. On *Mamore* the only age group of stags not seriously to be affected appear to have been in the lower age-group of three to five-year-olds.

On both *Knoydart* and *Lochiel* forests (Inverness-shire) there was heavy mortality among the older class of stag, whilst on *Ardverikie* (Inverness-shire), which had a fresh fall of snow at end of May, the toll was heaviest among the hinds. On *West Benula* (Ross-shire), during the first visit to the low ground after the snow had melted, no less than 43 deer carcases were found, comprising 12 hinds, 29 calves and 2 stags. On adjacent *Inverinate*, however, which is closer to the coast, casualties were far fewer than had been expected.

The picture from *Affaric* (Inverness-shire) was a sad one, for the December storms had already killed off a number of stags, and deaths continued until May. A number of hinds also succumbed, their carcases being found in groups of five or six behind rocks and small hillocks where they had sought to find shelter from the storms. Many of those that did survive were so weak in March, April and May that, instead of running away, they attempted to hide. By the end of May there was still a lot of snow on the hills, with a late fall on 29 May.

In Perthshire, during the first week of December 1961, there was a fall of snow measuring up to 18 in (45 cm) in depth on the roads around *Talladh-a-Bheithe*, and this killed off a good few calves, particularly stag calves, before Christmas. The death rate from March to May, however, was not much above the average despite the fact that there was deep snow about until the 7 April.

Conditions on *Reay* (Sutherland) during the 1961-62 winter were shocking, whilst on the other side of northern Scotland the deer on *Langwell* and *Braemore* (Caithness) also had a very poor winter due to the prolonged cold and wet weather. The death rate here, however, was only about average, consisting mainly of old hinds and the weaker yearlings. Nevertheless the deer were still in very poor condition in June, especially the hinds.

In north-east Scotland the winter was also prolonged and very severe on the Sutherland estate forests, with the first bad snowstorms arriving in early December and the severe winter carrying on right through to the end of March. Although the deer were in poor condition there was not a high death rate except amongst a few old stags and some calves. On the *Invercauld* estate (Aberdeenshire), although the winter had been particularly severe, the deer came through surprisingly well, though many started the summer looking extremely lean.

1964–65

The severe wintry conditions, which started about the 24 November, caused drifts to build up along many forestry fences, enabling the deer to wander into the forestry blocks, as a result of which a considerable number were shot. In the *Torrachilty* plantations near Garve (Ross-shire), which belonged to the Forestry Commission, 146 deer were reported to have been shot within the fence, whilst on the private woodland estate of *Novar*, near Evanton, over 500 deer were shot.

Others straying on to agricultural land were likewise slaughtered, whilst the poachers were also taking their toll.

1966–67

By the autumn of 1967 some of the forests in the Garve area of Ross-shire were not only feeling the effects of the slaughter of deer which had recently taken place on *Novar* and elsewhere, but during the winter of 1966-67 there had also been high mortality in some areas. In *Glen Etive* (Argyllshire) the winter was described as one of the worst for years, with a rainfall of 122 in (310 cm) and over 100 deer – hinds, calves and stags – had been found dead.

1969–70

Late calves, should the following winter be at all severe, will increase calf mortality tremendously, and this undoubtedly occurred in many parts of northern Scotland during the spring of 1970, following the severe winter of 1969-70. As a case in point, *Kinlochluichart* (Ross-shire) had a good, but rather late, crop of calves during the summer of 1969, but as a result of the severe winter that followed, the Hon. Spencer-Loch estimated that over 50 per cent of the 1969 calves had perished. The calf crop during the 1970 summer was also poor, and only about one hind in eleven or twelve was seen to have a calf at foot by the autumn – i.e. under 10 per cent.

1974–75

The winter of 1974-75 was notable for the amount of rain which fell in many districts, which caused more hardship to the deer than if the weather had been more severe. On *Glen Etive* (Argyllshire) there was a heavy rainfall which lasted continuously from October until late January, with only four fine days, and since this was followed by a very dry spring, the new grass came later than ever. As a result, Richard Fleming, the owner of *Blackmount*, reported that the deer were in the worst condition that he could ever remember.

There was a much higher mortality, especially among the stags on *Fersit*, than I have known in the nineteen years I have stalked there and the same applied to *Glenstrae*, where the deer had been shut out from the new forestry plantings. Out of 42 hinds in *Glen Etive* which were being fed, with 28 calves between them, only 2 calves survived the heavy floodings of the winter, being swept away whilst crossing to and fro from the feeding grounds.

There was little doubt that the spring mortality among the 1974 calf crop was considerable. On *Kinlochluichart* (Ross-shire), for instance, the calf crop during the summer of 1974 had been extremely good, yet very few yearlings were seen during the 1975 stalking season, which suggested that casualties among this class of deer during the winter and spring had been considerable. Fortunately there was a good calf crop on *Kinlochluichart* during the summer of 1975.

There is no doubt that, despite the comparatively mild – albeit extremely wet – winter of 1974-75, the first half of 1975 was extremely hard on the deer. For about six weeks between February and late March the weather had improved considerably and, instead of incessant rain, periods of warming sunshine enticed the deer to scatter out of the corries and on to the moss crop. Soon, it was hoped, the first spring grass would start to appear and give the weakened deer a chance to take in fresh nourishment and recover some of their lost condition. But it was not to be, for on 23 March the wind veered round to the north-east and with it came snow. April and May were bitterly cold, but another heavy fall of snow on 9 April, with drifting on the higher ground which lasted for several days, really hit the weaker animals very hard.

After this snowfall, followed by three mild days, the wind returned to the north-east and, with further snow showers which continued until 3 June, the grass never had a chance to grow. By that time some of the older stags were showing quite an advanced state of antler growth but their bodies, still covered by winter hair, were looking very thin.

On 4 June the weather suddenly turned very hot and this lasted for about a week, the warmth bringing on an abundance of grass and the heat forcing the deer to seek the higher ground, not only to be cooler but to escape from the flies. It was only during this short but hot spell that the deer had been able to put on any condition. Thus, the spring and early summer up to end of May had proved much worse on the deer than the winter had been and, as a result, casualties that spring, particularly among the older stags, weaker hinds and calves, were extremely high.

1978–79

Weather conditions during the early part of 1978 were particularly severe over much of the highlands, with a heavy mortality among the 1978 calves during the following winter. On *Braeroy* (Inverness-shire) it was estimated that at least 150 calves had been lost, whilst on *Strathconon* (Ross-shire), in addition to 64 calves, the carcases of 71 stags and 93 hinds of all age groups were found in the spring. Elsewhere, on the evidence of carcases found during March on *Coulin* (Ross-shire), it was apparent that winter mortality had been higher than normal, and this undoubtedly accounted for a shortage of deer on both *East Glenquoich* (Inverness-shire) and *Dalnaspidal* (Perthshire).

On *Reay* forest (Sutherland) there was a high mortality among the hinds and calves, but the stags came through the winter well. The reverse, however, was the case on *Ledgowan* (Ross-shire), where there was a considerable loss among the yearling stags. On *Monar* (Ross-shire) there was also a heavy mortality in the spring, principally among the younger deer.

1981–82

Despite the severe winter of 1981–82, deer casualties in some of the worst-hit areas were not as high as had been expected. Deer losses on *Glenartney* (Perthshire), particularly among the 1981 calves, were substantial and during the spring something between 150 and 200 carcases were found. *Braulen* (Inverness-shire) also lost a lot of deer during the spring, including some stags which died shortly after casting their antlers.

During the winter of 1981, following a break-in to the *Rannoch* plantation (Perthshire), approximately 600 deer had to be slaughtered by the Forestry Commission and Red Deer Commission.

On the island of *Rhum*, where winter conditions are never as severe as on the mainland, winter mortality, particularly among the older stags, was also high, being nearly twice the normal.

1983–84

Following the very wet winter in some areas, the death toll during the spring of 1983 was quite exceptional. Reporting on the losses on the *Lochiel* forests (Inverness-shire), J. S. Hunter wrote,

> In the early summer our stalkers reported coming across a very large number of carcases - chiefly old stags, hinds and calves. This must have been the result of a very wet winter; rainfall here for the four months October to January amounted to over 39 in [100 cm], followed by a very late and cold spring, so that there was no growth of grass before the end of May.

In consequence the cull of both stags and hinds had to be adjusted during the winter of 1983-84 - the former by as much as 40 per cent. The loss of deer on *Ben Alder* (Inverness-shire) was also considerable and over 250 deer of all ages, which included 50 stags, were found dead and, as on *Lochiel* forests, the stag cull that year was reduced by about 40 per cent. The toll on *Glenshiel* (Ross-shire) was probably about the same, for during the spring over 200 carcases were found scattered over the forest. On the Island of *Rhum* there was also a heavy winter mortality and the stag cull was reduced from 60 to 50.

On *Atholl* forests (Perthshire) there was a very heavy loss of deer after the Red Deer Commission had made a deer count, so any deer population figures they may have been working on for the area in which the census had been taken would have been rather misleading. Strangely enough, on *Glenfeshie* (Inverness-shire), which marches with both the *Glenbruar* and *West Hand* beats of *Atholl*, I was informed by the owner, the late Lord Dulverton, that his deer survived the spring, which had proved to be such a killer in many areas, remarkably well, with only about 4 per cent casualties as compared to only 1 per cent in 1982. He put this down to the abundance of heather on *Glenfeshie*, which took the pressure off the molina grass which had failed to develop the previous spring. Another factor which he considered most important was having maintained a stable population by high culling.

1988–89

As with the high losses of 1983-84, mortality among the deer in the western highlands during the winter of 1988-89 was extremely high, the main causes of which were a combination of too many deer - particularly hinds - and miles of forestry fencing which prevented the animals seeking shelter in their time of need. There was, of course, another factor which no deer forest owner, unless he is prepared to spend a considerable sum of money on artificial feeding, can control, and that is the climate. Commenting on these winter losses, Sir Donald H. Cameron of Lochiel wrote,

> The early part of the year produced atrocious weather and our rainfall at *Achnacarry* for the first three months of the year amounted to 57 in [144.8 cm]. Deer dislike the rain more than they do the cold, and as this was followed by a slow growth in grass, the conditions for the deer in the spring could not have been worse. The result was a very heavy mortality chiefly among old stags, as well as younger beasts and calves, and hinds. These deaths were due to *climatic conditions* and not to bad forest management [an accusation which was widely being raised in the Press and elsewhere].

The ratio of stags to hinds being culled on the three *Lochiel* forests during the past twenty-five years has varied between 1:1.25 and 1:50. During the winter of 1988-89 the stag cull amounted to 151 as compared with the 251 hind cull.

1990–94

Despite periods of heavy snow and a high rainfall in some areas, there were no reports of high winter mortality among the deer during this period.

During the early months of 1990, there was heavy rainfall over much of Scotland, and in particular in Inverness-shire and western Ross-shire. On *Ben Alder* (Inverness-shire) hind stalking had to finish early, due to heavy rain at the end of January washing away almost a mile (1.6 km) of pony paths, as well as part of the access road to Ben Alder lodge. Rainfall during January and February at the lodge was measured at 12.7 in (32.2 cm) and 19.3 in (49 cm) respectively.

During the winters of both 1991 and 1992, in each year there was a heavy fall of snow about mid-October, with drifting remaining in some areas above 1,000 feet (305 m) until the spring.

The winter and spring of 1992-93 were both wet and extremely cold, yet the deer recovered well, and by the autumn stag carcases were reaching the larder in remarkably good condition, with a good covering of fat around the kidneys and saddle.

CHAPTER 7

Poaching

On some forests, such as *Corriemoille* (Ross-shire), which are adjacent to main roads, the deer stock had, by 1948, been reduced to almost half of what it had been just prior to the War, due mainly to extensive poaching. In fact one owner in the area reckoned that out of a yearly kill of 25 stags he was able to shoot 10 and the poachers 15.

On the other hand, forests that were situated well back from main roads were able to hold their numbers well and some had more deer on the ground than formerly. Apropos poaching, a forest owner at the time said,

> Poaching had been bad this winter. It has had the effect of making the deer move away from the main road area and a beat which ought to have yielded eight stags gave us none last season [1947]. On the other hand the far-away beats seemed to have masses of deer, both hinds and stags, which had found out where safety lay.

At that date the fine for poaching was only £2, whereas a deer carcase was able to fetch anything from £6 to £8. A fine of this proportion was, of course, out of all proportion to the offence and, following a conviction and fine, a poacher's pocket was more than reimbursed the next time he pursued his unlawful business.

In my annual report in *The Field* (12/2/49) I stated,

> The fine should be made to fit the crime and this is surely to increase it tenfold. Deer should also be given a close-season, like all other game, and be included in the Night Poaching Act, for it is at night, by the aid of spot lights, that the majority

are taken. Offenders could then be dubbed with an additional fine for killing out of season as well as a prison sentence for their nocturnal activities. Only by such means can there be any hope of checking this menace.

During 1949 poaching was just as bad as, if not worse than, the previous year, the forests to suffer most being those adjacent to a main road, with most of the poaching being done at night from cars using a powerful spotlight to pick out the deer that had come down to feed on the grass near the roadside. The only way to prevent this activity would, perhaps, be by continual patrolling of the roads, but such an undertaking would be impossible. The heaviest toll to be taken was amongst the stags for, quite apart from providing more venison to sell, they seemed to frequent the roadside more than the hinds. The poacher invariably cut off the head, and one forest owner reported that he had found no less than twenty such grim reminders of the poacher's nightly toll.

As already mentioned, a fine of only £2 merely encouraged an offender to resume his 'profession' in order to make good the cost of the fine. One poacher, however, did get thirty days and his rifle confiscated because he was not in possession of a Firearms Certificate – a careless oversight on his part, for at that date it would only have cost him five shillings in the first instance, with little or no chances of its issue being refused.

On another occasion a poacher was employing a companion to drive some deer towards him. It was about 5.30 p.m. and, probably due to the uncertain light, his friend was mistaken for a deer and shot dead. Court proceedings were naturally taken out against him, but he was admonished! Had he killed a deer, then presumably he would have received a £2 fine and would, therefore, not have got off so lightly.

About the same time a poacher, who was caught red-handed on *Strathbran* forest (Ross-shire), turned out to be an Inverness-shire policeman! It would appear that he preferred a deer forest beat to the one allotted to him by his chief.

In 1951 the Poaching of Deer (Scotland) Bill had its second reading in the House of Lords, but was never passed. At that time, however, a proper close-season for deer in Scotland was even more important, for not only would it automatically have made the offence for poaching far more serious, but it would also have prevented the slaughter of deer, *without* authority, by farmers whenever hard weather brought the deer down to lower altitudes for shelter and sustenance.

At this period, poaching was not confined to the mainland and was particularly bad on Mull, where local butchers had venison for sale all the year round.

During 1951 poaching of deer was as bad as ever and a big toll was taken among deer which had been driven by the hard weather to seek some shelter on the low ground bordering the main roads. I wrote in my report for the year,

> Equally serious are the depredations made on deer stocks by some proprietors of deer forests, and owners or tenants of sheep farms, who organise winter deer drives with the sole object of killing as many deer as possible quite regardless of sex, size and condition, with the minimum expenditure of time or effort.

Deer carcases at that time (1951) were fetching around £10 each, so the results of a winter deer drive could be a very profitable undertaking. I concluded my report by saying,

> The only way this barbarous practice can be stamped out of the highlands is to give deer a proper close season, make it illegal for venison to be received or sold out of season, and make fines for poaching and non-observance of the close-season sufficiently severe to act as a deterrent to potential transgressors of the law.

At last the Government was becoming aware of what was happening in Scotland, but it was to be another eight years before any legal action was taken, and the Deer (Scotland) Act of 1959 became operative, with a further three years before the close season clause came into effect 21 October 1962.

In 1953 several owners were starting to report on the scarcity of the older and heavier class of stag, as well as the paucity of hinds in some areas, and it was becoming apparent that these were the two classes of deer that were suffering at the hands of the poachers or during the above-mentioned winter *battues*. For instance, one deer forest owner in the south Monadhliath district of Inverness-shire wrote to say,

> Each year there is a marked decrease in the number of the heavier beasts due to the shooting of these by the sheep farmers and others during the winter months and early spring. I have never seen so many wounded animals on the hill as there were this year. Some terribly maimed with twisted limbs, or a foot shot away. Most of these wounds appeared to be caused by gun shot, as the wretched animals had big swellings over the injured joint and between the haunches. Frequently at weekends gangs of men with every type of firearm go out to wound and maim the deer, callous to the suffering of wild animals as so many of them seem to be.

There were similar reports of 'a lot of wounded beasts about' from Perthshire and Ross-shire – particularly in the Kinlochewe district, where for many years, the roadside poacher had been able to take a considerable toll of the deer that wandered down of an evening to the strath alongside the Garve to Loch Maree road.

Three years later, mainly due to the low price being offered for venison, it would appear that poaching was becoming less attractive, and fewer cases were being brought to the courts. On *Glenlyon* (Perthshire) two hydro-electric employees were caught red-handed with a stag one Sunday night, whilst on another Perthshire forest two other poachers were also caught and fined. A few poachers were still active along the Garve–Loch Maree road (Ross-shire) – mainly local men who, although they had been caught several times in the past, would never give it up unless, and until, they were given heavier sentences. Wrote one forest owner,

> The greatest indiscriminate destruction of deer was being carried on by small – and not so small – proprietors who have acquired property since the

War. These men – as well as their tenant farmers – shoot every deer they can, either for cash or, what they call, in the interest of sheep farming.

By 1958 the price for venison was starting to improve (*see* page 210) and, as a new Deer Bill was under review, this encouraged the poachers to become more active and make as much money as possible before the more severe penalties included in the forthcoming Deer (Scotland) Act became operative.

In the Invergarry district alone, at least 27 stags were shot by poachers during the first fortnight of December 1958, whilst in *Strathconon* (Ross-shire) poaching was said to have reached 'insufferable limits.'

In the spring of 1959 poaching was particularly bad in the Kinlochewe district of Ross-shire, and Major J. L. Garton reported that 'over 400 deer of all types and sizes were taken out of one glen. It will take years to wipe out this murderous assault.' The Close-Season section of the 1959 Deer Act would not become operative until 21 October 1962.

By 1969 the price of venison in some areas was fetching 4s 11d per lb, which was more than double what it had been a few years previously, and this not only encouraged the poacher to become more active, but increased legal out-of-season killings on the grounds of marauding. In 1970 poaching was reported as being particularly bad on Mull.

During 1973 poachers in Sutherland were using a crossbow, and on *Gordonbush* two arrows were found, one having killed a hind but the other having missed its mark.

Poaching along the seven-mile coast-line of *Kingairloch* forest (Argyllshire) was particularly bad during the winter of 1973.

During the next eight years poaching and out-of-season killing of deer, under the cloak of marauding, continued to take its toll in some areas, but a much publicised 'stalker patrol' operating in the Garve district did appear to reduce poaching activity in that area. During 1978, however, a considerable number of deer were poached in the *Ben Hee* area of Sutherland, whilst on Mull the late Viscount Masereene and Ferrard reported that poaching had reached 'an appalling' level, and it was known that one gang had sold an estimated £15,000 of venison. Several local poachers had been caught, but received fines of only about £25 to £50, and the gear seems never to have been confiscated.

By 1978 poaching had also become a problem around *Ederline* in Argyllshire, which is surrounded by Forestry Commission plantations. W. Warde-Aldam, the owner of *Ederline*, wrote,

> It is very difficult to catch poachers who are quite prepared to carry away haunches and leave the rest . . . The Forestry Commission try their best, but it is a very difficult task to catch any poacher in the act over such a vast area. The situation is not helped by public pressure on the Commission for amenity and leisure. This, in many cases, means public access to most Forestry Commission roads or at least a liberal distribution of gate keys which can so easily be cut for a duplicate.

During the following year a poacher in the Newtonmore area was known to have sold over £2,000 worth of venison, yet when taken to court his fine amounted to only £140. In the same year two poachers caught near *Ledgowan* (Ross-shire) were only fined £50 each – the equivalent sale value, then, of one good yeld hind.

During 1981 poaching still remained a problem in some areas. In early October of that year two poachers were seen to kill four stags (one mature, one knobber and two calves) on *Loch Choire* (Sutherland), but unfortunately both men managed to escape.

Another form of poaching was reported by a guest while stalking in Perthshire. Apparently, an absentee neighbour's stalker was seen trespassing off his ground in order to give his wind to a herd of about 150 deer which were eventually moved on to an adjacent piece of ground. During the manoeuvre the stalker had, apparently, had to cross two different marches.

> The whole operation was skillfully operated, and having got the deer where he wanted them it was merely a question of letting them drift around and eventually work their way back up wind on to his own ground . . . the whole operation was skillfully executed and bore out local opinion that similar raids on his neighbour's deer had been carried out before.

Needless to say, any poaching activity is bound to leave a number of wounded deer, for understandably no poacher, the sound of his shot having alerted the stalker or police, is going to waste much time looking for a wounded beast that runs off. In 1973 three of the stags shot on *Fairburn* (Ross-shire) had previous bullet wounds, whilst on *Glencallater* (Aberdeenshire) four stags shot in 1979 had broken legs. During the same season two stags were found dead on *Remony* (Perthshire), one having starved to death on account of its lower jaw having been blown off.

On *Ben Hee* (Sutherland) a stag was shot in 1982 with a crossbow arrow deeply embedded in its spine. Needless to say it was in poor condition, its injuries including two cracked ribs. On the same forest two other crippled stags were shot, but unfortunately a third, which was hobbling about on three legs, could not be accounted for. 'These are, unfortunately, the signs of the times in my part of the country,' commented C. H. S. Garton, the owner of *Ben Hee*.

Not every wounded beast seen is the result of a poaching incident, for there are some people who either don't realise that the beast shot at has been wounded, or just don't bother to follow up or fail to report to neighbouring forests' stalkers that a wounded beast has been lost. But on forests in the vicinity of a main road the poacher must take the blame for these casualties.

In areas that don't have good road access, the poachers don't take the trouble to remove the complete carcase. On *Mamore* forest (Inverness-shire), for instance, in 1987 poachers left behind the forequarters of seven stags, only removing the most valuable parts of the cascase – the saddle and haunches.

In 1989 the head stalker on *Dalnaspidal* (Perthshire) was one evening collecting his sheep when he heard a shot from across the main A9 road which separates *Dalnaspidal* from *Dalnacardoch* (Perthshire) and saw two men running, as well as a herd of deer on the move. He quickly ran back to his house, which was about a mile distant, in order to telephone the police who, unfortunately, refused to set up a road block on the A9 but would, nevertheless, come immediately to investigate, arriving some thirty minutes later, with blue lights flashing. By this time, however, the poacher had left, but before doing so had succeeded in dragging the carcase off the hill, crossing over dual carriageways and concealing it, intending, no doubt, to return after dark. The following day the stalker found the gralloch of a hind near the spot from where he had heard the shot, but the poachers were not seen again.

Although I hold no brief for the modern deer poacher, the resourcefulness of one had the flavour of the exploits of that greatest deer poacher of all time, R. Gordon-Cumming, who, in about 1842, by his ingenuity was able to shoot a fine 11-pointer on *Braulen* forest (Inverness-shire), right under the nose of the keeper waiting for him, and still get away with the head. Our modern poacher, however, was not quite so ambitious as Gordon-Cumming for his quarry was only a hind which he had shot and left hidden in some bracken on the hillside, with the intention of fetching it at some later hour. In the meantime, however, the stalker, having heard the shot, had found the carcase in the bracken and, taking up a position some distance away, awaited the return of the poacher.

After a time the stalker noticed a small van coming up the glen and, as it failed to reappear from behind a small clump of trees that bordered the road immediately below where the hind was lying on the hill, he assumed that the poacher had returned and would shortly be seen walking up the hill for the carcase, whereupon he himself would creep down to the car and await the poacher's return 'red-handed'. But no poacher appeared, and after waiting perhaps a full hour the van was then seen to drive away from the glen. Puzzled as to what had happened, the stalker walked over to the patch of bracken, and to his amazement, found the carcase had gone! Apparently the poacher had realised the situation and, instead of walking up to the carcase, had crawled up under cover and, having tied a rope to the hind, had somehow managed to crawl back under cover, towing the hind behind him (*Field Sports*, Vol. 2, No. 12, December 1953). I think this particular poacher earned his venison.

The solution to maintaining control on the sale of illegally taken venison would seem to be carcase tagging – a system which I first proposed over forty years ago (*Country Life* 14/3/52), and have since repeated on numerous occasions both in the press and at meetings, being introduced at one as 'Mr Tag'! From a postal enquiry I carried out in 1981 among over 100 deer forest owners, it would appear that 72 per cent were in favour, 8 per cent against and the remaining 20 per cent – which included forests to which access was by boat only and where poaching was, therefore, not a problem – had no firm opinion one way or another. Up to date, however, carcase tagging has failed to receive support from the Red Deer Commission (*see* page 149).

'The Monarch of all he surveys' (Charles B. Barber 1845-94)

Rifle support: Jack McKinney, who has only one arm, uses a forked stick. Stalking at *Glencarron* (Ross-shire) in 1975.

A small portable and adjustable rifle support has become increasingly popular in recent years.

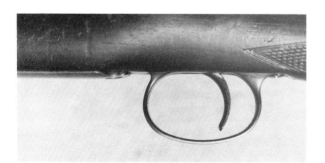

Detachable cheekpiece for rifle stock,
(left) raised, showing method of attachment and *(right)* clamped down in position.

Trigger pressure
(left) Most stalking rifles have a trigger that is straighter in design than one fitted to a match rifle for target work.
(right) With the deep curve of the match trigger, this ensures that digital pressure is always at the same point.

Mrs P. Fleming, with Ian MacRae, on *Black Mount* Forest (Argyllshire) during the early seventies.

What no stag! *(R McPhail)*
After the wartime character
of Mr Chad.

(i) A nervous pony has to be blindfolded.

(ii) The stag should be placed to the left of, and at right-angles to, the pony.

Loading up a stag on to a 'garron'

(iii) With one man supporting the head and shoulders of the stag, and the other the rump, the stag will be raised on to the saddle.

(iv) The stag's head should be strapped back, well clear of the pony's head.

Saddling up the ponies at Sron-phadruig Lodge before a day on *Dalnacardoch* Forest (Perthshire) in 1961. The pony on the left is carrying a *Glenquoich* type saddle suitable for both riding or carrying a carcase, whilst the one on the right has a *Glenstrathfarrar* saddle designed for carrying a carcase only.

Unloading the ponies at Sronphad-ruig Lodge, *Dalnacardoch*.

The end of a successful day.

The Norwegian Fjord or Vestlandet pony proved to be a trifle on the small side for carrying a large Highland stag.

One of the earliest vehicles used on a deer forest was the HAFLINGER, but it was not sufficiently robust for rough treatment.

By the seventies many forests were using a small vehicle called the GNAT, which on reasonable terrain, was an ideal vehicle for the single-handed stalker, provided he kept clear of deep holes and rocky terrain.

Another one carcase pick-up vehicle was the SNOWTRIC, but it was best suited for heathery terrain.

A metal sledge can also be attached for dragging an additional carcase off suitable terrain.

The six wheel AMPHICAT never achieved the success hoped, and it was also best suited for a non-rocky terrain.

The four-wheel KAWA-SAKI, as well as the similar HONDA, have both proved to be invaluable for the single-handed stalker. In their original 3-wheel version they could be a death trap, and were liable to overturn on steep or uneven terrain.

The 'Rolls-Royce' of recovery vehicles for non-rocky terrain has undoubtedly been the SNOW-TRAC, for it provides not only both shelter and comfort for its passengers, but can carry up to half a dozen carcases.
A SNOWTRAC on *Langwell* forest (Caithness) in 1975.

The other extreme was the BUCKTOTER – a barrow type frame – which relied solely on human endeavour to balance the supported load and provide 'motive' power.
(Left) A twin wheeled 'bucktoter', which was being used by the R. D. Commission on *Kintail* (Ross-shire), here being demonstrated by David Bowlby of Inverinate.
(Above) A single-wheel 'bucktoter' which has a metal bicycle type frame.

CHAPTER 8

Stalking and Other Incidents

Two Stags with One Shot

During the 1966 season there were a couple of reports of two stags having been shot with one bullet – a feat that should only ever occur by pure accident and not by design, but I realise it has frequently been achieved by poachers, and by stalkers during hind culling. On *Glencarron* (Ross-shire) a small beast moved up behind the stag being shot at and paid the price. At *Langwell* (Caithness) a guest fired at a stag at a range of about 100 yards (90 m) and, much to his surprise, killed another stag which had been standing some 30 yards (28 m) away to the right. The stag fired at ran away a short distance and required a further stalk before being finished off with a second shot. On skinning this beast, it was found that the first bullet had passed slightly behind the heart before ricocheting off a rib and entering the second beast in the chest, killing it stone dead.

A somewhat comparable event occurred on *Talladh-a-Bheithe* (Perthshire) in 1989, when a guest aimed at and killed, stone dead, a stag, only to see a second beast, standing some 20 yards (18 m) away to its left, collapse, the bullet apparently having ricocheted off a rock before striking it in the heart. If the guest was in search of a trophy, it was certainly his day for, whilst the beast originally aimed at was only a knobber, the second stag turned out to be a good ten-year-old 'royal'!

On *Kinloch* (Sutherland), during the 1992 season, two stags were killed outright by a single shot, the second and smaller beast having been obscured by the 'target' animal.

In 1987 on *Park* (Isle of Lewis) a stag and hummel resting side by side were also killed in similar circumstances, the former covering the existence of the hummel in the background (*see* page 86).

In 1979 a German guest staying at *Kingairloch* (Argyllshire) shot two stags with one bullet, but one of them required a second shot to finish it off.

On *Langwell* (Caithness) in 1971, one bullet accounted for two stags, the first beast having been shot through the heart before the bullet passed on to hit a second stag, standing nearby, just below the eye.

In 1974, Friday 13 was unlucky for two stags on *Corrour* forest (Inverness-shire), for on that day Mr Harvie-Watt fired a shot at the right-hand beast of two that were facing each other about 5 feet (1.5 m) apart, the range being about 80 yards (73 m). The bullet passed through the stag's body and, after hitting a rock directly behind, ricocheted on to the second stag, hitting it in the neck. Both animals got up but, after running about 40 yards (36 m), both fell dead.

Stags and Foxes

An unusual 'double' was achieved in 1969 by Colonel D. E. Baird, whilst stalking as a guest of Viscount Mountgarret on *Wyvis* (Ross-shire). On 9 October he shot a 6-pointer stag and immediately, at the sound of the shot, a fox was disturbed and was killed with a second shot. Unless the rifle used was a double-barrelled weapon, then I doubt if this feat could qualify as a true 'right and left', which requires that the weapon must be swung from one target to another, with no distinguishable pause and without the weapon leaving the shoulder.

During the 1967 season a number of stalkers reported an increase in foxes on their ground. On *Couldoran* (Ross-shire) Miss Huntsman, having shot a stag, was walking over to the carcase when two foxes – probably cubs of the year – got up under her feet and ran away. Apparently the stag and the two foxes had been sheltering together in the same heathery burn. On *Glencarron* (Ross-shire) Macrae, the stalker, whilst hind stalking, spotted two foxes curled up asleep on top of Ben Fahaig and, after a successful stalk, both were accounted for.

An unusual event was witnessed on *Talladh-a-Bheithe* (Perthshire) on 2 October 1972. While spying for a suitable beast to stalk, a stag was seen to disturb a fox from a clump of heather. At first the fox appeared to be extremely annoyed at having its slumbers disturbed in this fashion, and started to snap and snarl at the stag, who evasively moved around to get above the fox. The two then started to play a game of 'tag', with first one and then the other making a mock attack, the stag striking out with its fore feet and lowering its head whilst the fox took evasive action with a series of pounces. This game went on for about a quarter of an hour before the fox eventually got bored and ran off. On this occasion no attempt was made to achieve a stag/fox double.

Apropos a 'double' at deer and fox, I myself have twice achieved this whilst roe stalking during the rut, the last occasion being in August 1993. On each occasion I was using an artificial roe call to attract a buck and, despite the sound of the shot, the fox continued to approach and was finally killed within about 10 yards (9 m) of the dead buck some thirty seconds later. Clearly not a 'right and left' but certainly a 'double'.

In 1980 Ronald Kipper, the head keeper on *Amulree* (Perthshire) whilst positioning himself for a shot at a stag, happened to notice that he was being watched by a fox that was sitting some 50 yards (45 m) away from the stag. Without hesitation he shot the fox first and then the stag, the range on each occasion being about 120 yards (110 m).

During the 1995 season a guest at *Kingie* (Inverness-shire) shot a fox and a stag from the same firing position, taking the fox first.

Many years ago I was faced with a similar situation but, being more interested in a pair of 8-pointer antlers than a fox mask or brush, I took the former first. Needless to say, Reynard didn't hang around to see who was to be next, so I missed the chance of a stag/fox double.

Compassion and Aggression

In 1965 an unusual incident was witnessed by Colonel C. A. Peel on *Glenshee* (Perthshire). A stag, in company with other beasts, was shot, but before falling dead it stood swaying for a few minutes, during which time all but one of the other stags moved off. The remaining stag, not much different in size, approached the wounded beast and immediately started to lick its face, before moving off to join the others.

A comparable incident happened on *Struy* (Inverness-shire) in 1967, but on this occasion the onlooker was more aggressive. On 7 October a beast, after being shot, lay down and was obviously badly wounded. Whereupon a second stag, which had been standing some 120 yards (110 m) away, charged up towards the wounded beast, which then stood up but was immediately bowled over by the second stag, and then finally died. His assailant was then shot also.

The Continental Approach

Deer stalking in Scotland is very much a 'British way of life', and nowhere else in the world does any field sport entail so much crawling before a shot can be taken. With the introduction of the telescope sight, however, during the years preceding the Second World War, the average range of shot was considerably increased – and material wear on plus-four trousers likewise reduced! As mentioned on page 11, the introduction of the 'scope sight has, unfortunately, encouraged many shots to be taken at ranges beyond that at which the rifle and 'scope have been zeroed.

During the 1960s I accompanied a German guest who was anxious to shoot his first Scottish stag, though previously he had shot both stags and other large game in Europe. In five days stalking not once was he prepared to get his *loden* hose wet through crawling, but fortunately, on his last day on the hill, we were able to find a stag in such a position that a stalk could be made to within about 100 yards (90 m) from behind the cover of a large rock, provided a stooping posture was maintained during the final approach.

In 1975 the stalker on a Sutherland forest succeeded in getting the *Rifle* – who on this occasion happened to be a Spaniard – within range of a party of deer and, as the stalker and *Rifle* lay side-by-side in the heather, the former indicated to the *Rifle* which beast should be taken. He then handed him the rifle and told him to take the shot whenever he was ready. Whereupon the Spaniard leapt to his feet and charged in the direction of the stag, firing as rapidly as possible from the shoulder as he went. Eventually the stalker was able to overtake the *Rifle* and inform him that that was not the manner in which stags were normally shot in Scotland!

Language Problem

Lack of knowledge of the English language was undoubtedly responsible for the loss of two wounded stags in 1982. On this occasion a German visitor, having wounded a stag with his first shot, misunderstood the stalker's instruction to 'give it another', and unfortunately fired at a second beast which also ran off wounded. The following day was spent searching for the two animals, but with what success was never reported.

Blooding

I was unaware that the old and rather barbarous custom of 'blooding' a *Rifle* on killing a first stag was still being practised in Scotland, but apparently it still is, for occasionally I receive a photograph of someone – mainly an American visitor – who has been subjected to this quite unnecessary ritual, proudly standing over their victim.

Stalking a Dead Stag

During the 1987 season the stalking party on *Ben More* (Mull) wasted a full half day trying to approach a 'sitting' stag in a rather exposed position, only to discover, to their chagrin, that the beast was already dead, having been wounded across the march before moving on to *Ben More*, where it had died.

Back in 1938 I experienced a similar incident whilst stalking on Beinn a Chroin, *Balquhidder*, (Perthshire). We had spotted a 6-pointer lying among a party of resting hinds, with its head stretched out on the ground as though asleep. A stalk was attempted and we were within about 400 yards (360 m) of the deer when a change of wind revealed our presence, causing the hinds to run off. The stag, however, remained, and it was only after a slow and careful crawl to within a few yards that we finally realised the beast was already dead, having succumbed to a stomach wound received earlier that day on the neighbouring forest.

A Shot Not Required

An unusual event occurred on *Glenlochsie* (Perthshire) in 1965. The stalking party had approached a stag and the shot was about to be taken when the animal fell over, dead. It had apparently been wounded on a neighbouring forest and had wandered over the march on to *Glenlochsie*.

A Long Stalk

During the 1968 season John Glen, whilst staying as a guest of Captain Bailey at *Inversanda* (Argyllshire), had been promised a day's stalking on his own, so on the appointed day his host took him out at dawn for a short reconnaissance to see if a shootable beast was visible, handy to the lodge. About 8 a.m. an old 8-pointer was sighted, so John Glen decided to forego his breakfast and go straight after the stag thinking that, at the latest, he would be back for an early 'brunch'. Matters, however, did not proceed according to plan, and it was not until about 4.15 p.m. that the stag was finally shot within half a mile of the spot where it had first been spotted some eight and a half hours earlier.

Sleeping Deer

An unusual incident occurred on *Gaick* (Inverness-shire) during the 1988 season. On one misty day during October the stalking party walked right up to a three or four-year-old stag which appeared to be fast asleep. After walking round him once or twice the stalker prodded the beast with his stick, whereupon it rose to its feet and trotted off in no great haste. It is not known what – if anything – ailed him, but his juvenile age would seem to preclude that too much rutting activity had been the cause.

A similar incident happened on *Badanloch* (Sutherland) on 1 October 1975, when the stalker, accompanied by two guests, approached an unwounded stag and was able to prod it with his stick – a case of let sleeping stags lie!

A somewhat comparable incident occurred in 1969 on *Mamore* forest (Inverness-shire), when the stalker and ponyman went out to collect a stag that had been shot by a *Rifle* the previous day. As the *Rifle* had been stalking on his own, after gralloching it he had been forced to leave it out overnight. On the following day the *Rifle* had, unfortunately, been unable to accompany the stalker and ponyman back to the hill, but had given precise instructions as to where the beast could be found. Sure enough, when they reached the area, there was a stag lying some 200 yards (180 m) away. Imagine their surprise when at only about 30 yards; (27 m), it suddenly sprang to life and bolted off! They then spotted the dead stag lying some 80 to 100 yards; (80 m) away and it wasn't long before it was loaded on the saddle *en route* for the larder. The other beast – probably exhausted by the rut – must have been so sound asleep that it hadn't even heard the stalker and ponyman chatting to each other as they approached.

Stag Mounting a Dead Hind

On 21 October 1983, whilst a guest was out hind stalking on *Sannox* forest (Isle of Arran), a young stag was seen to approach a dead hind that had just been shot. Wrote Alan S. Ross,

> It tried for a while to get the hind on to its feet, and on one occasion succeeded in rolling the hind down the hill with its pawing. When this did not work, the stag tried to mate with the hind by lying

down on top of it. Rob, the stalker, then sent the ghillie forward in order to chase the stag away, but the stag had other ideas, and finally the ghillie had to beat a hasty retreat. When eventually, however, the stag saw all members of the stalking party approaching in a body, it realised it was time to go, and with no further ado, ran off smartly.

Hind Dying of Heart Attack?

In 1969 the *Ben Alder* (Inverness-shire) stalking party was watching a mixed herd of about thirty stags and hinds moving up a hillside at a distance of about 200 yards (180 m), when a hind in the group suddenly dropped dead. She was not old and was in perfect condition, and certainly there was no apparent reason for her sudden demise.

Friendly Red Deer Calf

During the 1969 stalking season a lady was returning by herself down to the loch on *Ben Alder* (Inverness-shire) in order to take the boat back to the lodge, when a red deer calf came rushing down the hill and started to lick her hand. It then followed her for a short while down the loch side before departing. It can only be assumed that the calf had, at one time, been bottle fed, probably by a shepherd. (*See also* Two hinds that went stalking, page 98).

Another Chance after Twelve Months

A visitor, stalking from the Invergarry Hotel (Inverness-shire) in 1957, had the unusual opportunity of killing a stag that he had wounded during the previous autumn, for not only did the stag have distinctive antlers but the old bullet wound was traceable in the carcase.

'Royal' and Snipe with One Shot

Shortly before the War, a guest on *Wyvis* (Ross-shire), after shooting a 'royal', found within a few yards of the carcase a snipe with its wing blown off. The snipe was still alive, but after being killed fortunately required only a pocket to bring it back to the lodge, for only one pony was out that day.

Birds Causing Panic among Deer

Odd incidents can suddenly create panic among deer, as exemplified by the following, which occurred twice on *Blackmount* (Argyllshire) during 1969 and was described by Robin Fleming as follows:

> We saw high up on the hill what we first thought to be a balloon or parachute, which sent the deer running off in a panic. We then realised that it was a flock of little birds flying in tight formation. The same flock was seen on another day, and once again the deer appeared to be terrified.

Unfortunately the birds were never positively identified, but it was thought they might have been either fieldfares or starlings.

Deer Eating Frogs

In 1984 a large number of small frogs were seen on *Balmacaan* forest (Sutherland), up to a height of 2,000 feet (610 m). In their search for minerals when growing new antlers, deer will eat anything, and my old friend, the late Dr Fraser Darling, once saw a stag wading in a shallow, peaty dub and eating frogs.

A Travelling Stag

In 1982 David Midwood, the owner of *Syre* (Sutherland), was accompanying his brother, who unfortunately missed a stag which had a very distinctive broken left antler. Two days later, whilst stalking at *Kintradwell* (Sutherland) as a guest of Simon Taylor, the owner, a stag was shot which, according to David Midwood, 'was the same beast of that I am quite sure – the head was identical in every detail, as well as the deportment of the beast' (*The Field* 13/11/82). The distance between *Syre* and *Kintradwell* is about 25 miles (40 km).

Stalking a 'Phantom' Stag

At times strange things happen which logical reasoning somehow fails to explain. Sport offers no exception and, indeed, possibly the greatest attraction of sport lies in the fact that the unexpected may step in to turn success into failure – or vice versa.

Some time ago a stalking friend of mine told me of a weird experience that he and his stalker had had with a stag just prior to the last War – and as his story seemed so unusual I asked him to write it down for me, promising that the names of those who witnessed these strange happenings would not be disclosed. This, apparently, is what occurred.

It was in August 1937 that a stag bearing only one antler of rather peculiar shape was first seen on a Sutherlandshire forest. He was seen in company with about a dozen other stags. The stalker, who was accompanied that day by the wife of the proprietor, decided that the one-antlered stag should be their quarry and, as all the beasts were lying down, with very good cover for approach, it appeared that the stalk would offer no great difficulty. For about the last 300 yards (270 m) the stalking party had to pass behind a small hillock, but when they arrived at the place selected for the shot, although all the other stags were still lying peacefully together, there was no sign of the one-antlered stag. He could have left the scene unnoticed during the 300 yards or so that the stalking party was out of sight – but subsequent events make one wonder.

A few days later the owner of the ground was stalking the ground himself and before long he chanced to spot a one-antlered stag which was lying down and which, from the description told to him by his wife, must have been the same beast that had given her the slip some days previously. He therefore decided to stalk it, and all appeared to be going well until, at about 200 yards (180 m) range, the stag just seemed to disappear. As the beast had been pretty well in view the whole time of the stalk, its sudden disappearance naturally puzzled him. In order to make sure, therefore, that he had not, during the course of the stalk, mistaken the actual spot where the stag was lying, he started to retrace his footsteps, but had barely gone more than about four hundred yards (365 m) from the stag when it re-appeared in exactly the same position as before, and was still lying down.

A repeat stalk was therefore made but once again, when about 200 yards from the stag, it just disappeared. This time, however, he continued the stalk and, when within about 100 yards (90 m) of the spot where the stag ought to have been,

'the air', according to his description, 'became absolutely evil despite the fact that it was a nice, bright day'. Although rather unnerved by the whole episode, the stalk was nevertheless continued, until at about forty yards (36 m) range from where the stag ought to have been, he 'could distinctly see the grass flattened as though something was lying on it'.

Anxious to get to the bottom of this, the rifle was withdrawn from its cover, a careful sight taken at the spot where it was presumed the shoulder *should* have been, and he was just about to pull the trigger when something wrenched the rifle out of his hands and hurled it to the ground some three yards (2¾ m) away. Thereupon 'the grass was seen to rise up as if a weight had been taken off', and shortly afterwards, at about 200 yards (180 m) range, the stag suddenly became visible trotting away. Whereupon 'the air became clearer'.

Some days later the owner of the forest, accompanied by Willie the stalker, found the same stag on a different part of the ground in company with a mixed party of other stags and hinds. A stalk was decided upon, and all went well until within about a hundred yards of the deer, when, as on the previous occasion, 'the air seemed to become evil', although the day itself was a nice fine one. This time, however, the stag remained in view the whole time and in due course, at about 90 yards (82 m) a shot was fired at it, 'although', in the words of the owner, 'I expected something to happen'. And something did happen, for apparently the bullet went clean through the one-antlered stag and killed another beast standing some distance behind. A second shot was fired at the same range and on this occasion the bullet 'was distinctly heard to strike but nothing occurred'. The stag ran off, but at about 150 yards (137 m) gave a chance for a third shot. Once again the bullet was heard to strike, but with apparently no ill effect on the stag, which then ran off.

Although the stag was not seen again during the remainder of the stalking season, the stalkers saw it during the winter months until February, when it disappeared altogether.

What is the explanation for this extraordinary train of events?

Its disappearance from the resting herd in the first instance can be explained by the fact that for a short space of time the entire herd was lost to sight during the stalk. But what of its disappearance on the second occasion when it was approached to within 200 yards (182 m)? The owner of the forest *could* have mistaken the exact spot, and although the grass was seen to be lying 'flattened as though something was lying on it', this *could* have been a shadow or play of the wind on the grass. But what about the rifle being knocked out of his hand? Nerves, wind, imagination or what? The owner of the forest was on his own on this occasion, so there was no chance of his stalker having 'accidentally' wrenched the rifle out of his hand. Nor, unfortunately, was there any witness to this event.

And what about the third meeting with this mysterious stag which, on this occasion, at least 'played fair' and remained in sight throughout the whole episode? The owner *may* have been mistaken in believing his first shot went right through the one-antlered stag and killed the one behind, because in his excitement and apprehension he *may* have aimed at the wrong stag, or perhaps missed, the bullet hitting another beast standing to one side. He was, I know, a very experienced deer-stalker and I cannot believe that he would ever dream of taking a shot at an animal knowing full well that another beast was standing directly behind for, unless the former was hit in some bony part of the body, the beast behind would most likely have been hit as well. Hearing the second and third shots strike something is no sure proof that contact with the stag had been made – it could have been a peat hag which can, at times, make the *Rifle* jump to the wrong conclusion. By this time, however, one can appreciate the emotions of the man behind the rifle, and even the most experienced shots *sometimes* have 'stag fever', when even a stag the size of a barn door will be missed!

One thing is certain, however, and that is that none of these shots had any effect on the animal – otherwise it would not have been seen on the ground for the next three to four months. What eventually did become of it will never be known, for whenever the subject was subsequently raised with the stalkers they all seemed strangely silent on the matter.

Not so very far away from the forest where the above occurred lies *Kildonan*, and on this ground a somewhat similar event occurred prior to the First World War, which is described by the Duke of Portland in his book *Fifty Years and More of Sport in Scotland* (1933). In the days before the railway passed through the Kildonan strath, stags used to come on to the ground from off the *Langwell* ground. One big stag, known locally as 'The Piper' – by virtue of the fact that his left antler, growing down over his cheek and then turning up again, somewhat resembled a pipe – visited *Kildonan* for three successive years, and although the *Kildonan* stalkers had several good chances of killing it, all tried without success. At last, in exasperation, Norman Fraser observed, 'This stag has a charmed life; he is either an evil spirit or protected by a witch, and nothing but a silver bullet will have any effect on him. If lead would kill him, he was dead long ago.'

It was a belief that witches had no power over silver, so, accordingly, some silver bullets were made by an Edinburgh gunsmith and everything was in readiness for 'The Piper's' return to *Kildonan* during the next season. Unfortunately, 'The Piper' did not keep his appointment, having, it was subsequently discovered, been poached by a shepherd on the *Braemore* ground - but whether the poacher had used lead or silver bullets is not recorded. I have often wondered, however, how the one-antlered stag my friend fired at would have stood up to silver bullets!

CHAPTER 9

Disturbance on the Hill

Sixty years ago, before mechanical transport and the ever-increasing stream of hikers, bikers and climbers invaded the Highland scene, the deer, stalkers, sheep and shepherds had the place pretty well to themselves, and when a carcase had to be taken from corrie or glen to the larder it was removed more silently – and perhaps with more respect to the departed – on the back of a garron (Highland pony) than today. The pony, alas, has almost disappeared from the stalking scene and in its place are a variety of noisy mechanical vehicles ranging from the commodious Snow-trac, capable of transporting four or five carcases depending on size, to the versatile Argocat and one-beast Honda. Such mechanical aids have undoubtedly removed much of the work-load from the stalker and ghillie, who can now spend most evenings, after a hard day on the hill, at home with the family instead of in the larder, skinning the carcases brought in that day. Today, few carcases are skinned in the forest larder, the majority being collected daily by a venison dealer.

Hikers, Bikers, Climbers

In former days few members of the public had transport to enable them to reach many of the more remote areas of Scotland, so the hiker was then seldom a problem. The motor car, coupled with improved forestry roads, has changed all that, and any spell of fine weather will bring hordes of hikers and mountaineers into the forests, particularly into those more mountainous areas that can provide a challenge for the climber.

One cannot blame anyone for wanting to visit and walk in some of the most beautiful country in Scotland, but during the comparatively brief stag-stalking season, lasting from about 1 August until

20 October and, to a lesser degree, during the winter hind-shooting, it would be only courteous if permission was first sought from the owner or head stalker, who would be in a position to say where people could go without causing too much disturbance to the ground. In some areas this is being done quite satisfactorily – in others the stalker is met with abuse (*see* page 63).

Initially, during the 1950s and early 1960s, it was the weather which dictated the amount of hiker or climber disturbance likely to be experienced, so bad weather, though unpleasant for the deer stalker, did have some compensation. Should, however, a fine spell of weather happen to coincide with the Edinburgh and Glasgow autumn bank-holiday weekend, hiker disturbance will be considerable, and some of the more accessible forests can be virtually cleared of deer during that period. Deer stalkers would therefore be advised to keep clear of these areas as well.

However, by 1964, with better rain gear and a more adventurous spirit among the youth, hiker invasion to the more accessible areas throughout the week was starting to mount. At that time, among the forests to report hiker disturbances were included *Ben More* (Mull), *Abernethy* (Inverness-shire), *Braemore* and *Strone* (Ross-shire), whilst stags on some of the *Balmoral* (Aberdeenshire) beats were also becoming noticeably scarcer, due, it was thought, to the continued passage of hikers to the high ground. Ordnance Survey work on *Corriegarth* (Inverness-shire) also caused some disturbance, whilst on *Morsgail* forest (Isle of Lewis) it was the constant noise of motor boats on Loch Langaval that caused most inconvenience.

During the 1965 season, due, no doubt, to a spell of wet and misty weather, hikers and climbers did not cause as much interference to stalking on either *Balmoral* or *Braemore* as in the previous season, but hikers were, nevertheless, out in force on *Ben More* (Isle of Mull), and the constant sound of motor boats roaring up and down Loch Langaval once again upset the stalking on *Morsgail*.

With more favourable weather than during the previous season, both hikers and mountaineers were out in force during 1966, causing considerable concern in some areas. Lord Burton wrote,

> The mountaineers are doing very serious damage to this forest [*Glenshiel*, Ross-shire]. The deer are being herded into two small areas where they are not only undisturbed, but also unapproachable. As a result they are probably over-grazing these two areas, and cannot be culled properly.

On *Inshriach* (Inverness-shire) two days were spoilt by hikers walking through the forest, whilst on a third occasion it was a party of ponytrekkers who disturbed the ground.

During the past thirty years or so skiing has also become an increasingly popular sport in Scotland, particularly in the Cairngorms and, although this has not interfered with any stag stalking, by 1965 the resident deer population in *Abernethy* (Inverness-shire) and its immediate area was starting to diminish on this account.

During the 1967 season considerable disturbance was created on *Culachy* (Inverness-shire) by hydro-electric engineers who selected the stalking season as being the most convenient time to work on the pylons which, more or less, follow Wade's military road through the centre of this forest.

Elsewhere, hikers again interfered with stalking in most of the usual areas, and in particular on *Inshriach* (Inverness-shire) and *Cluanie* (Ross-shire). Even *Balmoral* (Aberdeenshire), where the Royal Family and their guests were stalking, did not escape intrusion. Colonel W. G. McHardy, the resident factor, wrote,

> We have been plagued during this past season by a larger number of hikers than usual, and as a result many days stalking have been ruined. I have been in touch with the Red Deer Commission and hope to get a further distribution of their pamphlet on *Hill Walking and Stalking*, in the hope of educating many members of the public about the damage they can do by wandering about in a deer forest during the stalking season.

Maybe this pamphlet should also have been brought to the notice of one member of the R.D.C. itself, as the following incident might suggest:- On one occasion during the 1988 stalking season, Lieutenant-Colonel John Moncrieff had a stalk ruined on his forest of *Loyal* (Sutherland) by a hiker who, when approached and asked why he was on the forest in the middle of the stalking season, replied, 'I am one of you. I happen to be a member of the Red Deer Commission.' It would seem that he hadn't read the R.D.C. pamphlet, or maybe it was a case of 'Do as I say, but not as I do!'

The fine weather, particularly during the early part of the 1968 season, encouraged more hikers and climbers to the hill than normal, and many stalks were ruined. Mountaineers were particularly troublesome on *Easter Glenquoich* (Inverness-shire), and many days were spoilt by hill-walkers on both *Inshriach* (Inverness-shire) and on *Flowerdale* (Ross-shire). On Skye, a combination of both hikers and climbers caused most of the deer to move off *Strathaird*.

In 1969 on Mull, the car ferry greatly increased the number of hikers, and the deer on *Ben More* were being continually moved by them. *Cluanie* (Inverness-shire) suffered badly from hikers, and forests in the Aviemore area were beginning to report fewer deer in the area due to tourist pressure.

1970 turned out to be a tragic season for *Ben Alder* (Inverness-shire). On 28 August a hiker was seen climbing Ben Alder 3,757 feet (1,145 m). The following day his body was found at the foot of a 320 foot (98 m) high rock face. While the search party was looking for this hiker a hind was seen to fall over the rocks and break her back. But worst of all, one of the guests returning to London on the M1 motorway had a fatal accident. Tragedy never comes singly.

Fine weather during the 1972 season brought out hikers and climbers in their numbers and, to mention but one forest, *Affaric* (Inverness-shire) had several long stalks ruined at the last moment by the sudden arrival of hill-walkers.

Forests which reported increased hiker disturbance during the 1973 season included *Ben More* (Mull), *Affaric* (Inverness-shire), *Glencarron* and *Cluanie* (Ross-shire).

On *West Benula* (Ross-shire), at the beginning of the 1974 season, considerable disturbance of the ground was caused by a two-day exercise carried out by the R.A.F. Mountain Rescue Team, together with their dogs, and as a result the deer did not properly settle down again for about three weeks. Whilst one cannot fail to admire the great work these rescue teams do to save the lives of people who, through ill luck or foolhardiness, find themselves in difficult positions, there would seem to be at least six or seven other months in the year when an exercise of this nature could be carried out without interfering with the deerstalking season.

Although the generally poor weather of 1974 reduced the number of hill-walkers roaming the hills, it didn't seem to deter some of the climbers,

and on such forests as *Cluanie* (Ross-shire) that can provide suitable terrain for rock climbing, a number of stalks were completely ruined by climbers, whose brightly coloured anoraks were visible to the deer over a considerable distance.

Despite the extremely wet weather over much of Scotland during the 1979 season, it was mild, and disturbance from both hikers and climbers was as bad as ever. Hikers were particularly troublesome on *Glenlochay* and *Dalmunzie* (Perthshire), as well as on *Achnacarry South* and *Kinloch Hourn* (Inverness-shire), whilst on *Glenshiel* (Ross-shire) the deer were being continually disturbed by mountaineers. On *Inveraray* (Argyllshire) no fewer than nine days stalking were completely ruined due to hill-walking parties and climbers.

With so many days lost on some forests due to mist and then, when the mountains were clear, by hiker disturbance, it was not surprising that a number of forests had considerable difficulty in achieving their 1979 target cull.

Despite the atrocious weather of 1980, which restricted the activity of the climbers in many areas, hikers were out in force on most days. Twenty years or so ago hiking in the Scottish mountains was principally a weekend activity, but it has now become a seven-day occupation.

There is little doubt that some people – fortunately a minority – go into the forest with the sole purpose of interfering with any deer stalking that may be taking place. During 1981 the following note was left in one of the bothies on *Affaric* (Inverness-shire) which hikers are permitted to use:

> *This is the deer-culling season – so we've come all the way from Elgin in an attempt to curb this uncivilised practice – we went into the hills yesterday (5 October) to warn the poor deer of their imminent fate. Hope others will follow our example.*
>
> [Signed by two people who claimed to be members of The Deer Preservation Society (D.P.S.).]

There was another wet season in 1982, but this did not in the least deter the hiker, and a number of forests, which included *Blackmount* (Argyllshire), *Glenfeshie* (Inverness-shire) and *Atholl* (Perthshire), all reported an increase in hill-walkers, some of whom wore highly-coloured anoraks. For a change, however, the head stalker at *Inveraray* (Argyllshire) was able to report that 'not a single day's stalking had been spoilt by the hill-walkers thanks to their good co-operation, mainly in the Ben Bhuidhe area'.

Despite the bad weather, hill-walkers continued to disrupt stalking on many forests in 1983, four complete days being ruined by them on *Achnacarry South* (Inverness-shire). On *Glenshiel* (Ross-shire) Lord Burton was of the opinion that the continued disturbance of the hinds by hill-walkers during the late spring had caused abortion in animals already in very poor condition, and as a result successful calving was very low that summer.

The fine weather of 1984 brought out the hikers in larger numbers than ever. On *Dalnaspidal* (Perthshire), which has three Munros, this mountainous area of the forest is now virtually useless for stalking, due to constant invasion by mountaineers anxious to log their Munros. Munro is the name applied to a Scottish mountain of at least 3,000 feet (914 m), so named after Sir H. T. Munro who published a list of all such peaks in the *Journal of the Scottish Mountaineering Club* for 1891.

On *Strone* (Ross-shire) a party of hill-walkers were found camping well into the forest. On *New Kelso* (Ross-shire) climbers, as well as a party of geologists, also contributed to the disturbance of the ground.

On *Culachy* (Inverness-shire), during the 1984 season, an unusual intruder was a large, shaggy wild goat which disrupted a stalk by chasing five sheep through the corrie just as the stalking party were about to reach the selected firing point. Unfortunately the goat was travelling too fast and the range was too far, otherwise it might have received the bullet intended for the stag.

Not surprisingly, the fine weather of 1986 encouraged hikers to take to the hill in considerable numbers, and in some areas they seriously interfered with stalking. On *Dalnaspidal* (Perthshire), due to hiker disturbance, one area of the forest is now a complete waste of time to stalk on for, whereas in former years hill-walker disturbance was mostly confined to weekends, during 1986 they were out almost daily. On *Mar* (Aberdeenshire) hikers were a particular problem on the west end of the forest, whilst on *Culachy* (Inverness-shire) Wade's road running through the centre of the forest was attracting not only the hill-walker, but also the autocross cyclist only too

anxious to find a really rough track on which to test or break his motorcycle – and perhaps his neck as well!

On *Glenshiel* (Ross-shire) and *Cluanie* (Inverness-shire) the steep corries have now been ruined for stalking by the mountaineers. During 1986 members of the stalking party had a narrow escape from being killed or injured by falling stones dislodged by some mountaineer above them.

During the 1988 season an unpleasant incident occurred on *Dalnacardoch* forest (Perthshire) when during an actual stalk, a party of hikers was encountered – fortunately out of sight of the deer – in a burn. On being requested to leave, they flatly refused. By good fortune their presence had not unduly disturbed the deer, which had moved only a short distance away. It was possible, therefore, to continue with the stalk and eventually the stag was shot. By this time, however, the hikers had left, only to retaliate by stealing the keys from the Land-Rover parked further down the glen, thus delaying recovery of the carcase until the following morning.

During the 1989 season disturbance by hill-walkers continued unabated. On *Camusrory* (Inverness-shire) two complete days were lost by walker disturbance, whilst on another occasion a party of hill-walkers deliberately set about disrupting a stalk by moving about on the hill above the deer and shouting.

Knoydart (Inverness-shire) is one of the least accessible localities on the west coast and yet it has become a favourite area for the hill-walker, and deer stalking has suffered in consequence. Some of the best areas on *Camusrory* are now virtually useless for deer stalking, whilst on *Knoydart* forest itself the stags are no longer able to rut on the higher slopes, but are forced to keep to the lower ground.

Disturbance by hill-walkers during 1990 was particularly serious on the Isle of Arran's two forests of *Dougarie* and *Sannox*, the former having stalks ruined on no less than eleven different occasions, by the intrusion of hill-walkers. 'This sort of disturbance', comments S. C. Gibbs the owner, 'is making a proper management cull increasingly difficult and very time-consuming.' Neighbouring *Sannox* suffered even worse, with fifteen stalks being ruined not only by the presence of hill walkers, but also by parties of geologists.

During 1990 a new pastime entered the stalking scene, and that was the use of mountain bikes and all-terrain vehicles capable of tackling tracks never intended for transport of this nature. Wade's road, which runs over the 2,500-foot (760 m) high Corrieyairack Pass from Fort Augustus to Loch Laggan is rapidly becoming a 'motorway' for such types of vehicles, to the detriment of stalking in the forests of *Culachy* and *Corrieyairack* through which it passes.

During 1991 *Kinveachy* (Inverness-shire) had one day completely ruined by the appearance of a party of 'cowboys' riding around the forest on motor bikes.

Warning Notices

Although some estates have posted notices on the roads or gates leading to the forest, notifying would-be hill-walkers that stalking was in progress, such measures have met with only limited success.

On *Glenlochay* (Perthshire), for instance, during the 1976 season more stalks were ruined by hikers than ever before, despite large notices – eminently polite, I understand – advising safe routes for both climbers and hikers. *Affaric* (Inverness-shire) is another forest which has displayed notices along the glen, which stated, 'Affaric deer cull – please assist by keeping off the hills from 15th August to 15th October.'

The majority of people, I understand, respect these signs, but there are always those who are abusive and consider that the stalking party has no right to be out on the hill killing deer. Some hikers, during the early part of the season, were even found camping in some of the best corries of *Affaric*, thus driving the deer off the ground into the sanctuary, where they remained for about four weeks until the break-out for the rut.

Whether or not it was as a result of the above notice posted on *Affaric* will never be known, but during the following season many hikers visiting the forest were more co-operative, and quite a number even took the trouble to call round at the head stalker's house to enquire if it would be convenient for them to go into the hills.

Nevertheless, there were still those who considered that they had as much right to be in the hills as the stalkers, and on the very first day of the season three tents were found pitched high in a corrie where it was planned to stalk that day. On another occasion a stalk was ruined by a party of hikers who completely ignored a request by the ponyman not to proceed further into the glen as a stalk was in progress. The net result was that, with the ground cleared of deer, the stalking party had to proceed to another beat on the opposite side of the loch, which involved a diversion of at least six miles (10 km) for the three ponies, and with so much time wasted only one stag was shot, instead of the three which might have been taken that day had there not been this enforced change of beat.

It has been suggested that if the notices displayed had been officially worded 'By Order of the Red Deer Commission' they might have been more effective, but I personally doubt it. I do believe, however, that if, during the stalking season, some official propaganda could be put out on the radio and television, discouraging people from going into the hills during the stalking season, this would help.

On *Glen Shee* (Perthshire) a wandering party of hikers did, in the end, do the stalking party a good turn, for although the stag being stalked had been moved off the ground, the hikers happened, by chance, to blunder into another party of deer which, when disturbed, wandered back into the burn in which the stalking party lay concealed and so provided the *Rifle* with an easy chance.

On the credit side, in some areas such as at *Glenbanchor* (Inverness-shire), after signs had been displayed on the approach roads to the forest indicating that stalking was in progress, the hill-walkers have been very co-operative, and generally enquired first from the head stalker before proceeding to the hill. On other areas, however, such as at *Glencarron* (Ross-shire), the reverse has often been the case, and not only have the signs been removed or destroyed, but any verbal warning has proved to be an utter waste of time. Nevertheless, on *Glenfeshie* (Inverness-shire), which has an annual cull of about 186 stags, Hugh Blakeney, the factor, was able to report in 1993 that he was receiving 'more and more enquiries from hill-walkers and climbers who wished to climb the higher hills, asking whether they could go on the hill without disturbing the stalking'. It would appear that the Tourist Board had been largely responsible for this much-appreciated co-operation, for there is little doubt that in a number of instances, hiker disturbance has been caused by lack of knowledge on the part of the walker or climber as to whom to contact before visiting the area.

Not only do hill-walkers and hikers vastly outnumber the climbers, but individually they undoubtedly cause greater disturbance to the deer, for climbers, except when travelling to and from the climbing area, will generally be confined to a rock face which, in itself, is unlikely to be attractive to deer. Their route through the forest will probably keep to tracks well known to both deer and stalker. Hill-walkers, on the other hand, have no such fixed route to follow, and may therefore turn up anywhere – often in the middle of a stalk.

A slight difference may, perhaps, be drawn between a hiker and hill-walker, for whereas the former may be walking as a member of a youth club or a rambling group, and as such be more inclined to keep to recognised tracks and paths, the latter may turn up anywhere, wandering and camping wherever the will takes him or her. So too, perhaps, should a difference be drawn between a climber and mountaineer, for whereas both will require sound lungs and a head for heights, the latter will certainly require a rope at times to reach his target. In this chapter, however, reference to hiker and climber could equally well apply to hill-walker and mountaineer. The amount of disturbance caused among the deer by any party will be roughly the same.

Hydro-electric Projects

During the immediate post-War years a number of the less well-known forests were starting to produce trophies of a much superior standard than formerly, and this was undoubtedly due to what might be called a local migration from those forests where hydro-electric and other disturbing works were being developed. These included not only the erection of miles of ugly pylons across some of Scotland's wildest and most beautiful scenery, but also the building of dams across glens and corries so that large areas could be flooded, thereby depriving the deer of much of their former wintering ground. During this period, for the same reason, some owners, well away from the scene of operation, were able to report a

sudden influx of deer to their forests whilst others were – temporarily at least – having their stock much depleted.

Nevertheless, as was the case with disturbance among deer caused by low-flying aircraft (*see* page 66), it did not take the deer long to become accustomed to the various activities around them, and by 1954 several owners who had a forest adjacent to these projects were remarking that their deer no longer took the slightest notice of the vast explosions which were continuously going off in the neighbourhood. By this date some of the schemes, such as the one at *Lochrosque* (Ross-shire), were nearing completion, but others were still much in their infancy – and at their noisiest.

In 1963 stalking on *West Monar* and *Pait* (Ross-shire) was much interfered with, due to work on constructing a new cottage to replace the one that had been flooded over during the hydro-electric project work.

Sheep on the Forest

In the early 1950s there were few forests in Scotland that were entirely free of sheep, and many were the complaints from stalkers about the disturbance they caused. The opinion of one stalker was that,

> the presence of sheep in large numbers on the hill had an effect on the movement of the stags who were upset by the gathering for the sales. The hinds, on the other hand, appear more conservative and remain more or less on their own beats whereas the stags move to quarters where they will be less disturbed.

Another forest owner suggested that 'the stags objected more than the hinds to the smell of sheep dip'. Generally speaking, however, I believe it is the stalkers and *not* the deer that object most to the presence of sheep on the forest, for they have a nasty habit of popping out of the most unexpected places just when a stalk is nearing success.

Duncan MacLennan, head stalker on *Affaric* (Inverness-shire) until the late 1980s, did not view the presence of sheep on the forest too unfavourably. He once wrote in 1960,

> It is amazing how deer on some forests seem to get accustomed to the shepherds and their dogs. When moved off their ground during sheep

gathering, the deer merely do a circle out of the way of the shepherd and come back to where they had been feeding previously once the sheep had been gathered.

Duncan had the impression that he was unable to get a sitting stag to rise just by whistling, due to the fact that the deer had become so accustomed to the shepherds whistling up their dogs.

Disturbance from the Air

It is surprising how quickly deer have become accustomed to aeroplanes. At the beginning of the War, in the early 1940s, the deer used to get into a fearful panic at the approach of a low-flying plane, and it was the opinion of Duncan MacLennan that the pilots 'used to amuse themselves by chasing the deer around the hills'.

Fifteen years later, during the 1958 season, Duncan, along with a stalking party, was waiting on the edge of a large corrie for a party of stags to rise, when a jet plane came very low right through the centre of the corrie almost level with the stalking party and the deer, and at one time looked as though it would crash into the hillside. Naturally, in the confined space of the corrie, it made a fiendish noise, yet the stags never even moved and appeared to pay no attention whatsoever.

Further north in Sutherland, however, it would appear that the deer took rather longer to accustom themselves to the sound of aircraft, and even in 1965 at *Mudale*, during periods of low-flying by aircraft of the Fleet Air Arm, the deer were unsettled and difficult to approach.

By 1974, however, it was becoming apparent that in some areas low-flying aircraft were no longer causing deer much concern and on *Rhidorroch* forest (Ross-shire), for instance, which was continuously being used as a low-flying area, the deer no longer even troubled to look up at a jet which will, nevertheless, cause panic to farm stock. Deer on forests bordering Loch Ness, which is also a regular low-flying area, behave in similar fashion.

On *Kinloch Hourn* forest (Inverness-shire) stalking was considerably disrupted during the 1977 season by the daily journeying to and fro of helicopters and ground machines belonging to the North of Scotland Electricity Board who, at that time, were erecting a line of pylons across the forest. There was little doubt, moreover, that this somewhat noisy activity also deterred the arrival of stags from adjoining forests that would normally have been expected to visit *Kinloch Hourn* for the rut.

One day during the 1978 season the stalking party on *Ledgowan* (Ross-shire) had a stalk ruined by the arrival of a large military helicopter which landed on the bealach (pass) in the vicinity of some deer that were being stalked. The rotors were not turned off, but two occupants dismounted and, after walking around rather aimlessly for a few minutes, took off again. Whether they had spotted the stalking party was not known, but there was no doubt that the deer had spotted them, for they immediately cleared off.

Stalking on *Ardtalla* forest (Islay) in 1986 was also considerably disrupted by a military helicopter which, for two whole days, persisted in hovering over the best part of the forest.

In 1989, despite repeated requests to avoid the area if possible, a Sea-King helicopter for a number of days persistently hovered low over *Sannox* forest (Isle of Arran), thereby ruining a number of stalks.

Occasionally, both hill-walkers and climbers do get into serious trouble and a full-scale rescue operation, complete with helicopters, has to be summoned to their aid. Despite being in close proximity to such an event, the stalking party on *Glenbanchor* (Inverness-shire) was able, in 1991, to successfully complete a stalk.

Up to date no report has been received of any stalk being disrupted by the presence of hot-air balloons flying low over the forest, but I myself, whilst stalking roe in England, once saw an approaching buck put to flight when the balloonist turned on the jet to gain some height.

Nor have I received a report of any stalk being spoilt by the arrival of a hang-glider or microplane, but if it has not already occurred then it will doubtless do so in the not-too-distant future.

Sonic Boom of Concorde

The summer and autumn of 1969 saw a new cause for disturbance in the mountains – the sonic boom of Concorde during some of her trial missions over the Western Highlands. 'Words fail me how best to describe what I thought of that machine', commented J. H. Dewhurst of *Strone* forest (Ross-shire). 'About six times did it clear a very large area of ground completely of deer.' Other forests to report similar disturbance were *Achnashellach* and *Ledgowan* (Ross-shire), as well as *Glenkingie*

(Inverness-shire). On *Glenkingie* the last day of the season – 10 October – was virtually ruined by a sonic boom, but what made it even more frustrating was the fact that it also happened to coincide with the first completely dry day for about five weeks!

PART II

THE DEER
AND
OTHER WILDLIFE

CHAPTER 10

A Census of Scotland's Red Deer

What is the Deer Population in Scotland Today?

There have been various attempts – or should one say 'guesstimates' – in the past to estimate the red deer population in Scotland, and invariably, I think, the number has been very much underestimated. Until comparatively recently, since the formation of Deer Management Groups (*see* page 158, few forest owners ever took the trouble to make an annual census and, provided they were able to continue killing their quota of stags, probably thought it unnecessary.

In 1952, some seven years before the formation of the Red Deer Commission, which was formally constituted on 1 October 1959, I first raised the question of an annual census in my annual stalking review for *The Field* (23/3/52) when I stated,

> I can never understand why more owners of large forests do not make a point of having an annual count, for it seems quite illogical that any sound decision as to the correct number of deer to be killed can be taken before it is known what the stock is. The chief difficulty in making a census, of course, is that the deer population in any one area is in a state of continual flux. This applies mainly to the stags, who are great travellers. Any census should, therefore, be taken over an area – and a large one at that – rather than by individual forests.

In 1953 Dr Fraser Darling initiated a census of red deer which was carried on under the auspices of the Nature Conservancy until its suspension in 1959, by which time, after about six years, only about one third of the land occupied by red deer had been covered. From then on census work was taken over by the Red Deer Commission, with relevant results of the census area covered each year being published in their *Annual Reports*.

The ideal, of course, would be for each county to organise annually a census week, when all stalkers, ghillies and shepherds would combine to take a count of all deer on their ground at some fixed date. When this should be is a matter of opinion. I believe early March, before the stags have shed their antlers, would be best. On the other hand, I know at least one stalker who would favour an autumn census.

In my opinion October would not be a good month, for whilst one owner might be able to see a lot of deer on his forest, this will be due to an influx of stags coming in for the rut from neighbouring estates, whose count would, accordingly, be reduced by the departure of many stags – 'absent without leave' – in search of hinds elsewhere. Furthermore, the month of October marks the height of the stag stalking season, and deer will continually be disturbed by stalking parties, and it would, therefore, be possible for a wandering stag to be duplicated or even triplicated in the census.

An early March census eliminates these disadvantages, and if there should be a heavy covering of snow on the high ground, the area in which to look for deer will be considerably reduced – an important factor with depleted staff.

During 1959-60, under favourable weather, the newly appointed Red Deer Commission completed their first small census in an area where two local estimates had previously suggested that a deer population ranging from 80 to 300 existed. The R.D.C. count put the figure at 170 – about 20 deer below the average of the two local 'guesstimates'.

As no reliable census figures of deer stocks are available, the only method is to calculate, from the number of deer killed, the number of live deer that have to be on the ground to produce every *shootable* stag. Writing on American deer, A. Leopold in *Game Management* (1933) states that for mule and white-tailed deer a 'unit herd' of 24 animals is needed for each stag shot. This herd is made up of 5 stags, 5 yearlings, 7 dry hinds and 7 milk hinds; calves are excluded. Fraser Darling believed this figure might also be applicable to Scottish conditions, 'though the composition of the unit herd may be a little different'.

In 1951 the Scott Henderson *Report of the Committee on Cruelty to Wild Animals* was published, and this suggested that the red deer population in Scotland at that date was 'somewhere in the region of 100,000 and that before the war it probably approached 200,000'. I considered that both these estimates were too low, as indeed were all previous estimates as well as one or two subsequent ones.

For instance, the *Minority Report of the Committee on Close Seasons for Deer in Scotland* (1954) suggested that 'the total deer population in Scotland must be in the region of 120,000 of which about one-third are on land other than recognised deer forests'.

Another estimate quoted in the report, made by the Department of Agriculture for Scotland, suggested a 'total stock numbering 84,775 in July 1952', as compared to about '130,000' at the beginning of the War.

The possible inaccuracy of these estimates was qualified by the statement that they were based 'upon incomplete information furnished by returns obtained from a number of deer-forest owners'. Even so, these figures, in my opinion, were well below probability – the former by about 33 per cent and the latter by over 50 per cent – and emphasised the fact that no one – not even the Department of Agriculture for Scotland, or the majority of deer forest owners – had any knowledge as to the number of deer in Scotland as a whole or in any particular area.

The chief difficulty in making a census is the fact that the deer population in any one area is in a state of continual flux. This applies mainly to the stags, who are great travellers. For about ten months of the year some forests are frequented solely by hinds, and any census taken in these areas during the winter will give a completely different picture from one taken, say, in October, when the stags come in for the rut.

Stags should normally not be killed until they are six or seven years old. This does not mean that any stag carrying an abnormal or poor type of head should not be killed earlier. It should, but, assuming that deer stocks are at the required level and are of normal quality, the policy should obviously be to kill mature rather than young beasts. The opinion of the Departmental Committee of 1919, which was appointed to enquire and report with regard to *Lands used as Deer Forests* (1922), was that, allowing for normal wastage, 'at least 25 head of deer must on an average be kept for each stag killed'. That is to say, a forest yielding an average bag of 100 stags per season should have a deer stock of not fewer than 2,500; or a 25-stag forest a stock of 625 deer.

This ratio of 25 head of deer for each stag killed only refers to a *shootable* stag and not to immature beasts which may have to be shot in a population culling programme.

I therefore decided to make a statistical assessment of the probable deer population of Scotland by using the ratio of 25 live deer of all ages to each *shootable* stag killed, preferring this ratio to the one suggested (24 to 1) by A. Leopold in *Game Management* (1933) for mule and white-tailed deer, on account of the latter being more prolific breeders than red deer, and often bearing twins.

The first step was to find out how many deer were being killed on the various estates in Scotland. This necessitated sending out, in 1950, about 650 questionnaire forms to owners of not only the recognised deer forests (about 200) but also to those who had shootings, sheep farms etc, on which some stalking was being undertaken. The response was amazing and only about 5 per cent failed to reply.

As a result of the figures received, I estimated that in 1951 the stock of red deer in Scotland stood at around 222,545 as compared to 291,790 in 1938. Seven years later I repeated the exercise and by 1958 it appeared that the population had fallen to about 188,850.

In 1960 I was informed by V. P. W. Lowe of the Nature Conservancy that the red deer population of Scotland was then considered to be 'in the order of 150,000' – a figure which, although some 50,000 more than the number which had previously been stated in the House of Commons and elsewhere, I still considered to be too low.

In 1961 I therefore asked the Nature Conservancy if they would kindly supply me with the population figures for the area of Scotland in which the actual count had already been made. Although the population figures for individual estates were, quite naturally, confidential, the Conservancy allowed me to see bulk population figures for each county, with a list of properties over which the census had been taken. Altogether the census covered some 1,654,904 acres in eight of the fifteen or so counties in Scotland containing red deer, and it suggested that in this area there was a total population of 52,921 deer (16,101 stags, 26,283 hinds and 10,537 calves). Over the same area and covering the same properties, I estimated that, on a unit herd basis of 25 deer of both sexes for every stag killed, the deer population was about 55,175 – a difference of only 2,254 animals, or about 4.2 per cent. Considering the time taken for the Nature Conservancy field census – about seven years – and the statistical method which I used, I think the two results compare far more closely than one might have expected.

Why, therefore, did I believe that the 1960 Nature Conservancy's total estimate of 155,000 to 160,000 was still some 28,000 too low? In the first place, the Nature Conservancy, on the assumption that their field census had covered about a third of Scotland's red deer territory, had apparently assumed that by multiplying 52,921 by three an approximate deer population for the whole of Scotland would be obtained. This assumption might have been true had their census area been a complete third of Scotland's red deer country, and had the third covered been truly representative of the area in each county actually inhabited by red deer.

I have assumed that the range of red deer in Scotland covers about 5,830,700 acres (2,359,567 ha), of which about 54 per cent can be considered as true deer-forest ground, although some of it

may be under sheep. The census area was 1,654,904 acres (669,706 ha), and although over two thirds covered true deer-forest country, in a number of counties some of the best deer ground had been omitted altogether, including *Blackmount* in Argyllshire, *Strathconon* in Ross-shire and the vast *Reay* forest in Sutherland, to mention but three.

Indeed, in Argyllshire not a single recognised deer forest on the mainland was included in the census, and of the islands only *Mull* was covered. Yet it is well known that *Jura* has, for many years, held a high deer population. Among the counties omitted altogether from the census were Caithness and Banffshire, both of which contain such fine deer forests as *Langwell* and *Braemore* in the former and *Inchrory* in the latter. It is not to be assumed that I am being critical of these omissions – I mention them only to add weight to my argument that Scotland's red deer population has in the past been under – rather than over-estimated.

I have shown how close, in the 1,500,000 or so acres covered by the census, my calculated figure has corresponded to the field count. On a deer density figure – 52,921 deer in 1,654,904 acres (669,706 ha) – the field count works out at about one deer to every 31 acres (12.5 ha).

If this density of deer can be considered representative of the area actually covered by the census, and if it can be assumed that this area is representative of the rest of Scotland's deer territory which was not covered by the census – and I see no reason why it should not be – then this would give a total deer population in 1960 of about 186,900 – a figure that tallies to within one per cent of my 1958 estimated population of 188,850 deer. I came to the conclusion, therefore, that the Nature Conservancy estimate was still some 28,000 deer on the underside. Nevertheless, as Table 1 shows, the census figures of the Nature Conservancy that have been taken in the field do confirm that, provided the average kill of stags is taken for each estate – a kill that will not affect very much the existing deer stocks – the statistical method of assessing deer population over large areas is as accurate a method as any other, particularly when a field count is impracticable.

If it is correct to assume that Scotland's red deer population in 1958 stood at about 188,850 deer, then what density to the acre did this represent?

Table 1: Comparison of Nature Conservancy census figures with population assessed by statistics

COUNTY	(i) Total land acreage excluding inland water	(ii) Acreage of recognised deer forests in county	(iii) Approximate acreage inhabited by deer	(iv) Approximate acreage of deer census	(v) Actual deer count in census areas	(vi) Calculation of deer population in census area	(vii) Calculation of total deer population	Remarks on census conditions
Aberdeen	1,263,300	191,540	210,500 }	283,300 }	14,666	12,500	11,100 } 15,850	Principally true deer forest ground included in survey of both counties.
Angus	559,090	56,271	139,800				4,750	
Argyll: Mainland	1,469,444 } 1,990,521	261,190 } 356,341	367,400 } 497,700	248,804	4,078	4,125	17,425 } 25,375	No true deer forest included in census on mainland. Islands of Islay, Jura and Scarba omitted from census.
Islands	521,077	95,151	130,300				7,950	
Banff	403,054	69,037	80,000	—	—	—	2,800	County omitted from census.
Bute	139,711	—	40,000	—	—	—	1,000	County omitted from census.
Caithness	438,833	59,174	109,700	—	—	—	2,550	County omitted from census.
Dunbarton	154,362	6,700	15,000	—	—	—	600	County omitted from census.
Inverness: Mainland	1,916,768 } 2,695,094	837,866 } 931,330	1,277,800 } 1,377,800	499,800	20,046	23,025	55,750 } 57,875	Principally deer forest ground in census, but only about half of true deer forest ground included.
Islands	778,326	93,464	100,000				2,125	
Kincardine	242,460	14,500	20,000	—	—	—	750	County omitted from census.
Kirkcudbright	574,024	2,524	100,000	100,000	418	400	400	Mostly Forestry Commission ground.
Perth	1,595,804	241,522	997,300	276,800	5,392	5,700	22,625	Less than quarter of true deer forest ground included in census.
Ross: Mainland	1,573,358 } 1,977,248	751,104 } 809,504	1,482,900 }	246,200	8,321	9,425	40,275 } 41,475	All deer forest ground in census but less than quarter covered. Islands omitted from census.
Islands	403,890	58,400					1,200	
Sutherland	1,297,913	355,200	700,000	—	—	—	17,000	All deer forest ground covered in census, but less than quarter covered.
Misc. Counties	697,531	—	60,000	—	—	—	550	Counties not covered by census.
TOTAL	14,028,945	3,093,643	5,830,700	1,654,904	52,921	55,175	188,850	

Source of data
(i) From information supplied by H.M. Ordnance Survey. (ii) From information supplied by Dept. of Agriculture for Scotland. (iii) Author's estimates.
(iv) & (v) From information supplied by V. P. W. Lowe, Nature Conservancy. (vi) & (vii) Author's estimates, based on unit herd of 25 deer to each stag killed.

The recognised deer forests, which at that date numbered about 183, covered about 2,798,706 acres (1,132,580 ha), or about 21 per cent of the total acreage covered by the twelve principal counties involved. If the *Minority Report of the Committee on Close Season for Deer in Scotland* (1954) was correct in assuming that one third of Scotland's deer population was on ground outside the recognised deer forests, it would appear, therefore, that about two thirds of my above estimated figure of 188,850 – say 125,900 deer – were located on the 2,798,706 acres of deer forest, and this would work out at about one deer per 22 acres (9 ha). The remaining 62,950 deer would, therefore, be distributed on land outside true deer forest, and on such terrain I estimated the deer density as falling between one deer per 50 acres (20 ha) and one per 80 acres (32 ha). However, the area scheduled as deer forest was being continually reduced, and by 1950 was over 250,000 acres less than pre-War. So the poulation of deer outside the recognised deer forest may well be more than a third of its total, thereby reducing the deer density within the forests proper.

The question of deer density is a very complex one, and opinions vary from one deer per 10 acres (4 ha) to as much as one per 50 or 60 acres (20 to 24 ha). A lot depends, of course, on what type of pasture the ground consists of. On a good average hill pasture, one deer per 20–25 acres (8–10 ha) should not cause overstocking, provided the deer have the pasture to themselves and do not share it with sheep. Not all forest ground, however, is good average pasture. Some consists of nothing more than sterile wastes of rock and peat hag, and deer stocks on such terrain will be very light. Fraser Darling, in his *Herd of Red Deer* (1937) comments that 'such favourably placed hind forests approach a density of one to 25 acres (10 ha), but this is perilously near overstocking.' Allan Gordon Cameron, in his *Wild Red Deer of Scotland* (1923), believes that 'not less than one deer to 25 acres' is about ideal. Evans, in his *Account of Jura Red Deer* (1890), gave a density of one deer to 13½ acres (5.5 ha), but Jura was certainly vastly overstocked.

During 1964 the Red Deer Commission concentrated their census work over some twenty estates in south-east Sutherland which were bounded by the Golspie/Lairg/Kinbrace/ Helmsdale road, but excluding ground north of Loch Rinsdale, Lochnan Chlair and Loch Badanloch, and 7,622 deer were counted in an area of some 270,000 acres (109,263 ha) (*Red Deer Commission Annual Report*, 1964).

When I was making my inquiries in 1950 from nineteen estates in this same area, the return showed that the annual cull was approximately 284 stags. Multiplied by 25, this indicated that the total deer population in south-east Sutherland at that time was about 7,100 – which although some 522 less than the R.D.C. census, is not much when one considers that there is a difference of some fourteen years in the comparison and my figure covered nineteen estates against the R.D.C.'s twenty estates.

According to the *Red Deer Commission Annual Report* for 1970, the red deer population was then estimated to be in the region of 185,000, – that is about 2 per cent less than my 1959 estimate and 2.6 per cent less than my 1961 estimate. There had, however, been a heavy cull on hinds, and it was not surprising that stocks had fallen by about 4–5,000 animals in nine years.

A study of the deer population on an island forest obviously gives the best opportunity for confirmation as to whether or not this unit-herd figure of 25 live deer to every shootable stag killed is a reliable one. On *Rhum*, for instance, the pre-War population was estimated at 1,750 beasts, and it was possible, without disturbing this population level, to kill 70 stags per season, which works out exactly at one to 25. After the War, until *Rhum* was taken over by the Nature Conservancy with a deer population of about 900, the number of stags killed per season had to be reduced to about 35 – which gave a ratio of one stag killed for every 25¼ deer on the ground. In February 1951 a count taken on *Arran* revealed a stock of 996 deer (excluding 381 calves). Since 40 stags were being shot, this gave a ratio of one stag killed for every 24.9 (say 25) deer on the island – or including calves, one per 34 deer.

Mainland figures are not so easy to confirm, due to the seasonal movement of deer from one area to another. However, there is ample evidence that this unit-herd figure of 25 deer for every shootable stag is a fairly reliable one. For instance, an estimate in 1959 of the deer population on the various forests of the *Balnagown* estate – which covered some 131,000 acres (53,000 ha) – suggested that there were about 5,000 head of deer on the ground, of which some 212 stags would be killed per season. This works out at just over 23½ deer to every stag killed.

In a smaller area of 7,000 acres (2,800 ha) at *Tombuie* (Perthshire), I was informed by J. D. Hutchison that when the Nature Conservancy made their count it was estimated that the resident deer population (principally hinds) was approximately 150, and since the war the average number of stags killed per season had been six. Once again we find the ratio of one to 25.

On the other hand, some forest owners have informed me that if stocks on their ground are to remain more or less at a constant level, it is necessary to have at least 30 deer on the ground for each stag killed – while others place the unit-herd figure as low as 1:20. It is all a question, of course, of whether the forest is stag or hind ground, or a combination of both. Since, however, a unit-herd figure of 25 live deer for every *shootable* stag was adopted by the Departmental Committee, I have likewise used this figure as the basis for all my calculations.

During the preparation of my book *The Stalking Grounds of Great Britain and Ireland* (1960) I enquired from some 400 estates in Scotland, which included both recognised deer forests and all marginal sheep ground capable of yielding the odd stag or two, the average number of stags it had been possible to kill on the ground during the post-War years without influencing the stock very much. More than 400 owners were contacted and the results are summarised in Table 2 (page 77), which also includes an estimate of the deer stock in each county, calculated on the unit-herd basis of 25 live deer to every stag killed.

It will be noticed that on this basis the stock in Kincardine (*Glendye* forest) pre-War was about 1,000 head, whereas it was, I was subsequently informed, more than double that number. However, at that time the ground was considerably overstocked, since when considerable culling has taken place, so that my present assessment is perhaps, more realistic.

I am confident that my figure of 188,850 for deer stocks in 1950, as compared with 244,450 in 1938, was not an overestimate. Indeed, it may well have been an underestimate, for no account had been taken of deer poached in the numbers killed, which it has been suggested may well have added about 15 per cent to the total figure. The principal poaching casualties, of course, occurred in those areas which are most accessible by road or boat, and on the mainland some of the smaller shootings near main roads had their deer stocks reduced by as much as 90 per cent. On some Argyllshire and Inverness-shire islands it appeared that stocks had decreased by about 50 per cent compared to pre-War. As a broad picture, therefore, it was apparent that the deer population in Scotland in 1950 was about 23 per cent less than it had been in 1938.

According to the 1994/95 *Annual Report of the Red Deer Commission*, a total of 20,650 stags were shot in Scotland that year, of which 18,666 were killed in season and the remaining 1,984 out of season. Ignoring the latter, which had probably been shot unselectively as marauders, if the ratio of 25:1 is applied to those shot in season, both on hill *and* in woodland range, it would appear that the current deer population is possibly in excess of 400,000. Suggesting this possibility with the R.D.C. their reply (7/11/95) was as follows:- 'We do not agree with your assumption that the red deer population is now in excess of 400,000. Recent evidence from counts over 800,000 hectares (1,976,000 acres) of *hill* land in the past two years show that deer numbers are similar to that of the early 1980s. An extrapolation of that over the whole of the *hill deer* range would suggest a population of less than 300,000. Woodland populations are *continuing to expand* but these are of an unknown size and may be in the region of 50,000. (Italics mine.) Combining the hill land and woodland estimated figures together we arrive at a 'possible' red deer population of about 350,000 deer, which may be nearer the truth, for with the spread of deer into increasing afforested areas, the cull in these areas is generally one for reduction and not herd management.

Table 2: The average number of deer killed on the forests and shootings of Scotland in 1959, as compared to pre-1939 war, together with a comparison of estimated deer population

COUNTY	PRE-1939 WAR Average number killed			(4) Estimated Deer Population in 1938 (Col. 1 × 25)	POST-1939 WAR Average number killed			(8) Estimated Deer Population in 1959 (Col. 5 × 25)
	(1) Stags	(2) Hinds	(3) Total		(5) Stags	(6) Hinds	(7) Total	
Aberdeen	498	489	987	12,450	444	504	948	11,100
Angus	264	215	479	6,600	190	225	415	4,750
Argyll Mainland / Isles	924 / 440 } 1,364	795 / 451 } 1,246	1,719 / 891 } 2,610	23,100 / 11,000 } 34,100	697 / 318 } 1,015	638 / 261 } 899	1,335 / 579 } 1,914	17,425 / 7,950 } 25,375
Banff	117	137	254	2,925	112	133	245	2,800
Buteshire (Arran)	47	51	98	1,175	40	50	90	1,000
Caithness	190	176	366	4,750	102	83	185	2,550
Inverness-shire Mainland / Isles	2,816 / 224 } 3,040	2,322 / 155 } 2,477	5,138 / 379 } 5,517	70,400 / 5,600 } 76,000	2,230 / 85 } 2,315	1,947 / 63 } 2,010	4,177 / 148 } 4,325	55,750 / 2,125 } 57,875
Kincardine	37	105	142	925	30	64	94	750
Miscellaneous Counties	42	53	95	1,050	42	52	94	1,050
Perthshire	1,176	1,544	2,720	29,400	905	1,208	2,113	22,625
Ross-shire Mainland / Isles	2,003 / 142 } 2,145	1,257 / 107 } 1,364	3,260 / 249 } 3,509	50,075 / 3,550 } 53,625	1,611 / 48 } 1,659	1,051 / 17 } 1,068	2,662 / 65 } 2,727	40,275 / 1,200 } 41,475
Stirlingshire	24	17	41	600	20	17	37	500
Sutherland	834	413	1,247	20,850	680	366	1,046	17,000
TOTAL	9,778	8,287	18,065	244,450	7,554	6,679	14,233	188,850

CHAPTER 11

Shortage of Mature Stags and their Age

Shortage of Mature Stags

By 1960 many stalkers were commenting on the extreme shortage of the older-class stag, and this was only to be expected after the widespread poaching which had been taking place during the late 1940s and early 1950s (*see* pages 49–52.

Throughout the 1960s an increasing number of forests were reporting a scarcity of deer, and in particular the older class of stag, and various reasons were given. Marcus Kimball M.P. commented (*in lit.* 1966),

> Bad winters and heavy shooting by crofters, the Forestry Commission and the Department of Agriculture under the enclosed land concession in the Act has reduced the deer stocks of Sutherland considerably. The root of the trouble is the *butcher*, who will pay a good price for venison all the year round regardless of season or condition. I am seriously concerned about the future in my part of Scotland [*Mudale*, Sutherland]. Measures will have to be taken if the deer are to survive.

Within ten years (1974) however, venison prices had slumped to 25p per lb and 11½p per lb for stag and hind venison respectively (*see* pages 50, 51).

Lord Lovat was also critical of the wholesale destruction of deer 'during the winter, where due to snow drifting along fences, the deer are able to enter forestry plantations'.

During 1971, in order to try and remedy the shortage of matured stags being killed off towards the end of the rut, the British Field Sports Stalking Committee sent a circular to a number of forests on the desirability of shortening the open season for stags by two to eight days but, of those that replied, more than 50 per cent were against any change, so the matter was taken no further.

By 1982 reports were coming in from a wide area of Scotland that stag numbers – particularly among the more mature class – were getting less, because, it was suggested by A. D. Gordon (Atholl Estates), 'too many young stags had been shot when venison prices were so high three years ago.' Other Perthshire forests to report a shortage of mature stags were *Suie* and *Auchlyne*. P. F. J. Colvin, of the *Corriemulzie* Estates (Ross-shire), believed that roadside poaching during the winter and spring of recent years had probably been the largest factor in this shortage, but R. M. McNicol, head stalker at *Badanloch* (Sutherland), was firmly of the belief that the main cause of the shortage in his part of Sutherland was due to a big increase in the overall cull on local forests, with no let up despite the noticeable decline in numbers that had been apparent in recent years.

Other forests to report a decrease in the number of shootable stags included *Blackmount* and *Dalness* (Argyllshire), and also *Ben Alder*, (Inverness-shire), and there was little doubt that the shooting of approximately 600 deer in a combined culling operation by the Forestry Commission and Red Deer Commission, after a break-in to the Rannoch plantations during the previous winter, had made a large contribution to this shortage. In the past, *Ben Alder* had relied on stags coming in from the Rannoch area for summering, and also for the rut, but in the years prior to 1982 the number had gradually dwindled from perhaps 130 to only about 30 in 1982. Among the forests that, by 1982, were already reporting a shortage of mature stags were *Glencarron* and *Fairburn* (Ross-shire), and *Abernethy*, *Kinloch Hourn* and *Lochiel* forests (Inverness-shire). *Loch Choire* (Sutherland), also reported a shortage of mature stags in 1982, yet '20 per cent of their cull, that year, of 85 stags were beasts of over 11 years of age, with the oldest about 19 years'. This aging was carried out by the Red Deer Commission, who in a similar exercise at *Glenfeshie* (Inverness-shire), assessed the age of four stags at 16, 17, 18 and 19 years respectively – all remarkably high for a highland stag which, under existing conditions, seldom exceeds 11 or 12 years of age. Nevertheless. on *Glenmazeran* (Inverness-shire), the average age of the 30 stags shot during the 1990 season was estimated to be 10 or 11 years.

Apropos the average age of stags being culled in Scotland, a letter dated 14 November 1988, from the Red Deer Commission to all deer forest owners, estimated that 'the bulk of the stag cull comes from animals of less than 6 years old', and

concluded by stating that 'this state of affairs is clearly unacceptable to the sportsman and reflects badly on the management practices of many, *but not all* deer forests'.

There is no doubt that many promising heads are killed too early in life, and this particularly applies to the 10-pointer with bay tines, which is far more likely to develop into a 'royal' than a 10-pointer with triple tops in the form of a crown but no bays. No promising head should be taken until at least ten years of age, but how few do in fact reach double figures? The average age of all stags being shot in Scotland today is probably around four or five years, and those that reach the taxidermist for mounting about seven or eight. The average age for hinds, other than calves, is probably around three years.

By 1984, owing to the shortage of mature stags on the ground, a number of forests had already reduced their stag cull by as much as 50 per cent, and even more in one or two instances. As a case in point, Major Sandy Gordon of *Lude*, reported that deer stocks were so depleted on *Barisdale* and *Glenquoich* (Inverness-shire) that it was decided that only 7 and 30 stags respectively were to be shot in 1984 from his two forests, as compared with 30 and 60-plus in former years. Other forests to report a scarcity of mature stags at that time included *Sannox* (Isle of Arran), *Glenbanchor* (Inverness-shire), *Leckmelm* (Ross-shire), *Glenshee* and *Suie* (Perthshire), *Dalness* (Argyllshire) and *Kinloch* (Sutherland).

By 1985, reports on the scarcity of the more mature stag continued to increase as did their absence cause concern to forest owners. In the autumn of 1985 Anthony Hignett, the then owner of *Kildermorie* forest (Ross-shire), was informed by Louis Stewart, the senior Deer Officer of the Red Deer Commission, that mature stags in the North Ross Deer Group area, in which *Kildermorie* is situated, were probably down by about 13 per cent, although hinds were on the increase. Other forests to report on a shortage of mature stags included *Monar* and *New Kelso* (Ross-shire), *Glenspean* (Inverness-shire), *Blackmount* (Argyllshire) and *Badanloch* (Sutherland), from where Richard McNicol, the head stalker, wrote, 'The shortage of mature stags becomes more apparent with every season, and today we don't witness the fights which were once seen between stags competing for hinds.'

By 1988, forests to report a shortage of mature stags had become even more widespread, and included *Invercauld* (Aberdeenshire); *Blackmount* and *Conaglen* (Argyllshire); *Erchless*, *Glendessary*, *Glenfinnan*, *Inverailort*, and all the *Lochiel* forests (Inverness-shire); *Rhiedorrach* (Perthshire); *Fairburn*, *Ledgowan* (Ross-shire); and *Loubcroy* (Sutherland). On *Black Corries* (Argyllshire) and *Lochs* (Perthshire), however, the position had improved slightly and more mature stags had made their appearance during the rut.

Quite apart from both over and unselective shooting of stags, which was taking place in Scotland during the late 1980s - particularly on sheep ground - it should not be forgotten that by 1989 Scotland was beginning to feel the effects of an exceptionally high mortality which had occurred among the deer during the spring of 1983, with reported losses of 200 or more on some forests. Any losses among the male calves of that year would, of course, have been from the young entry which would have provided the mature stags (over 6 years of age) for the late 1980s.

E. Luxmore of *Glenspean* (Inverness-shire) reported that the deer on his forest had not recovered from the massive cull stipulated by the Red Deer Commission during the winters of 1978 and 1979, when 'over 1,000 deer were shot'. Formerly the annual cull on his forest had been about 25, but less than half this number can be shot today' (1990).

By 1990, in an attempt to raise the age status of stags on the ground, a number of the larger forests had started to reduce the stag cull accordingly. On *Glenavon* (Banffshire), for instance, whereas the stag cull in the early 1980s had been around the 100 mark, during the 1989 and 1990 seasons it had been reduced to 77 and 60 respectively. The hind cull of 150 for the winter of 1989 was, however, the highest for thirteen years, when 185 hinds were shot, and even that was well below the 1975 total of 220.

Other forests who, by 1990, had reduced their stag cull included *West Monar* (Ross-shire), *Glendessary* and *Glenfinnan* (Inverness-shire), *Dougarie* (Isle of Arran) and *Blackmount* (Argyllshire). On the last-named forest, whilst the overall quality of the stags had definitely started to show an improvement, proper control of stock and quality had unfortunately not been made any easier by the fact that long lengths of the Forestry Commission fences had fallen into disrepair and the deer were able to wander off the ground, some never to return.

The main reason for the shortage of mature stags is, undoubtedly, lease letting by the week or day, and the natural reluctance of some stalkers to take a paying guest - who may not be too physically fit - back to the lodge without having had the opportunity to fire a shot. So the first beast with antlers seen is often the target for the day.

Many stags are now being shot in small areas peripheral to a recognised deer forest, and the man in charge will probably not be a professional deer stalker familiar with the ground, but one that has been engaged to help out for the season. Most probably he will be a shepherd or forester, whose knowledge is about sheep or trees but not deer, so he cannot be expected to have much idea about selective culling, quite apart from the fact that he is probably just as keen as the guest *Rifle* not to return to the lodge without having had the chance to fire a shot. His predicament is also increased by the fact that many a guest *Rifle* - straight from an office desk and not trained for hard hill work - is only too anxious to shoot the first stag seen rather than face another hour or so of strenuous climbing in search of a cull beast.

Furthermore, on a hind forest which has to rely on stags coming on to the ground for the rut - and this applies particularly during a late season - any young stag seen will be shot in order that the planned seasonal cull figure - for which, perhaps, 50 per cent of the lease may already have been paid in deposit - can be met, regardless of the fact that by doing so they will be depleting stocks on their main source of supply - the larger traditional deer forest.

The shortage of mature stags has, of course, been partly responsible for late ruts in some areas, where seasonal rutting has now, largely, become a 'teenage' activity simply because few of the 'big boys' have been allowed to survive, having been shot by a trigger-happy trophy hunter. It is not surprising, therefore, that the rutting calendar has been put back a week or two to suit their age.

Prior to the Second World War there was virtually no short-term letting of stalking by the day or week, so the stalker of the 1930s never had to work to such a tight time schedule as does his modern counterpart. Furthermore, in those days there were no close-seasons for deer, so this gave the stalker freedom to cull the 'rubbish' whenever the opportunity provided itself, which included shooting stags in winter at a feeding point (*see* page 152).

During the last century, on many of the larger forests, all good trophy heads were strictly preserved and never allowed to be shot until fully mature. It is recorded that on *Dunrobin* forest (Sutherland) any stalker who allowed his charge to shoot such a stag was fined £1 – big money in those days – but doubtless it succeeded in preventing such a shortage of mature stags as exists today.

A good example of what can be achieved by selective culling and a general reduction in deer population was to be seen on the Island of *Rhum* (Inverness-shire), which is administered by the Nature Conservancy Council. Between 1958 and 1961 more than 100 stags were shot each season and, as a result, during the 1961 season there were more than sixty stags with antlers of twelve points or more, including one with sixteen points, which suggested that about 10 per cent of the stag population on the island were 'royals' or better. What can be achieved on *Rhum* ought to be possible on some of the self-contained estates elsewhere, *if* one could only trust a neighbour to spare young promising heads – but unfortunately one cannot. *Rhum*, of course, has the great advantage of being an island with no neighbour opposition. This can never happen on the mainland.

A century ago, J. G. Millais, in his *British Deer and their Horns* (1897), wrote that the greatest danger threatening the future quality of the red deer trophy was 'the fatal yearly tenant system, for a sportsman paying a big rent very naturally skins the place and spoils the forest as regards heads.' How much worse, therefore, is the position today, when stalking by the day or week is so readily available from a sporting agency, the majority of which are more concerned with the letting than the 'leaving'.

Age of Red Deer

Many of the early writers credited deer with living to fabulous ages, but it would appear that most red deer will die a *natural* death between the ages of 15 and 19, the majority being probably under rather than over 15 years.

The longest lived stag at *Warnham* Park, Sussex, where every animal is age-tagged, died in the winter of 1944 at the age of 17 years. During 1977 a 12-stone (76.2 kg) stag was shot on *Blackmount* forest (Argyllshire), which was estimated to be certainly 18 or may have been 20 years old. An even older stag was shot on *Kylestrome* forest (Sutherland) in its 21st year. It was not, however, a wild Scottish stag, but an ex-Warnham Park animal that had been brought to *Kylestrome* as a 3-year-old in 1960. This stag, which was given the name Wallace, got into a fight with one of his very large sons and was so badly injured that he had to be shot. 'He was', wrote Lady Mary Grosvenor in 1977, 'a greedy old boy and would eat pretty well anything offered, so latterly we were able to give him a worm dose in his feed every spring and this undoubtedly did him a lot of good and helped to keep him going'. At his death, he was a 10-pointer weighing 16 stone (101.6 kg).

The oldest recorded red deer of the present century was probably the tame hind of John Fraser, which died at the age of 31 years.

On *Loch Choire* (Sutherland) Lord Joicey informed me that, with the assistance of the Red Deer Commission, he arranged to have all the deer shot on his forest to be aged by tooth wear, and during the winter of 1983 seventy of the hundred hinds shot were estimated to be 6 years old or more. 'This was achieved', he wrote, 'through a careful policy of selective culling and not by chance.'

During the early 1970s some investigation was done by the Department of Forestry and Natural Resources, Edinburgh University, on the average age of deer being shot in south Ross-shire, as a result of which the average age of the stags was about 6½ years, whilst for hinds, the majority of carcases were only about 3½ years. 6 years old, therefore, is certainly an extremely high average for 70 per cent of any hind cull.

During the 1994 season the average age for the 63 stags shot on *Braulen* (Inverness-shire) was estimated to be 9¾ years, with the oldest (two) at 14 years and the youngest (three) at 7 years.

During the 1979 season H. J. E. van Beuningen estimated that there was an age variation of three to twelve years in the 20 stags shot on *Strone* (Ross-shire) with an overall average of 6½ years. I personally believe, therefore, that the average age for stags throughout the *whole* of Scotland will not exceed 4 or 5 years, whilst that for hinds is as low as 3 years.

CHAPTER 12
Hummels in Scotland

General

With the exception of the musk deer (*Moschus*) and Chinese water-deer (*Hydropotes inermis*), the males of all other species of deer carry antlers which are grown, shed and reproduced annually. In the majority of cases the growth and shedding of the antler is repeated with great regularity each year at the same period. Most male species of deer, which include red, sika, roe and fallow deer, carry their antlers for about six to eight months before shedding, following which the new antler growth starts to develop immediately. In some species, however, such as reindeer or caribou, the males – or bulls as they are more correctly referred to – shed their antlers after the autumn rut, although growth of the new antlers will be delayed until the spring.

Although many females of the hollow-horned ruminants such as cattle, sheep, goats, antelope etc. have horns, these male attributes are not normally possessed by female deer. The genus *Rangifer*, however, is the exception, and the majority of female reindeer, or caribou, possess antlers, similar in construction but considerably smaller than the males. Among some of the other species of deer, and in particular the roe (*Capreolus*) and American white-tailed deer (*Odocoileus virginianus*), there have been instances when the females have also developed these male attributes.

Antlers in themselves are a problem, for not only does the annual growth of a fine pair put a severe physical strain on the stag, but the more complicated and beautiful the adornment the less value are they as weapons of attack against members of their own kind.

The origin and purpose of the deciduous antlers has long puzzled zoologists and no one, as yet, has given an entirely satisfactory explanation. Darwin, in the *Origin of Species*, adopted the view that antlers were sexual weapons acquired by the males for fighting with their fellow males, and assumed that a male deer without antlers, i.e. a hummel or 'bald' stag, would be at a disadvantage during the rut or mating season. This theory, however, does not seem to be borne out in practice, and frequently in Scotland a hummel stag is able to hold together a large herd of hinds against antlered opposition. As weapons of defence, however, especially against a carnivorous predator, antlers, and in particular the more elaborate ones, are undoubtedly efficient. It is strange to find, therefore, that during the winter, at a time when some of the more northern species of deer such as the caribou are easy prey to the wolf, owing to the snow crust making escape by flight almost impossible, the bulls are without their main weapons of defence – the antlers. On the other hand female caribou retain their antlers until the spring.

With regard to the origin of antlers, it should be remembered that the earliest known deer were devoid of these appendages, and when antlers first made their appearance they were of simple fork formation. It is only in more recent times that the more complicated patterns of our existing forms have been developed.

A red deer stag that fails to produce any antlers is normally referred to as a hummel, which is a derivative of the word 'humble', as opposed to a stag with antlers being romantically described as 'noble'. In south-west England the hummel is referred to as a 'nott' stag, whilst in Germany it is known as *Mönch* or *Plattkopf* – literally a monk or flat head.

A hummel is quite distinct from a havier, which is a castrated male deer and, although without antlers, a hummel is certainly not impotent. Instead of normal pedicles from which antlers are grown and shed annually, should these appendages be present on a hummel they will consist of small stumps covered with a whorl of hair. No one has discovered how hummels, which occur more commonly in Scottish red deer than anywhere else in the world, are produced, but one fact is certain and that is that the 'poll' character of the hummel is not as prepotent as the poll in some breeds of cattle and sheep, and the male offspring will normally produce antlers. In breeding trials undertaken by G. Lincoln and John Fletcher and reported in *Deer* 1969–84, 45 male progeny of 2 hummels all developed normal antlers, including those derived from inbred crosses where a hummel stag was mated with its own daughters, suggesting no real genetic basis for the hummel state. The authors conclude that 'current evidence suggests that the major factor is environmental . . . *Nurture rather than Nature*' (*Deer* 6:4, p. 131).

Hummels are practically unknown in English deer parks, the only authentic case of which I am aware being a calf born to a Scottish hind that had been introduced to Warnham park, Sussex early in this century and was believed to be in-calf on arrival.

Dr Fraser Darling, in *A Herd of Red Deer* (1937) considers that,

> about one stag in a hundred is without antlers [and that the hummel character] is a genetic, sex-limited recessive, and perhaps this fairly numerous incidence, despite the fact that hummels are usually culled from the forests, occurs as a result of the relative success which hummels achieve as master stags. The genetic absence of antlers in no way affects the sexual rhythm or potency of the stag.

As a matter of interest, and to prove this point, I sent the testicles of two rutting stags of approximately similar age which I shot in October 1961, to the University of Glasgow, Department of Veterinary Pathology. One was an 8-pointer and the other a hummel. Dr Dunn wrote (1/11/61),

The testicles were very interesting. I passed them to Miss Morgan, of the Department of Histology here, and she found, oddly, that the hummel was much more highly fertile and must have shown a much greater degree of libido than the horned stag.

Hummels, like all male deer, pay no respect to forest marches, and any beast reported on one forest could well have been seen on one or more adjacent forests, thus resulting in duplication of the numbers reported being present in any one county or district. They are great wanderers, particularly at the onset of the rut, and one hummel can look very much like another without the distinguishing features of an antler. Once shot, however, it becomes a reliable statistic which enables one to work out the ratio of hummels to antlered stags in the area. Numbers of sightings, therefore, must be treated with caution when estimating this ratio.

As a result of a thirty-year survey, compiled from information received annually from over 100 deer-forest owners and stalkers etc., it would appear that one of the largest concentrations of hummels has occurred in the *Glenfeshie* (Inverness-shire) area, particularly during the late 1960s, when during a period of five seasons between 1964 and 1970 – excluding 1965 and 1969 when no reports were received – no less than twenty-eight hummels were shot on this forest, nine of which were taken in 1967 when the total number of sightings that year was about twenty. On a number of other occasions ten or more hummels were seen during the season, but doubtless some of these may have been duplicates. In 1970, however, eight of the ten seen were accounted for.

Hummels have also been much in evidence on *Glenavon* (*Inchrory*) forest in Banffshire and, during the past thirty years, thirty-four have been shot. *Glenavon* forest is only partially surrounded by good deer forest country – in the south by *Mar* and *Invercauld* in Aberdeen-shire and in the west by *Abernethy* in Inverness-shire – so the hummel population in the area is perhaps more resident than anywhere else on the mainland. In 1984 six hummels appeared on the ground and four were shot. The following year (1985) the surviving pair had been joined by a third, and two were shot, leaving one which managed to see the 1986 season through before becoming a casualty in

1987. As no newcomers had been noted during the latter season, one might have assumed that by the end of that year, the forest would be clear of all hummels. But not for long, for by the time the 1988 stalking season came round five had appeared on the forest of which four were shot. Two appeared again in 1989 but neither was shot. None were reported in 1993 stalking season, but four were seen in 1994, two being shot.

It may seem a mystery where such a large number of hummels can suddenly appear from on a forest, when the previous season none had been seen. Hummels, however, especially immature animals, can easily be overlooked when present among a party of hinds, particularly in wet or misty weather conditions.

A mature stag, whether antlered or a hummel, will often return, year after year if not shot, to the same area for the rut. As a case in point, during October 1942 whilst stalking on the *Forest Lodge* beat of *Atholl* (Perthshire), I spent several days after a particularly large hummel but failed to get a shot at it. Twelve months later, the hummel had returned to the same area near the Tarf and this time I was successful (*see* page 88).

During the 1966 season six hummels appeared on *Kinlochewe* forest (Ross-shire) and all were shot. Not surprisingly, the forest was free of hummels the following season.

Hummels have been reported from most of the west coast islands, and have been particularly numerous on *Park* (Eishkin) forest on the Isle of Lewis where, during at least three seasons, ten have been reported – 1979 (3), 1982 (2) and 1989 (0), the number in brackets denoting the number shot. On the same forest eight hummels appeared in 1985 (1), and six in both 1984 (1) and 1987 (3).

During the 1960s and early 1970s it would appear that hummels were perhaps more plentiful than today, and it was not unusual for some forests to report the appearance of eight or more on the ground during the season. In 1964 'about a dozen' were reported on *Meggernie* (Perthshire), whilst 'about ten' were seen on *Black Corries* (Argyll-shire), only three being accounted for in both forests. On several occasions six to nine hummels have been reported from *Blackmount* (Argyll-shire), the most successful culling operation being in 1970 when five of the nine seen were shot. There are still a number of hummels in the area, the highest cull in recent years being four in 1986.

One of the most versatile recovery vehicles of recent years has been the ARGOCAT, for being amphibious, carcases can be ferried over water.

The GLENCOE A.T.V., manufactured by Scot-track of Nairn, is capable of carrying larger loads than the ARGOCAT.
(G. Macdonald)

The GLENALMOND A.T.V., also manufactured by Scot-track of Nairn, is likewise capable of carrying larger loads than the ARGOCAT. The standard model is not amphibious, but one model supplied to a customer was upgraded by the addition of port and starboard air bags to enable it to be used to cross a loch. *(Scot-track)*

On forests divided by a loch a boat is generally essential. Retrieving a stag across Loch a'Bhraoin, on *Inverbroom*, (Ross-shire), in 1957.

Calling for the pony with a smoke signal.

Signalling, with the use of a two-way radio.

Whatever the transport, a certain amount of manhandling of carcase to more favourable ground may be necessary.

(i) Crossing a burn on *Glenveg* forest (Ross-shire).

(ii) A pull-out of deep heather.

(iii) In this sort of weather neither pony nor vehicle may be of much use (*Culachy*, Inverness-shire).

(iv) Dragging a stag down to more level ground for collection by pony or vehicle – one pulling whilst another holds a steadying rope.

Donald Cameron spying for a second stag on *Kinloch Hourn* forest (Inverness-shire).

Spying on the low ground above Loch Hourn, Inverness-shire.

Sandy, the author's labrador, frequently accompanied him to the hill. Spying on *West Benula* (Ross-shire).

A stag's view of stalkers spying.

The *Rifle*'s view of his stalker.

When bleeding, in order to accelerate the flow of blood, some stalkers will stand on the carcase in order to apply pressure to the heart.

(Below) The 'gralloch'.

(Below left) Poca-bhuide − at one time the recognised perk for the stalker.

(Below right) Removing a deer tusk, or canine tooth.

Killed by lightning – during July 1976 ten stags were killed by lightning on *Glenavon* forest (Banffshire). *(Anon)*

Fencing casualty – red deer calf with hind leg trapped in wire fencing.

Shortened hind limb of Sika deer as a result of being trapped in a wire fence.

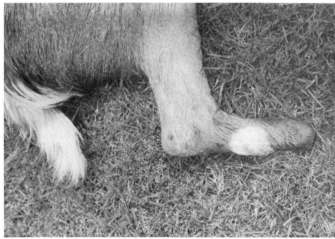

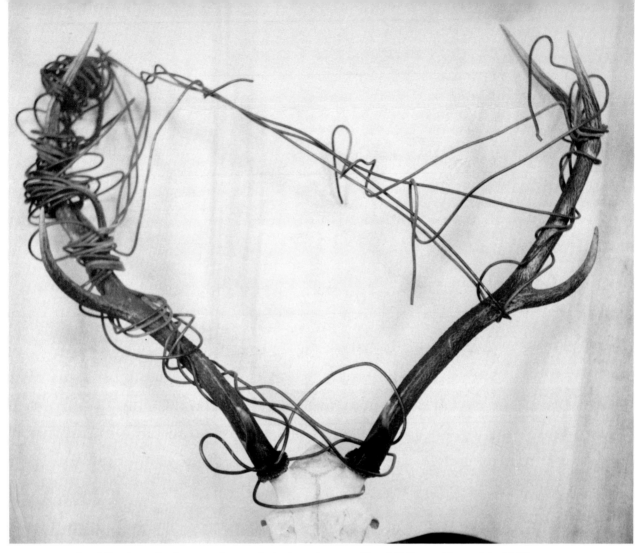

Steel fencing wire festooned around stag's antlers, on *Hunthill* forest (Angus) in 1955. *(Anon)*

Stag caught in nylon netting erected around a forestry block.

Forests on which four or more hummels have been killed in a season include *Glenogil* (1994) and *Invermark* (1964, 1978, 1994) in Angus; *Cruach* (1978) and *Glenkinglas* (1974) in Argyllshire; *Ben Alder* (1975, 1982) and *Gaick* (1983) in Inverness-shire; *Meggernie* (1974) and *Atholl* (1985, 1987, 1989) in Perthshire; and *Achentoul* (1988) in Sutherland.

Before the stag herds have broken out for the rut, several hummels may be included among them. In 1972 four hummels were observed among a party of stags on *Glenshiel* (Ross-shire), whilst in early September 1963, whilst stalking on *Dalnacardoch* (Perthshire), I saw three hummels included in a herd of about sixty stags.

Hummel and 'Royal' Shot in a Day

In 1991, on *Abernethy* forest (Inverness-shire), which now belongs to the R.S.P.B., the tenant, R. C. Naylor, shot a hummel on one day – his first ever hummel – and on the following day shot a good 'royal'. At least two stalkers, however, have succeeded in shooting a hummel and royal on the same day – D. V. Phelps on the *Derry* beat of *Mar* (Aberdeenshire) in 1956, and Richard Southby on *Ben Hee* (Sutherland) in 1980.

In 1976 I myself shot a hummel and large switch within the space of about ten minutes on *West Benula* (Ross-shire) (*see* page 89).

It is not often that two hummels are shot in a single day by the same stalking party, but this has occurred on *Ben Alder* (Inverness-shire) in 1972, and more recently on West Hand, *Atholl* (Perthshire) during the 1987 season. Prior to 1971 hummels were seldom seen on *Langwell* (Caithness) and none had previously been shot for at least eight years. In that year, however, two were shot on the same day, but by different stalking parties on separate beats.

Right and Left at Hummels

Although two hummels have occasionally been shot by the same stalker during a single day, it must be extremely rare for this to have been achieved as a true 'right and left'. Brigadier R. B. R. Colvin, however, informed me that during the 1967 season he had been able to achieve this on his forest of *Corrievarkie* (Perthshire) – a true 'right and left' entails swinging the rifle from one beast to another with no *appreciable* pause and *without* the rifle leaving the shoulder.

There appears, however, to have been an opportunity to achieve this on *Rhiedorrach* Forest (Perthshire) during the 1972 season, for on one occasion two hummels were seen standing side by side roaring, and looking like identical twins.

Hummel, Switch and 'Royal' Shot in a Day

In 1957 Major J. L. Garton had the unusual experience of killing a 'royal', a switch and a hummel, all in one day on *Kinlochewe* forest (Ross-shire) – undoubtedly a 'John Macnab' of deer heads, or perhaps a new 'Grand slam' target for members of the S.C.I. (Safari Club International).

Hummels in Combat

In 1964, on 7 October, a hummel was shot with hinds on *Coignafearn* (Inverness-shire). On the following day, another hummel had taken over the same party of hinds and was also shot.

Hummels have gained the reputation of being particularly wary and well able to hold their own against an antlered opponent. They certainly appear capable of looking after themselves when danger threatens, and indeed, they have to be in order to survive. In 1969 on *Kingie* (Inverness-shire), in order to avoid detection, a hummel was seen to squat on the ground like a hare until eventually flushed by the stalking party. On *Shielbridge* (Argyllshire), between 1964 and 1971, a hummel appeared annually but no one succeeded in getting a shot at it.

As to success in combat, unless both contestants are of equal age and weight I think the inferior animal will eventually give way before physical contact is made. It is a case of 'bluff and bulk' rather than 'brute strength and bloody ignorance' when it comes to a fight. On one occasion I saw an 8-pointer stag just walk away from his hinds when he saw a hummel approaching, the latter obviously a much heavier animal.

A few years ago, whilst stalking a hummel on *West Benula* forest (Ross-shire), I had anticipated the chance to witness a fight when a large switch arrived on the scene, but the hummel sized up its opponent and moved off to a safe distance some 400 yards away, where it remained to watch the switch rounding up his hinds. Eventually I shot the switch, whereupon the hummel, believing the coast was now clear from antlered opposition, returned to the hinds – alas, to pay the same penalty as the switch (*see* page 89). On *Mar* forest (Aberdeenshire), however, in 1966 a hummel was gored to death by its opponent.

Stalking a Hummel

During the 1979 season two hummels were recorded as 'first stags' in the *Auchlyne* (Perthshire) game book – both being achieved under rather different circumstances: one being shot by Peter Bigge as his first stag ever, whilst for the other, Mrs J. Bowser, the owner of the forest, had taken some forty-three years of stalking to shoot one.

From reports received from forests following the 1970 stalking season, it would appear that more hummels were seen that year than usual and at least fifty were shot, which represented about 33 per cent of the number actually seen. Whenever a hummel appears it is generally a 'hunted man', and an all-out effort is generally made to shoot it. Indeed two hummels on *Mudale* (Sutherland) proved to be quite a damaging diversion, for everyone tried in vain to shoot them. Neither ever gave the chance of a shot, and this must have saved the lives of quite a few other stags which might have been stalked instead. During the 1970 season hummels were particularly plentiful on both *Blackmount* forest (Argyllshire) and *Glenfeshie* (Inverness-shire), where respectively nine and at least ten different beasts were seen, five being shot on the former forest and eight on the latter. The late Lord Dulverton told me that, during the previous four years (1967–70), twenty-four hummels had been killed out of a total of 480 stags brought into the larder – about 5 per cent. In 1967, out of twenty hummels estimated to be on the forest, nine were shot. It did appear, therefore, that the proportion of hummels in this area was considerably higher than for Scotland as a whole.

On *Park* forest (Isle of Lewis) in 1987 two stags were killed with a single bullet when a neck shot was taken at a beast sitting broadside with, apparently, no other deer in sight. However, when the stalker went up to gralloch it, he discovered that there was another beast lying dead just beyond it, also with a bullet hole in the neck. It appeared that the two animals had been sitting side by side and since the rearmost beast was a hummel, it had escaped being noticed.

In 1981 a beast, at first thought to be a hummel, was shot on *Glenmuick* forest (Aberdeenshire), but on examination was found to be a stag whose antlers had been sawn off at the base. It was thought to have come from a deer farm, the nearest one to *Glenmuick* at that time being *Glensaugh*, some 20 miles (32 km) away.

Pseudo-hermaphrodite

On 6 October 1983, on *Achentoul* forest (Sutherland), a beast, thought to be a hummel, was seen rounding up a party of hinds and chasing other stags away in typical male rutting behaviour. However, when it was shot, Hugh Rose, the stalker, noticed that there were no external male genitalia but instead there was a normal vulva. It had a broad head with small cartilaginous knobs and two small rudimentary pedicles about ¼ in (7 mm) high on the skull. The neck was developed and covered in rough hair. Its age, from tooth wear, was estimated to be about seven years. Its weight, in the skin, was 144½ lb (65.5 kg).

The carcase was sent to the North of Scotland College of Agriculture's Veterinary Laboratory at Inverness, which carried out a partial post mortem examination, and extracts from their report were published in the 1984 *Annual Report of the Red Deer Commission*. The beast was identified as a pseudo-hermaphrodite, which gave it the appearance of 'a female, but, due to inadequate ovarian function, some male characteristics had developed'.

A comparable event took place on *Kildermorie* forest (Ross-shire) in 1947 when, on 12 October, the stalker observed what he thought to be a hummel. Two other stags were present, and all were reported to be roaring. On being shot, it was noticed that the beast was not, in fact, a hummel but a hind. The head had two coronets and the neck was swollen and rough, with a longish mane. In all other respects, however, the organs were female.

'White' Hummel

In about 1957 a white hummel, estimated to be about four years old, appeared on *Lochranza* forest, Isle of Arran, and Lady Jean Fforde, the owner of the forest, gave instructions that it should be spared. Nine years later it was still on the forest and able to hold hinds, but by then it could only be described as 'half-hummel', as it was now carrying a single antler. So far as I am aware, he had never passed his colour characteristic to any of the calves he had fathered.

Ratio of Hummels to Antlered Stags

As mentioned on page 83, Dr Fraser Darling suggested that in Wester Ross, where he carried out his research work, 'about one stag in a hundred is without antlers' – in other words a hummel. In order to obtain some figures to work on in an attempt to estimate the ratio of hummels to antlered stags for the whole of Scotland, I started to include, in the questionnaire form I have been sending annually to deer forest owners, a query asking how many hummels had been seen on the forest during the deer stalking season, and how many had been shot (see page xi). As a result of this enquiry, it would appear that on average, about thirty-eight hummels are being shot each season which represents just under 0.8 per cent of the total stag cull (Table 3). During the 1970 season, however, at least fifty hummels were shot.

Hummels, of course, have been shot on many areas outside the reporting forests but, like an opinion poll, reports from approximately 109 would seem to be a sufficiently large sample from which the hummel population for the whole of Scotland can be reliably calculated.

In their 1986 Report the Red Deer Commission estimated that the total red deer population in Scotland was about 290,000 of which about 83,000 would be stags, 155,000 hinds and the remainder calves of the year. The estimated annual

Table 3: Proportion of hummels to antlered stags shot in Scotland, 1963–1993 (inclusive)

	Number of Estates reporting each year	*Hummels shot*	*Stags shot*	*Hummels to antlered stags shot (%)*
Aberdeen	6	59	9241	0.6
Angus	6	86	10396	0.8
Argyll	12	124	13443	0.9
Banff	1	34	2960	1.1
Bute	2	8	2702	0.3
Caithness	3	9	3417	0.3
Inverness	30	314	39094	0.8
Perthshire	15	234	23025	1.0
Ross	20	168	22626	0.7
Sutherland	14	104	17963	0.6
Totals	109	1140	144,867	0.78

All figures are approximate.

cull then was around 41,500 of which 20,000 would be stags.

As indicated in Table 3, since 0.8 per cent of the stag cull on the forests under review were hummels – if this same percentage was applied to the total 1986 stag cull (20,000) for Scotland – this would suggest that the number of hummels being killed annually in Scotland would have been around 160. Furthermore, if we apply the same percentage figure of 0.8 to the estimated 1986 stag population (83,000) we arrive at a total live hummel population in Scotland then of approximately 660 animals.

By 1992 the R.D.C. estimated that the deer population had probably increased by about 3 per cent, so at that date the total hummel population might have been around the 700 mark. Since then, owing to an increased cull, particularly of hinds, the red deer population in Scotland has started to fall, and with it probably the overall hummel population.

From these figures, therefore, it can be assumed that just *under* one per cent of Scotland's stag population will be hummels – or putting it another way, there will be one hummel to every 126 stags, which is slightly lower than Fraser Darling's estimate of 1:100 for Wester Ross. In Table 3 it will be noted that for Ross-shire the percentage of hummels to stags was 0.7 per cent, but in both Banffshire and Perthshire it was around one per cent.

Havier

A hummel should not be confused with a havier (hevier), though in general appearance, if the latter is without antlers, it may be comparable. A havier is a stag that has been castrated and is, of course, infertile.

A stag without any testicles was shot on *Inversanda* (Argyllshire) in 1965, but whether a havier or a case of cryptorchidism was not recorded. Its antlers – each about 9 in (23 cm) in length and 1½ in (3.7 cm) in circumference, with one growing downwards, were still in velvet. A stag in similar condition was shot in *Invermark* forest (Angus) in 1982. It had a switch-type head, and weighed 14 stone. In 1976 a stag was shot on *Leckmelm* (Ross-shire) with short antler stumps about 10 in (25 cm) long and, although velvet was adhering to them, the stumps were quite hard. On examination it was found that the animal had previously been castrated.

Cryptorchidism

Cryptorchidism occurs when the testes fail to descend to the scrotal sac and are retained in the abdominal cavity, thus being held in a higher temperature than when in the scrotal position. Although hormonally normal, a cryptorchid stag is reproductively sterile.

In 1965 a stag was shot on *Glenfeshie* (Inverness-shire) which had both testicles undescended. A similar beast, a 9-pointer, was shot on *Ben Alder* (Inverness-shire) in 1973, which also had a monorchid during the same season.

Monorchid

A monorchid is a male deer with only one testicle or with only one testicle descended into the scrotum. 'Monorchids can and do breed. The abdominal testis is usually non-functional due to being maintained at too high a temperature for active spermatogenesis, but the scrotal testis is quite 'normal' (M. Woodford *in lit* 1948).

During the 1958 season, I killed a small 'royal' on *Garrygualach* (Inverness-shire) which turned out to be a monorchid.

Hermaphrodite

An hermaphrodite was killed on the *Glen Ey* beat of *Mar* forest (Aberdeenshire) by Major F. W. Strang-Steel in 1958, which was described as having 'the neck and head of a hummel with small bumps on its forehead and mane like a stag, but otherwise lacked the normal male organs and appeared to be female. It was a small but "elderly beast" (10 stone), and when shot was in company with other small stags.' I believe a somewhat similar beast was shot on *Wyvis* (Ross-shire) about 1930.

An hermaphrodite is any animal that combines the characteristics of both sexes. Thus, a hermaphrodite deer would possess both ovaries and testes, and probably antlers as well. They are, however, infertile (*see also* pseudo-hermaphrodite, page 86).

Three Hummel Stalks

I will close this chapter with an account of three of the most exciting stalks – one spread over two years – I have had in Scotland after hummels.

My first Hummel

I shot my first hummel in 1942 during a week's army leave which was spent at *Forest Lodge* (Perthshire), and although we saw him on several occasions, I had to return to my unit without so much as getting the opportunity for a shot. He seemed to have a charmed life. On one occasion, with a favourable wind and ample cover for a close approach, we reached a bank within about 110 yards (100 m) of the place where we had last seen the hummel rounding up his dozen or so hinds. So far it had been a 'cake-walk' and a hasty glance through the wavering grass showed the deer still to be in front of us, apparently undisturbed. However, after examining more closely all the deer before us, there was no sign of the hummel but, believing he must be hidden in some deep hole, we decided to remain and watch events.

We had scarce been waiting more than five minutes when a deep bellow on our left made us look in that direction, and there, a good 330 yards (300 m) away and in full view, stood the hummel roaring from the top of a small hillock. Before we could withdraw from our exposed position he had spotted us and immediately ran off to be followed by his hinds.

Two days later we found him again, but just as the stalk appeared to be nearing success, a much complaining cock grouse literally exploded into the air from under our very noses as we crawled our way through the heather and, of course, gave the show away. Before my leave was up I had one more stalk after him, but from the very start the wind was never going to be in our favour and, before we had approached to within a quarter of a mile, he had scented danger and taken his hinds away.

Twelve months later I was back on the ground for my October leave, and my first enquiry was to find out whether the hummel was still on the ground. He was, so on the day after my arrival we set fourth in high hopes, for only two days previously he had been seen by the stalker.

Eleven a.m. found us scanning that wild country across the Tarf, which over a century ago the sportsman/author William Scrope had found to be such a happy hunting ground. In those days of antlered monsters, if we are to believe the graphic pictures in his famous book on deerstalking (*The Art of Deerstalking*), or those portrayed by the pen of Colonel Crealock some fifty years later (*Deer-stalking in the Highlands of Scotland*), a hummel would surely have been considered poor quarry. But today his demise was desired as much as any 'royal'.

We soon spotted the hummel with eight hinds, less than three quarters of a mile away. Undulating ground, broken up by peat hags and a wee burn, gave us ample cover to approach the deer without once exposing ourselves. An occasional roar kept us informed that the deer were still in front of us. But once again he eluded us, for as we spied the deer from a peat hag well within shot, only an old 10-pointer stag appeared to be with hinds.

It was a shootable beast, and since a stag in the larder is worth two on the hill, rather reluctantly I shot it. At the sound of the shot, the hummel suddenly appeared, accompanied by three hinds, wading across the Tarf, a good mile away. They must have started to move out as soon as we had commenced our stalk.

But the following day our luck was to turn. Visibility was exceptionally good, and it was not

long before we spotted the thick, short-necked form of the hummel. He was about two and a half miles away and running his hinds on a small flat piece of rushy ground on the opposite side of the river Tarf to where we were watching.

Although we had to descend some thousand feet or so down to the river, broken ground and a deep burn made this task easy. Once at the river, however, our troubles began, for the deer, now less than 330 yards (300 m) away, were in full sight, and at no place could we make a crossing out of view of the deer. Either we could stay where we were and hope that the deer would move closer, or we would have to risk a crossing. We chose the latter and, selecting the most broken stretch of water and waiting for the sun to come out and perhaps dazzle the deer, we waded, almost up to our waists at times, through the fast-flowing river, moving only when all heads were down or turned away from us.

On reaching the far bank we still had a crawl of about 220 yards (200 m) up a small burn before closing the range to within about 130 yards (120 m), and it was during this crawl that disaster nearly aborted the stalk. Rounding a bend in the burn we bumped into a resting hind, who jumped up barking before rushing off across the river. The deer in front of us, including the hummel, immediately took alarm and started to trot off, but instead of running up the hill away from us, they swung round and started to follow the hind which was now across the river. This, indeed, was luck for it gave me a chance of a broadside shot at the hummel as he trotted past a bare 110 yards (100 m) away. We had at last broken the spell and bagged the hummel.

Hummel and Switch

Some thirty-five years later I had a somewhat similar chase after another hummel. At the time I was stalking on *West Benula* (Ross-shire) and had spotted a hummel holding some half dozen hinds. Provided we could get past the many beasts scattered along the hillside, the stalk appeared to offer no real difficulties. But as we were debating a suitable line of approach, another stag with long switch-top antlers, appeared on the scene to dispute ownership of the hinds. On the approach of the switch, all the beasts moved further into the corrie and had soon disappeared round the shoulder of the hill. The only chance now of coming to terms with the hummel was to rediscover him somewhere along the west-facing slope of Gleann Sithidh, and to do this would entail a long climb out to the head of the corrie.

It was well past midday by the time we had made the ascent, and although we soon spotted the switch, there was no sign of the hummel, so we decided to go for the former.

The switch, with about half a dozen hinds, was directly below us, and this entailed a lengthy slide down the hillside in full view of the deer, but eventually – moving only when heads were not looking our way – we reached a ridge some 110 yards (100 m) above the deer, from which an easy shot was possible.

At the shot a beast, which we had not previously seen, suddenly appeared some 440 yards (400 m) below the hinds and a quick glance through the telescope showed it to be the hummel. Fortunately we had not been detected by the hinds, who were now slowly walking away up the glen and, as they did so, the hummel started to follow them.

As soon as he had disappeared into a deep gulley, we quickly slid down a further 110 yards (100 m) to take cover behind a ridge, so as to cut him off should he emerge on the other side. When he did appear he was barely fifty metres away, so the shot offered no problems. The time interval between shooting the switch and the hummel had been less than ten minutes.

So ended an eventful and lucky stalk!

'An evil-looking beast'

In contrast to these two lengthy and exciting stalks after the elusive hummel, a beast shot in 1975 could not have been more simple. It was late in the afternoon when, on our way back to the lodge after a blank day on *Glencarron* forest (Ross-shire) we spotted a small group of stags which included a medium-aged 6-pointer with switch tops, so we decided to make a stalk for him. The approach offered no undue difficulties and, as I was about to take a shot, I happened to notice, barely a hundred metres away, the head and shoulders of a hummel sitting in a patch of deep heather, contentedly chewing the cud. It was a beast of about eleven years old, and when it reached the larder it turned the scales at 16 st 11 lb (106 kg), which turned out to be the heaviest beast of the season. It happened to be the first hummel that an American guest staying at the lodge had ever seen, and his only comment was, 'What an evil-looking beast'.

Not everyone's opinion is the same, however, for as my old father used to say – for every foul face there is an equally foul fancy – and on one occasion in 1982, when I shot a particularly large hummel, a young lady who had accompanied me on the stalk was so impressed with it that she asked for its head to be fully cape-mounted, and it now hangs above her bed in London!

CHAPTER 13

Non-typical Coloured Red Deer in Scotland

White Red Deer

During the past fifty years there have been a number of reports of white deer appearing on Scottish deer forests. A white-coloured deer must not be confused with albinism, for whereas 'white' deer have normal pigmentation of the eyes, the irises of the latter are pink. Albino deer are characterised by pink skin and a pure white coat, and not only may the nose be paler but the hooves more pigmented than in normal-coloured deer. So far as I am aware, no true albino wild red deer has occurred in Scotland during the past fifty years, but reports of the appearance of white or cream-coloured red deer are fairly widespread. The presence of white-faced, or bald-faced red deer occurs regularly in central Perthshire (*see* page 93).

For a number of years there was a white stag on *Brodick* (Isle of Arran), but on 1 December 1970,

at an estimated age of about thirteen or fourteen years, it had to be shot by the stalker as it was being aggressive to human beings. During the latter part of its life it had become very tame, spending much of its time on the low ground near the village, where it regularly received food from the residents. By this time the stag had been christened Angus. For a short period during the rut of 1967 Angus did succeed in holding a few hinds before being chased out by another stag.

For the first five years of his life Angus was without antlers, and to all appearances a hummel. Then, from about 1963 until 1969, it annually grew a single antler of three or four points on the left side, but in the following year another antler appeared on the right side and until July of that year it was an 8-pointer, with four points each side. However, during that month the right antler became damaged and subsequently fell off. Five months later, as already described, Angus had to be shot.

There is, apparently, a tradition among the Hamiltons that when the head of the family dies a white deer appears on the hill. This stag was born in the spring of the year following the death of Lady Jean Fforde's mother, the owner of *Brodick*. There was, apparently, some alarm in about 1960, when a rumour went round that there was a second white deer on the hill, but this was either not true or some loyal retainer must have killed it and buried it quickly!

In 1949 a white hind appeared on Mull, whilst during the same season a white stag, estimated to be in its fifth year, was seen on a number of forests in central Perthshire. In 1958 the white hind which had frequented *Kingie* forest (Inverness-shire) for many years was still alive, but a hind seen on *Culachy* (Inverness-shire) the previous year had disappeared.

In 1961 a young, cream-coloured hind, which was believed to be the offspring of a similar-coloured stag seen on the forest in 1956, was frequently to be seen on *Chesthill* (Perthshire).

During 1964 the white hind that had frequented *Kingie* forest (Inverness-shire) for a number of years gave birth to a white calf. No one was prepared to estimate the age of the hind. There had, however, always been the odd white hind on this forest since about 1926, when a white 13-pointer stag had been shot. Since then several white calves, both male and female, had been born, so it was estimated that the hind on the forest in 1964 was perhaps a granddaughter of the white 13-pointer.

During 1967 a very light coloured hind, which had been on the ground for a number of years, was killed on *Mamore* (Inverness-shire).

In 1969 a strangely-coloured calf was born on *Hunthill* (Angus), but when seen the following summer its coat had a dappled appearance which included a number of large white spots. It also had a white muzzle, suggesting that it had just pushed its nose into a bucket of meal.

In 1971 an almost white hind appeared on *Glenshiel* (Ross-shire) but its presence was not reported the following season.

During 1980 a pure-white calf was seen on several occasions on Sguman Mhor, *Kinveachy* forest (Inverness-shire) – presumably having been born on the ground, for there were no reports of it having been seen elsewhere. So far as I am aware, this is the first occasion a white red deer has ever been seen on *Kinveachy*.

At some time or another, however, white deer have appeared on many different forests, particularly on those west of Loch Ness, being descended from some white red deer that were sent to *Glenquoich* from Woburn about 1875.

On Christmas eve 1890 Mr Laycock shot a perfectly white hind on *Letterewe* (Ross-shire) that had been on the ground for a number of years.

Between 1926 and 1964 there have been a number of records of white red deer – mainly hinds – on *Glenkingie* (Inverness-shire). But it is unlikely that there is any connection between the white deer on *Kingie* and those on *Kinveachy*, for the two forests are separated from each other by about 60 miles (96 km) with Loch Ness intervening.

About forty years ago there was a white red stag and hind on *Glenshero* (Inverness-shire), and at about the same time a white switch was reported on *Dalnamein* (Perthshire). Both of these forests are within about 30 miles (48 km) of Kinveachy. During 1985 a white stag was seen on several occasions on *Glenshero*. It had the appearance of a young animal.

In 1962 a white red deer stag appeared on *Killiechonate* (Inverness-shire), whilst in the same year there was a white hind on neighbouring *Mamore*.

On 28 August 1982 R. A. Dubery saw a pure white calf on his forest of *Edinchip* (Perthshire) which was described as being 'very strong and active'. The calf was seen again on 20 October of that year but its presence was not reported subsequently.

A white calf was also seen on *Achnacarry North* (Inverness-shire) in 1982. Between 1926 and 1964 there have been a number of records of white deer – mainly hinds – on adjoining *Glenkingie* forest (*see above*), so it would appear that the white strain may still linger in the area.

For a number of years a white hind was seen on *Glenbanchor* (Inverness-shire) and in 1984 she had a calf, but it was of normal colour. In that year an almost pure-white hind was seen on *Glensanda* (Argyllshire) among a large group of normal-coloured hinds and calves.

In 1985 a white calf appeared on *Glenkinglass* (Argyllshire). Ten years later another 'extremely white' calf was seen in this forest.

In 1987 a cream-coloured yearling, as well as the usual white-faced deer (*see* page 93) appeared on *Suie* (Perthshire), and was seen on the ground the following year as a knobber. In 1988 an almost pure-white calf was seen on several occasions in the area.

For the third year running (1990) a white calf appeared on *Suie* (Perthshire), which is an area regularly frequented by white-faced deer (*see* page 93). It was a stag calf and was still present on the ground during the 1993 season, but with increasing years had become more cream than white.

During 1990 an almost pure-white hind was seen on several occasions on *Ben Loyal* forest (Sutherland). *Ben Loyal* adjoins *Kinloch* forest which formerly belonged to the late Lieutenant Colonel Douglas Moncrieff, who occasionally used to send deer up to *Kinloch* from his park at *Kinmonth*, near Perth, as fresh blood. The appearance of white deer at *Kinmonth* first occurred when a pregnant hind, recently received from *Woburn Park* in Bedfordshire, produced a white calf, since when other deer of this colour have regularly appeared in the park. Doubtless it was a hind from *Woburn*, although of normal colour herself, that may have been responsible for the white hind seen on *Ben Loyal*. *Woburn* no longer has any deer of this colour.

During December 1993 an aged cream-coloured stag, which had frequented the *Auchlyne/Suie* area for a number of years, was found dead.

White-faced or Bald-faced Red Deer

A typical white-faced or bald-faced deer has a white face similar to Hereford cattle, and there may also be white 'socks' above the hooves. In some specimens the whole of the face may be white, but in the majority of Scottish examples of this strain the white will be limited to a narrow blaze down the face, or perhaps even to only a small white patch on the centre of the forehead. In those animals that show a considerable amount of white on the face, the nose is often pink-coloured and one or both eyes may be 'wall' (opaque, white or with pale iris).

Towards the end of the nineteenth century some bald-faced hinds were presented to the Marquis of Breadalbane by the King of Denmark and, according to Millais (1897), these were released into the sanctuary of *Blackmount* deer forest (Argyllshire). Possibly as a result of this introduction, a bald-faced stag subsequently wandered on to *Achnacarry* forest (Inverness-shire). When bald-faced deer disappeared from Argyllshire is not known, for Robin Fleming, the owner of *Blackmount*, has no knowledge of any being seen on his forest in recent years.

About 1880 it would appear that the Marquis of Breadalbane also introduced some bald-faced deer to his park at *Drummond Hill* (Perthshire), which lies adjacent to Taymouth Castle. During the First World War, as a result of timber operations, the deer fence was breached and many of the bald-faced deer escaped on to the hill and joined up with the wild deer on neighbouring forests which included *Chesthill*, *Glenlyon* and *Remony*, and to this day occasional white-faced deer continue to appear on these Perthshire forests, as the following records show.

In 1960 a white-faced stag of eight points and weighing 15 stone was shot on *Remony*, and since that date a few deer of this description have been a regular occurrence on the forest. In 1970 another stag, featuring a good white blaze and having white 'socks' on its forelegs, was shot on the same forest.

During March 1983 a white-faced stag turned up on *Edinchip*, which is situated near Killin some 14 miles (22 km) south-west of *Remony* and, although it temporarily disappeared during July, it returned about the middle of October. Estimated to be about four years old, R. A. Dubery, the owner of *Edinchip*, described it as having 'a terrible switch-type head, with the top points almost touching.'

White-faced deer are generally present on *Suie* and *Auchlyne* (Perthshire), and during the rut of 1989 a white-faced stag and a similar-coloured hind were generally to be seen together, giving hope that there would be a white-faced calf in the following summer. In the event, three white-faced calves appeared on *Suie* during the following June, and in addition there were three similarly-coloured yearlings as well as an elderly stag of eleven points. There was also a three-year-old cream-coloured stag in the area. In 1985 a white-faced hind had given birth to a normal-coloured calf so it seems possible that this distinctive colour variation follows the male rather than the female line.

Elsewhere in Scotland, outside Perthshire, a white-faced hind, with two white patches on each haunch, was regularly to be seen on *Ben Hee* forest (Sutherland) during the 1974 season, but where it had come from was a mystery, for it had never been reported previously in the district. Its origin may have been the same as suggested for the appearance of the white hind on neighbouring *Kinloch* in 1990 (*see* page 93).

Between 1974 and 1977 a heavy, mature stag, which displayed a white patch on the back of its neck, was resident on *Dougarie* (Isle of Arran). It was a 10-pointer in 1977, compared with eleven points during the two previous seasons.

During a meeting of the Balquhidder Deer Management Group (see page 158) members unanimously agreed that none of these bald-faced deer in their management area should be shot.

Black Red Deer

During 1989 there was an unusual report from Charles Marsham, the owner of the *Rispond* Estate (Sutherland), that he had a stalk ruined on his forest by the sudden appearance of a 'black hind', which had been overlooked during the spy in the belief that it was a black peat-hag. So far as I am aware, this is the *only* report of a *black* red deer ever having appeared anywhere, either in a park or in the wild. When queried as to whether there was any possibility of the hind having been recently wallowing in black peat, or perhaps mistaken for a sika deer hind which, apart from a prominent white rump patch, might have appeared black in winter pelage and poor light, I was assured that it was neither, but definitely a black red deer hind. So far there has been no further reports of this unusually coloured deer.

To substantiate the possibility of it having been a sika deer, in recent years sika have been spreading their range into north-west Scotland (*see* page 119), and in 1989 there was a feral sika deer within 30 miles (48 km) of *Rispond*.

CHAPTER 14
Hinds and Calves

Hinds

Hinds are responsible for a population boom, and the only way to reduce the overall stock must be to cull hinds heavily. Once stocks have reached the desired level, and the overall sex ratio is correct, the number of stags and hinds to be killed must, thereafter, be decided on an area rather than an individual forest basis. Very few forests today are extensive enough to hold a balanced resident population of both stags and hinds – some forests are purely stag ground, whilst others may never see a stag from one rut to another.

It is essential, therefore, that there should be good liaison between owners and stalkers on adjoining estates so that, with a shared interest and knowledge of deer numbers, sex ratio and trophy potential over a wider area than a single estate, a worthwhile management plan can be evolved.

The essence of good herd management is not only to control the deer population compatably with the acreage and food available, but also to maintain a well-balanced stag/hind ratio not exceeding around 1:2.5. If there are too many hinds the rut will be prolonged, and 'run' stags are neither good venison nor in the best condition to face a really hard winter, resulting in a greater mortality among adult stags than hinds.

According to Darling (1937), the fertility of adult hinds is about 60 per cent, whilst the mortality of calves of under one year of age will be about 50 per cent. It has often been said that the more hinds there are on the ground the greater number of stags will be attracted for the rut, but this is not so. Nor is it true that 'a good stock of hinds is better than a deer fence', for whilst their presence may retain the stags for two or three months during the rut, for the remainder of the year a hundred or more hinds is not going to keep a stag at home if his fancy takes him elsewhere.

The condition of the hinds is most important, and if they have had a rough spring and summer they will come into condition late, the rut will be late and during the following summer there will *probably* be a lot of late calves also (*see* page 44). In 1960, following a hard winter and very wet spring, there was a heavy mortality among both hinds and calves at *Blackmount* (Argyllshire) during the summer.

On a number of occasions the Red Deer Commission has expressed concern over a rising deer population, particularly among hinds, and has urged estates to increase their cull. If venison dealers are paying good prices not much persuasion is required, but when it is down to 15 to 20 pence per pound (in season-carcases) or 5 to 15 pence per pound (out-of-season) as it was in 1971 this is a different matter. The price of venison is like a two-edged sword, for when it is high it suits both estate manager and poacher, but when it is low it probably assists in the survival of the deer. It is a case of 'why fill the larder with a lot of venison for which there is little demand or return?'

In response to R.D.C. advice, during the winter of 1966-67 many estates considerably increased their hind cull to well above the number that had been formerly practised. On *Invermark* (Angus) the cull that winter was over 200, which was about double the number usually killed. On *Glenavon* (Banffshire) the increase was even more spectacular, with a cull of 334 hinds as compared to a more normal cull of about 50 to 60 practised in previous years. In recent years it levelled out at about 140-150 per season. Other forests which that year increased their hind cull by about four times the average of previous winters included *Glenartney* (Perthshire) 283, *Langwell* and *Braemore* (Caithness) 227, *Struy* (Inverness-shire) 70, *Glencarron* (Ross-shire) 90, *Scatwell* and *Strathconon* (Ross-shire) 305, to mention but a few.

Pressure on the hind cull continued during the following seasons, and on the combined forests of *Strathconon* and *Scatwell* during the winter of 1967-68 the cull was further increased to 356, but on *Langwell* and *Braemore* it fell slightly to 201.

During the winter of 1967-68 197 hinds were shot on *Invermark* (Angus), which was about double the usual cull. Many other forests, during that winter, would have shot more but for the intervention of foot-and-mouth disease, which put a stop to hind culling for a time. As a result of this outbreak, *Glenavon* (Banffshire) was only able to

cull 76 hinds that year as compared to 334 during the previous winter. Even so, this was about a third more than the average number of hinds killed in earlier post-War years.

As mentioned on page 65, disturbance on the hill caused by afforestation and work on hydro-electric projects resulted in a number of local migrations of deer, and for a period of years hinds were reported as being scarce in some areas. In 1954, on both *Glenmoidart* (Inverness-shire) and *Inveraray* (Argyllshire), hinds were said to be becoming fewer each year, whilst in 1956 one forest owner complained bitterly that his ground, unfortunately, marched with a neighbour who had little or no interest in stalking and killed, indiscriminately, any beast that crossed the march. Hinds are more static than stags, and the result of overshooting will soon become apparent and will take much longer to recover.

In recent years many estates have once again increased their hind cull – some by as much as 100 per cent or even more. *Strathconon* (Ross-shire), for instance, shot 600 hinds and calves during the winter of 1992-93 as compared to 297 in 1989. During the same season *Mar Lodge* forest (Aberdeen-shire) shot 1,000 hinds and calves – an increase of about 600 on the 1989 cull total. *Langwell* (Caithness), with a cull of 1,040 hinds and calves during the winter of 1992-93, was about double the cull of the previous years, while the 255 beasts taken off *Glendoll* and *Rottall* (Angus) was about 66 per cent up on 1989.

Until 1977 the annual hind cull on *Kinloch* (Sutherland) had been about 20 beasts, but for the next ten years this was reduced to only 3 or 4. Then, in 1988, it was raised to 37, and was further increased to 100 during 1992-93. On *Ben Loyal* – a neighbouring forest to *Kinloch* – the hind cull, including calves, also increased considerably from 91 in 1989-90 to 217 during the 1992-93 season.

In addition to shooting, a few forests included the sale of live hinds to deer farms in their cull. In 1989, for instance, although both *Glenmuick* (Aberdeenshire) and *Gaick* (Inverness-shire) had reported hind culls of 170 and 200 respectively, only 110 of the former and 30 of the latter had actually been shot on the forest, the remainder having been caught and transferred to deer farms.

During the following three winters (1990-92) the hind cull on *Gaick* was maintained at around 200, the highest number being in the winter of

1990–91 with a total of 217. By the autumn of 1993 a cull of this number was thought to be excessive, so in future it will probably be reduced by about 20 per cent to around 160.

On *Rhiedorrach* (Perthshire), during 1990, there were more deer on the ground than at any time during the previous twenty-five years, and at that date it was estimated that the stock of deer numbered about 400–600 stags and 2,000–2,500 hinds. Prior to that year, the annual hind cull had been about 80, but was then increased to 140 in 1991–92 and 205 in 1992–93.

Although, during recent years, there has been a gradual build up of the hind population throughout much of the highlands, there are, nevertheless, some areas where the reverse has been the case. This was particularly apparent in some of the reports received in 1979, with considerable concern over their scarcity being expressed on *Glenbanchor* and *Abernethy* (Inverness-shire). Over all, the shortage of hinds that season appears to have been confined to some of the East Grampian forests. A shortage of hinds was also reported on *Glencallater* (Aberdeenshire) but, on the credit side, more stags than normal were showing up on the west side of the forest.

As a result of the recent increase in hind culls on some of the larger forests, it was not surprising that, by 1993, a number of forests were reporting a shortage of hinds, and these included *West Monar* (Ross-shire), *Dalnaspidal* (Perthshire), *Glenfeshie* and *Erchless* (Inverness-shire). So far as the latter two are concerned, *Glenfeshie* marches with *Atholl* forest in the south and the *Geldie* beat of *Mar* in the east, whilst *Erchless* is only about 4 miles (6 km) south of *Scatwell* and *Strathconon*, which have been culling heavily in recent winters. The heavy cull of hinds on *Strathconon* would also have been felt on *West Monar*, which is situated along its south-west march.

Pre-War a larger percentage of yeld hinds probably featured in the hind cull than today, for they undoubtedly provide better venison than a milker with calf at foot. Although a yeld hind will not have had a calf that summer, she is not necessarily barren and may well prove to be one of the earlier breeders the following summer – and is a welcome member, therefore, of any hind group. Today, many of the hinds shot will be milkers, accompanied by their 5–8-month-old calves, and whenever possible, any late calf should be shot also. On some estates the number of calves shot has been included in the total hind cull, but on forests which have separated the hind cull from the calves in their return, the latter has generally represented about 25 to 30 per cent of the cull.

Pre-War, when I estimated the total red deer population in Scotland to be just under 300,000, it would appear that the annual hind cull then numbered about 8,300. By 1950, when the deer population had fallen to just under quarter of a million, the hind cull was probably about 6,700.

According to the annual reports of the Red Deer Commission, the hind cull (excluding calves) during the past twenty-four years had gradually increased from 11,267 (10,622 in-season, 645 out-of-season) in 1971 to 33,195 (32,359 in-season, 836 out-of-season) in 1992-93. During 1994-95 the hind cull was reduced to 25,585 (24,987 in-season, 598 out-of-season). From these figures alone, it would appear that the hind cull in the early 1990s is now over three times what it was in the late 1930s.

Excessive hind stock on some forests has received a lot of adverse publicity in recent years, and one of the proposals suggested is to lengthen the legal hind season by starting in early September instead of 21 October, thus allowing it to run concurrently with the last six to seven weeks of the stag season. I am very much against this proposal, for I do not believe that *selective* shooting of either sex would be possible at the same time.

Far better to extend the hind season to either the end of February, so as to coincide with the legal date in England for female deer, or even prolong it to the end of March. Here again, this would not be setting any precedent, for as recently as 1984 Scotland made it legal to continue shooting roe does until end of March – a month later than in England.

Today, apart from mist and bad weather, there should be little difficulty in achieving a satisfactory hind cull, for the modern stalker no longer has to rely on the time-consuming process of using a garron to remove the carcase from hill to larder. Each year mechanical transport has become more versatile, and it is seldom that a carcase has to be manhandled over much distance before being loaded up on to a vehicle. Moreover, prior to the War, once the carcase had reached the larder the stalker and/or his assistant – often before having a meal or change of clothes – would then be faced with an hour or two of skinning, depending on the bag for the day, which was not the best preparation for a repeat performance on the next day. Today, apart from gralloching and removal of head and feet, little larder work is required before the carcase is collected the following day by a game dealer's van.

Although it would appear that, in many overstocked areas, the only good hind is a dead one, this description could hardly be levelled at a remarkably tame hind that at times actually assisted the stalker in his hind cull.

Two hinds that went Stalking

In 1967, when Willie Munro left *Moy* (Inverness-shire) to become head stalker on *Wyvis* (Ross-shire), a passenger in the back of his ancient Ford Prefect car was Bambi – a 10-month-old red deer hind which he and his wife had reared from a young calf of but a few days old.

Willie and Bambi soon become inseparable, and wherever Willie went Bambi was sure – or tried – to go. Indeed, at times it became quite a task for Willie to leave the house undetected, and many a time had Bambi run after the car when the Munro family set off on a shopping expedition.

When Willie went deer stalking Bambi had, at times, to be shut up in a paddock, otherwise she would accompany him to the hill – following every moment of the stalk and showing not the slightest fear when the shot had been taken, nor any sign of remorse for a fallen relative. Indeed, she would approach the shot deer with complete indifference and would then, in a disinterested way, either lie down and watch the deer being gralloched, or use the time to take a bite prior to escorting the carcase back to the larder. On many occasions Bambi had, in fact, actually assisted in the stalk for, by following her closely over an exposed flat or along a hilltop, Willie had been able to approach a deer which otherwise would have been impossible – in fact she had often acted as the perfect 'stalking horse', a method that, in the last century, was often used for approaching wildfowl and other game.

Although Bambi was generally to be found in the vicinity of Willie's house, she was free to

wander to the hill to consort with the wild deer should she so wish. It was hardly surprising, therefore, that when two and a half years old Bambi – who was now adorned with a red collar – was able to find a mate, and on 7 September 1969 she produced a daughter which was christened Trudie. I asked Willie why they had selected this particular name in preference to the names of Faline and Gurri – the principal female characters in Felix Salter's two famous books on *Bambi* and *Bambi's Children* – and was told that, when the birth was imminent, they had felt so certain that the calf would be a stag that they had decided to call it Rudolph – a name, perhaps, more applicable to a reindeer than a red deer. However, 'Rudolph' turned out to be a 'she', and so Trudie, whilst not too far distant in pronunciation from Rudolph, seemed more appropriate. It was not long before Trudie was following in her mother's footsteps, and whenever Bambi was allowed to follow Willie to the hill Trudie went along as well.

In 1970 Bambi had her second calf – also a daughter – which was christened Beauty, and although perhaps not quite so confiding as her mother or sister, she also was soon accompanying the stalking party to the hill, and showed not the slightest fear at the discharge of a rifle which had been fired only a yard or two away, or at the subsequent sight of blood from a fallen neighbour.

Bambi and her children obviously enjoyed human company, and if neither of the Munros were about they would wander off to join woodmen working in an adjacent plantation, or perhaps watch electrical engineers working on a power line.

Of the three, Bambi, in her fifth year, was always the most confiding, obviously preferring – or perhaps respecting – male rather than female company. This was evident in her behaviour to both Mrs Munro and any other lady visitor, and should she not get her way she would often jump up to give a tap on the shoulder with her foreleg. Once a lady visitor thought that, by wading out into the burn which ran past the house, she would escape Bambi's attention, but not a bit of it, for water held no terrors for Bambi – or, indeed, for any red deer! Bambi's distrust, however, of young women seems to have stemmed from the time when Willie's young daughter one day started to tease her. Bambi, however, soon put an end to that sort of nonsense by seizing young Kathleen – then only three years old – by the hair and pulling her, shrieking, across the lawn towards the river before father came to the rescue. Needless to say, Kathleen was henceforth much fonder of the ponies around the house than of Bambi and her children.

Any washing left hanging on the clothes-line proved irresistible to Bambi, and many was the occasion when an almost new pillow-slip or piece of underwear reached the ironing board with a hole chewed out of it, or other structural alterations! Bambi had also discovered that the rubber on windscreen wipers made good chewing-gum, so it was always prudent to remove these from your car whenever parked in the vicinity of the Munro home! Tractor oil, although invariably making her sick, was nevertheless consumed with relish as, of course, were also many of the other more usual household titbits, which included sweets, biscuits and bread. Her excursions with her two daughters to the adjacent forestry plantation of *Novar* were certainly not looked upon with much enthusiasm by the forester, and doubtless she would soon have paid the penalty of trespass with her life had she and Trudie not been wearing their collars.

Bambi's attachment to, and escapades with, the Munro family, although remarkable, was not unique, for shortly after the War, whilst stalking near Garve (Ross-shire), I became acquainted with a young hind that behaved in almost identical fashion. It all started one June day in 1944, when Peggy Urquhart, the sister of Murdo the stalker, found a wee hind calf of but a few days old standing near their gate. The calf was quite alone, and when approached, lay flat on the ground just as its mother had doubtless taught it to do when confronted with anything strange. After waiting a few hours to see if any hind would appear on the hill, of which there was a wide expanse in view from the house, when none appeared Peggy concluded that its mother had probably been shot by poachers during the night, for their house was but a few yards from the main Garve to Ullapool road and there was a lot of poaching going on in the area. The little orphan was, therefore, carried into a shed and given its first meal of milk from a bottle. Within days the calf was given the run of the garden, but for obvious reasons was always shut up at night.

With human beings the calf soon lost all fear, and by the time she was twelve months old would follow the Urquharts about everywhere. But she never got accustomed to Murdo's collie dog and, even when two years old, whenever the dog approached, up would go the hairs down her spine and, should the dog approach too close, a hard strike on the dog's head with one of its forefeet would be the only welcome it received.

By now she was no longer living in the hut, but was leading a perfectly wild existence on the hill just below the house. Yet she never wandered far away, and whenever she felt lonely would come wandering down to the house to see if her human friends were about, for there was nothing she liked better than to receive their affection. She was equally fond of the garden, and found its produce far more tasteful than anything she could possibly find up on the hill!

Like Bambi, if no one was at home she would often wander a short distance down the road until, perhaps, finding some road men, for she seemed to derive considerable enjoyment from sitting nearby to watch them at work! Her curiosity was great, and if anything unusual appeared she would trot up to it in order to give it a closer inspection. It was hardly surprising, therefore, that she found my camera, mounted on a tripod, a wonderful toy, and more than once sent it flying with a gentle nudge from her nose.

As far as strangers were concerned, one could never tell how she would treat them. In some respects she was, therefore, rather like a temperamental child, and if she trusted you, would allow herself to be patted freely and would repay the compliment by rubbing her head against you, or nuzzling you with her soft, twitching nose. At other times she would reciprocate any amorous petting by suddenly jumping up and cuffing you with a foreleg. Fortunately I generally found her in one of her most agreeable moods, allowing me to pet her freely like an overgrown dog, but whether it was the 'staggy smell' from my stalking clothes or what was inside them that pleased her I cannot say.

When three years old she, like Bambi, was allowed to accompany Murdo to the hill when he went stalking, and it is hard to imagine a more unique spectacle than that of a stalking party being followed a few yards in the rear by a hind! When the party sat down to spy she would lie down in the heather alongside, and even the sound of the shot and subsequent spectacle of a kinsman being gralloched failed to arouse any fear or 'fellow-feelings' within her, and she would even go and sniff around the entrails of the fallen monarch as though satisfying herself that the stalker had made an efficient operation of it!

In October of 1946 I was stalking on a neighbouring forest and was, naturally, very interested to see if any of the many stags who had chosen the hillside around Murdo's house for their rutting ground would persuade this young lady to join their harem. But no, and as far as Murdo knew she never ventured far from his house and was never seen in the company of other deer. In fact I was told that, whenever a stag looked as though contemplating a date, she would run down to the house as though dubious of his intentions!

But only to deceive; for in the autumn of 1947 I had the exciting news from Peggy Urquhart that her tame hind had had a son during the summer. What a Jekyll and Hyde existence this young lady had led in the Autumn of 1946! By day she would accompany the stalkers to bring about the downfall of, perhaps, the mate who had wooed her only the previous night!

It is amazing how seldom a hind, when in season, fails to find a mate, even though there may not, apparently, have been a stag resident within many miles of her. One of the most extraordinary cases in this respect is told by Tom Speedy in his book *Natural History of Sport in Scotland with Gun and Rod* (1920). He tells of a tame hind which was kept by itself in a small park within 2 miles (3 km) of Edinburgh. The nearest deer forest was that belonging to Lord Ancaster at *Glenartney* – a distance of about 50 miles (80 km) as the crow flies. Nevertheless, by some means or other, this hind was able to find a mate and produce a lusty calf. Yet matrimony does not always come to these isolated 'spinsters', for in 1948 there was another elderly tame hind near Drumnadrochit (Inverness-shire) who, although living within easy distance of 'stag ground', had apparently failed to find a mate and remained barren all her long life.

Now that the Urquhart's hind had a calf to care for, she was not nearly so confiding and, although she did not desert the playgrounds of her childhood days, she never brought her calf down to the stalker's house but kept the schooling of him to herself. Thus, his hereditary fear of human beings was never broken down like his mother's had been, and he remained a creature of the wild. Yet, if she had only known how soon her calf was to be an orphan, she would doubtless have remembered what good friends the folk that lived in the stalker's house had been to another orphaned calf only three years previously, and would have told him so.

But she was not to know, and when it was noticed that the two familiar figures failed to put in an appearance on the hillside for several successive days, fears for their safety grew. The mystery of their disappearance was soon to be known. A hind's body, bearing traces of the poacher's hideous work, was found 2 miles (3 km) away in the river which ran alongside the road, and almost immediately a calf, lost and distracted, returned to the hillside behind the stalker's house – so near, and yet so completely out of range of all the cares that human kindness so very much wanted to offer him.

By Christmas the little calf had disappeared also, and it is possible that a wintry spell of snow and frost found him unprepared to face it alone. Maybe he had now rejoined his mother in that vast sanctuary far beyond the range of any stalker's spyglass or poacher's rifle.

Over the years there have, of course, been many deer that seem to have preferred human to cervid company – Lea MacNally's tame hind at *Torridon*, which in 1982 had twins, was certainly one of them (*see* page 102) – but I doubt if any have adjusted their lives to quite the same extent as those two 'stalking hinds' of Willie Munro and Murdo Urquhart.

Calves and Calving

Over the years there has been a wide range of calving successes, which makes it impossible to generalise. Under normal circumstances one should be able to expect a good crop of calves to follow a mild winter, thus leaving the hinds in the best condition to raise a calf. On the other hand, a hind that is in poor condition may not be able to pull through to the spring, and although its loss will numerically improve the calving percentage among the survivors, it may also result in a number of late calves during the summer, which is not good for the future,

High winter-mortality among the hinds will, of course, mainly affect the more elderly, which, from a management point of view, is not a bad thing, for this will enable the stalker to reduce the total number of hinds he has planned to kill, and enable him to spend more time in selecting those to be weeded out.

Many stalkers, with adequate time to pick and choose the beasts to be culled, prefer to select hinds which are yeld - i.e. a female deer which has not had a calf the previous summer, but is not necessarily barren - but whilst this class of animal certainly provides the best venison, they might also provide better breeding stock for the future if left on the forest. In my opinion, therefore, the cull should concentrate on the worst and not the best, and this would include all hinds in poor condition and those with a late calf at foot - the latter being shot as well.

Bad weather and shortage of daylight hours will, of course, often preclude too much time being spent on selection and, as the days pass by and 15 February draws ever-closer, selectivity may have to go by the board if the planned cull figure is to be achieved.

Despite a late rut in 1947, calving during the following summer was about normal and, from a number of areas, stalkers were expressing concern that they were unable to find sufficient yeld hinds to kill. On *Mar* forest (Aberdeenshire) the stalker reckoned that approximately 30 per cent of his high-ground hinds of over two years of age were yeld, but on the low ground the percentage was probably nearer 20 per cent. During the same winter the late Captain W. D. M. Bell - the famous elephant hunter - estimated that perhaps only 33 per cent of the breeding hinds on his forest of *Corriemoillie* (Ross-shire) had produced calves that summer.

1950 followed a similar pattern, and stalkers over a wide area were having difficulty in finding enough yeld hinds for their cull.

After one of the worst winters and early springs for years, during which there was high mortality among deer of all ages, there was a serious shortage of calves during the summer of 1951.

At *Badanloch* (Sutherland), for instance, there was only about half the normal number to be seen, while on *Strathconon* (Ross-shire) only a very small percentage of the hinds had calves. On the *Atholl* forests of Perthshire it was quite common to see a parcel of fifteen to twenty hinds with only three or four calves amongst the lot of them. Rather more satisfactory, however, were the conditions on *Lochs* (Perthshire), where a count taken at the end of October showed that there were 268 calves on the ground to 415 hinds.

The winter of 1954 was extremely bad, and during the following summer many hinds - themselves in poor condition - produced a higher percentage of late calves than normal, some of which were undersized. On *Glenquoich* (Inverness-shire) a hind was seen to calve during the first week of October, and some forests estimated that casualties during the spring had amounted to perhaps the greater part of one year's breeding stock.

Nature, however, came to the rescue in 1956 with an exceptionally high crop of calves, which included, however, a large number of late calves. On *Ceannacroc* (Inverness-shire), for instance, a calf estimated to be barely a week old was seen on 10 September, whilst at the beginning of October, on *Corrievarkie* (Perthshire), 'a very young calf' was seen running with its mother.

During 1969 a large number of late calves were reported, particularly in Sutherland, one of the youngest being a three-day-old calf on *Borrobol* on 25 September.

The summer of 1972 proved to be an exceptionally good calving year, with some forests estimating that about 75 per cent of hinds had a calf at foot, and many of these had been early calves. Nevertheless, there were also a number of late calves, which included one still in its dappled coat on 14 September on *Scardroy* (Ross-shire). On 3 September D. Geddes, the head stalker on *Borrobol* (Sutherland), had actually witnessed the birth of a calf whilst out stalking - surely a unique event. During mid-winter of 1971, whilst out hind stalking, D. Geddes had, in fact, one day heard a stag roaring, so it would appear that this hind could well have been in season at that time.

The rut of 1974 was both late and prolonged, and it was anticipated that, as a result, there might be a lot of late calves the following summer, but this was not so. Nevertheless, two very late calves were seen on *Dougarie* (Isle of Arran) one on 10 August which had only recently been born, and the other during the last week of September which appeared to be about a month old.

The summer of 1979 also produced a good crop of calves, and on *Achnashellach* (Ross-shire) it was estimated that there was probably one calf to every three hinds. *Kinlochluichart* (Ross-shire) also had more calves that summer than was anticipated after the bad winter of 1978–79. Calving was also good on *Black Corries* (Argyllshire), but there were also a lot of late calves. On *Reay* (Sutherland) the stalking party came across a very small calf on 19 October which appeared to be only about a month old, as dappling on the coat was still visible.

Apart from *Dougarie* (Isle of Arran), which reported a good calf crop in 1977, there appeared to be a noticeable shortage of calves on many of the mainland forests that year, but for what reason it is difficult to say. One suggestion made was that the heavier hind cull that had taken place in previous years had left a larger than normal percentage of the hind population being in the two to three-year age group – i.e. the progeny of the 1975 summer, which was reported to have been a very good one on many forests. The calves from this age group, therefore, would not have been born until 1978.

True to expectation, the calf crop in 1978 was good, but due to the 1977 rut having been late, coupled with the fact that a large percentage of the hinds calving were 'first timers', it was only to be expected that there would be a lot of late calves that summer.

On many forests, which included *Glenmuick* (Aberdeenshire), *Black Corries* (Argyllshire), *Camusrory* and *Glenfeshie* (Inverness-shire), the calving rate was poor during the summer of 1993 and, with no calves at foot, hinds came into season early, resulting in an early rut in some areas. Some early calves, therefore, were expected in the summer of 1994.

Twin Calves

Unlike roe deer, twinning among red deer is a rare event and, when hind culling, it is very seldom that one finds twin embryos in the hind during the gralloch. Two calves following a hind is no certain proof that she is the mother of both. During the winter of 1970 a hind and twins were seen during late December on *Knoydart* (Inverness-shire), and the same party of three were seen again in February 1971. 'No mistake about them being twins', reported Andrew MacKintosh, and 'both hind and calves were very lean when last seen'. It is not known if they survived the winter, but thought extremely doubtful.

Twin embryos within a hind being gralloched were found by Howard Walker on *Brodick* forest (Isle of Arran) in 1967. The following August, whilst grouse shooting in the same area, he found the skeletons of two calves lying within about a foot (30 cm) of each other, and both appeared to have been still-born.

On the 14 August 1982 R. A. Dubery saw a hind, with two calves following, on his forest of *Edinchip* (Perthshire). He also reported that a few years previously he had also seen a hind with twins in the same area of woodland and suggests that the 1982 twin-bearing hind may have been a daughter. The year of 1982 also saw the birth of twins to the late Lea MacNally's tame hind at *Torridon* (*Torridon*, Lea MacNally, 1993).

CHAPTER 15

The Rut

The Mating Act

There are a number of people who travel to Scotland every autumn for deer stalking who say that they have never actually seen a stag mating with a hind during the rut. This, perhaps, is not really surprising for, apart from the fact that copulation often takes place at night, to watch deer for any length of time requires good clear weather, of which, unfortunately, there are not too many such days in October. As often as not, if the weather is wet, cold and windy, there will be little temptation to spend much time spying with 'scope or binocular, for both – particularly the former – will soon become fogged up and virtually useless. So what generally happens, therefore, is that, once the 'target' for the stalk has been selected by the stalker and an approach has got under way, the *Rifle's* main attention will be to follow the stalker's line of approach and instructions as near as possible, and not to watch deer. Indeed, the *Rifle* may never set eyes on the stag again until the moment of truth arrives and he is told to 'tak him noo'.

On 6 October 1972 a good 10-pointer stag was seen to serve three different hinds in quick succession on *Camusericht* (Perthshire), whilst in 1977, during a stalk on *Langwell* (Caithness), I myself, accompanied by Martyn Leslie, the then resident factor of the Portland Estates, witnessed the unusual spectacle of a matured stag mounting another stag which was itself engaged in covering a hind. A similar incident was photographed by F. Spencer Nairn in his deer farm at *Struy* (Inverness-shire).

Deer do not, of course, have to observe any 'legal season' for the rut, and although it should, in a normal season, be nearing completion by the last week of October, it will sometimes continue well into the following month. In 1955 Willie Grant, the stalker on *Talladh-a-Bheithe* (Perthshire) saw, during the last week of November, the same stag serve twelve hinds out of a herd of fifteen, all within a period of two and a half hours.

In 1978, on the last day of the season (20 October), two separate stalking parties out on *Coulin* (Ross-shire) both saw a stag covering a hind, one of the stags mounting the same hind twice within about five minutes.

During the 1962 season, whilst stalking on *Caenlochan* (Angus), the Hon. J. W. Leslie and his stalker saw a stag serve the same hind no less than six times, all within the space of about fifteen minutes, whilst during the same season on *Kildonan* (Sutherland), a 'royal', which was subsequently shot, was observed to cover the same hind eight times in about twenty minutes. Two other hinds standing nearby were completely ignored by the 'royal' and were obviously not in estrus.

On *Torosay* (Mull), on 30 October 1959, Lieutenant-Colonel Miller reported having witnessed a stag covering a hind 'several times'.

Although a hind will be in estrus for a period of only about twelve to twenty-four hours, with a herding species such as red deer the rut can be a very hard time for the stag, and there will be very little time for feeding and relaxation between serving the various members of the harem, should it be large. Under these conditions the stag will soon become 'run'. It has been estimated that during the three to four weeks of rutting activity, a stag may well lose as much as 25 per cent of its body weight, thus leaving it ill-prepared to face a hard winter should it follow swiftly after the rut.

Moreover, should a hind fail to be fertilised at the first estrus she will come into estrus a second, or even a third time, the interval between cycles being about two and a half weeks. In a large herd, therefore, with many hinds missing out on the first or second estrus, this will only prolong the rut and create a more severe strain on the master stag unless, of course, he has been shot or replaced by a successful opponent.

This, therefore, emphasises the importance of keeping hind stocks to a minimum and thereby maintaining a more balanced stag/hind ratio.

Swimming during the Rut

Red deer are excellent swimmers and, regularly during the rut, a travelling stag will swim across a Scottish loch in search of hinds. Stags are reported to have swum across Kilbrennan Sound from the Island of Arran to the Mull of Kintyre - a distance of 4½ miles (7 km).

Owing to the disturbance by the hydro-electric work it was noticed that, on *Strathvaich* (Ross-shire) during the beginning of the 1959 rut, the stags only visited the hinds by night, returning to the high ground during daylight hours. One day the stalking party saw a hind, accompanied by a yearling, swim across a recently completed reservoir - a distance of about 600 yards (548 m). The hind emerged fairly exhausted, but the younger animal appeared to be quite fresh.

During the 1976 season an 8-pointer with the excellent measurements of length, left 37½ in (95.3 cm), right 37 in (94 cm); beam 4¾ in (12 cm), and inside span 31¾ in (80.6 cm) was shot on *Sleat* Isle of Skye, by Norman Macpherson. Heads, generally, on Skye are not good and it was assumed that this stag may have swam across to Skye from *Scalpay Island* which, at low tide, would have involved a swim of not more than 100 yards (91 m). Another suggestion was that it might have swum to Skye from the mainland in the *Glenelg* area of western *Eilanreach* forest (Inverness-shire), but this would have involved a further swim of about 400 yards (366 m) across the Sleat to Kylerhea in eastern Skye. A stag and two hinds from *Warnham Park*, Sussex, were introduced to *Scalpay Island* in 1927, so *Warnham* blood had been in the breeding of deer from this island some forty-nine years previously.

On *Dalnaspidal* (Perthshire) a stag was shot, during the 1987 season, with an eartag indicating that it had been tagged as a calf on *Ben Alder* forest (Invernessshire). In order to reach *Dalnaspidal* it must have either swum across Loch Ericht - a distance of about 600 yards (548 m) at the narrowest point - or wandered the 15 miles (24 km) or so around the loch side. Not a great distance for a travelling stag and it could, of course, have been on the ground for some time before being shot.

The Rut of Post-War Years

General

Pre-War, the rut in Scotland was generally considered to take place between about

20 September and 10 October, and this resulted in the majority of calves being born during the first fortnight of the following June.

But what is a 'normal rut' today?

The difficulty today of classifying ruts into 'early', 'normal' and 'late' is that, with some of the former larger estates now divided up into smaller units, a small forest that now consists mainly of high ground above say 2,000 feet (610 m) may report a 'late' rut whilst an adjacent area of low ground, which was formerly part of the same estate, may have witnessed a slightly earlier rut – or vice versa. Formerly there would have been only one report for the whole area – now there will be two, which may differ.

Nevertheless, based solely on the rutting periods reported to me during the past forty-eight years, it would appear that during twenty-five autumns – i.e. 55 per cent of the seasons under review – little serious rutting was taking place before 1 October, as the following list indicates.

Incidence of early, normal and late ruts
(1947–1995)

Early Rut (14%)
(starting about mid-September)
1956   (p. 108)
1971   (p. 109)
1972   (p. 109)
1980   (p. 110)
1981   (p. 111)
1990   (p. 112)
1993   (p. 112)

Normal Rut (31%)
(starting about 25 September)
1948   (p. 107)
1949   (p. 107)
1957   (p. 108)
1959   (p. 108)
1960   (p. 108)
1961   (p. 109)
1964   (p. 109)
1968   (p. 109)
1970   (p. 109)
1979   (p. 110)
1984   (p. 111)
1985   (p. 111)
1986   (p. 111)

1987   (p. 111)
1991   (p. 112)

Late Rut (55%)
(starting early October)
1947   (p. 107)
1950   (p. 107)
1951   (p. 107)
1952   (p. 107)
1953   (p. 107)
1954   (p. 108)
1955   (p. 108)
1958   (p. 108)
1962   (p. 109)
1963   (p. 109)
1965   (p. 109)
1966   (p. 109)
1967   (p. 109)
1969   (p. 109)
1973   (p. 109)
1974   (p. 110)
1975   (p. 110)
1976   (p. 110)
1977   (p. 110)
1978   (p. 110)
1982   (p. 111)
1983   (p. 111)
1988   (p. 112)
1989   (p. 112)
1992   (p. 112)
1994   (p. 112)
1995   (p. 113)

As will be seen there was, more or less, a continuous six-year period of reported late ruts between 1973 and 1978 – being particularly late during 1975 and 1976 – yet there were surprisingly few reports of late calving during the following summers. This does not necessarily mean that late calving did not occur – it perhaps did but was not recorded. Furthermore, reports of late ruts often coincide with reports of bad weather when a fogged-up glass accompanied by rain and gale-force winds will have made any prolonged spying a complete waste of time, so, under such conditions, mating will often have escaped detection by the stalkers.

Even in a so-called 'normal year', the rutting period may be extended over the best part of four to six weeks, yet the bulk of calves will probably be born during the two middle weeks of June. A few calves are certainly dropped at the end of May, or late in the autumn, but they are not as plentiful as late rutting might suggest.

It has occurred to me that perhaps a late mating might result in an aborted calf but this possibility is not shared by John Fletcher who is of the opinion, (*in lit* 31 March 1995) that there is,

> no evidence at all to suggest that late matings will result in 'aborted calves'. If a fertile mating takes place late, then, in all likelihood, a calf will be born late. The only possible other contingency is that the embryo may be absorbed at an early stage. This is not strictly abortion but embryonic loss with no passage of foetus.

It would also appear that, from reports received from those forests where some form of artificial feeding in winter has been available, an earlier rut has followed. This is probably true if a comparison is being made between the feeders and non-feeders but, for an overall improvement over a large area, the majority of forests represented in, say, a Deer Management Group area, will all have to subscribe to a feeding programme (*see* page 155).

As mentioned on page 103, it is surprising how few people, other than the professional stalker or ghillie, claim that they have actually seen deer mating, and this has led to the belief that most matings must, therefore, take place at night. This may well be so, but it has been forced upon them by frequent intrusion on their habitual rutting areas by stalkers, ponies, recovery vehicles etc., and as a consequence it is only during the hours of darkness that rutting can take place without undue disturbance. Furthermore, stalkers are on the hill to kill deer and cannot, therefore, spend too much time watching them, and this must result, particularly on days of rain or poor light, in many matings never being witnessed.

Apropos late ruts and their effect on calving, Roderick Stirling of *Fairburn* (Ross-shire) commented (*in lit* 1982),

> while the rut, such as it is, appears to be getting later each year, it is noticeable that there is no difference in the dates when calves are born. I suspect the continuous wet conditions of recent seasons appear to make the stags look less active, for they are certainly quieter than in dry, frosty weather.

Throughout Europe the roe rut takes place during July and August. Because of what is referred to as delayed implantation, development of the foetus is arrested for about four months, so that the birth can take place some nine months later when survival conditions will be at their best for the young kid. This made me wonder if a reverse situation might apply to red deer whereby, following a late rut, there might be an *accelerated* implantation so as to ensure a summer rather than autumn birth. In order to see if there was any foundation for this speculation, I contacted Dr John Fletcher, who has made a close study of the gestation of red deer, both on the Island of Rhum and on his Reediehill deer farm at Auchtermuchty. His reply (12/2/95) stated that,

> there is really no doubt that the length of gestation (about 34 weeks) is extremely constant among red deer in different situations . . . There is some evidence that gestation may be a very few days longer in the European red deer which one might expect given their larger size; after all wapiti have a longer gestation and hybrids are intermediate. . . . I think that the confusion arises over the problems in detecting the time of mating. Few people appreciate that the hullabaloo that marks the rut precedes mating by quite a period of time. We think that the roaring, stinking, displaying and fighting serve a role in stimulating the hinds to come into heat but they are also a vital part of the stag's strategy in ensuring that the most successful male is in the prime position when the hinds start to come into heat. This means that the most obvious signs of the rut may be in decline or even finished before any hinds are actually covered.

According to Clutton-Brock, Guinness and Albon in *Red Deer Behaviour and Ecology of Two sexes* (1982), the gestation period for hinds on Rhum was 34 weeks (236 days ± 4.75 days for males, and 234.2 ± 5.04 days for females). Following their ten-year study on the Isle of Rhum the authors observed that they 'never saw a free-ranging hind mating with a stag of less than five years during the peak rut, though stags are fertile as yearlings'. That observation, of course, referred to an island population where the herd sex-ratios and age groups were being carefully monitored. On the mainland, however, there are no such barriers to contain the herd, and any stag wandering off a well-managed forest does so at his own risk. The inevitable result is, therefore, that seasonal rutting has now become, largely, a 'teenage' five to seven years age group activity simply because few of the 'big boys' have survived and, since younger stags invariably rut later than the more mature stags, the rutting calendar has, as a consequence, been put back a week or two to suit their age.

Dr Fraser Darling, in *A Herd of Red Deer* (1937), states that 'calving time is from about June 7th to July 15th in Highland red deer, and most of the calves are dropped between the 15th and 25th of June. There is a sharp falling off in the numbers calving early in July, and only occasional calves are born in August and September.

There is little doubt, therefore, that since the War the rutting season has gradually been pushed back a week or two, the main reasons being a lower age-group of participating males and a lowering of the general condition of the deer, particularly the hinds, which is most important for an early rut.

Pre-War the 'normal' rut generally took place between about 20 September and 10 October, and by about 5 October most of the big stags would be so badly run as to be not worth shooting. That was why, in those days, although there were no legal close-seasons for deer, most stag stalking, as a sport, would terminate on or about that date.

Before the War, also, many deer forest owners augmented the deers' winter fare with some form of additional feeding, and on those forests where no such additional feed was available the deer had access to large tracts of good wintering ground much of which, due to wide-scale afforestation and hydro-electric exploitation, is now denied them. Moreover, particularly during the post-War years, many forests either carried a small stock of sheep or had, in effect, become a large sheep farm, and with an increasing deer population, this has reduced the natural food available for the latter.

Fortunately, in recent years, more forests are now supplying some additional winter feed, and if the overall deer population can also be reduced, particularly among the hinds, so as to maintain a closer sex ratio than as at present – not to mention some restraint on the number of mature stags being shot – then the traditional rutting season of late September may well return to the Scottish highlands.

An early and more active rut, however, generally means a rapid loss in condition, and by mid-October many of the larger beasts will be run and just not worth shooting.

Summary of Scottish rutting seasons since 1947

1947 A late rut, with little roaring or rutting activity before October. On *Dunrobin* (Sutherland) it was not until 20 October that the first roar was heard.

1948 After the late rut of the previous year, it was either described as back to normal or early. For instance, on both *Mar* (Aberdeenshire) and *Dunrobin* (Sutherland), some stags were even roaring during the last week of August, and by mid-September the stag parties on the majority of forests had started to break up. One of the late forests was *Coignafearn* (Inverness-shire), where the stags were only just beginning to join the hinds when stalking finished on 4 October.

1949 A very passive rut and, although on some forests a few stags had started to roar by 12 September, less roaring was heard than usual, particularly during October which can be a very noisy month.

1950 Generally a late rut which had hardly got under way before the termination of stalking. On *Coignafearn* (Inverness-shire), a lot of the big stags were still together on 10 October, and there were plenty of hinds about at that date without a stag. The late rut was reflected in the good average weight that season. It must be appreciated that in those days many forests terminated stalking as soon as the rut had got properly under way – which was often before or about 10 October.

1951 The season will be remembered for the abnormally late rut, and quite a few owners and their guests had to return south during the first week of October without having heard a single roar.

1952 Another late rut, and on many forests it was not until the first week of October that any roaring was heard. After stalking for a week or two on *Mar* forest (Aberdeenshire), General Shanker wrote, 'I found everything out of joint this season, and it was not until October 12 that we heard any sporadic roaring.'

1953 A late rut, and even up to 10 October there were plenty of stags about in shootable condition. Although on many forests roaring had started on about 15 to 20 September, stags seemed reluctant to break out properly and, even by 10 October there were still many parties of hinds about without a stag.

Once the stags had broken out the rut was brief and it was noticeable that many stags, after spending only three or four days with hinds, were quite finished.

1954 An extremely late rut and, although some sporadic roaring was heard on a few forests on 7 September, many stalkers had to wait until the first week of October to hear their first roar. Generally speaking it was not before 10 October before the rut was under way and was then brief, being over after about ten to fourteen days. Nevertheless, during December, a few big stags were still running odd hinds on *Corrievarkie* (Perthshire) right up to 31 December, the main rut on the forest having taken place 8–24 October.

1955 Another late rut. The reason for a late rut would appear to be a combination of a dry spring and wet summer. The winter of 1953–54 had, for the most part, been mild right up to end of January, with grass and heather still well forward. This was followed by a period of severe frosts which killed off everything, with the result that by June there were practically no young heather-tips available for either deer or grouse. The spring, however, was fine, but the bitter east winds of March, April and May, dried everything up to such an extent that there was little grass showing until June. Thereafter the summer and autumn were extremely wet.

1956 Following a dry spring and favourable summer, the rut was early and by the end of September was well under way, making it difficult after 10 October to find a shootable stag. Because of the much-run condition of the stags, a number of forests wisely decided to end their stalking by about 6 October. Others, however, continued stalking for another fortnight, and this was the subject of a number of complaints by some forest owners and tenants who deplored the practice of killing stags after 10 October. It was, of course, perfectly legal to do so, for it was not until 1962 that a legalised close season for red deer in Scotland became effective (*see* page 142). William Scrope, the sportsman/author of the early nineteenth century, had commented,

> In this state of running they [the stags] are rank and wholly unfit for the table. Such deer a good sportsman never fires at: but many may be found

at this time, not so forward, but perfectly good, and they are of course easily distinguished.

In an early season, as Scrope observed, there are still some stags to be found 'not so forward but perfectly good' and, provided one is selective, these should be targets for the closing days of the season.

'People who can boast that they have shot a wonderful head on October 20th', commented Brigadier Colvin (*in lit* 1956), 'are unworthy of owning a deer forest.'

1957 Although stags started to roar somewhat earlier than in recent years, with desultory roars being heard on many forests from about 10 September onwards, it was not until the last week of the month that the stags started to form their herds. Even so, there was remarkably little activity and stags appeared scarcely belligerent. Once the rut had started, however, the stags quickly went out of condition and by 10 October most of the older-class beasts were completely run.

1958 From all over Scotland the story was the same – a late rut, with the majority of the stags taking little interest in the hinds until about 4 October. Even so, a week or so later there were small parties of stags wandering about as though it was still September.

The first roars were heard about mid-September on some forests, which included *Kinlochewe* (Ross-shire) and *Culachy* (Inverness-shire). However, on the latter, Lea MacNally, the head stalker, had seen a stag covering a hind on 29 November, and reported hearing a few stags still roaring on 4 December.

1959 After one of the driest summers and autumns for many years, the start of the rut followed no fixed pattern, being in full swing by 20 September on Mull (Argyllshire), but being late in both Aberdeenshire and parts of Ross-shire.

Owing to the disturbance caused by the hydro-electric work on *Strathvaich* (Ross-shire), it was noticed that, at the start of the rut, the stags were only joining the hinds by night, returning to the high ground for the day.

1960 Generally speaking the rut was late although, on the two adjacent forests of *Knoydart* and *North Morar* (Inverness-shire), stags were heard to roar rather earlier than usual, and by 28 September the rut was in full swing. Thereafter the stags went out of condition rapidly. Oddly enough, at *Arnisdale*, which lies opposite *Knoydart* across Loch Hourn (Inverness-shire), the rut was described as 'very late', not commencing until about 4 October. It was about a week later before it got properly under way on the *Atholl* estate forests.

1961 Rather variable across the country, being rather early in Angus but late on the west-coast forests.

1962 The rut, with few exceptions, was extremely late everywhere, and it was often the smaller stags which were first to join the hinds. Indeed, since the War, late ruts were becoming a norm. Late rutting is closely associated with the condition of the deer in the spring, and unless their winter fare can be augmented by artificial feeding this pattern will continue. One of the few forests to report an early rut was *Ardverikie* (Inverness-shire), where the deer had received additional food from November to May.

1963 Once again another late rut, and the stags were able to maintain their condition right to the end of the season.

1964 The rut was very variable, being slightly early in Aberdeenshire and Angus, but late on the island of Mull and western Sutherland.

1965 The rut was late in all counties except, possibly, Perthshire, and out of 131 forests reporting, only 20 (15 per cent) described it as early. On *Brodick* (Isle of Arran) a stag was heard roaring on 27 December, whilst on 4 February the stalker on *Killilan* (Ross-shire), during hind stalking, saw an aged stag in company with about thirty hinds, 'roaring away in great style'.

1966 Another late rut, and on many forests, it was mid-October before there was any real rutting activity. Even so, it was a fairly *passive* one and many reports suggested that it was the younger, rather than older class of stag, who first came to the hinds.

It is the behaviour of the hinds that regulates the pattern of the rut and after the long winter, and wet spring and summer, particularly in the north-east, the hinds were in poor condition.

1967 A late rut which enabled some forests to complete the cull before the stags had become run.

1968 Due to the fine weather, and as a result of an increasing number of owners supplying some form of winter feeding for their deer, the rut in many areas, was slightly earlier than in previous seasons.

1969 In contrast to the previous season, the rut was late, with little activity on many forests until the second week of October. On those forests which regularly fed their deer in winter, the rut was slightly early.

1970 Although some stags were heard roaring early in September, it was not until the first week in October that any rutting activity was apparent. On *Ben Alder* (Inverness-shire) the first stag to be seen with hinds was not until 8 October, and as late as 1 December a stag was seen to be serving a hind.

Any hind that is seen to be served during the hind stalking season should be shot if possible, for late breeders are not good stock for the forest.

1971 Following a fine, dry autumn in most areas, the rut was generally early with the odd stag roaring as early as late August on *Ben More* (Mull), and by 6 September on *Ben Alder* (Inverness-shire). By the beginning of October many of the larger stags were so badly run as to be not worth shooting. In consequence, several forests ended stalking about 9 October. *Wyvis* (Ross-shire) in fact wound up on 5 October – the earliest for thirty years.

1972 Over the whole of Scotland the rut was early. On *Langwell* and *Braemore* (Caithness) it commenced about 9 September, which was a full fortnight earlier than usual. At *Knoydart* (Inverness-shire) some stags were roaring on 4 September, and by the 24th of the month the rut was well under way. A fortnight later the bigger stags had all finished and left the hinds. Further north, the rut was later.

The early rut, and exceptionally fine weather, meant that by the time any of the larger stags had reached the lower-placed forests, they were probably too much run to be worth shooting.

1973 An extremely late rut and, on those forests which had completed stalking by 10 October, hardly a run stag had come into the larder. Even when it did break out, it was a comparatively subdued affair.

A noticeable feature of this season was the non-belligerency which some of the older stags, in company with their own party of hinds, displayed to the younger generation of stags who, as often as not, were allowed to hang about in the vicinity of the harem.

During the rut this year, on a number of occasions on both *Blackmount* (Argyllshire) and *Kinlochluichart* (Ross-shire), hinds were seen to mount each other as domestic cattle will often do, which might suggest that they were already in season, but no stags were able to take advantage.

1974 Apart from at *Langwell* (Caithness), where the rut commenced about 19 September, on the majority of forests, and in particular those in Aberdeenshire, Banffshire and Perthshire, it did not get under way until about the first week of October.

1975 An extremely late rut, and on some of the low-ground forests stalking had finished without the stalking party ever having witnessed any serious rutting in progress.

Throughout much of Scotland there was little rutting activity until the second week of October. On 10 October over 150 stags were seen lying peacefully together on *Ben Alder* (Inverness-shire), and not a single roar could be heard.

1976 Once again the rut, particularly in the eastern part of Scotland, was late and many forests were able to select unrun beasts right up to 20 October. As always there were exceptions, and the rut on *Ben More* (Mull) was described as being very early, with a stag seen with hinds during the first week of September.

1977 Another late rut, with little activity on many forests until second week of October. On *Kylestrome* (Sutherland), for instance, there were bunches of twelve or more shootable stags still together in mid-October, whilst on 7 October about 200 stags were seen herded together on the home beat of *Wyvis* (Ross-shire). There was a similar position on the *Atholl* group of forests (Perthshire), and even as late as 27 October there were groups of mature stags, numbering several hundred, low down where they had been all season. It was considered unlikely that any of them would ever go to hinds as the latter were, by then, mainly accompanied by younger beasts. On *Kingie* (Inverness-shire) the rut did not commence until about 20 October – the last day of the season.

1978 Once again the rut was extremely late, and on many of the western forests there was little activity before the second week of October. On *Blackmount* (Argyllshire) the rut was described as 'incredibly late *apparently* . . . yet the yeld hinds shot in November and early December would seem to disprove this, for the calf embryos were all well formed'.

The wretched weather of 1978 may have been partly responsible for stags showing little appetite for the rut, and it was Lord Burton's opinion that 'the stags on *Dochfour* (Inverness-shire) were probably more interested in seeking shelter than women!'

1979 The rut followed a very irregular pattern this year, being early on some forests and extremely late on others, even within the same county. On *Glenartney* (Perthshire) the odd stag was roaring by 27 August, and an early rut followed. Elsewhere in Perthshire, however, there was little rutting activity before October.

On *Glenquoich* (Inverness-shire), although the stags which had been fed during the winter started to rut about 11 September, it was not until the third week that the majority joined in.

Both on *Kingairloch* and *Blackmount* (Argyllshire), as well as on some of the islands and elsewhere in the county, little activity was to be seen before October.

Apart from *Wyvis* (Ross-shire), which reported a slow and prolonged rut starting about mid-September, all the Wester Ross forests, and those in north-west Sutherland, saw few stags with hinds before the first or second week of October. It was a similar pattern in Aberdeenshire, Angus, Banff and Caithness.

1980 A rather earlier rut than in recent years, with many stags roaring by mid-September, and rutting by end of month. On *Kinloch* (Sutherland), however, a stag was seen with hinds on 8 September. On *Langwell* (Caithness) the rut started on the low ground about mid-September, but on the high ground it was about a week to ten days later.

On some forests such as *Kinveachy* (Inverness-shire) and *Wyvis* (Ross-shire), most of the big stags were completely run by about 12 October, and not worth shooting after that date. On *Ben Alder* (Inverness-shire) it was the earliest rut since 1972.

1981 Although conditions varied considerably from county to county, the general opinion was that the rut was earlier than usual, with the first roars in many areas being heard by mid-September. Indeed, on *Glenfinnan* (Inverness-shire) some roaring was heard during three days on about 26 August, but there was no real break-out until beginning of October.

On *Dunrobin* (Sutherland) the rut was the earliest for many years. This was put down to the excellent condition of the deer, especially the hinds, due to general winter feeding and removal of cattle from the forest.

Winter feeding does, undoubtedly, encourage an earlier rut, and this was shown on *Letterewe* (Ross-shire) with the 'feeders' joining the hinds long before the general break-out of the stag herds had occurred.

A bonus of the early rut of 1980 was the excellent showing of calves during the following summer.

1982 The rut this year was described as being one of the latest and quietest on record, and over much of Scotland it was not until the end of the first week of October that there was any real activity.

There were, of course, exceptions, such as on *Scardroy* (Ross-shire), which reported an early rut, with stags roaring by 6 September, while on adjacent *Strathconon* (Ross-shire) the first stag to be shot with hinds was on 16 September. It was, however, a woodland stag, and it was not until a fortnight later that any of the hill stags started to go with hinds.

An amusing incident was witnessed on *Ledgowan* (Ross-shire), when a rutting stag was seen to chase a party of hinds in and out of some old ruined buildings near the loch side.

1983 It was an extremely late rut, and over much of Scotland there was little activity before 12 October, and even then it was a very subdued affair with less roaring than usual. On both *Invercauld* and *Glencallater* (Aberdeenshire) very few of the larger stags had joined up with the hinds before about 18 October, although by this date some of the smaller stags had already been running with hinds. As a result, some stags were still holding hinds well into November.

One fine sunny day on 15 November, D. S. Bowser and his stalker were out on *Suie* (Perthshire) when they came across three good stags, each of which was holding twenty-five to thirty hinds and, although behaving in typical rutting fashion, only once was a roar heard. In addition, there were two good stags without hinds, but each was trying to cut out one or two hinds from those being held by the other three stags. 'Except for the lack of noise,' commented D. S. Bowser, 'one would have thought it to be the middle of October rather than mid-November.'

1984 The pattern of the 1984 rut was back to normal, with much roaring and great activity on most forests by the end of the first week of October, when the rut reached its peak. There were, as usual, exceptions, for *Gordonbush* and *Loch Choire* (Sutherland), *Hunthill* (Angus), *Dunbeath* (Caithness) and some Perthshire forests all reported late ruts.

During the season, it was noticed that on those forests which were situated adjacent to (or had part of the ground under) afforestation, such as at *Fasnakyle* (Inverness-shire) and *Kildermorie* (Ross-shire), there was a noticeable difference of about a week to ten days in the pattern of the rut between the woodland and true hill stags. Roaring among the former generally started about 19 September, but it was not until the end of the month that much activity was to be seen or heard among the high-ground deer.

1985 The rut was about normal and the majority of forests reported seeing activity by the last week of September. On *Braemore* (Caithness) the first stag with hinds was seen on 6 September, while on neighbouring *Langwell*, a stag with hinds was shot on 18 September – the same date as the first stag with hinds was being shot on *Glenartney* – Perthshire. In many areas stags lost condition rapidly, and in consequence a number of forests finished stalking about 13 October, and so missed out on the best stalking weather of the season.

1986 The rut followed a more or less normal pattern, with roaring on many forests being evident from about mid-September onwards, but no real activity until early October.

1987 The rut was similar to the previous year, and when it did occur it was of brief duration. By

20 October most of the more mature stags had finished and left the hinds.

1988 The rut throughout Scotland was a particularly passive affair, and although a few forests reported the odd stag roaring during the early part of September – indeed, the first roar was heard on *Achentoul* (Sutherland) on 4 September – it was not until the latter part of the month, or beginning of October, that it really got under way. Even then there was little real activity, and on *Fairburn* (Ross-shire) it was described by Roderick Stirling as 'the non-event of the year', with parties of fifteen stags or more still together without hinds even on 15 October.

It was suggested that the poor condition of the hinds in some areas may have been responsible for the late rut.

1989 As in the previous season, the rut throughout Scotland was late and a rather passive affair, and apart from an odd roar in mid-September, there was little activity before the first week of October.

1990 Compared to previous seasons, the rut over much of Scotland was early, and well before mid-September the odd roar had been heard on a number of widely separated forests, which included *Invercauld* and *Mar* (Aberdeenshire); *Dunbeath* (Caithness); Ardgour (Argyllshire); *Auchlyne* (Perthshire); *Knoydart, Camusrory* and *Achnacarry, South* (Inverness-shire); *Corriemulzie* (Ross-shire); and *Ben Armine* (Sutherland), to mention but a few. On *Glenmuick* (Aberdeenshire) the first roar had been heard on 30 August.

1991 Throughout Scotland the rut followed no fixed pattern and, while the majority of forests in the east – including those in Aberdeenshire, Angus and Banffshire – reported a late start (around 6 or 7 October), on some of the western forests of Argyllshire, Inverness-shire and Ross-shire the rut was much earlier. On *Knoydart* (Inverness-shire) the first roar was heard on 28 August and within a week the first stag was seen with hinds. *Kingie* and *Glenfinnan* (Inverness-shire) had also heard a stag roaring before the end of August, but on *Affaric* (Inverness-shire) the rut was about a fortnight later than normal. In Sutherland, the rut got under way about ·25 September, with a lot of fighting being witnessed on *Ben Loyal*.

1992 Although many forests reported the odd roar before mid-September, it wasn't until the following month that rutting really got under way. Generally speaking, the stags were slow to break out – influenced, no doubt, by a mild spell of weather during the early part of October. On *Ardtalla* (Isle of Islay) the first roar was heard on 2 September, and during the following week a well-run stag was shot. On the mainland, however, the vast majority of all stags shot before mid-October were in excellent condition.

1993 Compared to recent years, the rut over much of Scotland was early, and during the first week of September the first roars had been heard on a number of forests, ranging from *Langwell* (Caithness) in the north-east to *Killiechonate* (Inverness-shire) and some of the west-coast island forests. On *Glenmazeran* (Inverness-shire) the rut was early, but in the case of one individual stag it proved to be a prolonged one, for it was seen with hinds on 20 September and was still holding its harem some nine weeks later (19 November)! On *Achentoul* (Sutherland) there were still odd stags with hinds at the end of November. On *Glenfeshie* (Inverness-shire), although the rut was appreciably earlier than in 1992, beginning during the last week of September, there was still, during the early part of October, a herd of about 300 stags not broken out. *Gaick* (Inverness-shire) had a very late rut, with little activity before the end of first week in October.

1994 Although on many forests over much of Scotland the first roar had been heard by mid-September, little serious rutting activity was apparent until about 10 October. In Caithness, although the odd stag was heard roaring by 13 September, the rut was late, with no real break out until about 10 October. In Perthshire, on the various forests of the large *Atholl* estate, there was no real break-out until about 15 October. Further south on *Glenartney*, however, the rut had been well under way some ten days earlier.

The rut on the forests in the western half of Sutherland was earlier than elsewhere in the county, and on *Kylestrome (Reay)*, where stalking terminated on 13 October, many of the larger stags were well run.

In Inverness-shire, there was considerable variation throughout the county, with those forests in the western part of the county experiencing a slightly earlier rut than in recent years. On *Ardverikie* the first roar was heard on 19 September, with the rut well under way before the end of the month.

In Aberdeenshire the rut was about two to three weeks later than usual, and on some forests continued well into November.

1995 Once again it proved to be another late rut, and over much of Scotland there was little activity before about 10 October.

In Argyllshire, following a fall of snow on 27 September, there were signs that the rut was about to commence, but with the return of milder weather, all activity quickly evaporated. On the Isle of Islay, however, the rut was in full swing by mid September, with an odd roar having been heard as early as 7 September.

On Arran some stags were also head roaring by 18 September, but it was not until mid October before the rut got under way. On *Glenartney* (Perthshire), although a stag had been heard to roar on 5 September, it was wishful thinking, for there was little activity before the following month. On *Glenshee* (Perthshire) the first stag holding hinds was shot on 2 October.

In Inverness-shire, although throughout much of the county a late rut was reported, on *Kinveachy* it proved to be one of the earliest for many years, due, it was thought, that the deer now had access to some agricultural land that was formerly occupied by sheep.

On *Dunbeath* (Caithness) the rut was also early, being under way by about 26 September, but was of short duration. In neighbouring Sutherland, however, most forests reported late ruts, with no real breakout until the second week of October.

But not all stags follow a set time-table!

CHAPTER 16

Introduction of Park Deer to the Forest

Red Deer

For well over one hundred years it has been the practice to transport English park deer to Scotland, either as fresh blood for native stock or as an introduction to a new area. The first introduction of which there is record seems to have been to the Isle of Arran (Bute) in 1859 and to *Morsgail* (Isle of Lewis) in *c.*1850, with 6 stags and 14 hinds from *Knowsley* Park (Lancashire) being shipped to the former and an unrecorded number, from an unknown park, to the latter.

From records available it would appear that, since about 1900, there have been over one hundred separate introductions of park deer to Scottish forests, involving, perhaps, some 500 deer, the majority of which have been obtained from *Warnham Court* Park, Sussex, and from this park alone, between 1894 and 1962, no less than 262 deer (115 stags and 147 hinds) had been supplied to various forests. These figures do not include the more recent introductions to deer farms.

Being an inland forest of 26,400 acres (10,684 ha) the deer most influenced by the introduction of *Warnham* blood must be on *Rhum* (Inverness-shire), for between 1925 and 1928 19 stags and 21 hinds from this park were introduced.

Other island forests which, more recently, have benefited from *Warnham* blood include *Tarbert* (2 stags and 2 hinds in 1938) and *Ardfin* on Jura (2 stags and 4 hinds in 1937), whilst in 1936 2 stags and 3 hinds were introduced to *Langass* on North Uist.

On a number of occasions between 1906 and 1929 at least 6 stags and 15 hinds from *Warnham* were introduced to *Sandside* (Caithness), and during this period two of the best stags shot on the forest were both 15-pointers. Extending to 7,500 acres (3,035 ha), part of *Sandside* was originally fenced, but this barrier has long gone into disrepair, so for many years now the deer have been able to wander on to adjacent forests.

Some 25 miles (40 km) to the south of *Sandside* are situated the forests of *Langwell* and *Braemore* (Caithness) which, during the early 1930s, had introduced 9 stags from Warnham, and more recently, during the mid-1980s, it has been the practice of releasing, annually, on *Langwell* an ex-*Woburn* Park stag for the rut.

Other forests in northern Scotland which have benefited from the introduction of *Warnham* blood are *Glencanisp* and *Kinloch* (Sutherland) where, in 1938, 2 stags and 14 hinds were received by the former and 2 stags and 7 hinds by the latter, to be followed by a further stag and 2 hinds in 1948.

In addition to these *Warnham* deer, *Kinloch* had also introduced, in 1939, 2 stags and 2 hinds from *Savernake* Park (Wiltshire) and 3 stags and 2 hinds from *Caledon* Park (Co. Tyrone).

Also, in Sutherland, during 1960, 6 stags and 8 hinds were introduced to the forests of *Kylestrome* and *Lochmore*, which together formed part of the extensive *Reay* forest belonging to the Westminster Estate.

Other English parks to supply deer to Scottish forests during the present century, have included:

Park	Forest
Arundel (Sussex)	*Letterewe* (Ross) *c*.1910
Eastwell (Kent)	*Letterewe* (Ross) *c*.1910
Grimsthorpe (Lincolnshire)	*Glenartney* (Perth) *c*.1923
Knowsley (Lancashire)	*Arnisdale c.* 1929, *Braulen c*.1911 *Struy* 1912 (Inverness) *Strathconon* (Ross) 1902
Stoke Park (Buckinghamshire)	*Cairnsmore* (Kirkcudbright) 1910
Studley Royal (Yorkshire)	*Feighn* (Ross) *c*.1909
Windsor Park (Buckinghamshire)	*Balmoral* (Aberdeen) 1938 *Brodick* (Arran) pre-1939

There have been innumerable occasions when red deer calves have been caught up and interchanged with other forest calves. Some of these calves may, undoubtedly, have had park blood in them.

On at least three occasions red deer have been obtained from the continent – Caucasian red deer to *Ardnamurchan* (Argyllshire) during the last century, Carpathian red deer to *Attadale* (Ross-shire) in about 1885, and Hungarian deer to *Letterewe* (Ross-shire) in 1910.

An exceptionally heavy stag weighing 25 st 4 lb (160.5 kg) was shot during 1953 on *Glenfiddich* (Banffshire) by C. Ormiston. In the previous year a much larger 13-pointer was killed by poachers on nearby *Innes* estate, but unfortunately its exact weight was not recorded. Sawn off at the predicles, the antlers, with a length of 41 in (104 cm) and beam of 7 in (17.8 cm), weighed 18 lb (8.1 kg). An even heavier stag was shot in 1955 by Robert A. Campbell on Cabrach, *Glenfiddich* (Banffshire). It weighed 26 st 6 lb (167.8 kg) gralloched (including heart and liver), or 23 st 12 lb (151.5 kg) without heart, liver, lungs and kidneys – a remarkable weight for any wild highland stag. Furthermore, during that period several other oustanding stags were either seen or shot in the area.

There seems little doubt that these great beasts were strays from *Pitgavenny*, near Elgin (Morayshire), where, in 1940 and again in 1943, Captain A. Brander-Dunbar had turned out twelve deer which he had obtained from *Warnham Park*. *Pitgavenny* is about 20 miles (32 km) from Cabrach – no great distance for a wandering stag.

In neither instance was there any doubt that, during the previous ten years or so, these deer had led anything but a feral existence, nor had they received any form of artificial feeding on *Glenfiddich*. On the whole, the stags on *Glenfiddich* weigh light, for during the inter-War years the average had only been about 13 stone (82 kg) without heart and liver.

In many respects it is perhaps unfortunate that there is not some law which would make it illegal to release any deer without some mark of identification such as an ear tag, but this would doubtless take some gilt off the gingerbread when the *Rifle* discovers that his trophy was, in fact, a park-fed animal and not a true hill stag. I am sure this is the reason why, in the past, many deer forest owners seem to have been reluctant to publish details of park deer introductions to their forest.

The 20-pointer shot by Lord Burton on Coire-nan-Gall, *Glenkingie* (Inverness-shire) in 1893 was a case in point. Between 1874 and 1905 *Glenkingie* was rented by Lord Burton from *Lochiel* and added to his *Glenquoich* forest. The stag had been seen on *Lochiel* ground during the three previous seasons, although none of the *Glenquoich* stalkers had apparently set eyes upon it before it was shot by Lord Burton, who always maintained that it was a genuine wild stag. The Earl of Ilchester, however, thought otherwise, stating that he himself had sent some *Stoke* Park stags to *Glenquoich* (which marched with *Glenkingie*), and this was undoubtedly one of them.

As a result of these numerous introductions to forests throughout Scotland, there is little doubt that a 'record head' or heavy weight claimed for some particular forest has signified the demise of one of these 'evacuees', either on its home ground or as a stray from some adjoining or even more distant property, for stags are great travellers. The large stags killed in the *Glenfiddich* area and the *Glenquoich* 20-pointer are but good examples.

Whatever the reason may be to introduce park blood to a Scottish deer forest, selection of the 'stud' animal is important, and multi-pointed stags should be avoided, for although they may look impressive in a deer park or on a study wall, they are out of place on a Scottish hillside.

Wapiti

On a number of occasions prior to the First World War, North American wapiti (*Cervus canadensis*) were introduced to a number of forests, which included *Glenmuick* (Aberdeen) *c.*1904; the Inverness-shire forests of *Killiechonate* (1912), *Mamore* (*c.*1904) and *Meoble* (*c.*1910); and

Cairnsmore and *Cumloden* (Kirkcudbrightshire) early in the century. But nowhere did the introductions achieve the successes that were hoped for. The largest introduction, consisting of about thirty evenly sexed animals, which had been purchased from Sir Arthur Grant of Monymusk (Aberdeenshire), was made to *Mamore*, but the wapiti proved unsuitable for forest life and didn't remain long.

Prior to the War some wapiti were kept in an enclosure of about 200 acres (81 ha) at *Meoble*, to which native red deer hinds, caught up on the forest, were introduced for the rut and subsequently released on the hill. I was informed (*in lit.*) by J. A. P. Charrington, who was proprietor of the forest during the late 1950s, that 'there is still present a distinct type of head showing traces of wapiti blood'.

At *Killiechonate*, some fifty years after their arrival on the forest, I was informed by Major Pilkington (*in lit*) that 'traces are still to be seen in the backward thrust of the tops' on some of the stags in the late 1950s.

Although the wapiti at both *Cairnsmore* and *Cumloden* in New Galloway were retained in deer parks, it is believed that some of the cross-bred wapiti/red may have escaped, and joined up with the wild red deer in the area. In recent years some of the best Scottish trophies have come out of the south-west of Scotland which enjoys a much milder climate than elsewhere, quite apart from providing access to vast areas of woodland. These Galloway heads are certainly the equal of some of the best heads shot in Scotland during the past century (*see* pages 176–178).

Ten-pointer found dead on *Alladale* forest (Ross-shire) in 1994, with its antlers trapped in the branches of a birch tree. *(H. Munro)*

Old tin bucket caught on hind's head, *Badanloch*, (Sutherland).

Metal caps of shotgun cartridges found in stomach of stag shot on grouse moor.

Stag shot on *Glencarron* (Ross-shire) in 1975, suffering from bloat.

Prolapse on stag shot on *West Benula*, (Ross-shire).

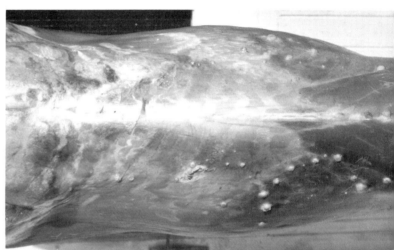

Scars left on carcase by warble fly.

Deer tick – *Ixodes ricinus*.
(*G. B. Thompson*)

Twisted nasal bones or maxillae on one-antlered stag.

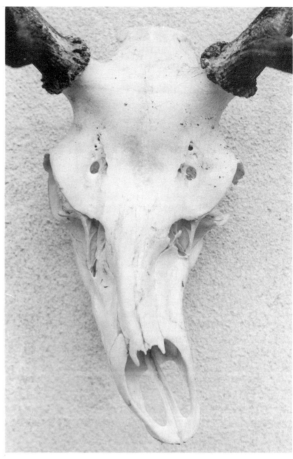

Twisted maxillae of stag shot on *Braeroy* (Inverness-shire) by Alastair D. R. Simpson in 1995.

Overgrown hooves of Sika stag.

Undershot jaw, or *Brachygnathia*.

Winter casualty. *(Lea MacNally)*

Hind, with crossbow bolt in head.

Fox caught in trap placed beside dead hind carcase.

At times the hydro-electric pipe-line on *Lochrosque* (Ross-shire) proved to be quite an obstacle when retrieving a stag carcase.

Carcase tagging — an official metal tag should be stapled to the ear, limb and/or body of every carcase.

Hummel and switch shot by author on *West Benula* (Ross-shire) in 1976.

Head of hummel.

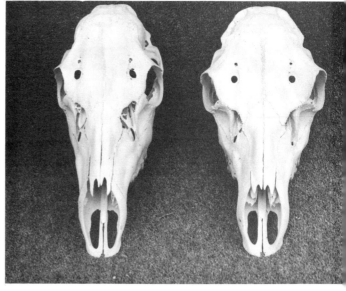

Comparison of hummel *(right)* and hind *(left)* skulls.

Hummel. *(Lea MacNally)*

Hind on *Lochluichart* forest (Ross-shire) — Its slimmer facial outline makes it distinguishable from a hummel.

Since 1964 a number of white calves have been born on *Kingie* forest (Inverness-shire).

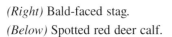

(Right) Bald-faced stag.
(Below) Spotted red deer calf.

CHAPTER 17
Red Deer in Woodland

In the 1930s most of the stalking in Scotland was done by forest owners and their friends, and licensed stalking, by the day or week, was practically unheard of. There was, therefore, better control over what was being shot; and if a promising young 'royal' was spared one year, in all probability it would return to the ground the following autumn, without having had to run the gauntlet of licensed short-term paying guests all anxious to return home – often across the Atlantic – with a trophy 'rack'.

The deer, also, had a better chance of surviving a harsh winter, for it is only within the last fifty years that much of their favoured wintering ground has been submerged under the man-made lochs of the Hydro-electric Board or cut off by ill-advised strip-planting by the Forestry Commission. Fences, however, can never be permanent, and it is seldom long before a heavy snowfall, lack of maintenance or old age will permit infiltration by hill deer.

For the woodland stalker the vast amount of afforestation which has taken place in Scotland has provided a type of stalking that is 'continental' in its methods – still-hunting at dawn and dusk, with little or no crawling – shooting from a high seat and calling the stag or buck during the rut. The hill stalker would probably be more successful if he, too, left the lodge before daybreak so as to be at the first spy point by daylight but, with a quarry that is generally visible all day, this is unnecessary.

Deer that have access to woodland not only weigh heavier but often produce better antlers and, in areas where they are not being constantly harassed by the forester, some stags will take up permanent residence in the forest, venturing out on to the hill in the autumn only to join up with the hinds for the rut. In forests, therefore, adjacent to or not far distant from forestry blocks, there is always the unexpected thrill of finding one of these woodland monsters rounding up a party of hinds that had, perhaps, the previous evening been without a stag. There is no doubt that an increasing number of stags, weighing in excess of 18 stone (114 kg) are being shot on the open hill, the stags having temporarily vacated their woodland retreat for the rut.

Furthermore, as more and more hinds take up permanent residence in woodland, so may the calf crop per 100 hinds increase from about 40 to 45 on the open hill to about 70 in the forest. Allowing for normal mortality among calves, this means that the annual cull of about 15 to 18 per cent now possible on the hill will have to be increased to about 23 to 26 per cent in woodland.

Woodland stalking in this country is still in its infancy and the professional Scottish stalker, used to conducting a stalk after a deer always visible on the hill, has a lot to learn in order to match up to the skill of the continental *jäger* who relies on patience and field craft to outwit his quarry which is seldom seen before the moment of shooting.

In England, where, apart from *Martindale* in Cumbria, red deer are largely woodland animals, the open season for shooting stags extends throughout the winter, thus enabling stags to be shot when foliage is at its minimum and they are more easily found.

Now that large areas of Scotland are providing comparable habitat to that enjoyed by red deer in England, it seems logical that the Scottish woodland stag should be treated similarly. I suggest, therefore, that Scotland's red deer be divided into two types – one mountain and the other woodland – and while the close-season for the former should remain as at present, for the woodland type the close-season for both sexes should be extended until the end of February which, although two months earlier than for stags in England, corresponds to that for female deer in England.

The immediate reaction to such a suggestion will undoubtedly be that to have different close-seasons for the same species will cause confusion. But would it? Already more than one species of deer are resident in the woods that straggle the English/Scottish border, and different close seasons, therefore, already operate for the same species within a matter of yards, depending on which side of the border the deer and/or stalker is standing when the shot is taken. Why should not woodland red deer, therefore, be shot *only* on a 'tagged' licence? (*See* page 148.) Each woodland estate in Scotland wishing to shoot stags after 20 October would have to apply for the necessary number of tags, which would have to be affixed to any carcase shot between 21 October and 28/29 February before being sold. These tags would not be transferable and, once removed from a carcase, would not be re-usable. Allowing ten days for dealers to collect carcases legally shot on the open forest up to 20 October, any stag carcase received after 1 November would have to have an official tag. They would, in fact, become legal out-of-season stags.

The issue of tags to those wishing to shoot woodland stags after 20 October would not in any way involve the thousands of crofters which, the Red Deer Commission, has always alleged, would make any tagging scheme in Scotland unworkable. Furthermore, if sika stags and hybrids were included in the tagging system, this would satisfy those forest owners who say they cannot cull sufficient sika stags before the close-season starts on 21 October.

Woodland areas would, in effect, become 'control areas' and under Section 8(i) of the Deer (Scotland) Act 1959 the Red Deer Commission would have to describe such areas 'by reference to a map' and specify the approximate extent of that area' – the minimum extent of which, in my opinion, should be not less than 1,000 acres (405 ha), preferably surrounded by some sort of fence, not necessarily deer-proof.

CHAPTER 18

Sika and Other Deer Species

Sika Deer (*Cervus nippon*)

For over a century there have been sika deer in Scotland, the first being introduced to *Tulliallon* (Fifeshire) in about 1870.

Since then there have been a number of further introductions, and at the present time there are sizeable feral populations in the counties of Argyllshire, Caithness, Inverness-shire, Ross-shire and Sutherland. Outside red deer country, some Japanese sika deer were introduced to *Dawyck* park, Stobo in Peebles-shire and, due to escapes over the years, there is now a sizeable feral population in the area.

Argyllshire

About 1893, 11 Japanese sika deer *C.n. nippon* (2 stags and 9 hinds) were caught up in *Fawley*

Court park near Henley (Buckinghamshire) and released into an enclosure at *Carradale* Point on the Mull of Kintyre (Argyllshire). However, as the enclosure was only fenced in on the land side, it wasn't long before the deer, by swimming round the end of the fence, were able to reach the mainland, and since that date a thriving population of sika deer has been established along the Mull, and latterly have spread north of the Crinan canal on to *Carse* in Knapdale, where some hybridisation with wild red deer in the area has occurred. In 1964 an alleged sika/red hybrid was shot on *Carse* weighing 15 stone (95 kg) 'clean'. This weight would be exceptional for a pure Japanese sika stag, which normally weighs about 8 to 10 stone (55 kg). An even heavier hybrid stag was shot in 1974, with an *estimated* weight of about 18 stone (113 kg). In that year fifteen stags and five hinds had to be shot as it was considered that the sika population had become too high.

Also, in that year, sika deer were reported from one or two new areas. On *Ederline* (Argyllshire) a stag – the first sika ever seen on this forest – was shot. It had probably wandered up to *Ederline* from *Carse* which is about 25 miles (40 km) away to the south.

Caithness

During the 1920s the Duke of Portland introduced some Japanese sika deer from his park at *Welbeck* (Nottinghamshire) and released them along the Berriedale river which runs through his forest of *Langwell*. They soon acclimatised themselves and a thriving feral population still remains in the area.

Inverness-shire

The first sika deer to reach Inverness-shire were those brought by William D. Mackenzie from *Fawley Court* (Buckinghamshire) and released on *Glenmazeran* (Inverness-shire) early this century. By about 1949 it was thought that sika deer at *Glenmazeran* had become extinct in the area, but within ten years they had started to reappear on the forest.

In about 1926 a sika stag was seen at *Alvie* (Inverness-shire), whilst another, about the same time, was seen in the Braemar district (Aberdeenshire). Both these stags had probably come from *Glenmazeran* – distances of about 12 miles (19 km) and 28 miles (45 km) respectively.

During 1987 two sika stags were shot on *Kinveachy*, where only one had ever been previously killed. The sika deer in this area had probably originated from *Glenmazeran*, which is about 10 miles (16 km) distant.

Early in the present century Colonel E. G. Frazer Tytler released 8 sika deer, which he had obtained from *Rosehall* (Sutherland), on to his *Aldourie* Castle estate at the head of Loch Ness, and it was from these two introductions of sika to *Aldourie* and *Glenmazeran* that the species has now firmly established itself in the woods and glens along the eastern shore of Loch Ness as far south as *Aberchalder* and probably beyond. In this range

they are particularly numerous on *Glendoe*, from where they frequently wander on to *Culachy*.

Further inland from the Loch, a few are to be seen on *Corriegarth* and *Brin* (Flichity) estates, and on all areas offering suitable terrain.

In 1977 a sika stag was shot on *Glencannich* (Inverness-shire). It would appear that this particular stag – the first sika ever seen on the forest – first made its appearance in 1971, and during the next six years was seen on a number of occasions. The main concentration of sika deer in this area are, as previously mentioned, in the woods along the eastern shore of Loch Ness, but to have reached *Glencannich* on the western side would have involved a swim of perhaps a mile (1.6 km) across the loch. Previously the odd sika had been seen at *Balmacaan* (Inverness-shire) which is only about 5 miles (8 km) distant to the east, so it could have come from there. Nevertheless, the original deer to reach *Balmacaan* would have been involved in a swim across Loch Ness.

In 1993 a sika stag was seen on *Erchless* (Inverness-shire), which lies due west of Inverness, some 10 miles (16 km) north of *Balmacaan*. The most likely origin of sika deer to this area, however, would be from the *Aldourie* estate, which is situated some 12 miles (19 km) away to the east near the head of Loch Ness.

In 1993 an 8-point sika stag, weighing 11 st 5 lb (71.6 kg) was reported from *Glendessary*. This is a heavy weight for a *pure* Japanese sika stag which seldom exceed 100–110 lb (47 kg) clean weight. It would appear, therefore, that this stag was either a sika/red hybrid, or perhaps, a Japanese/Manchurian cross of which there are several in England. Where this stag came from is not clear, for the nearest resident population of sika is probably in the woods south-west of Loch Ness – a distance of about 26 miles (42 km) away.

Some 10 miles (16 km) or so further west, a young sika stag and hind were shot by Drew Harris, the head stalker at *Kilchoan* (Knoydart), and a presumed red/sika hybrid was later seen on the ground, but not shot.

Ross-shire

The first introduction of sika deer to Ross-shire took place in 1889 when 6 deer were received by

Sir Arthur Bignold from Viscount Powerscourt, who had an estate in Co. Wicklow, and taken to *Achanalt* (Ross-shire). At first the deer were kept in an enclosure, but in 1915, owing to feeding restrictions during the First World War, the deer were released on to the open forest. They adapted themselves well, and soon spread their range to neighbouring forests.

During the 1970 season a sika stag appeared on *Wyvis* (Ross-shire), and when first seen was in possession of about twenty red deer hinds. There were a few resident sika deer on neighbouring *Kildermorie*, but none on *Wyvis*, the original source of the sika to this area being *Achanalt* (Ross-shire), which is situated some 12 miles (19 km) west of *Wyvis*.

Nine years later an 8-point sika stag was shot on *Wyvis* by its owner, Viscount Mountgarret. When killed, it was running with about fifty red deer hinds, having previously succeeded in chasing out not only a 'royal' red deer stag, but also two 10-pointers, which, despite their considerable superiority in weight, appeared to be afraid of the sika. When shot, the sika stag weighed 8 st 6 lb (53 kg) – about 5 stone (31.5 kg) lighter than the average weight of the red deer stags on *Wyvis*.

By the early 1990s the sika deer were becoming established in the forestry plantations around *Coulin* (Ross-shire), and two were seen during the 1994 stalking season.

Sutherland

About 1947 the first sika stag arrived at *Rhidorroch* (Sutherland), having wandered up from *Rosehall* (Sutherland) – a distance of about 13 miles (21 km). Sika deer were first introduced to *Rosehall* towards the end of the last century. This stag was followed, some two years later, by a hind and calf, since when their numbers have steadily increased.

In 1984 a sika/red hybrid, which had been following some red deer hinds, was shot on *Rhidorroch*, as well as a good 8-point sika stag, the latter estimated to be about 10–11 years of age.

About five stags and ten hinds are being shot annually on *Rhidorroch*. 'I have a policy at *Rhidorroch*', wrote E. Scobie, the owner (1987), 'that if I see ten stags of *any* age, I will try and

shoot five of them during the season. In this way the population has remained more or less stable.' According to E. Scobie, sika deer 'seem prolific in producing stag calves'.

In 1974 a sika/red hybrid stag 'in excellent condition' was shot on *Ben Hee* (Sutherland) on 15 October. The nearest resident sika populations to *Ben Hee* are in the two Forestry Commission blocks of Craggan and Loch Choire on *Shin* forest, a distance of about 10 miles (16 km). Originally, the sika deer on *Shin* forest had probably wandered up from *Rosehall*, from where they are now spreading westwards along Glen Cassley, and have now reached *Kylestrome* and *Gobernuisgach*.

By 1993 the number of sika deer on *Kylestrome* (Sutherland) were rapidly increasing and causing some concern, and during that season five stags – four in a forestry block and one on the hill – were shot. A suspected sika/red hybrid stag was also seen in one of the glens, but all attempts to shoot it failed.

During the same season a sika stag was shot on *Gobernuisgach* (Sutherland), which is situated about 8 miles (13 km) to the east of *Kylestrome*.

Although the original source of sika deer to this north-west part of *Reay* forest could have come from *Achanalt* (Ross-shire), the more probable source would certainly seem to be *Rosehall*, for not only is the distance considerably shorter – about 24 miles (38 km) – but access along Glen Cassley is much easier than the more mountainous route from *Achanalt*.

Although sika deer have been at *Langwell* (Caithness) for over sixty years (*see* page 120), they seldom wander across the county boundary on to *Achentoul* (Sutherland), which is situated only some 15 miles (24 km) away to the north-west. However, during the 1993 season two sika stags were shot on this forest – the first to be seen there for about ten years.

Sika deer are not popular with either the Forestry Commission or Red Deer Commission, and during 1989 the R.D.C. were invited to control the deer for three years in the two Forestry Commission blocks of Craggan and Loch Choire, on *Shin* forest (Sutherland). 'Dung counts estimated population of approximately 150 deer in each block and the cull to maintain the Loch Choire population at a constant level was set at 30 stags and 30 hinds.' The deer on Craggan, however, 'were to be culled as hard as possible' (R.D.C. Annual Report 1991).

Both blocks, separated from each other by about 9½ miles (16 km) of open hill, are well fenced, Craggan consisting of 1,287 acres (521 ha) of afforested ground – principally Lodgepole pine and 282 acres (114 ha) of open hill, and Loch Choire comprising 1,119 acres (453 ha) of mixed Lodgepole pine and larch.

Apart from a non-observation of legal close seasons for sika deer in Scotland during the first year, conventional culling methods were used, which included daylight stalking, night shooting from a vehicle using a hand-held spotlight and, on two occasions, deer drives. Stag culling started in Craggan on 10 September 1990 and continued until 31 January 1991. However, once the hind season had started on 21 October 1990, the emphasis was always on killing hinds. In Loch Choire, stags and hinds were culled between 5 November 1990 and 21 February 1991.

The total sika culls in these two blocks, in relation to the target cull set, were as follows:

| | Target Set | | | Actual Cull | | | |
	Stags	Hinds	Total	Stags	Hinds	Calves	Total
Craggan	30	30	60	40	15	6	61
Loch Choire	30	30	60	26	13	10	59

If it is assumed that the calf cull was equally divided between the sexes, the final cull would appear to have been as follows – the figure in brackets denoting by how much the target had been achieved or not:

	Stags	Hinds	Total
Craggan	43 (+13)	18 (−12)	61 (+1)
Loch Choire	31 (+1)	28 (−2)	59 (−1)

During the next two years the majority of culling was achieved by daylight stalking, and night shooting using a vehicle-mounted spotlight. Other culling strategies tried included 'trials with baits and the use of dogs'.

The dogs were used to move the deer to posted *rifles*, but as only four deer were shot during five drives, the method was not considered successful. So far as 'baiting' was concerned, 'in an attempt to entice deer into areas where they might be shot, treacle feed-blocks and salt-licks were laid out', but the deer were not interested in such supplementary feed, and only one deer was shot by this method.

During 1991–92 (Year 2 of the three-year cull project) both 'stags and hinds were shot from 10 September, to take advantage of the rut when hinds were more often seen. 16 stags, 15 hinds and 8 calves were shot between 10 September and 20 October 1991 . . . Night shooting began on 1 October and the 'walk-up' light method was used intensively.'

In Year 3 (1992–93), due to the fact that deer numbers and damage levels had been reduced on Craggan, it was decided to shoot only in the Loch Choire block, where damage levels remained high. In that year, during a sixteen-week period, a total of 70 deer, consisting of 27 stags, 25 hinds and 18 calves, were shot, the most successful method being the use of a vehicle-mounted spotlight. To improve this method, several roadside clearings had been created, and on these areas alone, 19 deer were shot (27 per cent).

At the end of the three-year cull project, the total number of sika deer shot by the R.D.C. in *Shin* forest amounted to 299 (135 stags, 108 hinds, 56 calves).

To conclude their 1992 annual Report, the R.D.C. stated,

Sika can breed very rapidly and a high culling effort is required to control numbers. To maximise the hind cull it is essential that culling starts at the beginning of the rut (early September) when hinds are most often seen. Culling should be carried out both day and night and a variety of methods should be used – e.g. daylight stalking, walk-up lights and vehicle-mounted spotlight . . . Nationally, sika control may well prove impossible given the wide extent of suitable habitat and the inability to control numbers within the original introduction sites. Within legal seasons, sika should be shot on sight. This may at least slow down population spread although it is unlikely to prevent it.

Weight

The average weight of the culled sika deer from *Shin* forest varied from between 30 lb (13.7 kg) and (28 lb) (12.8 kg) for male and female calves respectively, to 88 lb (40 kg) and 53 lb (24 kg) for stags and hinds of five years of age and over. No details are given as to how the deer were weighed, but probably excluded head and feet.

The average 'pluck' weight of an adult sika stag will be as follows:

	lb	kg
Heart	1.5 – 2	0.7 – 0.9
Liver	3 – 3.5	1.4 – 1.6
Lungs	1.75 – 2	0.8 – 0.9
	6.25 – 7.5	2.9 – 3.4

Antlers

Table 4 shows some of the best Scottish heads which I have personally measured, or have had brought to my attention. All these antlers are from stags believed to be typical Japanese sika deer (*Cervus nippon nippon*). They are considerably smaller than the Manchurian (*C. n. manchuricus*) or Manchurian/Japanese cross-bred sika, which occur in some areas of England. For comparison, antlers of the best recorded sika head from north Lancashire (1954) had lengths of 21¼ in (54 cm) (left) and 22 in (56 cm) (right), and a C.I.C. score of 307.30 points. A large stag from this area may weigh up to about 150 lb (68 kg) 'clean'.

The C.I.C. medal categories for sika deer are as follows:
Japanese sika deer – *Bronze* 225.00–239.99,
Silver 240.00–254.99,
Gold 255.00 +
Manchurian, Chinese etc. – *Bronze* 300.00–349.99,
Silver 350.00–399.99,
Gold 400.00 +

Fallow Deer (*Dama dama*)

The distribution of fallow deer in Scotland has never been as widespread as in England, the majority being retained in deer parks, one of the largest being owned by Lord Ancaster at *Drummond Castle*, near Crieff (Perthshire) which was said to number about 400 deer in 1896. Many of the fallow deer at large today were formerly present in a deer park, but in the woods around *Dunkeld* (Perthshire) there has been a completely wild population of fallow deer for around two hundred years, which provides some of the most testing fallow stalking to be enjoyed anywhere in the British Isles (*see* page 124).

Argyllshire

On the mainland a few fallow deer occur in the *Inveraray* district, but their present status is unknown. In 1960 they were estimated to number under fifty head. About 20 miles (32 km) west of Inveraray, there used to be some fallow deer in the *Poltalloch* area, but none have been reported from this district for many years.

A few fallow deer may remain near *Carradale* on the Mull of Kintyre, but it seems doubtful, for by 1949 they were said to be 'not numerous' in

Table 4   Sika deer antlers

Locality	Date	No. of tines L. R.	Length (cm) L.	R.	Beam Circ. (cm) L.	R.	Inside Span (cm)	Tip to tip (cm)	C.I.C. Score	Shot by
Langwell (Caithness)	1982	4 + 4 = 8	53.8	57.8	8.3	8.0	37.8	51.5	252.8	G. K. Whitehead[3]
Tulliallan (Fifeshire)	1994	5 + 6 = 11	51.3	49.5	9.5	9.5	38.0	51.1	272.2[1]	?[2]
Langwell (Ross-shire)	1979	4 + 4 = 8	54.0	51.0	8.0	8.0	38.0	?	235.4	?
Langwell (Caithness)	1937	4 + 4 = 8	42.0	42.5	7.6	7.4	30.2	33.5	197.0	?
Skipness (M. of Kintyre)	?	3 + 3 = 6	42.5	40.0	9.0	9.0	40.5	43.2	194.7	S. Gair[3]
Skipness (M. of Kintyre)	1935	4 + 5 = 9	39.9	38.2	7.4	7.4	25.0	30.3	186.8	G. K. Whitehead[3]
Skipness (M. of Kintyre)	1930	4 + 4 = 8	38.0	36.6	7.6	7.5	31.0	36.8	184.0	G. K. Whitehead[3]

[1] This head has a long back-tine in the crown area of each antler, the one on the right side terminating in a fork. These additional points in the crown area have contributed no less than 61.1 points, giving it the highest C.I.C. score yet reported for Scotland.
[2] Measured by Allan Allison.
[3] Owner's measurements.

the area, with perhaps 'less than 10 remaining'. There is, however, a thriving sika deer population all along the Mull of Kintyre (*see* page 119).

Fallow deer may still be present – or were until recently – on some of the islands off the west coast of Argyllshire, and these include *Islay, Mull* and *Scarba*.

On *Islay*, where the deer were probably introduced during the fourteenth century – or even as early as AD 900 by the monks as one historian suggests – their number in the Landy district, during the middle of the last century, was estimated to be around 500 head. A century later (1960), however, their numbers had fallen to about fifty.

The fallow were first introduced to *Mull* in 1868 by Colonel Greenhill Gardyne, when he liberated a few deer at *Glenforsa*. By 1952 the number in the area was estimated to be around fifty head but, following the heavy cull of red deer in the *Glenforsa* plantation around 1961 (*see* page 142), doubtless any fallow deer seen in the area during culling operations suffered the same fate.

On the island of *Scarba*, which lies just north of Jura, a small herd of perhaps under fifty deer are maintained. There were, formerly, a few fallow deer on the *Isle of Cara*, but the last deer was shot in 1908.

Perthshire

According to Millais (1913), fallow deer were introduced into *Dunkeld* forest by a Duke of Atholl early in the nineteenth century, though it is believed that some further new blood may have been introduced about 1880. The deer have never been enclosed, and their range in the *Dunkeld* area is probably not much different to what it was at the beginning of the century. Two of their favourite areas are in Craigie Barns and Drumbouie woods, which lie between Cardney and Dunkeld. The former is very rough terrain – ideal for the deer, concealed by heather which in many places grows up to waist high, but a heart-breaking place to stalk in, with its steep crags and gulleys. It is an area where quiet approach is well-nigh an impossibility, and although the deer will frequently lie very tight, only taking flight when almost stepped on, the uneven ground and thick cover provide the stalker with little opportunity for even a snap shot.

The deer are mainly of the common-coloured variety, being light brown and spotted in summer, but darkish-brown to grey in winter, with barely a trace of spots. There are also a few light-menil-coloured deer.

In 1959 the number of fallow at *Dunkeld* was estimated to be about 200 – about half of the pre-War population.

Fallow deer were also introduced to the woods around *Atholl* castle towards the end of the eighteenth century, but they did not survive there for long.

In 1985 a buck was shot on *Lude*. It was only the second deer of this species to have been seen on the ground, and was believed to have come from *Dunkeld* – a distance of about 10 miles (16 km) away.

During the 1994 red deer stalking season a fallow buck was shot in woodland on *Boreland* – the first ever to have been seen on the estate. It had probably wandered up from either *Dunkeld* or the Loch Lomond area – a distance of about 25 miles (40 km) or 18 miles (29 km) respectively (*see* page 125).

Elsewhere in Perthshire a few fallow deer have been reported in the woods around *Tombuie* (Bolfracks), which lie some 12 miles (19 km) to the west of *Dunkeld*.

Ross-shire

Formerly there was a well-scattered population of fallow deer in the woods along Strath Bran which extended westwards from about Garve in the east to just beyond Achnasheen in the west. Included in this 20-mile (32 km) range are the forests of *Ledgowan*, *Lochrosque*, *Strathbran*, *Achanalt*, *Kinlochluichart*, *Corriemoillie*, *Strathgarve*, *Inchbae*, *Strathrannoch* and *Scatwell*, but as the woods have gradually been felled so have the deer disappeared. Not all these forests, however, had a resident population of fallow deer, but wandering deer could be expected anywhere. Throughout much of this range, there were also sika deer (*see* page 120), and identification between these two similar-sized species was, understandably, confused at times.

In about 1960 the number of fallow deer in the woods around *Lochrosque* was estimated to be in the region of 100, and although at about that period there were, perhaps, about a dozen fallow still to be seen on occasions near *Strathgarve*, as a resident population this deer had completely disappeared from *Strathrannoch*.

Elsewhere in Scotland, during the mid-1950s there were some fallow deer on the Forestry Commission ground of Creag nan Eun, which is situated between *Glenmoriston* and *Balmacaan* (Inverness-shire), but there have been no recent reports from that area. There have, however, been reports of the odd sika deer (*see* page 120), and there is always the possibility of confusion between the two species.

In 1960 fallow deer were said to be quite numerous in the woods alongside Loch Lomond, having swam over from *Inchmurrin* island (Dunbartonshire) where they had been introduced during the sixteenth century. There are none there today, but since early in the present century a few have made their headquarters in the *Buchanan Woods* which are situated near the south-east corner of the loch.

Prior to the War there was also a few fallow deer at *Arisaig* (Inverness-shire), which, it is believed, were introduced about 1860 and survived until about 1950, when the last one died.

Since the early part of the last century there have been a few free-range fallow in Dumfries-shire, which are probably descended from deer introduced to *Raehills* near Moffat in about 1780. Although by the end of the following century this deer would appear to have become extinct in the area (Grimble 1898), by 1948 a herd, numbering about 100 deer, were reported in some of the large woods about 3 miles (5 km) from *Raehills*, with scattered animals elsewhere in the district (Whitehead 1964).

Antlers

Few Scottish fallow buck heads have been measured, but the following buck, killed in *Drummond Castle* Park (Perthshire) pre-1912, and exhibited at the *Country Life* exhibition of 1913, would appear to be about the best:

Points	Length	Beam	Inside span
10+15=25	30 in (76.2 cm)	4⅜ in (11.1 cm)	24⅜ in (61.9 cm)

As a comparison the best recorded wild buck from New Forest (Hampshire) has a length of 28⁷⁄₁₆ in (72.3 cm).

The C.I.C. medal categories for European fallow deer are:
Bronze 160.00–169.99, *Silver* 170.00–179.99, *Gold* 180.00 +.

Weight

A good wild buck should weigh about 140 lb (63 kg) 'clean' – but some park animals can be considerably larger. Millais (1906) records a *Drumlanrig* buck that weighed no less than 24 stone (152 kg) as he fell and 18 stone (114 kg) 'clean'. *Drumlanrig Castle* at Thornhill (Dumfries-shire) was the residence of the Duke of Buccleuch.

Roe Deer (*Capreolus capreolus*)

The roe deer – one of the two indigenous deer at present surviving in Scotland – has been a native there since the pre-historic period. Its range, however, has not been quite so constant, and there was a period during the eighteenth and nineteenth centuries when it was extinct in all Scottish counties south of about latitude 56°N. Today there is not a county in Scotland where the species cannot be found provided the habitat is suitable.

Although the roe is normally a woodland species, there are a few areas in Scotland – notably in Angus – where the roe spend much of their time on the hill, and in such terrain provide an opportunity to stalk in a conventional manner, the final approach, as often as not, being made at a crawl. Such roe stalking, in my opinion, far surpasses the continental method of waiting and shooting from a high seat – a method now widely practised throughout England and Scotland. One cannot, of course, expect a 'gold medal' class trophy on a 'hill buck'.

In many areas of Scotland there are a number of localities where both roe and red can be shot during the same day, and doubtless there have been occasions when a double – but not a 'right and left' – at these two species has been achieved.

Not surprisingly, the quality of trophy varies according to habitat, and all the best recorded trophies have been shot in areas that provide both woodland and agricultural crops.

For many years prior to the War, the *Pitgavenny* (Morayshire) roe head, obtained by W. S. Tegner in 1928, was considered to be one of the best heads to have come out of Scotland this century, but apart from a length of 10⅝ in (27 cm) and long, slender, forked tops, it lacked both weight and volume, and can in no way compete with the massive trophies of today.

There is no reason to doubt that some massive heads did formerly exist in Scotland but, as in England, prior to the War most roe of either sex were shot during winter shotgun drives when, of course, the antlers of the bucks would have been cast and new growth still in velvet, so it was impossible to assess their potential. It was not until 1966 that The Deer (Close Seasons) (Scotland) Order made it illegal to kill roe bucks in the winter months unless they were causing serious damage to crops or forestry etc., so it is only since about this date that these fine trophies have started to appear.

Until after the War few roe stalkers in Britain, and in particular those in Europe, appreciated the excellent quality of antlers being produced by roe in Southern England, and many land owners were only too happy to allow any keen and reliable stalker to shoot the deer for a quite nominal sum in order to reduce damage to crops, woodland or gardens to a minimum. Word, however, travels far and fast, and it was not long before an ever-increasing number of continental sportsmen started to come to England to shoot roe, for it was considerably cheaper here than in the eastern bloc countries, from where the best trophies were to be found.

On many estates, both in England and Scotland, the letting of roe stalking is now being handled by a sporting agency which, naturally, is more interested in money from lettings than in leaving deer on the ground after the tenant has departed with his trophies.

Already, in parts of southern England where commercial trophy stalking has been taking place for a number of years, the *average* age of trophy bucks being shot is now nearer three than four or five, as formerly. The trophy standard has, therefore, when assessed under the C.I.C. formula, suffered accordingly, for it is in those years beyond three that both weight and volume will continue to increase and elevate the score. Length, however, may well start to shorten slightly, as bulk increases, but it will be minimal. Moreover, quite apart from providing the stalker with a superior trophy, a five-year-old buck will have had the chance to sire more kids than if he had met his demise at the age of three. This is only good herd management. Let's hope, therefore, that those who negotiate trophy letting will bear this in mind.

The best Scottish trophies in any quantity are to be found in the counties of Aberdeenshire, Angus, Fife and Perthshire, but from time to time an outstanding trophy may also be taken in any of the other southern counties.

In 1973, for instance, a fine trophy was shot by K. Clark in Berwickshire, and was exhibited at the 1981 World Exhibition of Hunting at Plovdiv, Bulgaria, where it was assessed at 181.73 C.I.C. points.

The summers of 1992 and 1993 produced some excellent trophies from Scotland, and out of twenty-two gold medal trophies recorded by R. Prior (*Shooting Times and Country Magazine* 17–23/2/94) seven had a C.I.C. score in excess of 150, the largest of which was a buck shot by C. E. Van der Straten Waillet in East Fife (206.2 C.I.C. points) – almost 3.0 points more than the previous Scottish best trophy shot by P. Wilson in Perthshire during 1976, details of which are as follows:

Length 27.8 cm (L), 28.4 cm (R); weight 783 g; volume 340 c.c. – C.I.C. points 203.35

It is to be hoped that news of such top-quality trophies being currently available in Scotland will not result, as unfortunately has already happened in south-east England, in a spate of wealthy trophy hunters coming to skim off the best before replacement bucks have had a chance to reach *maturity*, and that Scottish roe bucks will continue to produce not only top-quality trophies, but also have a few years in which to sire good progeny.

Carcase weights vary considerably according to habitat, and whilst some bucks from Fifeshire have been recorded at 64 lb (29 kg) 'clean' weight, bucks from the west coast will seldom exceed 40–44 lb (19 kg).

C.I.C. Medal categories for European roe are: *Bronze* 105.00–114.99, *Silver* 115.00–129.99, *Gold* 130.00 +

White roe deer

During 1983 a pure-white roe deer, accompanied by a normal-coloured kid, appeared on *Dalnaspidal* (Perthshire) during grouse shooting in August, and was on the ground some two months later.

Reindeer (*Rangifer tarandus*)

Reindeer were formerly plentiful in Scotland, and probably did not become extinct until about the ninth century, although some historians have suggested they may have lingered on for a further two or three hundred years. Since then, however, several attempts have been made to reintroduce this deer but without much success.

In about 1790, fourteen reindeer were released on the *Atholl* forest (Perthshire) at various times, but the longest period any deer managed to survive was about two years. Reindeer were also introduced to *Mar* forest (Aberdeenshire) by the Earl of Fife at the beginning of the last century but, according to Scrope (1839), 'they all died, notwithstanding that all of them were turned out on the summits, which are covered with dry moss on which, it was supposed, they would be able to subsist.'

One of the largest introductions of reindeer was made by a certain Mr Bullock in about 1820 when, according to Harper (1945), he introduced, over a number of years, about 200 animals on to the *Pentland Hills* (Lothian), but they did not survive for long.

More recently, on 2 June 1949, following a proposal by Mikel Utsi, a reindeer-herd owner in the Jokkmokk area of arctic Sweden, The Reindeer Council of the United Kingdom was formed, with Sir Frederick Whyte K.C.S.I. as Chairman and Dr E. J. Lindgren as Honorary Secretary. The object of the Council was to 'encourage experimentation in reindeer breeding in suitable areas in Scotland and/or overseas, and to engage in any appropriate activity ancillary thereto'.

The immediate concern of the Council was to support a proposal for an experiment with twenty-five first class breeding and draught animals from Scandinavia, which would be transported to the British Isles and cared for by trained herders for a minimum of three years, without cost to this country (or, if they prove a nuisance, destroyed). When the herd's survival seems assured, the owners will be prepared to sell breeding animals to appropriate individuals or institutions, in accordance with the Council's advice.

After two years of waiting, the Reindeer Council in February 1951 received permission from Mr McNeill, the Secretary of State for Scotland, for the importation of twenty-five reindeer. The proposal had, apparently, been rejected earlier by Mr McNeill's predecessor, presumably on the grounds that there was some doubt as to whether the reindeer could be reared under Scottish conditions along with red deer and sheep without detriment to the latter; or that they might introduce or develop some disease on arrival. All imported deer have, of course, to undergo a period of quarantine on arrival in this country. (Whitehead 1964)

Eventually, on 12 April 1952, 8 reindeer of 'mountain type', consisting of 1 four-year-old draught ox, 2 three-year-old bulls, 2 two-year-old females and 3 one-year-old female calves arrived at Rothesay Dock (Isle of Bute) from Sweden and, after a period of quarantine in the Edinburgh zoo, finally reached *Rothiemurchus*, near Aviemore (Inverness-shire), and were released into a fenced-in enclosure of approximately 300 acres (120 ha) near Loch Morlich. This area was subsequently increased by a further 70 acres (28 ha) when the north side of Airgiod Meall 2,118 feet (645 m) – known as Silver Mount – was added, as it was thought that the deer would benefit from some higher ground. In their native home, much of their life is spent at altitudes of between 4,000 and 6,000 feet (1,219 and 1,829 m).

As already noted, all the original reindeer were of 'mountain type' so it was decided that some 'forest-type' animal should be acquired, and accordingly, on 27 October 1952, a bull and nine young females of this type were obtained and, after a four-week period of quarantine, were eventually released in the reserve on 26 November. Three months later they were joined by a female and her calf of 'mountain type', which had been transferred from London Zoological Gardens.

During the first year of the experiment five of the original eight 'mountain type' reindeer, plus a calf which had been born shortly after arrival, died, and by the spring of 1953 only three remained alive. The 'forest type' reindeer, however, fared slightly better, and by the end of May 1953 eight of the original ten were still alive.

In their native habitat a herd, if required, should be capable of tripling itself within three years, but this certainly didn't happen at *Rothiemurchus*, and by 1962, despite further introductions, the herd remained at the 1954 level.

At the present time the reindeer now have the run of about 6,000 acres (2,428 ha) on the northern slopes of the Cairngorms, which the Reindeer Company lease from Highlands and Islands Enterprise. In 1990 a further 350 acres (142 ha) of hill ground was leased from the *Glenlivet* Estate (Crown Commission), and part of the herd was temporarily moved there. Surrounded by a fence, the *Glenlivet* area, which was formerly the site of an old hill farm, is some 30 miles (48 km) north of the Cairngorms Reindeer Centre, which has its headquarters at Glenmore, Aviemore.

In June 1994 the Cairngorm Reindeer herd numbered 114, of which 38 were bulls, 61 cows and 15 oxen (castrated males). Included in that total are 29 calves of the year. The figure of 114 is the highest number yet achieved in its forty-two years existence. The majority of calves are born in May and early June, but occasionally the odd calf will be born in April, or early July, but late calves are not welcome. According to information from the Cairngorm Reindeer Centre (*in lit* 1994), the gestation period is about 218–223 days – about a fortnight shorter than for red deer (*see* page 106).

At the beginning of May 1995 the Centre received, as a gift from M. Pierre Marc, his entire herd of 38 reindeer, which had previously been kept in the Jura Mountains of eastern France. After a short period of isolation, the newcomers were then integrated in the herds at Cairngorm and *Glenlivet*, and by the autumn of 1995 the total herd belonging to the Reindeer Centre numbered 129 adults and 30 calves of the year – a total of 159.

From what has happened during the past two centuries, it would appear that the Scottish highlands are not really a suitable habitat for Scandinavian reindeer, and should any beast wander out of the Cairngorm reserve, there would seem to be no possible chance of this deer ever building up a feral population in the manner the sika deer has achieved in Scotland and elsewhere in the British Isles.

Muntjac (*Muntiacus reevesi*)

The muntjac, which was first introduced to England by the 11th Duke of Bedford in his park

at *Woburn* (Bedfordshire), now has a large and expanding feral distribution in England, their range now extending as far north as about Staffordshire and Warwickshire – still some 200 miles (320 km) south of the Scottish border.

Unless a liberation is made in Scotland, it seems improbable that this small Asiatic deer will ever establish itself north of the border until well into the next century.

Chinese Water-Deer (*Hydropotes inermis*)

Since about 1940, due to break-outs from both *Woburn* and *Whipsnade* (Bedfordshire), this small antlerless deer has gradually established a feral population within about 60 miles (96 km) of *Woburn*.

Unless a liberation is made north of the border, it seems most unlikely that this Asiatic deer will ever establish itself in Scotland.

Wild Goat (Feral) (*Capra hircus*)

Although there are no truly wild goats in Britain there are a number of feral goats in Scotland, some of which have been living a free and undomesticated existence for centuries, particularly along the western seaboard and adjacent islands.

The record length of 44⅝ in (113.3 cm) came from a billy shot on Isle of Bute c.1931, whilst the record head from a goat shot during the past half-century was from a nine-year-old shot at *Rowardennan* (Stirlingshire) in 1958 by D. Barry, with the following measurements: Length 36⅜ in (92.4 cm), horn circumference at base 7⅛ in (18.1 cm) and tip to tip span of 39 in (99.1 cm). Two years previously the same stalker had shot another large billy on *Ben Lomond* (Stirlingshire), the horn measurements of which were only about 3 in (7.6 cm) less in both length and span measurements respectively.

Any pair of horns with a length of 30 in (76 cm), and comparable span or greater, is good for Scotland.

Areas in Scotland which have produced some fine goat trophies during the past half century have included *Cairnsmore* (Kirkcudbrightshire), *Dochfour* (Inverness-shire), *Inversnaid* (Stirlingshire) and *Rhum* (Inverness-shire).

CHAPTER 19

Eagles and Other Wildlife

Golden Eagle

Among all field sportsmen and women, the deer stalker, armed with telescope and/or binoculars, if he or she is a keen naturalist as the majority undoubtedly are, has probably more time to study other wildlife that share the mountainous domain of the stag than has the fisherman or birdshooter.

Among the raptors, eagles, of course, figure most prominently in their reports and there is no doubt that this magnificent bird now has a wide range over much of northern Scotland.

General increase

In the years immediately following the Second World War the golden eagle had, in some parts of Scotland, become extremely scarce, but by the early 1960s it was already starting to show a steady increase in many areas. On *Glenshee* (Perthshire), for instance, one or two were to be seen almost daily, yet a few years previously it was rare to see even one during a whole season. Eagles were also becoming plentiful on *Arnisdale* (Inverness-shire) but, in spite of this, ptarmigan were also in greater numbers than ever before.

By 1962 eagles had started to increase in Angus, and J. Svensson, who rented *Hunthill* forest, wrote, 'Golden eagles are much more plentiful, attracted, no doubt, by the relatively large numbers of blue hares'. Eagles, however, do not nest on this forest.

On *Killilan* (Ross-shire) the increase in eagles during the 1970s also seemed to coincide with an increase in the hare population.

In that year a considerable increase in the number of eagles was reported from *Glencannich* (Inverness-shire), whilst on *Glenfernate* (Perthshire) the stalking party had one or two good opportunities for a shot spoilt by eagles diving over the deer and causing them to shift. On a number of occasions the eagle would then follow the fleeing deer and so keep them moving for a considerable distance. In this manner a number of stalks were also spoilt by eagles on *Kinlochluichart* (Ross-shire) and the Hon. Spencer-Loch told me that he himself had never experienced deer being moved so often by eagles as during the 1969 season. One day he was watching a herd of stags moving quietly along when they happened to flush a grouse. Immediately an eagle appeared on the scene and gave chase whilst the deer all ran off in panic.

On *Corrievarkie* and *Talladh-a-Bheithe* (Perthshire), however, the eagle and some of the other raptors started to disappear during the mid-1960s and, whereas in about 1960 as many as six eagles were sometimes seen on the wing together,

six years later they had suddenly become scarce, and in 1966, for the first time in many years, no peregrines nested on the forest.

In 1964 Brigadier Colvin and his keeper saw no fewer than six eagles all together in flight near the *Dalnacardoch* march, and during the spring of that year David Rose, the local Nature Conservancy keeper, reported that there were four eyries in his area, each of which had two eaglets, and all but one successfully flew.

During 1970 it was reported that five pairs nested on *Killilan* (Ross-shire), of which at least three succeeded in raising a family. Three pairs were also seen that year on *Aberchalder* (Inverness-shire), and on both *Scardroy* (Ross-shire) and *Glenshee* (Perthshire) several pairs were reported. On the last-named forest blue hares were extremely numerous, and not only did they attract the eagles but also, on several occasions, gave warning to the deer of the stalking party's approach.

On *Glenlochay* (Perthshire), although prior to 1976 there was only one eyrie on the forest, in that year there were four pairs nesting in the glen.

Training the young entry

During 1969 Duncan MacLennan, the head stalker on *Affaric* (Inverness-shire), twice watched an eagle teaching its young to take ptarmigan. The old bird, accompanied by youngsters, would attack and narrowly miss the ptarmigan before it temporarily took refuge in the grass. This was repeated and, after several practice stoops, the ptarmigan was allowed to go. It had, apparently, served its purpose but had, nevertheless, had a pretty unnerving experience.

In the same year a grouse was in similar trouble on *Borrobol* (Sutherland), for here the stalker saw one caught in flight by an eagle, who in turn passed it on to another eagle which was presumed to be a young bird. After playing about with it for a few minutes, the second bird flew off with it. No reprieve for this grouse.

Varied prey of the eagle

On 11 October 1978 Jim Munroe, the understalker on *Dougarie* (Arran), saw an eagle swoop on and kill a buzzard, the latter being subsequently picked up. Shortly afterwards the same eagle made an attack on a late calf, but without success.

In 1986 M. R. Warren reported an unusual incident on *Glenfinnan* forest (Inverness-shire), when an eagle was seen to stoop on a kestrel, thereby making the latter release its prey.

Eagles, Geese and Swans

Whilst stalking on *Braemore* (Ross-shire) on 8 October 1968 Lt-Col. P. C. Mitford witnessed a skein of geese, which were flying south at about 2,900 feet (988 metres), put to rout and complete disarray by an eagle which started to circle above them. He wrote,

> It made no attempt to attack them, but the geese just broke formation, dropped in height, and then flew due west until clear of the golden eagle. They then reassembled their formation, with, apparently, a new leader, and continued on their way.

On *Ben Armine* (Sutherland) a skein of geese was also seen to have its formation broken up by an eagle (1962).

During 1966, whilst stalking on *West Benula* (Ross-shire), the late Hon. Mrs David Bowlby told me that on one occasion she saw 'three wild swans on the wing being attacked by an eagle, which succeeded in bringing one down. After a fight on the ground, the swan succeeded in getting away.'

A somewhat similar incident was witnessed by Duncan MacLennan, on *Affaric* during the 1975 season. He described the incident as follows:

> One evening, in early October, on our way back to the lodge, we heard a gaggle of geese overhead. On looking up we saw the geese at no great height, one end of the 'V' formation being strung out much more than the other. As we watched we suddenly saw what appeared to be a black ball come hurtling down out of the clouds above. It proved to be an eagle which had singled out a goose and both birds went hurtling down towards the river at a terrific speed. Just as we thought they were bound to crash on to the ground, the eagle pulled out of the dive and swung back upwards again, whilst the goose disappeared over the river bank and was not seen again. The remainder of the skein, now much scattered, were visibly seen trying to re-organise their formation.

On *Remony* (Perthshire), in 1972, a skein of geese were seen flying southwards along the valley of the Acharn burn when, approaching the steep face at the head of the valley, they were confronted by an eagle which was circling high above them. Immediately, they broke up in confusion, some alighting and others scattering in all directions with much clamour. The eagle, however, apparently took no notice and continued to circle above the higher ground.

On *Dalness* (Argyllshire), on two successive days, a pair of eagles were seen diving on to Greylag geese that were passing south-wards over the forest, but no casualties were involved (1976).

On 8 October 1993, a single wild goose was seen by the stalking party on *Glenkinglass* (Argyllshire) to be descending in a series of wide circles, closely followed by an eagle. Unfortunately the outcome of this particular confrontation was not known, for both birds shortly afterwards disappeared from view behind the hill.

Attacking a stag

On two occasions in 1992 (11 and 14 September) the stalking party on *Ardgour* (Argyllshire) witnessed an eagle repeatedly dive at, and actually strike, a fully grown stag. Reporting this incident, Allan Cameron, the head stalker, wrote, 'While I have seen eagles attacking calves before, I have never seen an attack on a stag in this fashion.'

Attacking a hind

In 1979 on *Glenquoich East* (Inverness-shire) an eagle was observed attacking a hind. It landed on her back and tried, unsuccessfully, to drive her over a steep place. On releasing its hold, the eagle then pursued the hind for nearly a mile (1.6 km) before abandoning the chase.

In 1995 on *Kinlochlvichart* (Ross-shire) a pair of eagles were disturbed from a freshly-killed hind carcase from which the head skin had been stripped off.

Attacking calves

There have been a number of reports of eagles both attacking and killing red deer calves.

During the 1968 season Anne, Duchess of Westminster, approached to within 20 metres of an eagle that had just killed a calf. In 1965, F. M. Cameron, the head stalker on *Rhiedorrach* (Perthshire), told me that on one occasion while he was stalking a stag, a golden eagle stooped twice at a young red deer calf, and actually landed on its back. Fortunately, about this time, the stag was killed and the sound of the shot frightened the bird away.

On *Ben Damph* (Ross-shire) in 1990 the stalking party, from a distance of under 200 metres, were able to witness a pair of eagles attack and kill a red deer calf.

In 1962 R. N. Richmond-Watson describes how he saw an eagle attempt, unsuccessfully, for about fifteen minutes to separate a calf from its mother on his forest of *Arnisdale* (Inverness-shire), whilst on *Forest Lodge* (Perthshire), during the same season, an eagle was seen to attack a wounded stag. Describing this event T. P. Stewart writes,

> When the beast, which had been wounded, made off it was immediately attacked by an eagle which swooped two or three times at the head, and then hovered above it. The stag tossed its antlers at the eagle . . . and eventually the eagle appeared to realize that the stag, although wounded, was still too strong for it, and made off.

Shortly afterwards the stag was given another shot and killed.

In 1969 a young eagle was seen attacking a calf on *Talladh-a-Bheithe* (Perthshire), the hind apparently making little effort to protect it. Eventually, however, the eagle gave up and flew off, the calf returning to its mother, apparently unharmed. On *Dalness* (Argyllshire) an eagle was seen to make an attack on two hinds, each with a calf, but no casualties resulted (1976).

An abortive attack on a well-grown calf in 1978 was witnessed by G. Ruggles-Brise on his forest of *Ledgowan* (Ross-shire). He described the incident as follows:

> On Sunday, 1st October, whilst driving on the road between Achnasheen and Kinlochewe, I spotted an eagle high above *Lochrosque*. Stopping the car to have a better look at the bird through binoculars, I immediately spotted a second eagle. I then noticed a deer calf which was running down the hill towards the road and was being systematically attacked by both eagles, each stooping at it alternately. On one occasion an eagle

actually landed on its back, but the calf was able to dislodge it before disappearing into a gully about 200 metres from the road, and the eagle then broke off the attack. There was no doubt that the eagles really meant business.

During the 1988 season, from *Loch Choire* forest (Sutherland), an eagle was watched, from over the march, repeatedly swooping down and striking a calf that appeared to have a broken leg, but whether the eagle had been responsible for the injury was not known. During a brief rainstorm, which temporarily obscured visibility, the eagle apparently succeeded in making the kill, for the calf was subsequently found to be dead.

A somewhat comparable incident was witnessed on *Achentoul* (Sutherland) in 1992. During a stalk a hind and calf were disturbed, and as they were running off, the calf was repeatedly attacked by an eagle which on one occasion actually succeeded in landing on its back and plucking out a bunch of hair before disengaging.

Attacking a stalker

In 1948, whilst stalking on *Lochs* (Perthshire), Colonel Charles Younger, accompanied by Alex Walker the stalker, whilst waiting for a stag to rise was attacked by an eagle which had to be fought off with sticks.

Interference with stalking

In 1994 on *Coulin* (Ross-shire), a stalk was interfered with by an eagle swooping at the party of deer being approached.

During the 1987 season a small stag weighing 8 st 5 lb (53kg) was shot on *Glenmuick* (Aberdeen-shire) with about 7 metres of netting trailing from its antlers, which made walking in long heather somewhat difficult. While closing in for the shot, an eagle landed on the ground some 20 metres behind the stag, and commenced to follow it for a further 30 metres or so before, on spotting the stalking party, it flew off. It was presumed that the eagle had considered the stag to be wounded, and was contemplating a handy meal. Either way, in the end it doubtless returned to consume the gralloch.

On *Ledgowan* (Ross-shire) a pair of eagles were seen, one day in 1988, to be mobbing a herd of about twenty to thirty deer. Whilst the birds probably had no serious intentions towards life or limb, they nevertheless caused considerable panic among the deer.

In 1990 E. Luxmore, whilst waiting for a stag to rise so as to provide a better target for a shot, saw a golden eagle land on a rock just behind the stag's head, and if he had moved a few yards to one side, he says he 'could have killed both stag and eagle with one shot'.

Much as the increase in eagles is welcomed by the majority of stalkers, there are some, like Judge R. A. R. Stroyan – the owner of *Boreland* forest (Perthshire) – who now consider there are far too many of them!

This opinion is also shared by a deer forest owner in Aberdeenshire who, in 1992, considered that there were 'far too many raptors about – eagles, buzzards, hen harriers, peregrines, merlins, kestrels, sparrowhawks and one goshawk were all seen during one day stalking – God help the grouse!'

Other incidents

An unusual event occurred on *Affaric* forest (Inverness-shire) in 1958. A party had been stalking high up in Coullavie Corrie, and shot a stag high on the east edge. In order to facilitate the long drag down, Duncan MacLennan, the head stalker, decided to leave the head behind which he did after cutting off the antlers on the frontal bone as they were to be retained.

Some two or three days later Duncan MacLennan was once again out with a stalking party in Coullavie Corrie, but on this occasion on the west face almost opposite to where the stag had previously been shot. All at once an eagle appeared carrying in its talons a bulky object which at first appeared to be a lamb. As it soared over their heads, Duncan gave a loud shout which had the effect of making the eagle release its grip on the burden, which landed close to the stalking party. It turned out to be the severed head of the stag shot a few days previously.

On one occasion in 1969, on *Talladh-a-Bheithe* forest (Perthshire), a wounded stag was lost, the mist having come down before it could be located. The beast, however, was found on the following morning, having apparently only just died, as it was still warm. It was immediately bled,

but for some reason not gralloched, before the party left in order to collect the boat in which to convey the carcase across the loch *en route* to the larder. When they returned some three hours later, they found that an eagle was already having a meal off a haunch.

In 1961 on *Monar* (Ross-shire), where eagles are described as numerous, one bird was found sitting on the gralloched corpse of a stag which had only been shot an hour before.

Sea Eagle

In 1975 the sea eagle, also referred to as the white-tailed eagle, was re-introduced to the Isle of *Rhum* and, by 1979, sightings of this fine raptor were being reported from both *Mull* and *Eishken* (Isle of Lewis).

By 1984 the late Viscount Masserene and Ferrard reported that the sea eagle was now 'firmly established' on his forest of *Ben More* (Mull) and, by coincidence, the blue hare population on the island had steadily declined in numbers. Although the main prey of this eagle is fish, water fowl and scavenging after gulls, according to David A. Bannerman, in Volume V of *The Birds of the British Isles* (1956), 'these eagles destroyed many of the hares that swarmed about the island' of Masvaër, off Tromsö, in Norway.

The sea eagle – once said to have been more numerous in parts of Scotland than the golden eagle – probably ceased to breed on the mainland about 1889, but seems to have continued nesting on the island of Skye until about 1916.

During the 1994 season on *Torosay*, Isle of Mull, David Bennett, the stalker, reported seeing a sea eagle lock talons with a golden eagle during a long encounter, carried out in full view of the stalking party.

Raven

On *Glenfeshie* forest (Inverness-shire) the late Lord Dulverton and his head stalker, Alec Davidson, during the 1968 season, witnessed a strange concourse of ravens around an eagle. Describing the event, Lord Dulverton wrote,

> About two dozen ravens were grouped together on the ground, and in the middle of the group was a golden eagle. We watched them for some

minutes, and formed the impression that perhaps the eagle was sick, and the ravens were only biding their time to attack it.

However, this was probably not the case, for all the birds, including the eagle, soon took flight and disappeared from view, so Lord Dulverton concluded that perhaps

the birds had all been feasting together on a gralloch or some other carrion, for they were only about 300 metres from where a stag had been killed a few days previously.

On *Ledgowan* (Ross-shire), in 1981, a stag was shot and, after being gralloched, was left for collection later in the day. When they returned a pack of ravens flew off, the birds having attacked the carcase, leaving a number of beak holes on the body. The gralloch, however, lying nearby had been ignored completely.

It is, perhaps, interesting to note that in old hunting parlance, the collective name for the raven was 'an unkyndenes of rauenes' (*Boke of St Albans* 1486). On *Ledgowan*, also in 1981, a stag was shot, and whilst the stalking party were waiting for the hinds to move off before approaching the carcase, an eagle glided down and pitched momentarily on the dead stag.

On *Achnashellach* (Ross-shire) many more ravens than usual were seen during the 1984 season, and during one stalk no fewer than twelve flew around the stalkers as if monitoring their final approach, and indeed, while the carcase was being removed from the scene, one bird had already started to feed on the gralloch. It is often said that the presence of ravens during any stalk is a good omen, and it certainly was on this occasion.

On two occasions in 1994, on *Auchlyne* (Perthshire), the deer were disturbed by ravens circling around, and 'dive-bombing' them, which caused them to move away.

Geese – *Migration and Weather Forecasting*

An early or late migration of geese in the autumn is said to forecast the severity of the winter to follow. During the autumns of both 1979 and 1980 the geese were reported to be flying south about a fortnight later than usual, and two mild winters followed. Conversely, in the spring of 1981, by 13 February many geese had already

passed over *Affaric* (Inverness-shire) on their way northwards, and according to the 'goose weather forecast', a mild spring followed.

The southward migration of geese in the autumn of 1991 was, however, early and by 15 September the skeins were already crossing the northern coast of Sutherland on their way to the fertile plains of Perthshire and elsewhere. The snow in October of that year, and the arctic conditions of December that followed, proved once again that the geese had got their sums right, as they have done on many other occasions too numerous to mention.

Despite the severe winter of 1981–82, deer casualties in some of the worst-hit areas were not as high as had been expected. Deer losses, however, on *Glenartney* (Perthshire), particularly among the 1981 calves, were fairly substantial, and during the spring something between 150 and 200 carcases in total were found. *Braulen* (Inverness-shire) also lost a lot of deer during the spring, including some stags which had died shortly after shedding their antlers. Even on the island of *Rhum* (Inverness-shire), where winter conditions are never as severe as on the mainland, mortality was also high, being nearly twice the normal, the casualties including a lot of the older stags with large antlers. On *Glenfeshie* (Inverness-shire), however, which at that time had an estimated resident deer population of about 750 stags and 1,000 hinds, the natural mortality in the spring, which had been carefully monitored by the Red Deer Commission, was estimated at only about 1 per cent.

During the autumn of 1979 the geese were much later than usual in flying south, and in the winter that followed, apart from one fairly heavy snowfall at the end of January in some areas, particularly Inverness-shire, the weather, otherwise, couldn't have been better and by mid-March there was sufficient grass to make the deer less dependent than usual on the moss crop.

So once again the geese had got their long-range weather forecast correct!

Red Kite

An event of ornithological interest was the appearance, in 1993, of three red kites at *Ledgowan* (Ross-shire). They were seen soaring above Glen Docherty – the first occasion this bird had ever been seen on this forest. Their appearance was associated with a release programme in the Highlands by the R.S.P.B. using Swedish birds and according to N. Fox – a member of the Society – they have already started to breed along the Great Glen, so the birds seen at *Ledgowan* could well have been Scottish bred birds.

The kite became extinct in Scotland as a breeding bird just over a century ago, when there was a nest in Perthshire. The kite is, of course, a scavenger rather than a predator, being particularly fond of fish entrails.

In 1992 a kite was one day seen at *Torosay*, on the Isle of Mull.

Short-eared Owl

During the 1963 season there was a small influx of short-eared owls in some areas, and in particular at *Glencallater* (Aberdeenshire), but they were not as numerous there as they had been in 1959 when a similar influx occurred.

Snowy Owl

At *Gordonbush* (Sutherland), a snowy owl was seen on 2 September 1980 at very close range. A regular visitor to northern Scotland, it is only in recent years that the species has remained to breed, having successfully nested on Shetland, but not yet on the mainland.

Hen Harrier

In 1966, on *Tombuie* (Perthshire), two hen harriers were seen to strike a flying grouse, and would no doubt have followed it to the ground and killed it, had not the birds seen the stalking party standing not far away. After a short while the grouse recovered and took wing, apparently little the worse for wear apart from the loss of some feathers.

Peregrine Falcon

During the 1990 season Sir Seton Wills had the rare opportunity of witnessing at *Glenavon* (Banffshire) a peregrine falcon attacking some greylag geese, and after one or two abortive attempts, the falcon, from a great height, finally succeeded in bringing a goose down to the ground – 'a truly great sight' was his comment.

On *Glencarron* (Ross-shire) a peregrine was seen to attack a ptarmigan whilst in flight. Feathers flew as the bird fell to the ground, but after a few minutes it seemed to recover and was able to fly off, more frightened than hurt.

An unusual event was witnessed by Lord Allerton in 1972, on *Dalnamein* (Perthshire), as he was shooting a stag. At the sound of the shot a covey of grouse, that had been sitting in the heather nearby, suddenly rose, and as they flew off one was killed by a peregrine, the head of the grouse being completely severed from the body.

Voles and mice explosions

In 1987 an abundance of mice and voles attracted a large number of owls and kestrels. It was the same on *Kingairloch* (Argyllshire), with many more sparrow hawks than usual preying on the hordes of rodents that had erupted on to the hill. It is amazing how the word gets around, and an increase in prey will often produce a complementary influx of predators to the area.

In 1990 there was a similar explosion of mice and voles on *Glenshee* (Perthshire), which was followed by an influx of owls to the area. 'In this year', reported Tim Healy, head stalker on *Glenkinglass* (Argyllshire), 'literally thousands of voles appeared on the forest, and in their wake came a large number of raptors, which included tawny and short-eared owls, as well as kestrels, hen harriers and buzzards.' In that year an osprey was also seen on *Glenkinglass*, but its appearance there, of course, was in no way connected to the vole invasion, for it is almost entirely a fish-eater.

During the 1993 season an unusually large number of kestrels were about on *Kingie* (Inverness-shire), and it was assumed that their presence was due to the abundance of mice and voles in the area.

Miscellaneous

During the autumn of 1965 there were a number of interesting observations of unusual birds appearing in strange localities. These included a great grey shrike (*Lanius excubitor excubitor*) on *Glenfeshie* (Inverness-shire), and a single snow bunting (*Plectrophenax nivalis nivalis*) on *Hunthill* (Angus). About twenty waxwings (*Bombycilla garrulus garrulus*) appeared on *Torosay* (Argyllshire) on 2 November but only stayed for a few hours. This was the first report of

any waxwings visiting *Torosay*. All three species are migrants.

In 1965 a capercaillie (*Tetrao urogallus urogallus*) was one day seen flying high up on the Cruach, *Blackcorries* forest (Argyllshire) – an area without any trees for miles. This spectacular bird is, of course, a resident in many areas of Scotland including Argyllshire and Perthshire.

PART III:
MANAGEMENT

CHAPTER 20

The Annual Cull

Introduction

Regarding the annual cull, this should obviously be based on the results of a census, and not on any hereditary figure which may even date back to pre-War days.

Since the War, deer in Scotland have been subjected to a number of disturbing factors, which have completely upset their pattern of life. These have included afforestation with miles and miles of fencing, the flooding of former wintering grounds and the erection of pylons during the development of hydro-electric schemes, not to mention hikers, bikers and climbers which are now able to penetrate areas which in former times, except during the stalking season, deer had practically to themselves (*see* page 60–67).

During 1952, reports from forests over widely separated areas, suggested a noticeable decrease in the deer population, and these included *Inveraray* and *Blackmount* (Argyllshire), *Coulin, Monar* and *Kinlochewe* (Ross-shire), and *Glenquoich, Glengarry* and *Inchrory* (Inverness-shire). On the other hand, a slight increase was apparent in a few areas, and it would appear that a local migration had occurred.

For instance, on *Auch* (Argyllshire) in 1968, N. W. Braid Aitken reported that, due to disturbances elsewhere, 'there is now a tremendous population of deer on *Auch* after the rut and all through the winter, and as a result I am finding it highly embarrassing in correlating the living space with that of the sheep stock.' He commented that not only had the fencing-off of the hills by the Forestry Commission changed the habits of the red deer, but the new close-season dates for red deer (*see* page 142) had 'made a big difference here and something may have to be done about it'. Major

Warde-Aldam also commented on the 'ever increasing disturbance with the normal movements of red deer by the forestry deer fences', which were then being erected all round *Ederline* (Argyllshire). On *Rhiedorrach* (Perthshire), by 1968, deer stocks had also started to increase, and Mr Shoosmith, the tenant, wrote, 'The number of deer is quite exceptional – I estimate we saw 1,000 in one day.' Lord Allerton, the tenant on *Dalnamein* (Perthshire), also commented that he had 'not seen more stags on the ground than there were this year (1968)'.

On other forests, by the late 1960s the reverse was the case, and to mention but two, on both *Coignafearn* and *Inshriach* (Inverness-shire) there was a noticeable decline in the number of stags. Hinds too, on both *Flowerdale* (Ross-shire) and *Ben More* (Mull) were decreasing in number, due, in the latter case, to poaching in the spring. On *Kinloch Hourn* (Inverness-shire), however, since the removal of the sheep during the early 1960s, more stags were coming on to the ground.

From reports received from forests in 1969, it would appear that the overall deer population of Scotland was on the decrease, and this was partly confirmed by the 1969 South Ross deer count, for when compared to a similar count made four years previously, it revealed that the stag population had been reduced by 11.3 per cent, hinds 3.5 per cent and calves 6.8 per cent – an overall reduction of 6.5 per cent. Nevertheless, despite the evidence of these figures, on the basis of reports received from about 120 estates, the stag cull in 1969, compared to that of 1968, was up by about 2.3 per cent and the hind cull by 5.3 per cent.

In 1976 considerable concern was expressed by the R.D.C. who estimated that the total deer population in Scotland, in spite of an increased cull on many forests, then totalled some 269,600. Indeed, it was estimated that the annual cull of around 35,000 deer was at least 10,000 below the number of calves that were being born annually, so the inevitable result would be that, during the next hard winter, not only would there be serious damage to woodland and farmland by invasion, but grave hardship to the deer themselves by starvation. As a result, the Red Deer Commission recommended that for the next few years the annual cull should be increased by *at least* 33 per cent.

By 1976 some forests had, during the previous few years, already stepped up their cull of both stags and hinds by more than this amount and, to mention but one, the increase at *Coulin* (Ross-shire) had been more than doubled. Others would like to have done so but, due to a number of reasons which included shortage of staff and hiker disturbance during the stalking season, had found it impossible. At least two forests reported that, had their guests shot more accurately, the cull would have been higher!

Forestry, more than anything else, has undoubtedly been responsible for not only restricting the range of red deer in Scotland, but also encouraging marauding, due to deprivation of winter habitat. For instance, when the Forestry Commission fenced in Guisachan hill above *Hilton* (Inverness-shire) during 1978, the deer in the area were deprived of their long-established wintering ground and, in consequence, had wandered eastwards, with the result that about 70 to 80 had to be killed in *Glenurquhart* during the spring as marauders.

On *Glenspean* and *Tulloch* (Inverness-shire), where the normal cull for each property prior to 1976, had been about 25 stags, due to forestry activity in the area, over 700 stags and about 300 hinds were shot in the following two years. Such slaughter could not, of course, be selective as, irrespective of age, damage to forestry was the same, and both mature and young unfortunately received the same treatment – a bullet.

A strong wind which blows constantly for any length of time in one direction can, on occasions, give a completely false picture of deer population on an individual forest, and this is exactly what occurred on *Langwell* (Caithness) during the 1978 season. For weeks on end there was a strong west wind blowing, which had the effect of moving several hundred deer off the forest on to and beyond the Caithness/Sutherland boundary, and in consequence there were fewer deer on *Langwell* than was normal during the early part of the season. As a result of this local migration, many more deer than normal appeared on *Achentoul* (Sutherland) during the early part of the season and, on two occasions during the last fortnight of September, groups of stags, estimated to number between 400 to 500 beasts, were seen on the eastern part of the ground.

During the 1984 season stags of all ages were reported to be few on the Rannoch side of *Ben Alder* (Inverness-shire), showing that the area had still not recovered from the shooting of approximately 600 deer by the Forestry Commission and Red Deer Commission, following a break-in to the Rannoch plantations during the winter of 1982. On the brighter side, however, C. H. S. Garton was able to report that on *Ben Hee* and *Corriekinloch* (Sutherland), there were not only more stags – both young and mature – on the ground, but also hinds, the latter having been only lightly shot in recent years.

Nowhere in Scotland has there been a greater increase in the overall hind population since the War than in Angus, and the total cull of hinds on the six major stalking grounds of the county – *Invermark*, *Hunthill*, *Glenprosen*, *Glenmoy*, *Glen Doll* and *Rottal* – had increased from about 316 in 1984 to 1,059 during the winter of 1989, with *Invermark* (335) and *Hunthill* (231) making the largest contribution.

In contrast to the large hind population, however, there was a distinct shortage of stags in all age groups reported on some forests -- some by as much as 33 per cent down – and these included *Hunthill* (Angus), *Glendessary* and *Glenfinnan* (Inverness-shire). Overall, from one hundred reporting forests, the total stag cull in 1989 was about 3,977 compared to 4,172 of the previous year – a reduction of about 4.7 per cent.

A deer count on *Abernethy* forest (Inverness-shire), on 26 October 1990, suggested a total population of about 807 deer, divided up into 239 stags, 414 hinds and 154 calves. This total figure was down by some 144 from what it had been in October 1989, the most significant reduction (101) being among the hinds.

On *Glenfeshie* forest (Inverness-shire), in 1993, the stag cull was increased from an average in recent years of about 150 to 186, to which could be added a further 15 from neighbouring *Killiehuntly* on lease - a total of 201. The reason for the increase was that in February 1992 the Red Deer Commission carried out a count which indicated that there had been a considerable increase in numbers over the past few years, due to deer coming on to *Glenfeshie* from the south, and the cull, therefore, was increased accordingly.

There is no doubt that during the past three or four years some of the larger forests have considerably increased their hind cull - some by as much as 100 per cent. *Strathconon* (Ross-shire), for instance, in 1992 shot 680 hinds and calves as compared to 297 in 1989. *Mar Lodge* (Aberdeen-shire) in 1992, shot 1,000 hinds and calves - about 600 up up on three years previously. In the same year *Langwell* (Caithness), with a cull of 1,040 hinds and calves, about doubled the cull of 1989, whilst the 255 beasts taken off *Glendoll* (Angus) in 1992 was about 66 per cent up on 1989.

On the other hand, *Gaick* (Inverness-shire), which had a hind cull of 204 during the winter of 1992–93 due to an increased cull among hinds on neighbouring forests, subsequently believed that this number had, perhaps, been excessive, and would, in future, reduce it by about 20 per cent.

Until 1977 the annual cull on *Kinloch* (Sutherland) had been 20 hinds, but for the next ten years it was reduced to only 3 or 4. Then, in 1988, it went up to 37, and during the 1992–93 season to 100. 'Although there are still too many hinds on the forest', writes A. W. G. Sykes, the owner of *Kinloch*, 'the numbers are gradually coming into balance between the sexes.' In 1993 the stag cull was about 30. On neighbouring *Ben Loyal* the hind cull - including calves - also dramatically increased from 91 in 1989 to 217 during the winter of 1992-93.

Some areas, however, have recently reported a shortage of hinds, and these have included *Erchless* (Inverness-shire), *West Monar* (Ross-shire), *Dalnaspidal* (Perthshire) and *Glenfeshie* (Inverness-shire).

Shooting hinds – 19th century

In former days it was the practice of deer stalkers to shoot hinds, if such an opportunity occurred, while stag stalking. Thus, one of the earlier exploits recorded after the afforestation of *Braulen* was on 23 August 1849 when, according to a Scottish newspaper, the Master of Lovat 'dropped a very handsome stag and hind right and left in *Glenstrathfarrar*'.

Recent hind culls

According to the anual reports of the Red Deer Commission during the ten-year period between

1982 and 1992, the average total number of hinds and calves shot both in and out of season each year varied between 15,093 (14,676 + 417) in 1983/84 to 27,454 (27,103 + 351) in 1991/92. The highest percentage of hinds shot out of season was during 1984/85, when it amounted to 3.2 per cent of the total killed. This out-of-season percentage has gradually decreased from 3.2 per cent (1984/85) to 1.3 per cent (1991/92). This compares to an out-of-season cull of stags of about 11 per cent. In 1970, based on venison dealers returns, this figure had then been as high as 22 per cent.

Calf cull

According to the R.D.C. annual reports, the number of calves shot in hind/calf culls had gradually increased from about 17 per cent in 1986 to 29.7 per cent in 1991/92.

The 1960s

When the Deer (Scotland) Act became operative in 1959 three years grace was given to enable owners of forests and marginal ground to reduce, where necessary, their deer stocks before the Close-Season section of that Act become operative on 21 October 1962. Unfortunately (as noted on page 204), in 1958 the price for venison had started to improve, and this encouraged both marginal land owners and poachers to make as much money as possible before the more severe penalties included in the Act would become operative. To assist in reducing the stock of deer on some marginal ground, cullers from the Red Deer Commission were called in, and on one of these areas – *Ross of Mull* – I was informed by the late Lord Massereene and Ferrard that during the spring of 1961 about 300 deer of all ages and sexes were shot.

Much more disturbing, however, to deer forest owners on Mull than this cull on the *Ross* was the situation at *Glenforsa*, which belonged to the Department of Agriculture. Both Lord Massereene and David James M.P. informed me that, during 1961, consignments of up to fifty carcases had been seen ready for dispatch from Salen pier. The total number of deer that had been killed on *Glenforsa* - many of which had doubtless come in from adjacent forests - was never published, but as I remarked at the time (*The Field* 4/1/62),

> If it is their ultimate aim to eliminate all the deer from their ground, then they should not do so at the expense of the neighbouring forests. If *Glenforsa* is to be clear of deer, then it must be fenced. No one, I am sure, would then object to complete extermination *within* the fenced-off area.

In the mid-1960s, based on experience on the Isle of Rhum, the Nature Conservancy recommended that, to maintain a stable population level, about 16 to 17 per cent of the deer stock should be culled each year. This is what was generally referred to as a 'one-sixth cull' policy. If, of course, stocks have to be *reduced*, provided the shooting is *selective*, it doesn't really matter what percentage is killed until a resident population that contains a well-balanced sex-ratio has been obtained. As was the comment in my 1965 review (*The Field* 24/2/66),

> But once the desired stock level is reached I doubt if a one-sixth cull can be maintained on many of the higher-placed forests where the deer have to endure far more severe winters than those on sea-girt *Rhum*. Moreover, when winter strikes, the deer on Rhum are unable to wander off into hostile woodland, from which an unknown number will never return, thus upsetting any cull plans being followed on the local forests. I do not consider, therefore, that it is correct to assume that conditions on *Rhum* are applicable to the mainland where, through various causes, natural or man-made, winter and spring mortality is higher, and if a 16-17 per cent annual cull is taken off many of the mainland forests, the deer population will steadily decline. I am not suggesting that there is no room for a reduction of deer stocks in some areas – *I am sure this is necessary* – but once a desirable level has been reached, it will not be possible to kill, annually, anything like 16-17 per cent and still maintain that level. In my opinion, provided that *sufficient* numbers of hinds are culled – which at present on many forests are not – then the annual kill should not be more than about 10-12 per cent, and on some of the higher placed forests, as low as 8-10 per cent. If adequate winter feeding is provided artificially, of course, then the winter and spring mortality rate from natural causes will be lowered, and the annual cull can be increased a bit.

The 1970s

In 1973 not only did the high price of venison encourage a heavy cull, but just prior to the season a request was sent out by the Red Deer Commission to all deer forest owners to increase their cull, these two factors making it probable that a record number of stags would be killed that year. As a result, many forests did just that. *Caenlochan* (Angus), for instance, increased the cull from 90 in 1972 to 140 in 1973, which was stated to be an all-time record. Quite a number of other forests, which normally would have killed about 40 to 50 stags, increased their cull by about 50 per cent. One of these was *Coulin* (Ross-shire).

Stag carcases during that season were fetching, on average, about £75 to £80 apiece, with very large ones worth well over £100. The venison revenue, therefore, for a fifty-stag forest was in the region of £4,000 which was about £1,600 more than in 1972 and ten times the receipts for the same number of stags in 1968. Unfortunately, however, during November of that year, there was a sharp fall, and dealers were quoting 30 pence per lb for hind venison (*see* page 205).

Within three years, however, the price of venison had about doubled to what it had been in 1974, and many forest owners were, therefore, only too happy to comply with the request of the Red Deer Commission to increase their cull, particularly as they predicted that 'one hard winter will take a heavy toll and must cause severe damage'. Fortunately, the following winters were not as severe as predicted, and as a result the estate culls, combined with a lower winter mortality than had been anticipated, had not kept pace with a rising deer population, which was then currently estimated by the Red Deer Commission to be around 296,600 deer. At the time, an annual cull of around 35,000 deer was estimated to be at least 10,000 below the number required to keep pace with the annual number of calves being born.

By 1976, although a number of deer forests, particularly in Angus and parts of Wester Ross, were reporting a considerable increase in their deer population, there were other areas where the reverse was the case, and this particularly applied to estates bordering forestry in which a large cull had taken place in previous years.

Moreover, with all the will in the world, some forests were already killing up to the limit of their staff, and with only one stalker and perhaps two ponies, thirty to fifty stags was probably the maximum number that could be handled in a relatively short season that could so easily be shortened by bad weather. Those, too, were the days before the highland garron had been replaced by the various array of mechanical transport now available.

Many forests, of course, rely on the rut to bring in the stags, but a late rut, as has been happening in recent years, inevitably reduces the number of stags that can be shot before the season ends on 20 October, and should there be many days lost through mist or bad weather, time for killing stags is even further reduced.

As I suggested in my review of the 1976 season (*The Field* 24/2/77),

> a solution to the problem would seem to be that, so long as the Red Deer Commission considers that the deer population in Scotland is too high, it should be possible, as a *temporary* measure, for any deer forest owner to apply to the R.D.C. for official sanction to continue the stag cull until, say, the end of October, or even longer if essential, and the hind cull by a fortnight until the end of February – a date which happens to correspond to that when hind stalking ends in England (Deer Act 1963).
>
> Such limited extension to either sex would not cause any cruelty or hardship to the deer, and indeed the reverse would be the case, for it would help reduce winter mortality which could be high if the winter is severe. Such an extension would also enable those estates which are already working to capacity to increase their cull with existing staff and equipment, and unless some such action is undertaken, it will be quite impossible for many estates to increase their cull by 'at least 33 per cent' as advocated by the Red Deer Commission.

The 1980s and Onwards

I have often wondered how many deer forest owners – particularly the absentee landlord or those whose presence on the forest only amounts to a month or so during the year – ever adjust their annual cull according to the previous year's calf crop and winter mortality, but instead work to a traditional book-figure dating back, perhaps, many years. This particularly applies to forests on which the bulk of stags will be shot by a paying client, when a satisfactory book balance at the end of the financial year is of more importance than a well-balanced sex ratio of deer on the forest.

There are, of course, a great number of forest owners who do take a great interest in their deer, and who will adjust the cull to meet the circumstances. For instance, the death toll in the spring of 1983 was exceptional, and many forests took this into account when planning the cull for the following autumn and winter. On the *Lochiel* forests (Inverness-shire) the stag cull was reduced by about 40 per cent, and the hind cull was also reduced considerably. On *Ben Alder* (Inverness-shire), where about 250 deer of all ages had perished, the stag cull was reduced by about 40 per cent, whilst on *Rhum* only 50 stags, instead of the usual 60, were shot.

The bulk of the spring mortality is evident on the larger estates which carry a resident population of both sexes, and when any undue losses do occur, the stalkers, on the evidence of carcases seen, are fully aware of the seriousness of the situation and can reduce their cull accordingly. Not so, unfortunately, on the smaller forests or marginal sheep grounds which mainly have to rely on stags coming on to their ground for the rut, and whose proprietors are probably quite ignorant of – or don't care too much about – what is happening elsewhere. The net result is that they continue to kill, if possible, the same number – or even more – than has been killed previously, unable to realise that the supply is not a bottomless pit and sooner or later may dry up completely.

A. D. Gordon, of the *Atholl* Estate (Perthshire), wrote in 1983,

> Far too many stags are being shot by the smaller forests, late on in the season – also by the Forestry Commission – not to mention those which are being killed out of season. This will undoubtedly tell on numbers during the next 5-10 years, and is already becoming critical on the west coast.

Apropos the shortage of stags in some areas due to over shooting, the following is an extract from a communication I received in 1983 from Major Neil Ramsay who ran a sporting agency. It referred to one particular area which totalled some 44,000 acres (18,000 ha) and comprised two separate but adjacent deer forests, and which had been let by his agency for seven or eight years. Throughout these years it had, apparently, been possible, by putting one *Rifle* out during the earlier part of the season and two in October, to take some 100 stags annually without any trouble. He wrote,

> Quite suddenly it became apparent that the stags were no longer there. Some embarrassing weeks took place in 1982 and refunds were negotiated. The estate held a conference attended by the stalkers and myself, and the decision was taken to let only 24 stags in 1983. Even this figure proved to be unobtainable . . . In 1982 I stated that I feared that there were other areas where I believed it is only a matter of time before *overshooting* catches up, but few forest owners thought it could happen to them. I had hoped that I was not being too unduly pessimistic. Apart from one or two specific areas there is, sadly, little to show that my pessimism was misplaced and many estates condone the shooting of stags, as if there was an inexhaustible supply . . . In the olden days it was the Head Stalker who told the Laird how many stags could be shot, and few would dare to question his word!

It is also, perhaps, true to say that in those days there was 'no gold in them thar hills' as there is today in rents, trophy fees and sales of venison. According to Major Ramsay (*in lit.* 1982), I understand that mainland stags of normal quality should be able to command a price of £110–£115 plus VAT on the European and home markets, whilst a figure of £131 plus VAT could be obtained from Americans, whom he has found to be excellent sportsmen and who have been extremely acceptable to the estates that received them.

Not everywhere, fortunately, was it a tale of doom and gloom, for at *Coulin* (Ross-shire), during August 1983, the deer were as plentiful as ever and, due to the late rut that year, remained on the ground throughout the season, whilst on neighbouring *Applecross* (Ross-shire), an early season census showed that there were '926 more deer on the whole peninsula than had been computed'.

Accordingly, the stag cull that season was increased to 167 – a figure that was about twice what was being taken off the ground before the 1914-18 War, and about three times more than the pre-1939-45 War cull. In 1983 an increase in the stag population on *Lude* (Perthshire) enabled the cull to be raised from the more usual total of about 10 to 45.

And from elsewhere in Scotland, since 1984, there have been similar reports of a territorial rise or fall in the Scottish deer population, the root of the problem being that in few *areas* – as distinct from *stalking units* – is there a well-balanced sex-ratio of deer, and this can only be achieved by a larger cull of hinds. If deer, of both sexes, were equally spread around the stalking units, this would not be too difficult to achieve. Unfortunately this is far from the truth, and Scotland's 300,000-plus deer population have the range of many hundreds of estates, varying in size from the Atholl forests which extend to some 78,000 acres (32,000 ha); to hundreds of smaller units of under 3,000 acres (1,200 ha), many of which have only a resident population of hinds and rely on the rut to bring in the stags. Owners of such areas are, understandably, reluctant to kill too many hinds, believing that more hinds on the ground will attract more stags. Unfortunately, if the stags are being heavily culled elsewhere, the bonanza of stags will never arrive. An *area* cull, therefore, of both stags and hinds *agreed* among *all* members of a local Deer Management Group, would seem to be the only solution to obtain a more balanced sex-ratio (*see* page 158).

CHAPTER 21
Tagging

Carcase Tagging

Poaching and out-of-season killing of deer is nothing new or unique to Scotland - it is practised throughout the world where game still survives. Some countries, however, have been able to tackle the problem more effectively than others, and it is wise, therefore, to take heed of what remedies have been proved successful elsewhere and try them here.

I first became acquainted with the tagging system in 1951 whilst on a stalking trip to Germany, and on my return to this country, at the request of Hastings, the late Duke of Bedford, I prepared a short paper on how a similar scheme might work here so that he could present it to the House of Lords during the second reading of the Poaching of Deer (Scotland) Bill on 13 March 1952.

The tagging of deer carcases is universal throughout the United States of America, and immediately any deer has been killed a tag, which has been applied for prior to the commencement of the hunting season, must be attached to the carcase and remain there until the carcase has been cut up.

Some states, such as Kentucky, issue three tags per beast: one to be attached to the hindleg where it must remain until the carcase has been processed and packaged; another to be attached to the skin, whilst the third tag will be attached to any other part of the deer - generally the head - which has become separated from the carcase for speedy despatch to a taxidermist for mounting. I am not, of course, suggesting that anything so complicated should be used in Britain!

In some states of the U.S., in order to help sex identification, it is also illegal to remove the sex organs from any tagged carcase.

In the United States the main object of tagging carcases is not only to restrict poaching but to control the number of deer being shot, for in most states, it is illegal to buy, sell or 'barter' any edible part of a deer, thus making the disposal of venison difficult.

So far as this country is concerned, this is the manner in which I envisage a tagging scheme should operate:

1. A deer carcase could only be accepted by a game dealer provided it had the official metal tag of the forest or property on which it had been shot. Every proprietor would, therefore, have to have an official metal tag, which would have to be stapled to the ear or limb of every deer carcase by means of special pliers, whether it was hanging in his larder for subsequent disposal to friends or disposed of to a game dealer. The tags would not only be serially numbered but would also bear the official number or prefix of the estate in question. It might also be desirable to have the date on which the beast was killed punched on to the tag in the same manner as many dairies date the metal caps of milk bottles. Once the seal of a tag had been broken, it would be invalid.

2. *Licensed* game dealers would only be permitted to accept *full* carcases so tagged – and those tags would have to remain on the carcase in the refrigerator until it was cut up. If any licensed game dealer was caught trafficking in untagged carcases, or holding any carcase in his refrigerator with the seal broken, unless some satisfactory explanation was forthcoming, he could be heavily fined and his licence to deal in game withdrawn.

3. There must be some authority to operate the scheme. If applied to Scotland only, then the obvious choice would seem to be the Red Deer Commission. If applied to England and Wales as well, which would obviously be advisable, particularly as the deer population of the other two larger species - fallow and sika deer - are increasing, it would be necessary to form a Deer Control Association to operate it.

4. It would be the duty of every estate that holds a resident stock of red, sika or fallow deer to provide details to the controlling body of the estimated live stock of deer, by species and sexes, at, say, 1 April, and also of the number of male and/or female deer it planned to cull during the following autumn and winter.

5. If, in relation to stocks, the cull plan was approved, the appropriate number of serially numbered tags would then be issued to each applicant. If, during the season, it was found desirable to kill more deer than originally planned, then a further application would have to be made for additional tags, with reasons for doing so. In an emergency, this could be done by phone, with a follow-up written application.

6. Within ten days after the end of the appropriate shooting season a report would be submitted indicating the number of deer that had been killed, and any *unused tags returned*. At the same time details would be given as to how the carcases had been disposed of, and the name and address of the appropriate dealer. Information would also have to be supplied on the number of carcases that had been cut up privately as gifts to friends etc., and for these carcases, the tag, with the seal broken, would have to be returned.

7. If, during the winter, marauding deer of either sex needed to be killed, either out of season, or on ground not normally occupied by deer, the owner of such ground would have to apply for a certain number of tags to cover the required number, and give reasons for doing so. If approved, then the necessary tags valid for, say, four weeks – would be supplied, and at the end of this period any unused tags would have to be *returned*, together with a statement as to the number of marauders killed and to whom the carcases had been disposed.

8. Twice a year each licensed game dealer would have to make a return to the controlling body, giving the number of carcases still held in stock at that date.

9. Each licensed game dealer would be required to keep an accurate register of purchases and sales, and such registers would be examined periodically along with refrigerators, larders etc. to see that no untagged carcases were present.

Not all venison, of course, reaches the larders of the licensed dealers, and quite a lot of business in the home trade is done for cash with hotels etc. This is an obvious loophole in any venison disposal scheme, and can be eliminated by making it illegal for hotels and restaurants etc. to purchase venison from anyone except a licensed dealer. In 1975–76, for instance, venison receipts by dealers were 1,484 fewer than the number of deer reported killed by estates, which would suggest that during that particular year a larger number than usual were being disposed of privately.

One of the principal objections to the tagging scheme, voiced by the Red Deer Commission and others, is the fact that, in addition to the recognised deer forest owners, a large number of crofters also have the right to kill deer on their smallholdings. So far as killing deer in season is concerned, this is perfectly true, but during the close-season, when most stags seek the low ground, they only have this right to kill when the deer are actually 'on any arable land, garden grounds or land laid down in permanent grass (other than moorland and unenclosed land) forming part of that land, or on such woodlands, as the case may be' (Deer (Scotland) Act, 1959). Elsewhere, it would be necessary to obtain authorisation in writing from the R.D.C. before any deer could be killed out of season, and this would include moorland and unenclosed land adjacent to arable land etc.

The issue of tags to crofters should not offer any real problem, for it is an annual occurrence for deer in large or small numbers to wander, particularly in winter, on to the farms situated marginal to deer forest territory. If, therefore, it is the *accustomed practice* of a smallholder to shoot the odd stag or hind in season, the crofter would simply apply for his stag or hind tags in the same way as any deer forest owner. For marauders that have to be killed *out of* season, application for the necessary number of tags would have to be made by letter or telephone, *as and when* marauding occurred. Any crofter who, in the past, has been in the habit of killing perhaps two or three marauders, would have no difficulty in obtaining the required number of tags, but if the demand appeared *unreasonable*, his application might have to be investigated before the full number was issued. That, surely, is sound deer management and conservation, and does not in any way interfere with a crofter's right to shoot what he has always considered necessary in the past.

I imagine the number of crofters who might wish to apply for tags would be well below 5,000 for, even at one deer per croft, the total number of carcases should not be much more than the number of 2,439 (stags and hinds) which appear in the 1992 R.D.C. report as having been shot 'by others' on 'land other than estates'.

There would be no question, of course, of a crofter being able to apply for a tag on the off-chance that a deer *might* some day visit his holding. Furthermore, tags would be identifiable only to the property to which issued, and this would be some control over any attempt to set up a 'black market' in tags.

One forest owner in Perthshire, who is strongly in favour of tagging, considers that the main objection might come from the stalkers themselves, but I have not found any evidence of this – in fact quite the reverse – and a number have written to say that they are 'one hundred per cent behind any scheme that might reduce poaching'.

In Argyllshire it is said that poachers in one area sometimes get rid of poached deer carcases to their farmer friends, who then claim to have shot the beasts on their croft. This could happen, I suppose, up to a point, but the farmer in question, before he could dispose of the carcase, would still have to apply for a tag, and if his demand for tags appeared to be unreasonably large for the area in question, the issue of further tags could be withheld until the matter had been properly investigated.

A forest owner in Sutherland reported that he knew one dealer who was buying poached venison, only to sell immediately to another dealer who, as the law stands at present, was able to buy and sell it as 'legally purchased' venison. Tagging, of course, would prevent this sort of thing happening, for not only would the first dealer (legally) be unable to purchase an untagged carcase but the tag, indicating its origin, would also have to remain on the carcase at the time of purchase by the second dealer.

It has been suggested that some owners might apply for more tags than required, and sell the surplus of unused tags to a local crofter or even a poacher, in order to cover beasts shot elsewhere without a tag. Another possible source of the 'black market' tag could be for an owner to decide that due, perhaps, to a shortage of deer, his planned cull would have to be reduced, thus leaving him with a number of marketable, unused tags. In both instances, to dispose of them privately would be illegal, and each tag would be easily identifiable specifically to the estate it was issued to.

However, to prevent over-application for tags, it might be advisable for each year's application to be based on the average number of deer, of each sex, which had been killed on that land during the previous five years. If, for any reason, a forest requested an increase in the number, reasons for doing so would have to be submitted so that the matter could, if considered necessary, be investigated before the extra tags were released.

Any carcase-tagging scheme should apply to Britain as a whole and not just Scotland, and should include fallow and sika, for the number of estates, particularly in Scotland, where these deer occur is not large and would not add to the administrative problem. Their inclusion would, however, preclude untagged carcases of young red deer being disposed of as sika or fallow deer. It would also get over the problem of sika/red crosses. To start with, however, there is no point in considering roe, for not even the most persuasive poacher would be able to palm off even a yearling red deer as a roe!

In their 1974 *Report* the Red Deer Commission stated that 'it seems clear that many of those who advocate the introduction of a statutory carcase-

Young red deer hind.

Bambi and daughter *Trudie*
– tame hinds on *Wyvis*
(Ross-shire).

(*Below*) Two hinds that
went stalking on *Wyvis*
(Ross-shire).

Stag roaring.

Stags fighting. *(Lea MacNally)*

(Above) The rut — a shootable stag not yet run.

(Right) Stag serving a hind. *(Lea MacNally)*

(Below left) Wapiti — crossing with this North American relation has not met with much success in Scotland.

(Below right) Strong heads are being produced by stags on enclosed deer forests and farms. *(Anon)*

Red deer stag in woods along Dee-side, Aberdeenshire.

A young Galloway forest provides an ideal habitat for this stag. *(Jack Orchel)*

Sika stag. Typical features of sika deer are the white metatarsal glands and white caudal patch.

A good sika stag shot by the author at *Langwell* (Caithness) in 1982.

Rear view of 11-point sika deer antlers, with long back tines, the right-hand one terminating in a fork. It was shot on *Devilla* forest, near Tulliallan (Fife) in 1994. *(A. Allison)*

Fallow buck. Many of the feral fallow in Scotland today were formerly enclosed in deer parks.

(Left) Roe buck. This deer now occurs in all suitable localities throughout Scotland. *(Jack Orchell)*

(Below left) Bull reindeer on the *Rothiemurchus* reserve (Inverness-shire).

(Below right) Wild goat on *Ailsa Craig*, Ayrshire.

(Right) 'Royal' from *Glencanisp* (Sutherland) shot by R. A. Vestey in 1953. A matching left crown and a stronger right bay tine would have improved this head.

(Below right) 11-pointer from *Dunrobin* (Sutherland) shot by F. J. Pryce-Jenkins in 1948.

(Above) 'Cup' or crown of true 'royal' 12-point head.

(Below) 3-a-top of 12-point head, but this should not be considered a 'crown' to make it a genuine 'royal'.

Typical 'switch', *Inverbroom*, Ross-shire (1956).

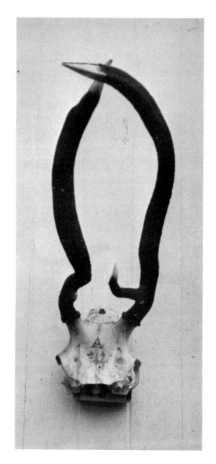

Very narrow, cross-beamed switch head.

Handlebar type 'switch', with straight beam ends, *Glenburn* (1946).

Some 'switch' type heads.

Handlebar type 'switch' from *Cairnsmore* (1962) with turned up beam ends.

tagging scheme tend to overestimate the possible beneficial effects which might result, and underestimate the enforcement problems which would exist under "Scottish conditions."'

Nevertheless, the R.D.C. indicated that they 'would be prepared to co-operate in a voluntary scheme restricted to out-of-season carcases only, with a view to exploring the problems and difficulties of operating such a scheme.'

It is not clear whether 'out-of-season carcases' refer only to those deer which have been included on the estate returns, or to those which have been obtained from the venison dealers records, which, presumably, will include the majority of carcases registered in the estate returns.

In the estate returns for 1974 – the year in which the R.D.C. made their offer of co-operation – out-of-season carcases totalled 768 (634 stags, 134 hinds) which represents only 3 per cent of the total number of carcases (25,225) reported from the various estates. From information obtained from venison dealer records, which include details of deer killed on land other than estates, out-of-season carcases totalled 2,377 (2,023 stags, 354 hinds) which represents almost 9 per cent of the total carcases received (26,842).

If the trial was restricted to those estates which regularly supply the R.D.C. with details of their annual cull, the issue of tags, when application is made for deer to be culled out of season, should not offer any problem, but I very much doubt if there would be any *voluntary* applicants from the majority of those shooting deer out of season on land other than estates.

The main purpose of carcase tagging is to prevent or reduce the illegal killing of deer, and no poacher is going to voluntarily participate in any scheme designed to prevent him pursuing his chosen activity. Carcase tagging must, therefore, be an enforcement and not a voluntary participation, and any proposal that a voluntary trial involving less than 9 per cent of the cull would seem to be a waste of time.

On a properly designed tag, all the information as to origin, date, species, sex etc. would be available and would remain as *'attached evidence'* on each individual carcase, no matter where in Great Britain it might happen to be, thus avoiding the lengthy process of having to seek out an estate record book – perhaps several hundred miles away in the far north of Scotland –

to check if a carcase found in a lorry south of Carlisle, had been legally taken. The absence of a tag would indicate that it had been taken illegally – as simple as that.

Carcase-tagging is not only a control on the number of deer being shot but is also a method of controlling who does the shooting. To the game dealer, it is an assurance that the venison has been taken legally, and could well ensure better-quality meat reaching the consumer. It is never intended to be a measure of control on the shooting plan, which must always remain the responsibility of the owner or occupier of the land.

Whilst one cannot deny the fact that the number of crofts, marginal to deer forest country, on which the odd deer or two are killed must outnumber the recognised deer forests, it must not be forgotten that it is the deer forest owner who is largely responsible for Scotland having any red deer at all and who, in rents, rates, employment of stalkers etc., pays a considerable sum of money for this privilege – a cost which is not borne by either the crofter or the poacher. It seems logical, therefore, that the deer forest owner should be the one to make decisions about the management and future of the deer.

In 1980 I decided, when contacting deer forest owners and stalkers for information for my Annual Review, to seek their opinion on this controversial subject. The result was much as I expected, for it showed that 72 per cent were in favour of carcase tagging, whilst 8 per cent were against. The remaining 20 per cent, which included those forests to which access was only possible by boat, and where poaching had, therefore, never been a problem, had no firm opinion one way or the other. Since over 70 per cent of owners indicated that they were in favour of a carcase-tagging scheme being put into operation, it would appear reasonable for the Red Deer Commission to support their wish.

In 1980 I suggested that money to run the scheme could be obtained by charging £1 for the issue of a single tag – a small outlay when a single red deer carcase was then worth about £100 or more. Such a charge would, at that time, based on the number of deer being killed, have brought in about £40,000 to £50,000 per annum. Today a figure of around £57,000 might be available – or even double if the cost of a tag was raised to £2, which doesn't seem unreasonable

During 1995 the R.D.C. were considering a universal tagging system, not so much to combat poaching, but to improve hygiene standards, and thus enable any substandard venison to be traced back to source of origin. Whether any such 'tagging' system will be included in the *Deer (Scotland) Amendment Bill*, currently being discussed at the beginning of 1996, remains to be seen, but it seems probable that the title of the *Red Deer Commission* will be changed to *Deer Commission for Scotland* so as to include its responsibilites for all species of deer throughout Scotland

Calf Tagging (Marking)

Between 1963 and 1984 the Red Deer Commission marked, with ear tags, 1,620 wild red deer calves over a wide area of Scotland and, by 1992, of the 354 tags which had been so far recovered from carcases of deer that had been shot (316) or had died a natural death (38), only 12 – all of which were stags – were recovered from carcases that had died more than 10 miles (16 km) distant from the place of marking.

Calves for tagging must be caught during the first two or three days after birth, for when disturbed they will be too weak to run far before lying down again, when capture can be made with a large landing-net.

During the 1980 season a number of calves that had been tagged elsewhere were shot on *Atholl* forest (Perthshire), two of which, both nine-year-olds, were killed on the *West Hand* beat – a distance of about 8 miles (13 km) from where each had been tagged. In the same season two eight-year-old stags, both of which had been tagged on *Dalnamein* (Perthshire), were shot on *Forest Lodge* – the distance from place of tagging here being about 10 miles (16 km). Another eight-year-old, which had also been tagged on *Dalnamein*, travelled a considerably longer distance before ending up in the larder in *Inchrory* (Banffshire), which was a good 35 miles (56 km) away from its birthplace.

So far as I am aware, this would appear to be the furthest distance from the place of tagging yet recorded for a stag. In their 1978 Report, the Red Deer Commission recorded the recovery of a tag from a stag that had been shot at *Abernethy* (Inverness-shire) – a distance of 25 miles (40 km) from where it had been tagged on *Atholl*. By 1980, as a result of their tagging operations, the R.D.C. had discovered that 62 per cent of deer which were tagged when calves were shot within 2 miles (3.2 km) of their birthplace. Stags, as one would expect, are inclined to travel longer distances than hinds, and only about 5 per cent of hind carcases have been recovered beyond 10 miles (16 km). On 13 October 1992, an 11-pointer stag, weighing 16 stone (101 kg), was shot on *Rhiedorrach* (Perthshire) by Mrs D. Jackson, with an ear tag indicating that it had been tagged as a calf on *Dalnamein* (Perthshire) in 1981 – a distance of about 25 miles (40 km) from where it was finally shot.

CHAPTER 22
Artificial Feeding

Pre-1939–45 War

Prior to the 1939–45 War the majority of the larger forests in Scotland were in the habit of providing some additional food for their deer – particularly the stags – during winter and early spring (*see* page 153). The desire to supply this additional, and often necessary, food was, I am afraid, more for a cosmetic rather than humanitarian reason, for invariably it was to assist the stag in producing large antlers, whilst the hind was ignored and even discouraged from partaking in the extra food.

In those pre-War days the most popular artificial food was maize, with locust beans and Indian corn a close second. Other items on the winter menu included dried sugar beet (*Strathvaich*, Ross-shire), kiln-dried barley (*Kintail*, Ross-shire) and B.O.C.M. red-labelled nuts (*Glencanisp* and *Kinloch*, Sutherland).

Between 1937 and 1939 some special feeding-cubes were being manufactured by I.C.I. and they received good reports from those forests that tried them. *Glenmazeran* (Inverness-shire) claimed

that antler growth was accelerated, whilst in the opinion of *Inverbroom* (Ross-shire) a darker-coloured antler resulted. Prior to the War I.C.I. cubes were tried on the following forests and probably others not recorded:

Aberdeenshire
 Balmoral

Argyllshire
 Ardtornish
 Black Corries
 Glen Etive

Inverness-shire
 Ardverikie
 Glenfeshie
 Glenmazeran
 Killiechonate
 Struy

Perthshire
 Lochs
 Meggernie

Ross-shire
 Inverbroom
 Wyvis

During 1936 the stags on *Knoydart* (Inverness-shire) were being fed at four different points on the forest with maize and locust beans but, as comparatively few stags came to the feed, the experiment was not pursued. Generally speaking, the climate on *Knoydart* is mild and, since the stags have access to ground along the sea shore, additional feed in winter was not considered necessary.

On the nearby island of *Rhum*, however, where between 1929 and 1938 about 120 stags and a few hinds were fed from November to April with maize, feeding was considered an unqualified success, for not only did the feeder stags start to shed their antlers earlier – some as early as 12 March and all by 1 April – but mortality among the older stags was reduced to practically nil.

Normally the weather on the west-coast islands does not reach the severity of that on the mainland, but pre-War the deer on the Island of *Scarba* (Argyllshire) were fed with hay and maize whenever the winter was particularly severe, the food being regularly sent over from the mainland.

Prior to the War, feeding deer with hay and locust beans was tried on *Scatwell* (Ross-shire) for a few years, but was not a success. During the winter the stags used to hang around all day waiting for the food, but as soon as the spring arrived, they moved out on to *Strathconon* where they remained until the next winter. The result was that none of the home-fed stags were ever killed on the ground of the owner who had gone to the trouble and expense of feeding them in winter!

Between 1906 and 1939 *Strathconon* (Ross-shire) also fed their stags in winter with a little maize, potatoes and hay. The late Colonel H. C. S. Combe, the owner, was not in favour of any artificial feeding, for he once told me that it was, unfortunately, only necessary because his neighbours did it – otherwise many of his stags would probably have wandered off the ground.

Before the War, winter feeding with maize was tried on *Caenlochan* (Angus), but after two years the trial was discontinued. During the first year, only a very few stags came to the feed, but in the second year they came in such numbers that it was impossible to provide sufficient food for them all. Furthermore, as soon as the stalking season came round they returned to the neighbouring forests, so it was considered pointless to continue.

In the early 1930s, feeding the stags on *Glenmoidart* (Inverness-shire) was tried for a few years, mainly with the intention of encouraging the stags to winter on the forest, but no particular improvement in either weight or trophy was noticed, so it was not persevered with.

During this period it was also the practice to feed the stags on *Kingie* (Inverness-shire) with a mixture of locust beans and Indian corn but, after feeding had been discontinued, practically all the stags, especially during a hard winter, went off the ground either down *Glengarry*, or to *Achnacarry* and *Glendessary*, only to return in early summer.

On *Mudale* (Sutherland), feeding the stags with maize was commenced in 1936 and continued until 1939, with good results, for it was found that a large number of stags which had previously only been visitors for a few months, coming in from *Reay* forest, were encouraged to remain on the forest throughout the year.

At *Braeroy* (Inverness-shire) the deer were fed regularly for three months from 1 January to 1 April with Indian corn. If any stag with poor antlers came to the feed it was shot, and this soon raised the standard of head on the forest.

On *Glencanisp* (Inverness-shire) it was the practice to feed the deer with maize from early November until the first week in April. In 1937 it was estimated that 20 tons of maize was being consumed by about 100 stags during these five months – an average of about 2¾ lb (1.2 kg) of maize per stag per day. During the following winter 180 stags came to the feed daily, and during this period they consumed 25 tons of maize – or just under 2 lb (0.9 kg) per stag per day.

Hinds, however, were discouraged from coming to the feed, and when in periods of snow they attempted to do so, were kept away by shooting odd beasts on the feeding ground.

Prior to 1962 the red deer in Scotland were not protected by any close-season, so it was legal to shoot either sex throughout the twelve months.

Before describing what has been happening on the forests during the more recent post-War years, mention should be made of an experiment tried at *Alvie* during the first quarter of this century.

Alvie (Inverness-shire), which extended to about 6,500 acres (2,630 ha), of which about a third were woodland, was purchased by R. B. Whitehead in 1906 and remained in his possession until 1924. The new owner, having

Tables 5:   *Winter feeding on Scottish deer forests prior to 1939*

County	Maize	Locust bean	Indian corn	Unspecified	Hay
Angus	Caenlochan				
Argyllshire	Blackmount	Dalness			
Caithness	Langwell	Langwell	Sandside		
Inverness-shire	Affaric	Arnisdale	Arnisdale	Fasnakyle	Alvie
			Braeroy		
	Glencannich		Corrour	Glenaladale	Corrour
		Glenkingie	Glenkingie	Glenfinnan	
	Glenmazeran				
				Glenquoich	
	Glenmoidart	Glenmoidart			
		Killiechonate	Killiechonate	Inverailort	
	Knoydart	Knoydart			
				Lettermorar	
		Mamore	Mamore		
	Rhum, Isle of				
	Scalpay, Isle of				
Perthshire	Dall	Dall	Dall		Glenartney
	Lochs				
Ross-shire	Benula			Braemore	
	Cluanie	Cluanie			
	Dundonnell				
	Glenshiel	Glenshiel			
	Glomach	Glomach	Glomach		
	Killilan	Killilan	Killilan		
		Kinlochewe		Kinlochewe	Kinlochewe
	Kinlochluichart				
	Leckmelm	Leckmelm			Strathconon
	Strathconon	Scatwell			Scatwell
	Strathvaich			Strone	
	Wyvis				
Sutherland	Corriekinloch				Badanloch
	Kinloch				
	Mudale				

shot a lot of deer in Austria was, therefore, familiar with continental methods of deer management and decided to introduce similar methods to *Alvie*. His first step was to fence in two sides, but this was not a success for a number of his stags – often the best – wandered on to neighbouring forests and were shot. So there was nothing else that could be done to remedy the situation except complete the fence all round, and this was done. With the fence complete, all inferior animals –

both stags and hinds – were systematically culled until eventually only about 150 stags remained within the forest, of which about half were over six years of age. From then on the fence served a double purpose – it kept the bad stags out and the good stags in.

Describing the *Alvie* experiment, H. F. Wallace in *Hunting and Stalking the Deer* (1960) wrote,

A certain amount of artificial food was given to the deer – clover hay in racks to avoid waste (with a few locust beans and turnips in the spring being provided) – immediately after the rut . . . The hinds did not come to the feed. In consequence the stags came into condition earlier the following season, and before the hinds. This prolonged the rut.

In the above-mentioned woodland, high seats were erected and the majority of stags were shot at dawn and dusk in continental fashion.

Today, although the deer still have access to about 1,000 acres (400 ha) of standing timber, the fence has long since gone into disrepair.

Post-1939–45 War

By 1950, when deer stalking in Scotland was slowly getting back to normal after the War years, little artificial feeding was being undertaken. Unfortunately, many areas of Scotland's former deer habitat were never to be the same as in previous years, for much of their former wintering ground was now being denied to them by miles and miles of forestry fencing, and low ground flooded in connection with the development of various hydro-electric schemes.

The answer to the problem was there for all to see – a better control of the deer population both in number and sex-ratio, and some form of winter feeding in selected areas, as had been widely practised in Scotland before the War.

In my review for 1950 (*The Field* 24/2/51) I suggested that the use of silage might help to solve the problem of winter feeding. Silage can be made in pouring rain – which should, of course, suit Scotland – so weather wasn't really a problem, and on a number of forests there are generally some acres of long grass which, when cut at their best, would be a good deal better than nothing at all. During January of 1949 the late Duke of Bedford started to put out some silage, as well as old heather, in his park at *Woburn*. The red and sika deer quickly devoured the heather, preferring it to good hay. The sika deer then started on the silage, and shortly afterwards the fallow deer followed their example. At first, however, the red deer would not even look at it, but after about a fortnight they, too, started to taste it, and it was not long before they were also taking it as enthusiastically as the sika deer.

By 1960 many stalkers were commenting on the poor quality of the Scottish deer compared to pre-

War. In some cases this situation had been brought about by general ignorance on the part of some amateur stalkers on the type of deer to be shot, which, in consequence, had resulted in a large number of promising immature beasts being killed and inferior beasts left to breed. However, it was the post-War development of short term stalking tenancies by day, week or month, and consequent greater pressure from the trophy hunter, that was the main culprit.

During 1959 R. A. Vestey was one of the few owners who regularly fed their deer in winter, the type of feeding used being red-labelled nuts produced by British Oil & Cake Manufacturers (B.O.C.M.) (*The Field* 31/3/60).

Another estate which, during the early 1960s, regularly fed their deer in winter with whole maize was that of the Duke of Sutherland. This is done, wrote J. M. L. Scott, the Duke's agent,

to keep the stags at home. We start off very lightly in November by giving an average of about ½ lb (0.25 kg) or less per head and this we keep up when the hard winter starts when it is increased by 1 lb (0.5 kg) per head or even a little more. We find it is better to feed at night for if we feed in the morning the stags are inclined to lie about the feeding place for most of the day when they should be out foraging for food.

Following the severe winter of 1961, when many forests had deep snow from mid-November until March or April, the spring was very cold with little natural food available apart from moss-crop. Fortunately, one or two forests were able to continue feeding during these early months and this was, undoubtedly, the salvation of many deer. During periods of snow cover, hay was put out for the deer on *Kinveachy* (Inverness-shire).

By 1967 it would appear that only a few forests had started to feed their deer in winter, and those that had were all convinced that it had been worthwhile. C. S. R. Stroyan commenced feeding his deer on *Monar* and *Pait* (Ross-shire) during 1966–67 and he reported that 'the effects of my first year of feeding were satisfactory and more good antler growth was observed'.

By 1968 an increasing number of owners had begun to supply some sort of winter feeding for their deer, if only during periods of severe weather.

There are, of course, many people who violently disagree with any form of artificial feeding for wild deer, and although it is inclined to make them dependent on human beings for their winter fare, one must remember, also, that *man* has been responsible for depriving the deer of much of their natural and ancestral wintering grounds (*see* pages 60–67).

Personally, I believe some form of winter feeding for deer in Scotland is now a necessity, not only for the deer's benefit but also to minimise the damage done by marauding.

A number of the smaller or higher forests will have very few deer on their ground to feed during the winter months, yet it seems hardly fair that the owners of such property should expect a neighbour, who has a large and resident stock of deer, to bear the full costs of feeding stags which, in a matter of months, will wander on to his ground and thereby provide both himself and his guests with some good sport.

In an article entitled 'A surplus of deer on Scotland's hills' (*The Field* 20/2/69) I suggested that,

> the answer to the problem is to have communal feeding areas designated in each natural block of forests. In each feeding area the food would be paid for by all the forest owners in the district on a deer-shot-per-season basis. In other words, a 100-stag forest would pay double the amount paid by the 50-stag-per-season forest.

The obvious organisation to monitor these schemes would seem to be the local Deer Management Groups which have gradually been developed in many areas of Scotland since the late 1960s (*see* page 158).

One of the benefits of winter feeding, quite apart from an improvement in antler growth, is that it may encourage an earlier rut. During the autumn of 1962 the rut was late over much of Scotland, but one of the few forests to report an early rut was *Ardverikie* (Inverness-shire), which at that time was one of the few forests feeding their deer from November to May.

Barrisdale (Inverness-shire) was another forest to regularly feed their deer, and from 1930 to 1938 the stags were lightly fed on maize and locust beans. Following the War, feeding was recommended but, following the death of the owner, Charles Williams, was once more discontinued in about 1955. Seven years later, however, feeding recommenced and during the winter of 1965 about 80 stags were coming to the feed.

Cluanie (Ross-shire) was another forest which, by the early 1960s, was regularly feeding their deer, and in 1968, when throughout Scotland the general pattern of the rut was late, by 12 September a number of the older stags had already started to collect harems together. In 1969 the pattern was similar.

During 1968, on both *Achdalieu* and *Achnacarry North* forests (Inverness-shire), where winter feeding had been practised for about two years, the stags broke out for the rut almost a fortnight earlier than elsewhere.

One of the best trophies shot in 1969 was a 13-pointer killed on *Meggernie* (Perthshire) by Lady Wills length 34 in (*87.6 cm*) [L]; 36¼ in (*92.1 cm*) [R]; beam 5 in (*12.7 cm*); inside span 26⅝ in (*67.6 cm*). This particular stag had been one of the *Meggernie* feeders, and when first coming to the feed in 1963 was an 8-pointer. In 1964 he was a 'royal', and although reverting to 10 points in the following year, was a 'royal' again in both 1966 and 1967. In 1968 he had 13 points, and this was repeated in 1969 when he was shot.

During the 1960s the stags on *Cluanie* (Inverness-shire) were already showing the benefits of winter feeding, and two of the best trophies shot in Scotland in 1968 came from there.

At *Glenquoich* (Inverness-shire) the stags which had received supplementary food during the winter commenced rutting about 11 September – but it was not until about the third week that the non-feeders joined in.

Talladh-a-Bheithe (Perthshire) first started to feed their stags in 1961, during a two-month period from 1 January to 1 March and, as a result, about seventy-five stags regularly came to the feed. During this period they consumed about 2½ tons of maize at a cost of about £52, which worked out at just under £1 per day or about 3d per stag per day. Suprisingly, but rather disappointingly, only about a third of the stags seen at the feed during the early months of 1961 showed up during the rut some eight months later.

By 1970 maize was not only in short supply but had become very expensive, so experiments were made, in collaboration with the producers, of feeding the deer with Rumevite, but so far as I am aware no reports have been published on the success or otherwise of these trials.

By the late 1960s *Glenartney* (Perthshire) had also started to winter feed, but at that period it would appear that less than 15 per cent of Scottish deer forest owners were doing any form of feeding. Since it was mainly only stags that came to the feed, and therefore only a very small proportion of the total deer population in Scotland that were really gaining any benefit from it, there were those who considered it to be a waste of money.

In 1969 *Glencarron* (Ross-shire) started to experiment with a Leyman Automatic Feeder, which was being marketed in Texas at a cost of $235. The advantage of this type of feeder is that it feeds automatically with a specific amount of feed at a given time each day, not requiring any human attention so long as the feed-hopper, which can hold about 1,000 lb (450 kg) of corn or pellets, lasts out. One advantage of this apparatus is that it can be installed further up the glen than a unit that requires daily attention. I understand that it worked with moderate success for a number of years, but is no longer in use.

During the 1971 season some really excellent stags, both in body and antlers, were seen on *Langwell* (Caithness), and this was put down not only to the previous mild winter, but also to artificial feeding and the influence of park blood (*see* pages 114–116).

Winter feeding, however, will never produce 'royals' out of switches, and on *Braeroy* (Inverness-shire), which had started winter feeding in 1967, although the generally poor type of head typical of the area had got heavier in the beam, no real improvement was apparent.

S. J. Loder (*Talladh-a-Bheithe*) was convinced, however, that winter feeding was well worth the effort and expense. In 1972 he wrote,

Our continuing policy of careful culling for the preservation of good heads and increased winter feeding has undoubtedly improved the standard of the stags very markedly over the past 18 years . . . Winter feeding was again carried out on *Talladh-a-Bheithe* (11th year) and *Camusericht* (4th year) and has continued longer into May. On *Camusericht* the benefits are beginning to show after only four years. We are hoping to start feeding hinds as well soon.

During the winter of 1971–72 a record number of stags came to the feed on *Ben Hee* (Sutherland).

By 1973 an increasing number of forests were providing some extra feed for their deer during the winter and spring, and one forest even continued feeding until well into June. Feeding undoubtedly helped to keep a high proportion of the stags on the ground, and so dissuaded them from wandering down to the low ground where they would probably have been shot as marauders.

In 1976 *Ledgowan* (Ross-shire) started to put out small quantities of hay for about 25–30 stags, 'with obvious beneficial results as both weight and quality of antlers are now starting to show improvement' (G. Ruggles-Brise *in lit.*)

Following one of the mildest and wettest seasons in recent years, the condition of the hinds on *Dalnaspidal* (Perthshire) during the winter of 1979 was poor in comparison to the stags, due, no doubt, to the fact that, whilst stags would come readily to the feeding points, the hinds appeared reluctant to do so and had spent much of the winter on the more exposed and higher ground.

The reluctance of hinds to take food, even under the severest of conditions, was also noticed on *Strone* (Ross-shire) where twenty-three hinds and calves were found dead in the snow. Throughout the winter the stags had taken readily to the food put out for them, but never the hinds, although they were generally to be seen hanging around the feeding points on the lower ground. In contrast to this apparent reluctance, in the early 1970s I several times witnessed the hinds coming to the feed at *Cluanie* during the spring months.

Apropos winter feeding, Michael Wigan of *Borrobol* (Sutherland) was of the opinion (*in lit* 1979) that over-intensive feeding only resulted in the deer being enticed off their natural wintering ground, with the inevitable result of a high mortality. That might be true in his part of Sutherland, but I cannot agree in general terms for, as already noted, in many areas of Scotland the Forestry Commission and the various hydro-electric schemes have already deprived the deer of much of their natural wintering grounds, and winter feeding has undoubtedly been the salvation of many thousands of deer.

On neighbouring *Badanloch*, which, along with several other forests in Scotland, started winter feeding in the early 1980s, results have been quite outstanding. *Badanloch*, of which only about 100 acres (45 ha) are above 1,500 feet (457 m), has always carried a large stock of deer, but mostly hinds. Since the commencement of winter feeding, the result has been a gradual increase in the resident stag population, and whereas in the 1930s there was a limit of 30 on the annual stag cull, today there is no difficulty in taking off 50.' According to Richard McNicol, the Head Stalker (*in lit* 1993),

Badanloch can no longer be described as a hind forest. I have never seen so many stags during the rutting season. Some stags seem very content with only one or two hinds and, in consequence, hinds are very broken up due to the heavy presence of stags.

CHAPTER 23

Deer Management Groups

During the 1960s there was a growing interest in the formation of local Red Deer Management Association Groups, and by 1970 the first three were in operation – one in Inverness-shire (Monadliath Red Deer Management Association), another in Perthshire (The Balquhidder D.M.G.), and the third in Mull (Mull D.M.G.). The main purpose of these groups – which had the blessing of both the Red Deer Commission and British Deer Society – was to improve the management of deer and encourage more liaison between proprietors; and they were undoubtedly a step in the right direction. Subsequently they became known as Deer Management Groups (D.M.G.).

From the three above-mentioned D.M.G.'s in 1970 the number has gradually increased, and by the end of 1994 totalled forty-eight, with the largest number (twelve) operating in Argyllshire (*see* page 159).

As will be seen from the list at the end of this chapter, although it would appear that, by the end of 1994, no D.M.G. operated in Aberdeenshire, part of this county is being covered by the East Grampians D.M.G. (Angus) and another part by the Cabrach-Glenfiddich D.M.G. (Banffshire).

Composed of landowners, stalkers, factors and farmers, D.M.G. meetings provide an excellent opportunity to discuss problems of local and common interest, such as winter feeding, marauding, poaching, sales of venison and the preservation of good trophy heads. As an example of what a D.M.G. can achieve, in 1989 the Balquhidder D.M.G. unanimously agreed that none of the white-faced deer in their management area should be shot (*see* page 94).

Deer have no respect for boundaries, and their movements are dictated by sex, food, and the weather. Very few estates are large enough to hold all their deer throughout twelve months of the year, so any deer management problems in an area must be dictated by geographical contours rather than a march fence.

On the practical side, a Deer Management Group should be responsible for organising an annual or bi-annual deer census in their area, and this is already being done by some groups. The ideal would be for several adjacent groups to liaise together, so that a few days could be set aside in order that all groups, covering a reasonably large area, can be out on the hill together taking their census.

Another suggestion I proposed in 1969 was that there should be communal feeding-areas designated in each natural block of forests, which would, in effect, be an area covered by one, or perhaps two, adjacent Deer Management Groups (*The Field* 20/2/69). In recent years, of course, more and more of the larger estates are providing some form of winter feed for their deer, if only to prevent them straying on to hostile territory. (*see* page 155).

Some groups have been extremely successful in what they have achieved, to the benefit of all concerned including the deer. Unfortunately, from some comments I have received or read, the same cannot be said for all groups and, once the initial enthusiasm had worn off, commercialism rather than deer management became the primary interest of some members of the group. Commented one deer forest owner (*in. lit.* 1980),

This is due, to a considerable extent, to the indolence of the officials into whose hands the group has fallen. In consequence, while some proprietors continue to take a responsible attitude, others have been 'commercial' in the extreme, and this has resulted in some areas that were once heavily populated hind ground now being completely without deer.

Fortunately, within this particular group area, there is one large landowner who is doing his utmost to retain a reasonable stock of both stags and hinds. This, however, could bring problems in a severe winter when the feeding of hinds was involved, for should the deer be forced to seek shelter on the ground of a commercially minded neighbour the results of sound management could all be ruined practically overnight.

The purpose of a Deer Management Group must be to instil a spirit of co-operation between all concerned, and this can only be achieved by all parties being represented on the committee – not just the larger forest owners, some of whom are often absent in the south during the critical months of winter.

Commenting on Deer Management Groups, in his booklet *Scotland's Red Deer* (1993), Hugh MacNally writes,

In every group will be found a nucleus of enthusiasts, without which no group would be formed to begin with. Whether these be field staff or owner/executive does not matter, the enthusiasm does. Unfortunately not all members of a D.M.G. join for enthusiastic reasons, and broadly speaking, most groups are composed of two types of persons – the 'Donald Dubhs' and the 'Weary Willies'. The success or failure of a Group will be in direct proportion to the ratio of 'Donalds' and 'Willies' in that Group. Each plays a vital role in their success or failure, each in his own way can sabotage a Group by passive or more vehement resistance for a wide range of reasons. An owner through lack of expertise at ground level. A stalker, because of obstacles placed in his way, lack of confidence in his own ability, unwillingness to work with others, or plain disbelief in the facts and figures at his disposal. In a D.M.G. of any size one can expect to find mixtures of all these components, and it is left to

the 'Donald Dubhs' who do believe, and can do, to rouse and convince the 'Weary Willies'. Often it can be a losing battle.

Nothing can beat a system of dedicated volunteers believing in what they set out to achieve, and in the context of D.M.G.'s no one knows this better than Red Deer Commission staff. Any form of compulsion raises the level of passive resistance and leads to all sorts of counter-movements. That is a main reason R.D.C. have refrained so long from using mandatory powers, preferring to actively encourage the formation of management groups as a way forward. Some Groups have clearly proved that the principle and positive practice does work.

Despite these somewhat derogatory remarks, I still hold to an opinion expressed some fifty years ago, that the future of Scotland's red deer must lie in the hands of successfully run Deer Management Groups.

Deer Management Groups
Aberdeenshire

Angus
East Grampians D.M.G.

Argyllshire
Ardchattan/Glenetive D.M.G.
Blackmount D.M.G.
Cowal D.M.G.
East Ardnamurchan D.M.G.
Inveraray/Tyndrum D.M.G.
Islay D.M.G.
Jura D.M.G.
Knapdale/Kintyre D.M.G.
Morven D.M.G.
North Mull D.M.G.
South Mull D.M.G.
West Loch Awe D.M.G.

Banffshire
Cabrach-Glenfiddich D.M.G.

Bute
Arran D.M.G.

Caithness
Northern D.M.G.

Inverness-shire
Cairngorms/Speyside D.M.G.
East Loch Shiel D.M.G.
Harris D.M.G.
Knoydart D.M.G.
Mid-West Association of Highlands Estates
Moidart D.M.G.
Monadhliath D.M.G.

Skye D.M.G.
West Inverness (Lochaber) D.M.G.

Kindcardineshire
Kincardine D.M.G.

Kirkcudbrightshire
Galloway D.M.G.

Morayshire
Northern D.M.G.

Peebleshire
Borders Sika D.M.G.

Perthshire
Aberfoyle D.M.G.
Balquhidder D.M.G.
East Glen Lyon D.M.G.
East Loch Ericht D.M.G.
Glenartney D.M.G.

Glenelg Peninsula D.M.G.
South Loch Tay D.M.G.
South Perthshire D.M.G.
Strathtay D.M.G.
West Grampian (Tayside) D.M.G.
West Rannoch D.M.G.

Ross-shire
Aird & Mid-Ross D.M.G.
Gairloch Conservation Group
North Ross Deer Group
South-west Ross D.M.G.
Wester Ross D.M.G.

Sutherland
East Sutherland D.M.G.
North-west Sutherland D.M.G.
West Sutherland D.M.G.

CHAPTER 24

Letting or Leaving

Compared to other field sports in Scotland – such as grouse shooting, and particularly salmon fishing on one of the better Scottish rivers (where a fine spell of weather can so easily ruin a complete week's sport) – deer stalking must rank as one of the least expensive. A charge of £200 to £250 or so per day will not only include the opportunity to shoot a stag, but also provide the exclusive services of a professional stalker as well as the use of transport, equine or mechanical, to convey the carcase into the larder. The venison, of course, remains the property of the estate, but the guest will normally be permitted to take away the antlers. I say normally because it is not unknown for a stalker to demand, in addition to his tip of perhaps £25 to £50 depending on the day's sport, a further £10 to £20 from the *Rifle* should he wish to take the head away, as the majority most certainly do (*see* page 23).

For a day's driven grouse shooting the cost will probably be based on about £75 to £80 per brace, or half that figure for walked-up grouse (1994). So with a party of eight guns on a 100-brace driven grouse day, the individual cost per gun works out at about £1,000, on top of which there will be a tip of about £25 to £50 per gun depending on the bag.

For salmon fishing on one of the better Scottish rivers, the cost could well run into four figures for two or three rods, with no guarantee of a fish at the end of a week.

Hotel Stalking

By the early 1950s there was an increasing demand for rented stalking for short periods, varying from a fortnight down to the odd day. In consequence, hotels had become the tenants of quite a number of forests and the facilities they provided were, in some instances, extremely good value for money.

Among the 'path finders' in the hotel stalking business were Captain and Mrs Leslie Hunt, who owned the Invergarry Hotel near Fort Augustus and leased the stalking rights over six or seven different forests in the area, which at one time or another included *Ceannacroc*, *Culachy*, *North* and *South Dundreggan*, *Balmacaan* and *Killiechonate* (all in Inverness-shire).

During the 1957 season ten guests at the Invergarry Hotel shot their first stags, one of which was a 'royal'. Altogether some 127 stags were shot by hotel guests on the seven forests rented that year by Captain and Mrs Hunt, who themselves were both practical deer stalkers and knew just what their stalking guests required – hot baths, late meals, good drying facilities and a tolerant attitude towards muddy boots!

Following his fortnight's stalking at the Invergarry hotel, I received a letter from the late Louis Petyt from Belgium, who stated,

> With six rifles out every day, each on a different forest, we were bringing back up to five stags per day – a number which could certainly have been six but for some poor marksmanship. The organisation was tip-top, and a really exceptional good lot of stalkers.

It was extremely pleasant to receive such bouquets from an overseas visitor whom I had introduced to Scottish stalking.

How different was the experience of another party of Belgians who, during the same season, rented a well-known deer forest in Ross-shire. It would appear that no ponies or ghillies were provided, so the carcases of the twenty-eight stags shot during their stay were left out on the hill to feed the birds and rot. Needless to say, they were amazed at this wastefulness, but otherwise were favourably impressed with Scottish stalking as compared to a woodland *battue* with dogs and beaters – the general practice in Belgian forests.

The daily rate to stalk from one of the sporting hotels in the early 1950s was about 10 guineas

(£10.50), irrespective of whether a stag was killed or not, and this fee covered the stalker's wages and hire of a pony, for mechanical transport was still waiting in the wings.

For every stag shot there was a sliding scale of charges which started at about 10 guineas for anything under a 10-pointer and ended up at about 25 guineas (£26.25) for the shooting of a 'royal' or above. The venison was the guest's property, but could be sent away in parcels at a charge of one shilling (5p) per package, plus postage. Tariff at the hotel was, of course, extra.

Another hotel was able to provide stalking for their guests at the rate of £3 per day, part of which would be refunded at the rate of ten shillings (50p) for each stag killed!

At that date £20 for shooting, say, a 7-pointer, or £35 for a 'royal' may have sounded pretty expensive to many people, but was it? In those days some of the best forests, yielding, say, 60 to 100 stags per season, had little difficulty in finding a tenant prepared to pay anything from £3,000 to £5,000 a year for his sport, which on a 100-stag forest worked out at about £50 per stag, which was £15 more than it would have cost a guest at a sporting hotel to shoot a 'royal'. Furthermore, the tenant would also have had all the worries of running the place and providing house staff, not to mention the fact that 7-pointers, for which the hotel guest would only be paying £20, would far outnumber the 'royals', yet all his beasts would have cost him more than double this figure.

In 1959, stalking was available for guests staying at *Druimavuic* lodge near Appin (Argyllshire), the rent of the lodge being £50 per fortnight in September, with an additional charge of £10 per stag and £5 per roe buck. This included the services of a stalker, ghillie and pony. Neighbouring estates to *Druimavuic* are *Dail* and *Ardchattan*.

In 1961 stalking was available from the Cluanie Inn, Glenmoriston on *Glenshiel* (Ross-shire), which belonged to the Dochfour estate.

In an article to the *Field Annual* (1950) on Scotland's red deer, I suggested that, since there appeared to be such a demand for this type of sporting hotel, would it not be a good opportunity to form one or two state forests, complete with suitable accommodation, that would be attractive to not only British sportsmen but also visitors from abroad. By mentioning 'state forests' I was

...

not, in any way, proposing the nationalisation of deer forests, but merely suggesting state ownership of one or two areas in Scotland that might otherwise fall into disuse or be broken up. Two properties which have changed hands during the past half century, and which would appear to have been ideal for such a purpose, would have been *Knoydart* and the isle of *Rhum* (Inverness-shire). On a state-owned forest all traditional methods of stalking would be maintained, which would, of course, include the use of ponies.

I suggested that,

> charges for stalking should be by the day, and be based on a fixed rate for the services of the stalker, ghillie, pony etc., with a sliding scale for the type of head shot. There should also be a heavy fine for shooting young and promising heads, unless the 'error' was due to the stalker's faulty instructions ... The venison should remain the property of the forest and be sold at a controlled price to the public . . . any such scheme should include amenities for fishing and shooting as an alternative form of amusement for guests on bye days . . .

Forestry Commission Stalking

In about 1973 an unusual situation developed at *Ederline* (Argyllshire), which marched with the Forestry Commission property at *Eredine*. At that time, although much of *Eredine* was surrounded by a deer fence, there happened to be an area of about 1,600 yards (1,460 m) in width between the two properties, on one side of which there was only low stock-fencing which permitted the deer to move freely between the two properties and beyond. Apparently the Forestry Commission wished to replace their stock fencing with a proper deer fence, which would then completely surround *Eredine* and thereby prevent all further movement of deer between the two properties.

Normally, when the Forestry Commission erect a deer fence round their property, it is to keep deer *out*. On this occasion, however, the intention was to keep the deer *in* and thereby 'maintain a constant stock of red deer within the forest in order to provide a permanent facility for day-permit stalking'. It would appear that the F.C. felt that they could only maintain a proper control of deer within their forest if this area could be completely fenced in, thus preventing the flow of any transitory animals. The F.C. also claimed that

'there will be no loss to the taxpayer from erecting this fence', as they expected to make 'a net profit' out of permit stalking for both red and roe deer.

In my opinion, if both red and roe deer are to be tolerated by the Forestry Commission in their woodlands in sufficient numbers to make day-permit stalking worthwhile, then it would surely be better to replace any existing deer fencing with stock fencing, and thus permit the movement of deer from one property to another. Furthermore, from a sporting point of view, the permit stalker would at least have the satisfaction of knowing that he was stalking a completely free-range wild deer rather than one whose movements were being restricted by a 6-foot (1.8 m) fence.

During the 1974 season the West of Scotland Conservancy of the Forestry Commission were charging £25 for a 5-pointer, and this price was progressively increased according to the trophy value, subject to 10 per cent VAT. In addition, there was a charge of £1.50 for every hour spent with the forest ranger.

In the early 1980s, in addition to a fee based on trophy quality, the F.C. had raised their outing fee to £21.90 for a period of three hours, which would be further increased at the rate of £7.30 for each additional hour in excess of three. Clients were fully informed of all trophy and outing fees before proceeding into the forest.

Permit stalking

By 1995 permit stalking was available on the majority of forests administered by Forest Enterprise (Forestry Commission), with only slight variation in charges and conditions between areas.

At time of application a non-returnable booking fee was required. In the North Scotland Region the booking fee in 1995 was £100 in respect of a weekly stalking permit – a week consisting of eight or nine outings, each lasting approximately three hours. Should an outing have to be cancelled due, perhaps, to inclement weather, then another outing, if possible, would be arranged. Should the client have to cancel the entire week's reservation, then, provided at least eight weeks notice had been given, the booking fee might be refunded at the discretion of Forest Enterprise.

In areas where permit stalking had been booked on a daily basis, a booking fee of £40 was charged, part of which would only be refundable if cancellation had been received at least four weeks in advance of the reserved date.

In all areas, before any client was taken out, he would be required to fire a group of sighting shots at a target and produce a result to the satisfaction of the accompanying ranger or other authorised person (*see* page 3).

All clients had to have third party insurance to the value of £1,000,000.

During the 1995 season the South-Scotland Region was charging £75 (including VAT) for a single stalk or outing of up to three hours duration for a roe buck or £35 for a roe doe, whilst for a week's stalking, based on nine separate outings each of three hours duration, the inclusive charge for roebuck stalking was £640, or £310 for does.

For red deer in the same region, the outing charge (including VAT) was £92 for a stag or £40 for a hind. For eight successive outings, each lasting approximately three hours, the fee was £720 for a stag or £310 for hind, the fee, in either case, being irrespective of the number of deer shot.

A stalk or outing lasting three hours, was deemed to have commenced the moment the stalking party entered the forest area.

For red deer, as well as sika deer, in both North and South Regions of Forest Enterprise, the weekly charge for stags was the same, namely £720. In the North Region, however, the charge for a week's hind stalking was £380 – some £70 more than in the South.

For roebucks the charge varied according to whether the stalking was taking place in a forest designated as a Band 'A' or Band 'B' area, the weekly charge in Band 'A' being £660 compared to £620 in Band 'B'. A forest was classified Band 'B' if it was subject to disturbance from various sources, such as recreation, road works, sporting events etc.

There is no guarantee of trophy quality of bucks in any of the North Scotland Forest Enterprise woods, and 'clients are expected to shoot every buck presented to them by the ranger, regardless of trophy quality' (*in lit* 20/2/95). For a doe, however, irrespective of whether it was shot in a Band 'A' or Band 'B' area, the charge was the same, namely £380.

Comparing these charges to those that were operating at the same period in the north of England (South Lakes Forest Enterprise), they were slightly higher, but in effect, for bucks, were cheaper, for they were 'fixed', whereas in England prices were based on trophy quality assessed under the C.I.C. formula, and this could result in the overall charge for a medal-class trophy being considerably higher.

At the time of writing (mid-1995) the following additional conditions apply:

Trophy charges

Except in Forest Enterprise forests in England, no additional fees for trophies have been levied in their woodlands north of the border and, once shot, the head becomes the property of the client, who will also be responsible for any preparation work. By special arrangement, however, rangers will be prepared to offer advice and assistance.

Wounded deer

If, during an outing, an injured deer is encountered, irrespective of where or in what manner that injury has been sustained, stalking will be suspended so that the injured deer can be shot. Should this interfere with or disrupt the day's outing, additional stalking time will, if possible, be arranged.

Should a deer be wounded by the client, then all further stalking that day will be suspended until it has been accounted for. In some regions a fine is also imposed upon any client *missing* or *wounding* a deer, the amount being, for example in the South Region of Forest Enterprise, £20 for a miss or £25 for a wounded beast. If a long pursuit after a wounded animal is required, then a client could be charged an additional penalty based on a rate of £15 per hour.

Venison

Once the deer has been shot, the carcase remains the property of the Forestry Commission, but it may be purchased by the client at an agreed price. For carcases, however, that have been badly damaged by the shot or shots, or have failed to be recovered within twelve hours of being shot, the Forestry Commission reserves the right to charge the client the market price for that carcase, which then becomes his property.

Stalking times

The main stalking periods for permit stalking in Forest Enterprise woodlands are as follows:

Roebucks, May–mid-August

Roe does, 21 October–mid-February

Red and sika stags, late September–20 October

Red and sika hinds, 21 October–mid-February

No stalking is permitted on Sunday in any Forestry Enterprise woodlands in Scotland.

See page 8 for close-season dates for all species of deer in Britain.

Agency Stalking

Outside Forestry Commission property, the cost of stalking arranged through an agency during the 1981 season worked out at about £180–£220 per stag, which would include accommodation and VAT. Without accommodation the cost was about £60–£80 – or possibly even less in some areas – irrespective of the quality of the trophy.

From letters received, however, at that period, it was apparent that some agencies were, in fact, demanding an additional trophy fee, although no mention of any such surcharge had been included in the booking contract. This, understandably, annoyed a number of clients, particularly those from abroad who, on the Continent, were accustomed to paying extra for exceptional trophies, and would not have objected *if* full details of what the extra cost was likely to be had been clearly stated on the contract. As a result, a number of clients found that an extra £100 to £200 had been added to the bill, and some adverse criticism appeared in the German hunting paper *Wild und Hund*, describing it as a sort of blackmail, as the trophy had already been shot and it was too late to object.

A number of deer forest owners – particularly those who take an active interest in their deerstalking, as distinct from the absentee landlord who engages an agency to arrange the stalking – will never allow a good head to be shot before it is fully mature. Unfortunately, today, during the rut or as a consequence of hiker disturbance, many a spared stag wanders off the forest never to return. During the 1979 season, over thirty stags (10-pointers or more) left *Loch Choire* (Sutherland) for the rut, but not one returned to its habitual wintering ground, presumably having been shot. It was usual for *Loch Choire* to lose a few wanderers each year during the rut, but never as many as that during a single season.

Some forests, of course, which are predominantly hind ground have to rely on the arrival of stags for the rut, but the stalkers should be selective and considerate to neighbours. Such an area is the southern beat of *Kinlochluichart* (Ross-shire), but in the late 1970s the number of stags coming on to the ground was steadily decreasing due to excessive slaughter elsewhere, with, on one occasion, 'as many as 18 stags in a day having been shot on a neighbouring forest' (Hon. Spencer-Loch *in lit*).

A century ago Millais, in *British Deer and their Horns* (1897) wrote that the greatest danger that threatened the future quality of the red deer trophy was 'the fatal yearly tenant system, for a sportsman paying a big rent very naturally skins the place and spoils the forest as regards heads'. How much worse, therefore, is the position today when stalking by the day or week is readily available in some areas from a sporting agency which, understandably, is more concerned about the 'letting' than the 'leaving'.

In the end, of course, it should be the landowner and his head stalker who should decide the number and *quality* of deer being shot, and this is observed on many estates. Unfortunately, however, there are large areas of Scotland owned by people who seldom, if ever, set foot on the forest, and whose main interest is to make money out of stalking, and not produce 'monarchs of the glen'.

Stalking challenge

During the 1960s the *Balnagown* estate, which owned forests in both Ross-shire and Sutherland, was providing stalking for guests wishing to use bow, shotgun or handgun (pistol or revolver), but fortunately all these unsuitable weapons, irrespective of whether they are of modern design, are now illegal for deer (*see* page 19). In 1975 there was an advertisement in a Texan store inviting Americans to come to *Invercauld* (Aberdeenshire) and try to achieve the prestigious 'John Macnab', but I understand there were no applications.

Deer farming

Andrew Allan established a large deer farm on *Strathgarve* (Ross-shire) in 1971, when he fenced in about 1,500 acres (600 ha) and introduced deer from a number of English deer parks, which included *Warnham* (Sussex), *Woburn* (Bedfordshire), *Studley Royal* (Yorkshire) and *Wootton* (Staffordshire). As a result of these introductions, the herd had, by 1983, grown to over 500, which included about 100 stags, a third of which were 'royal' or better.

The farm comprises a sheltered south-facing area of hill varying from about 450 feet (137 m) to 2,500 feet (760 m). The ground has been limed, and during the winter and early spring months the deer receive a supplementary diet of roots, hay and at times maize, so with this fare it is hardly surprising that some heavy stags with fine trophies have been shot there. In 1979 two stags, one weighing 31 stone (197 kg) and the other 28 stone (178 kg), were shot on the farm, the best trophy that year being a 16-pointer with the following measurements:

length 38¾ in (97.5 cm) (L), 39⅛ in (99.4 cm) (R); beam 7 in (17.8 cm) (I), 6½ in (16.5 cm) (R); inside span of 26 in (66 cm) (*see* also page 176).

PART IV:
ANTLERS, WEIGHTS AND VENISON

CHAPTER 25

Antlers

Description

In describing or measuring an antler the correct terminology should be observed.

'Royal'

A 12-pointer stag head with all its *rights* (*brow*, *bay* and *tray*) on each side and three points on each top in the form of a *cup* or *crown*. A 12-pointer with straggling tops should not strictly be referred to as a 'royal' but merely a 12-pointer.

Switch

A head consisting of only the main *beam*, with or without *brow* tines. An antler with brow and bay, but without any point or tine above the *bay* may be referred to as having 'switch tops', but it is not a switch.

Points

All tines, including the uppermost spike end at the top of each antler, can be referred to as a point.

Tines

These refer to points below the terminal end of each antler. As an example, a 10-pointer (5+5) only has four tines or points on each antler with an additional point on each top, to make it 10 points.

Velvet

During development the antler is covered with a vascular, sensitive integument coated with hairs, which is referred to as *velvet*. Growth of the new antler, dependent on the age and size of the deer, takes about four months to develop. The colour of the velvet varies from a light reddish-brown to dark grey. The velvet on a white red deer stag will be almost white.

10-pointer

A ten-pointer (5+5) will have four tines on each side, with the terminal top of the beam being included as a point.

Hummel

A male red deer that never produces any antlers (*see* pages 82–90)

Beam

The main stem of an antler. The beam measurement refers to the circumference. If only one beam measurement is to be taken – as is normal practice unless the antlers are being assessed under the C.I.C. (Conseil International de la Chasse) formula – this will be measured at the smallest circumference between the brow and tray tines.

Measurement of Antlers

Unless a head (trophy) is being measured under the formula approved by the C.I.C., the following measurements should be taken:

Length

Measured along the outside curve of each antler from the base of the coronet to its extremity (tip).

Beam

The circumference of each antler (beam) is taken at the thinnest part between the bay and tray tines – or, if the former is missing, between the brow and tray tines.

Span (inside)

The widest *inside* measurement between the two main beams of the antlers.

Spread

The widest overall measurement of the antlers at any place, whether it be between outer edge of beams or tips of tines.

Points or tines

Any point except the tip of the main beam, can be referred to as a tine.

The C.I.C. medal categories for red deer (*Cervus elaphus*) are as follows:

Scottish and Norwegian
    Bronze 160.00–169.99; *Silver* 170.00–179.99; *Gold* 180.00+

Europe, Western
    Bronze 165.00–179.99; *Silver* 180.00–194.99; *Gold* 195.00+

Europe, Eastern
    Bronze 170.00–189.99; *Silver* 190.00–209.99; *Gold* 210.00+

Velvet – late shedding

Following a normal winter and spring, mature stags will cast their antlers during the early part of April, and by the last week of August the velvet will be shed, so that by September most of the older stags should be in hard antler. A bad winter followed by a late spring will delay the whole process of antler replacement, and this has occurred on several occasions in Scotland during the past fifty years or so.

Antler growth and development depend on the severity of winter the stags have had to endure and availability of food during the spring and formative months of antler growth. When winter feeding occurs, antler shedding and regrowth is accelerated.

The most massive, but certainly not the most attractive, head obtained during the 1956 season was a royal killed on the *Glen Ey* beat of *Mar* forest (Aberdeenshire) by Mr Henderson, which had a beam of 6½ in (16.5 cm). The stag was shot on 19 September and, except for one tray tine, the rest of the antler was still in full velvet, with no signs of fraying, though the beam was hard underneath. This stag weighed 20 stone (127 kg), including heart and liver. It so happened that

some ten years previously, whilst photographing deer on *Mar* forest, I had seen a head so remarkably similar to this one that I am certain it must have been the same stag. Assuming, therefore, that the stag photographed in 1946 would then have been not less than six or seven years old, then its age when shot was probably not less than seventeen years.

During the 1958 season a number of stags were extremely late in shedding the velvet off their antlers, and from *Kinlochewe* (Ross-shire) Major J. L. Garton reported that 'stags were seen in full velvet whilst others were roaring late on in September – something which had never been seen before.' On 2 October a fairly well-run stag was shot in charge of hinds. It had still not shed the velvet from the top of its antlers.

During the same season a number of stags on *Blackmount* (Argyllshire) were still in velvet on 20 September, whilst on *Mar* (Aberdeenshire) 'some very good stags were still in velvet about October 6'.

The winter of 1961–62 was a particularly severe one in parts of Scotland, and indeed some forest owners considered it to be possibly the worst in their experience. The position was worsened by the fact that few forests at that time were providing any winter feed for their deer.

Throughout much of Scotland, stags during the spring of 1962 were late in shedding their antlers, and on *Mamore* and *Glenshero* (Inverness-shire) quite a number of stags that had wintered badly were still carrying their previous year's antlers into early June, whilst on the Sutherland Estate forests the stags were about three weeks late in shedding. On the *Lochiel* forests (Inverness-shire) there was little evidence of any new antler growth by the end of May. On *Affaric* (Inverness-shire) a number of the older stags succumbed during May, still in possession of last year's antlers; whilst by early June, only about 2 in (5 cm) of new antler was evident in some of the younger stags, instead of about 12–14 in (30–36 cm) which, in normal years, would have been visible. On the lower ground, however, stags that had access to crofts had their antlers well developed by early June. On the *Atholl* forests (Perthshire) it was about the first week in April that the older stags first started to cast their antlers. On *Ardverikie* (Inverness-shire), however, where the deer had received some winter feed, antlers were shed early, the first of the feeders having cast their old antlers by 4 March. Elsewhere, however, on the open forest, antler shedding was somewhat later than usual.

A dry spell of weather during August and September will sometimes cause the velvet to dry up on the antler, thus making it difficult to fray off. During the 1976 season there were a number of reports of this occurring on forests widely separated. On 13 October a stag in full velvet was seen with hinds on *Borrobol* (Sutherland). During the same season, in contrast to this late cleaning, an old stag which had spent much of its time in the woods around *Dalness* (Argyllshire) had discarded all trace of velvet by 2 August.

Following the atrocious weather of the 1982–83 winter and spring, the deer during the autumn of 1983 were not in the best condition, and many stags were late in shedding velvet. On *Gaick* (Inverness-shire) many of the mature stags were still in velvet around the middle of September, whilst on both *Kinlochluichart* and *Letterewe* (Ross-shire) it was October before the antlers of some of the older stags were clean of velvet. It was hardly surprising, therefore, that antler quality was poor that year.

During the last week of the 1987 season a small stag, about the size of a small hind, was found dead on *Affaric* (Inverness-shire) having died, perhaps, two days previously. Both antlers, about 6 in (15 cm) and 12 in (30 cm) long, respectively were still in velvet, with the latter antler growing down the side of its face.

On *Ledgowan* (Ross-shire), during the 1991 season, a stag was shot on 10 October with antlers still in full velvet. The animal was in very poor condition and quite unsuitable for venison.

Malformed Antlers

Abnormalities in antlers come in all shapes and sizes – some hereditary, some from disease and some by accident – and it is impossible to describe more than a selected few.

An unusual head was shot on *Glen Ey* forest (Aberdeenshire) during the 1954 season. The right antler was described as being 'long and very thick, with six points in best 'royal' style, but the left antler, which had three points, was only about 18 in (46 cm) long, and came out at right angles to the head.'

Quite a number of single-antlered stags were seen on a number of forests during 1972, which included *Ben More* (Argyllshire), *Strathconon* and *Glencarron* (Ross-shire).

On both *Strathvaich* (Ross-shire) and *Glen Clunie* (Aberdeenshire) a stag with identical short antler stumps was shot on each forest. At first glance it appeared as though the antlers had been broken off above the coronet, but I am certain that this was not so, and the antlers in each case had never been more than stumps. If the antlers had been broken off – and it would have required a tremendous wrench to have fractured both together – the stumps would have had sharp edges. Instead, the surface of both stumps were quite smooth. A comparison, perhaps, could be found in a piece of pottery which, if broken after firing, will be rough and jagged, whereas if the break has occurred before firing it will be smooth and glazed. I have yet to discover the reason for these truncated antlers which I have seen on several occasions.

Towards the end of 1976 a number of stags were seen on the *Atholl* forest (Perthshire) with broken antlers, due, it was thought, to a calcium deficiency. During the following season a large number of stags were seen on *Ben More* (Mull), also with broken antlers.

During 1968, on *Mamore* (Inverness-shire), one stalker shot, during the same day, three abnormal-headed stags – two with only one antler and the third with its left antler growing down the side of its face, which necessitated the stag having to turn its head to one side when feeding.

On *Strathmore* (Sutherland), during the 1977 season, Mrs H. Gow shot an uneven 8-pointer which had a normal brow, bay, tray and fork on the left side, but on the right a long club-shaped tine which sprouted from just above the brow tine and then hung down behind the main beam. Also in Sutherland, during the same season, Mrs Nicholson shot a 13-pointer on *Clebrig* which had two short tines, both about 3½ in (9 cm) in length, sprouting *backwards* on one antler from a position level with the brow tine.

An interesting 9-pointer stag was shot on *Ben Armine* (Sutherland) during the 1990 season, with all five tines on the right antler sprouting from the coronet.

On *Glensanda* (Argyllshire) Mrs Arthur Strutt shot a stag in 1991 with a deformed antler which curled upwards and then inwards, resulting in the antler tip almost penetrating the eye.

Soft and Spongy Tines

Several stags shot on *Kinloch* forest (Sutherland) in 1949 had very poor antlers, with the top points quite soft and rotten. When first handled, it was possible to bend the points as though they were made of rubber, but after a few months drying out they became extremely brittle and any attempt to bend them caused the tine to snap off.

During the 1966 season the points of some of the antlers of stags shot on *Inversanda* (Argyllshire) were reported to be soft and spongy and, according to the tenant, Captain E. A. S. Bailey, 'some liquid could be squeezed out of them.' Some eleven years later, on *Glenshero* (Perthshire), the tines of two of the stags shot that year were also described as being 'soft and spongy'.

On *Kinlochluichart* (Ross-shire), during 1971, antler growth was generally bad, and the antlers on some of the stags killed had very soft points. A quarter of the stags killed on *Coulin* (Ross-shire) that autumn also had poor antlers, many of which were not only broken, but also appeared soft and rotten.

Swinging Antler

When the pedicle or skull from which the antler grows is injured in, perhaps, a fight, accident or even by a bullet, or altered by disease, the antler will be affected. If, however, a pyogenic process has affected the base of the pedicle and surrounding skull, the growth of the antler may be entirely destroyed and, as the ossifying centre has been destroyed, no further antler can ever be grown from that pedicle. Any antler which existed at the time of the pyogenic attack may either be shed or remain attached to the skull by skin or gristle only. I have shot several stags with short antler stumps so attached, and whenever the stag moved the antler swung freely alongside the animal's face.

One-antlered Deer

A true one-antlered deer, which has no pedicle development on the deficient side, is really a half

hummel, irrespective of the number of tines on the antlered side (*see* Hummels pages 82–85).

Cromie

A typical cromie head should be stunted, goat-like in appearance, with the two beams, normally void of any tines, spreading back over the neck. Occasionally, however, a cromie-type head will have tines, and a good example of a multi-pointed cromie was shot in 1955, on *Ardlussa* (Jura) with the following measurements:

No. of points	Length		Beam
	L.	R.	L. and R.
5+3=8	13 in (33 cm)	15 in (38 cm)	4¼ in (10.8 cm)

Cromie heads are much rarer than formerly, and are generally associated with antlers grown by stags on the Isle of Jura (Argyllshire). During the 1955 season five such stags were seen on *Ardlussa*, including the above-mentioned 8-pointer. In 1992 a half-cromie, with only one antler directed backwards, was shot on *Ardtalla* (Islay).

During the 1994 season a cromie was shot on the *Islay* Estate (Argyllshire), the first since 1985.

Multi-antlered heads

Bifurcation of the main beam at or near to the coronet will often give the appearance of an additional antler, but unless there are three or four *distinct* pedicles, such heads can only at best be described as being pseudo-three- or four-antlered.

Three-antlered heads

Prior to the War, recorded three-antlered heads have included the following: 10-pointer (5+4+1) from *Langwell* (Caithness) in 1873; an 8-pointer (4+3+1) from *Struy* (Inverness-shire) in 1893; a 12-pointer (6+5+1) from *Craig* (Argyllshire) in 1926; a 10-pointer (3+2+5) from *Lochs* (Perthshire) (no date), and from a number of other forests including *Kinlochewe* (Ross-shire) in 1925, *Barrisdale* (Inverness-shire) in 1926, *Strathconon* (Ross-shire) in 1927 and *Black Corries* (Argyllshire) (c.1964).

During the past fifty years, seldom did a season pass without the report of a three-antlered stag having been seen on one forest or another, but nowhere are reports repetitive enough to suggest that this condition is hereditary.

In 1950 a good example of an 11-pointer three-antlered stag was shot on *Black Corries* (Argyllshire) by David Whateley. The left antler, measuring 32 in (81.3 cm) in length was of normal format, with six well-developed points all being particularly good. The main right antler, with a length of 33 in (83.8 cm), sprouted from a misplaced pedicle that was lower on the skull than normal, and although void of any lower points, had three tines on top. The third antler, some 5 in (12.7 cm) in length, and carrying a small fork on top, sprouted from the area on the skull normally occupied by the right pedicle.

A stag with three antlers was found dead near Fort Augustus (Inverness-shire) in 1959, the measurements of which were as follows:

	Left	Right	Extra Right
No. of points	6	5	2 = 13
Length	30¼ in (76.8 cm)	23½ in (59.7 cm)	29¼ in (74.3 cm)
Beam	4¼ in (10.8 cm)	4¼ in (10.8 cm)	3⅝ in (9.2 cm)
Span (between left antler and right antler [back])			23¾ in (60.3 cm)

In 1964, a three-antlered stag was shot on *Glenfeshie* (Inverness-shire), and during the same season a similar-antlered stag was seen on *Culachy* (Inverness-shire) but not shot.

In 1968 Miss Sally McCorquodale shot a good three-antlered stag on *Suisgill* (Sutherland), the third antler, which carried a well-developed brow tine, growing from a third coronet situated adjacent to the left antler. This particular stag, which had a total of eleven points, had been stalked unsuccessfully on the same beat some two seasons previously, and had wintered on *Suisgill*.

During the same season another good three-antlered stag was shot on an *Atholl* forest (Perthshire) by W. H. McAlpine but, as will be seen from the following measurements, the *Suisgill* head is slightly the better:

During the 1976 season an 18-stone (114 kg) stag with three antlers was shot on *Strathmore* (Sutherland) by Mrs Heather Gow, an old wound on a foreleg suggesting that this *might* have been the reason for the additional antler.

In 1984 a three-antlered stag was shot on *Kildermorie* (Ross-shire), with a short spike antler of about 12 in (31 cm) in length placed centrally on the skull, midway between a normal left antler of four points and a right antler of two points, thus giving it a total of seven points.

During the same season a three-antlered stag was seen but not shot on *Ben More* (Mull), with one antler curving down to the ground, another sprouting from the centre of the frontal bone and the third, being of normal location, carrying five points.

A good example of a pseudo three-antlered head, with the third antler growing from a bifurcation of the right antler, was shot on *Kylestrome* (Sutherland) by Lady Mary Grosvenor in 1969, who informed me that this particular stag, thought to be about ten years old, had frequented the forest for a number of years. A 'royal' in 1966, the stag grew a slight 'aberration' on the right antler in 1968, but the following year, when shot, the right antler had bifurcated just above the bay tine to give a long spike antler. The left antler had five points, with a fair 'cup' on top, whilst the right antler had a brow, bay and three on top, but no tray.

Thirteen years later in 1982, a genuine three-antlered stag was also shot on *Kylestrome* with all three antlers growing from separate pedicles. The extra antler, however, consisting only of a stumpy spike some 4 in (10 cm) long, sprouted directly in front of the right antler which, similar to the left, was of switch type, with a short brow tine at the base.

A three-antlered stag of twelve points was shot on *Kinloch* (Sutherland) in 1977, having brow,

Forest	Shot by	Number of points			Length of each antler			Inside
		Left	Right	Third	Left	Right	Third	Span
Suisgill (Sutherland)	Miss S. McCorquodale	5	4	2 = 11	26½ in (67.3 cm)	27½ in (69.8 cm)	18 in (45.7 cm)	14½ in (36.8 cm)
Atholl (Perthshire)	W. H. McAlpine	2	4	1 = 7	24¾ in (62.9 cm)	25 in (63.5 cm)	16½ in (41.9 cm)	– –

bay, tray and a fork on the right side, with two completely separate but slightly shorter antlers on the left side, one having four points emanating from a distinct coronet, and the other with three points, but without any coronet.

A curious three-antlered stag was shot on *Kinlochluichart* (Ross-shire) in 1980, for not only was the left antler bifurcated into a large fork about halfway up its length, but there was an additional antler in the form of a single spike, erupting from the centre of the frontal bone. In the same year a stag with a small third antler protruding from the skull was shot on *Ledgowan* (Ross-shire), whilst a three-antlered stag was seen with hinds on *Langwell* (Caithness), but not shot. One antler appeared to have been broken off above the bay tine, with the third antler just below.

In 1989 a 7-pointer stag was seen on *Rottal* (Angus) with what, at first, was thought to be three antlers, but when shot it was found that two of these grew from a bifurcated beam, so only two pedicles were present.

In 1990 a good three-antlered stag was shot on *Gaick* (Inverness-shire) by A. Bezzola, the two outer antlers having four and three points respectively, with the inner one consisting of a long switch-type spike sprouting from a separate pedicle.

During the 1992 season three-antlered stags were seen on a number of forests, which included *Achnacarry North* (Inverness-shire), *Kinlochluichart* (Ross-shire) and *Ben Loyal* (Sutherland).

Four-antlered heads

Four-antlered heads, with separate pedicles for each antler, are undoubtedly rare, and unless the beast has been actually shot to enable a closer examination, a bifurcation of one or both main beams, when viewed at a distance through binoculars, has sometimes given the impression of four sepatate beams.

In the early 1960s there was a head in one of the outbuildings at *Strathconon* (Ross-shire) which was always referred to as the 'four-horned stag', but in reality, due to bifurcation close to the right coronet, three branches sprang from the one pedicle.

During 1976 a stag believed to have four antlers, was seen on *Meggernie* (Perthshire), but was not shot. The situation was similar at *Fairburn* (Ross-shire) in 1980, so the head was never physically examined.

A perfect example, however, of a four-antlered trophy was obtained by a visitor from Denmark in 1977, whilst stalking on *South Dunrobin* (Sutherland), for each of the four antlers grew from a separate pedicle, and each pair were remarkably well matched as the following details show:

	No. of points	Length	
		Left	Right
Front pair	2+2 = 4	26 in (66 cm)	23 in (58.4 cm)
Back pair	2+3 = 5	27 in (68.6 cm)	26 in (66 cm)
	4+5 = 9	Inside span 23 in (58.4 cm)	

This stag was first seen on 13 September with about a hundred other deer on *Kintradwell* (Sutherland), near the march where it adjoins *Gordonbush* and *Kildonan*. After a lengthy stalk, a shot was taken from a range of about 150 yards (136 m), but unfortunately missed. After the shot, the stag ran off in a south-westerly direction on to *South Dunrobin*, where it was eventually shot some 6½ miles (11 km) from where first seen on *Kintradwell*.

A wide four-antlered stag was shot on *Glenmazeran* (Inverness-shire) by Jan Huybs with the following measurements:

	No. of points		Length		Inside span
	L.	R.	Left	Right	
Front pair	1	1 = 2	5⅝ in (14.3 cm)	5½ in (14 cm)	8⅝ in (21.9 cm)
Back pair	4	4 = 8	26½ in (67.3 cm)	26½ in (67.3 cm)	30¼ in (76.8 cm)
		5+5 = 10			

The single lower antler beam extended outside the main antler brow tines.

In 1989 Angus MacKenzie shot an 11-pointer stag on *Loyal* (Sutherland) with four separate pedicles and coronets – albeit one of the antlers measured only 3¾ in (9.5 cm) in length. The other three antlers measured 24 in (61 cm), 22½ in (57.2 cm) and 13¾ in (34 cm).

In 1992 a stag with four separate pedicles was shot on *Kylestrome* (Sutherland), but all four antlers were short, consisting of two switch-type beams in front and a pair of longer spikes behind, both measuring about 4 in (10 cm) in length.

Palmated Antlers

Although palmation of the upper tines is frequently to be observed among park or deer-farm stags, there are few records of its occurrence among genuine wild Scottish stags.

On *Strone* (Ross-shire) a stag was killed with palmated antlers. *Strone* is situated adjacent to *Inverbroom* forest, where, in 1955, another stag with remarkably similar palmation had been shot by L. J. Haes, suggesting that there might be some relationship between the two.

In 1974 a 15-pointer with a palmated left antler was shot on *Glenavon* (Banffshire).

Peruke, Perruque

Castration or severe damage to the testicles will often cause malformation of the antlers, accompanied by an exuberant growth of velvet. Such malformation occurs most frequently among roe bucks.

A peruke stag was shot on *Leckmelm* (Ross-shire) in 1976.

Deer farm and Park Deer Trophies

In 1986 a large 19-pointer, with antlers about 39 in (99 cm) in length was shot on *Strathgarve* (Ross-shire) by S. A. C. Morgan, but stags from this ground can no longer be considered to be of true Scottish blood, for since the early 1970s Andrew Allan has fenced in about 1,500 acres (606 ha) and introduced deer from a number of English parks, which have included *Warnham*, *Woburn*, *Studley Royal* and *Wooton* (J.C.B.). As a result of these introductions the herd at *Strathgarve* had, by 1983, grown to over 500, which included about 100 stags, a third of which were 'royal' or better. About ten trophy stags have been shot in most years. *Strathgarve*, therefore, is more of a wild deer farm than open deer forest, and certainly not the ground on which I once stalked some forty years or so ago, when it was an open forest and I had to rely on stags coming on to the ground from off the adjacent forests of *Wyvis* and *Garbat* (Ross-shire).

During the 1986 season Mike Wyndham-Wright, a taxidermist in Oban, informed me that he had received, from overseas visitors, a number of trophies bearing twenty points or more, some of which were still in velvet – their origin obviously a deer park or deer farm, such as the one at *Strathgarve*.

Another enclosed deer forest of about 350 acres (142 ha) is owned by Colin Gibb at *Inshewan* in Angus, and some fine trophies, more resembling Scottish than English park blood, have been shot there.

In 1992 W. Dodgson from Utah, U.S.A. shot a particularly good 14-pointer at *Inshewan* with the following measurements:

	Left	*Right*
Length	41¼ in (104.8 cm)	41⅜ in (105 cm)
Beam	6⅛ in (15.5 cm)	6⅛ in (15.5 cm)
Inside span 34 in (85.6 cm)	Weight 13 lb 9 oz (6.2 kg)	

Assessed under the C.I.C. formula this trophy had 193.58 points.

The big heads of Galloway

In recent years some of the best red deer heads have been shot in south-west Scotland, the majority of which have been shot on Forestry Commission property. At the end of the last century, apart from some red deer in *Cumloden Park*, near Newton Stewart, which belonged to the Earls of Galloway, there were few wild red deer at all in this part of Scotland, and it is only since about 1908 that they have started to appear on the open hill and in particular on *Cairnsmore* and *Merrick Hills*, the former, for many years, being leased by the Duke of Bedford.

James Nicholson, formerly the headkeeper on the *Cairnsmore* estate, gave me the following account of their first appearance on the ground. 'In the winter of 1908', he writes, 'I was living at Talnotry and saw, one morning, a hind and that year's calf, accompanied by a yearling on the Craigdews side of the Grey Mare's Tail burn, and that, as far as I know, was the commencement of the red deer at *Cairnsmore* and *Bargaly*.' Craigdews is about five miles (8 km) from *Cumloden Park* from where the deer probably originated.

Shortly after this the 11th Duke of Bedford introduced a stag from an English park – believed to be *Stoke Park*, Buckinghamshire – and according to the late (12th) Duke, this was the only occasion on which park blood had been introduced to the ground. However, I was informed by the late Captain C. E. Lucas – father of the present owner of *Warnham Park* – that his records show that, in 1900, one three-year-old stag and two hinds were ordered, to be dispatched to *Cairnsmore* and this was followed, two years later, with a further order for seven hinds. Whether these deer ever reached *Cairnsmore* to be released on the hill will probably never be known. For a number of years, however, there was a small deer park at *Cairnsmore* in which a number of red deer and wapiti hybrids were kept, but according to the late Duke these were never released on the hill but eventually returned to *Woburn*.

Early in the century two bull wapiti were introduced to *Cumloden Park*, and since then both wild and park deer have been obtained from Ross-shire and *Woburn* respectively. Over the years, and in particular during the War, the wild deer in the area have been infiltrated by escapees from *Cumloden Park*.

Many thousands of acres of former hill pasture in Galloway are now under forestry, and this has provided an ideal environment for the deer. There is little doubt that both habitat and the introduction of park blood early in the century has been responsible for the excellent quality of the deer in this part of Scotland.

It is only during the past thirty years or so that the Forestry Commission first started to make a charge for trophy shooting in some of their forests. But it is only recently that any trophy shooting has been permitted in Galloway, all the culling having been previously done by F.C. personnel.

One of the best heads to come out of Galloway was a 14-pointer, shot in Glen Trool by Willie Laurie of the Forestry Commission in 1981, which when assessed under C.I.C. formula scored out at 185.09 points – some 4.36 C.I.C. points more than the 'official' Scottish record trophy shot by C. E. Lucas at *Braulen* Inverness-shire in 1905 (180.73) points. The latter, however, must be designated as 'official' because it had been assessed under an international jury at the trophy exhibition in Budapest 1971.

In 1974 a 'royal' was shot in Galloway by I. Watret and sent to the 1981 International Exhibition in Plovdiv, Bulgaria, where it was assessed at 173.38 C.I.C. points (bronze medal).

An even larger Galloway royal, with an 'unofficial' score of 181.74 C.I.C. points (gold medal) was shot by a Forestry Commission ranger during the 1983 rut on Rowantree Hill, *Glentroop*

forest, which is only about 2 miles (3.2 km) from where the 14-pointer had been shot in 1981. Its carcase weight (clean) was 220 lb (100 kg), and since its age was estimated to be only six years by P. Radcliffe, Red Deer Research Officer of the Forestry Commission, had it been allowed to survive another four or five years, its antlers could well have made a new Scottish record. Although scoring some 3.35 C.I.C. points less than the previously mentioned 1981 14-pointer, it is a far more attractive head. Its tops, perhaps, could not be described as true cups, but they are well matched as compared to the straggling upper tines of the 1981 trophy.

Table 6 (page 178) compares the measurement of these two Galloway heads with the official Scottish record trophy from *Braulen* (Inverness-shire).

Trophy shooting is undoubtedly big business today, and many American and continental sportsmen will pay astronomical fees to shoot an outstanding trophy, even though its range may be restricted within a deer fence. On the Continent the antlers of deer are assessed according to the appropriate C.I.C. formula, and any score achieving a certain total qualifies for a gold, silver or bronze medal award – as well as a considerable increase to the basic trophy fee which, for exceptional trophies, may run into thousands of pounds.

It is only during the past thirty-five years or so, however, that the Forestry Commission first started to charge for trophy animals, but until about the early 1980s no permit shooting for red deer in Galloway had been allowed, all the culling being done by Forestry Commission personnel. Had, however, the 1983 'royal' been taken in one of the areas where permit shooting was allowed, then the charge to the permit holder, based on the 1981 Forestry Commission fees, would have been in the region of £800.

In eastern Europe, however, both these heads would only have ranked as bronze medal category, and would, in consequence, have cost slightly less – say about £600. However, it must be appreciated that a trophy of around 180 C.I.C. points, whilst outstanding for Scotland, is only small fry in eastern Europe, where a number of gold medal trophies with scores in excess of 250 C.I.C. points are shot each year, the twentieth-century world record head from Bulgaria (1968) having a score of 273.60 C.I.C. points. In fact, to wound and lose

Table 6   Two best Galloway red deer heads compared with the Scottish record head

	Galloway 1983			Galloway 1981			Braulen 1905		
	Left (cm)	Right (cm)	C.I.C. points	Left (cm)	Right (cm)	C.I.C. points	Left (cm)	Right (cm)	C.I.C. points
Length of antler (beam)	106.4	100.2	51.65	100.5	108.4	52.23	109.5	111.5	55.25
	(41¹⁵⁄₁₆ in)	(39⁷⁄₁₆ in)		(39½ in)	(42⅜ in)		(43⅛ in)	(43¹³⁄₁₆ in)	
Length brow tine	29.9	31.6	7.68	37.4	37.0	9.30	32.4	30.6	7.87
Length tray tine	25.2	20.5	5.71	25.5	24.6	6.26	24.1	26.8	6.36
Circum. coronet	21.0	21.0	21.00	22.9	22.7	22.80	22.1	21.8	21.95
Circum. lower beam	15.5	14.9	30.40	13.2	13.6	26.80	13.9	13.5	27.40
Circum. upper beam	13.9	14.1	28.00	15.3	15.4	30.70	12.3	13.0	25.30
Weight	5.4 kg		10.80	4.75 kg		9.50	5.05 kg		10.10
Inside span	84.0		3.00	94.0		3.00	77.0		2.00
	(33in)			(37 in)			(30¼ in)		
Number of tines	6	6	12.00	7	7	14.00	6	7	13.00
Beauty points									
Colour (0–2)			2.00			1.50			2.00
Pearling (0–2)			1.50			1.50			2.00
Tine ends (0–2)			1.50			1.50			2.00
Bay tines (0–2)			2.00			2.00			2.00
Crowns (0–10)			4.50			4.00			3.50
Penalty points									
Defects and									
irregularities (0–3)			—			—			—
Total C.I.C. points			181.74			185.09			180.73

For other Galloway trophies *see* pages 179, 181–187, 190

Some of the Galloway heads are displayed in the Forestry Commission Deer Museum at Clatteringshaws, New Galloway.

a gold medal trophy stag in Hungary could well cost the unlucky sportsman more than the price to shoot a Scottish record head, for the fine is based on 50 per cent of the estimated price of the lost trophy, which could well run into several thousand pounds. In this country, if a deer is hit and lost but only slightly wounded, the Forestry Commission imposes a fine, which in 1981 was £15. Should, however, the deer have been badly wounded and was not recovered, then, in addition to the £15 penalty, the client was also charged the value of the lost venison, so for a large Scottish stag the fine could well have amounted to about £160. See wounded deer - page 11.

As already mentioned, apart from red deer in *Cumloden* deer park, Newton Stewart, it is only since about 1908 that any red deer started to appear on the neighbouring *Cairnsmore* and *Merrick Hills*, and it is also recorded that, on at least one occasion, the late Duke of Bedford did introduce some park blood to the area. Although,

therefore, the deer in Galloway cannot be considered as representing pure indigenous Scottish blood, they are an excellent example of the quality of deer that an ideal environment can produce.

Best Reported Heads of the Stalking Seasons 1948–1995

Table A, Length   *179–185*

To qualify for inclusion in this Table, one or both antlers must have a length of 36 in (91.5 cm).

Table B, Inside Span   *185–188*

To qualify for inclusion in this Table, there must be an inside span measurement between each antler of 33 in (84 cm).

Table C, Scottish Multi-pointed Antlers 188–190

To qualify for inclusion in this Table the antlers must have fifteen or more points.

Sources of measurement

I.C.N.A. – I. C. N. Alcock
G. – Gray & Sons (taxidermist)
J.M. – John Macpherson & Son (taxidermist)
K.M. – K. MacArthur
O.M. – Owner's measurements
W.A.M. – W. A. Macleay & Son (taxidermist)
P.D.M. – P. D. Malloch & Son (taxidermist)
A. de N. – A. de Nahlik
G.K.W. – G. Kenneth Whitehead
M.W-W. – M. Wyndham-Wright (taxidermist)
R.W. – Rowland Ward

Table A – length

Antlers of a genuine wild Scottish red deer stag with a length of 37 in (94 cm) are well above average.

The largest recorded antlers of any stag in Scotland this century came from a 13-pointer shot by Captain C. E. Lucas at *Braulen* (Inverness-shire) in 1905, which had a length of 43⅛ in (109.5 cm) left, and 43¹³⁄₁₆ in (111.5 cm) right (*see* Table 6, page 178).

Since 1948, measurements of over 1,000 red deer antlers have been received from deer forests in Scotland, but for inclusion in this book a minimum length of 36 in (91.5 cm) has been set. During four seasons, however, none of the heads reported quite achieved this minimum figure, so for the years 1977, 1978, 1985 and 1992 the antlers with the longest beam have been included.

During this period the longest six heads, with antlers measuring 40 in (101.6 cm) or more, were reported from the following forests: *Kinrara* (Inverness-shire) and *Strathconon* (Ross-shire) (*see* page 181) and in Forestry area in Ayrshire (*see* page 183).

In 1995 a good fourteen-pointer of silver medal class was shot on Forestry Commission land on the Isle of Arran by Martin Corney, which scored out at 174.97 C.I.C. points. It had an average length of 31.6 in (80.4 cm), beam 5.4 in (13.7 cm) and inside span of 26.4 in (67 cm).

TABLE A – LENGTH

Date	Forest	Shot by	Number of points	Length		Inside span	Beam average	Source
			Left Right	*Left*	*Right*			
1948	Dunrobin, Sutherland	F. J. Pryce-Jenkins	6 + 5 = 11	37¼ 94.6	37½ 95.3	29¼ 74.3	4⅜ 11.1	J.M.
	Invercauld, Aberdeenshire	Baron Carl Ivel-Brockdorf	5 + 6 = 11	35¾ 90.8	37 94.0	27 68.6	4½ 11.4	J.M.
	Cairnsmore, Kirkcudbrightshire	?	6 + 6 = 12	36½ av. 92.7		32⅛ 81.6	5 12.7	J.M.
	Lochrosque, Ross-shire	Lt. Col. P. F. Benton Jones	5 + 5 = 10	36 91.4	35½ 90.2	29¼ 74.3	5¼ 12.3	J.M.
	Dunbeath, Caithness	Miss Judy Currie	4 + 4 = 8	35 88.9	36 91.4	31 78.7	5 12.7	J.M.
1949	Glenfeshie, Inverness-shire	J. Kennedy	= 8	37½ av. 95.3 av.		32½ 82.5	4½ 11.4	J.M.
	Knoydart, Inverness-shire	C. Jenkinson	5 + 6 = 11	37¼ av. 94.6 av.		27½ 69.8	4½ 11.4	J.M.
	Killilan, Ross-shire	Mrs E. G. M. Douglas	= 8	36½ av. 92.7 av.		30½ 77.5	5½ 14.0	J.M.
	Killilan, Ross-shire	Mrs E. G. M. Douglas	= 12	36 av. 91.4 av.		25¾ 65.4	5½ 14.0	J.M.
	Strathconon, Ross-shire	Maj. J. D. Lloyd	5 + 4 = 9	36 av. 91.4 av.		28¾ 73.0	4½ 11.4	J.M.

Year	Place	Name	Points	Measurement			Initials
1950	Benula, Ross-shire	G. A. Wolfkill	= 10	37 av. / 94.0 av.	30 / 76.2	5 / 12.7	W.A.M.
	Loch Choire, Sutherland	G. L. Wood	6 + 6 = 12	36 av. / 91.4 av.	26¾ / 68.0	4½ / 11.4	J.M.
	Mar, Aberdeenshire	Sir George Schuster	6 + 5 = 11	36 av. / 91.4 av.	25½ / 64.8	4⅞ / 12.4	J.M.
	Braeroy, Inverness-shire	R. Manningham-Buller M.P.	5 + 5 = 10	36 av. / 91.4 av.	23 / 58.4	5⅛ / 13.0	J.M.
1951	Meoble, Inverness-shire	J. A. P. Charrington	4 + 4 = 8	36½ av. / 92.7 av.	35½ / 90.2	4¾ / 12.1	J.M.
	Inverinate, Ross-shire	Mrs D. A. S. Bowlby	5 + 5 = 10	36 av. / 91.4 av.	29¼ / 74.3	5 / 12.7	J.M.
1952	Glencallater, Aberdeenshire	W. P. Scholes	5 + 5 = 10	36¼ av. / 92.7 av.	31¹⁄₁₆ / 78.9	5¼ / 13.3	G.K.W.
	Glenmazeran, Inverness-shire	Hon. Mrs Rhodes	6 + 6 = 12	36 av. / 91.4 av.	27 / 68.6	4¾ / 12.1	J.M.
	Eilanreach, Inverness-shire	Capt. The Hon M. E. Joicey	5 + 5 = 10	36 av. / 91.4 av.	28½ / 72.4	5½ / 14.0	J.M.
	Knoydart, Inverness-shire	A. L. Wills	5 + 4 = 9	36 av. / 91.4 av.	28¼ / 71.8	4¾ / 12.1	J.M.
1953	Glenfiddich, Banffshire	C. Ormiston	5 + 5 = 10	38½ av. / 97.8 av.	30¼ / 76.8	5⅛ / 13.0	J.M.
	Glendye, Kincardine	Maj. D. B. Foster	5 + 5 = 10	37 av. / 94.0 av.	34½ / 87.6	5 / 12.7	J.M.
	Glenkingie, Inverness-shire	G. Kenneth Whitehead	6 + 6 = 12	36⅛ av. / 91.7 av.	26¾ / 67.9	4¾ / 12.1	G.K.W.
	Glencanisp, Sutherland	E. Vestey	6 + 6 = 12	36 av. / 91.4 av.	29 / 73.7	4½ / 11.4	J.M.
1954	Dall (Loch Etive), Argyllshire	R. D. T. Gibson	5 + 5 = 10	36 av. / 91.4 av.	30 / 76.2	5⅞ / 14.9	G.K.W.
1955	Dougarie, (Arran) Bute	A. D. A. W. Forbes	6 + 6 = 12	36 av. / 91.4 av.	31¾ / 80.6	5 / 12.7	P.D.M.
	Cluanie, Ross-shire	H. Know	4 + 6 = 10	36 av. / 91.4 av.	25 / 63.5	4¾ / 12.1	W.A.M.
1956	Glendessary, Inverness-shire	R. Upton	4 + 4 = 8	36½ av. / 92.7 av.	29½ / 74.9	5 / 12.7	O.M.
	Scatwell, Ross-shire	A. J. Macdonald-Buchanan	7 + 7 = 14	36 av. / 91.4 av.	26⅜ / 67.0	5½ / 14.0	J.M.
1957	Strathconon, Ross-shire	Maj.-Gen. W. A. Fox-Pitt	6 + 5 = 11	37½ av. / 95.3 av.	28 / 71.1	5½ / 14.0	J.M.
	Lochgair, Argyllshire	A. G. Ferguson	6 + 6 = 12	37 av. / 94.0 av.	28¼ / 71.8	4⅞ / 12.4	J.M.
	Affaric, Inverness-shire	G. C. Shakerley	7 + 6 = 13	36¼ av. / 92.1 av.	27½ / 69.9	4½ / 11.4	J.M.
	Glenquoich, Inverness-shire	W. G. Gordon	5 + 5 = 10	36 av. / 91.4 av.	33 / 83.8	4⅜ / 11.1	J.M.
1958	Balmoral, Aberdeenshire	H.M. The Queen	6 + 5 = 11	35 av. / 88.9 av.	30½ / 77.5	4¾ / 12.1	J.M.

1959	Kinrara, Inverness-shire	Lord Bilsland	5 + 6 = 11	39½ *100.3*	40 *101.6*	27½ *69.8*	5 *12.7*	G.K.W.
	Glencalvie, Ross-shire	A. N. Hickley	4 + 5 = 9	37¾ *95.9*	37 *94.0*	32 *81.3*	4 9/16 *11.5*	G.K.W.
	Benmore (Cowal), Argyllshire	J. Maxwell	7 + 6 = 13	37½ *95.3*	36½ *92.7*	32¼ *81.9*	5 *12.7*	J.M.
	Glencanisp, Sutherland	R. A. Vestey	6 + 5 = 11	37 *94.0*	37 *94.0*	31 *78.7*	4¾ *12.1*	J.M.
	Loch Choire, Sutherland	Duke of Sutherland	6 + 7 = 13	37 *94.0*	36 *91.4*	30½ *77.5*	5½ *14.0*	J.M.
	Boreland, Perthshire	C. S. R. Stroyan	6 + 6 = 12	34½ *87.6*	36½ *92.7*	31 *78.7*	4¾ *12.1*	G.K.W.
1960	Hunthill, Angus	J. Svensson	5 + 5 = 10	35 *89.0*	36½ *92.7*	34 *86.4*	4¼ *10.8*	O.M.
	Glen Ey (Mar), Aberdeenshire	Major F. W. Strang-Steel	6 + 6 = 12	36½ *92.7*	35½ *90.2*	26 *66.0*	5 *12.7*	J.M.
1961	Arnisdale, Inverness-shire	Col. C. L. Hanbury	5 + 5 = 10	36¾ *93.3*	38 *96.5*	35¼ *89.5*	5 *12.7*	J.M.
	Ardgour, Argyllshire	Nigel A. Alington	6 + 6 = 12	36½ *92.7*	36 *91.4*	30¾ *78.0*	4½ *11.4*	J.M.
	Glenbanchor, Inverness-shire	Col. A. W. A. Smith	6 + 6 = 12	36½ *92.7*	35 *88.9*	29 *73.7*	4 *10.2*	J.M.
1962	Glenquoich, Inverness-shire	W. G. Gordon	7 + 6 = 13	36 *91.4*	36½ *92.7*	25 *63.5*	5¼ *13.3*	J.M.
1963	Galloway (F.C.), Kirkcudbrightshire	R. W. Hunter	6 + 6 = 12	37½ *95.3*	35½ *90.2*	29½ *74.9*	4¾ *12.1*	H.M.
	Garraries (F.C.), Kirkcudbrightshire	K. MacArthur	6 + 5 = 11	37¼ *94.6*	36⅝ *93.0*	34¾ *88.3*	4⅞ *12.4*	O.M.
1964	Carrick (F.C.), Ayrshire	R. W. Hunter	6 + 5 = 11	36¼ *92.1*	36 *91.4*	30½ *77.5*	5 *12.7*	H.M.
	Glenquoich, Inverness-shire	G. H. Bullard	6 + 5 = 11	35 *88.9*	36 *91.4*	30 *76.2*	4¼ *10.8*	H.M.
	Garraries (F.O.), Kirkcudbrightshire	J. Bridgeman	5 + 5 = 10	35 *88.9*	36 *91.4*	27¼ *69.2*	4 9/16 *11.5*	K.M.
	Glenkingie, Inverness-shire	Major Allan Cameron	5 + 6 = 11	34 *86.4*	36 *91.4*	30⅛ *76.5*	4⅛ *10.5*	H.M.
1965	Carrick (F.C.), Ayrshire	R. W. Hunter	6 + 6 = 12	39 *99.0*	39½ *100.3*	31 *78.7*	5½ *14.0*	H.M.
	Ardmore (Islay), Argyllshire	Lady Rosemary MacTaggart	7 + 6 = 13	38 *96.5*	36 *91.4*	27 *68.6*	5¼ *13.3*	H.M.
1966	Garraries (F.C.), Kirkcudbrightshire	R. A. Cimatti	6 + 5 + 11	41⅜ *105.0*	41⅜ *105.0*	29½ *75.8*	5¾ *14.6*	R.W.
	Strathconon, Ross-shire	J. Macdonald-Buchanan	6 + 6 = 12	40 *101.6*	39½ *100.3*	32½ *82.5*	5¼ *13.3*	J.M.
	Glen Ey (Mar), Aberdeenshire	Lady Strang-Steel	5 + 6 = 11	38 *96.5*	36½ *92.7*	24½ *62.2*	5½ *14.0*	O.M.
	Affaric, Inverness-shire	Miss Sylvia McClure	6 + 5 = 11	37 *94.0*	37¼ *94.6*	28½ *72.4*	4¾ *12.1*	J.M.
	Grannoch, Kirkcudbrightshire	R. G. B. Parker	6 + 5 = 11	36 *91.4*	37 *94.0*	29 *73.7*	5¼ *13.5*	J.M.

	Glenquoich,	W. G. Gordon	6 + 5 = 11	36½	34	32½	4½	J.M.
	Inverness-shire			*92.7*	*86.4*	*82.6*	*11.4*	
	Garraries,	R. A. Cimatti	6 + 6 = 12	36½	36½	21⅞	4½	R.W.
	Kirkcudbrightshire			*92.7*	*92.7*	*54.3*	*11.4*	
1967	Strathvaich,	R. Williams	4 + 4 = 8	39	38½	28½	4¾	J.M.
	Ross-shire			*99.0*	*97.8*	*72.4*	*12.1*	
	Glenquoich,	W. G. Gordon	6 + 6 = 12	38½	38	26	5⅞	J.M.
	Inverness-shire			*97.8*	*96.5*	*66.0*	*14.9*	
1968	Cluanie,	A. E. N. Hughes-	5 + 5 = 10	36	39	32½	5½	J.M.
	Ross-shire	Onslow		*91.4*	*99.0*	*82.5*	*14.0*	
	Cluanie,	Miss A. H.	6 + 5 = 11	37½	38½	31¼	5	J.M.
	Ross-shire	Robertson		*95.3*	*97.4*	*79.4*	*12.7*	
1969	Glenquoich East,	Lord Burton		39½	39½	30¼	5½	O.M.
	Inverness-shire			*100.3*	*100.3*	*76.8*	*14.0*	
	Gatehouse of Fleet,	I. Fowler	7 + 5 = 12	38½	37¾	33	5½	O.M.
	Kirkcudbrightshire			*97.8*	*95.9*	*83.8*	*14.0*	
	Cluanie,	A. N. Robertson	5 + 5 = 10	38	37⅛	26¼	4⅞	R.W.
	Ross-shire			*96.5*	*94.3*	*66.7*	*12.4*	
	Meggernie,	Lady Wills	6 + 7 = 13	34½	38	26⅝	5	R.W.
	Perthshire			*87.6*	*96.5*	*67.5*	*12.7*	
	Glenquoich,	C. R. V. Holt	6 + 6 = 12	36½	35	?	?	O.M.
	Inverness-shire			*92.7*	*88.9*			
	Cluanie,	Miss E. G.	5 + 6 = 11	35¼	36¼	29½	5½	O.M.
	Ross-shire	Robertson		*89.5*	*92.1*	*74.9*	*14.0*	
1970	Garraries (F.C.),	K. Macarthur	4 + 4 = 8	38	39	34½	5⅛	K.M.
	Kirkcudbrightshire			*96.5*	*99.0*	*87.6*	*13.0*	
	Garraries (F.C.),	K. Macarthur	5 + 4 = 9	37½	37	25	5⅝	K.M.
	Kirkcudbrightshire			*95.3*	*94.0*	*63.5*	*14.2*	
	Garraries (F.C.),	J. Good	4 + 5 = 9	37½	36	33	4 7/16	K.M.
	Kirkcudbrightshire			*95.2*	*91.4*	*83.8*	*11.2*	
	Invercauld,	Dr R. B. Dominick	6 + 6 = 12	37¼	37¼	24½	4¼	R.W.
	Aberdeenshire			*94.6*	*94.6*	*62.2*	*10.8*	
	Glenquoich,	A. D. Gordon	6 + 7 = 13	37	37	27	5½	O.M.
	Inverness-shire			*94.0*	*94.0*	*68.6*	*14.0*	
	Struy,	M. A. Spencer-	4 + 4 = 8	36	36	27	5¾	O.M.
	Inverness-shire	Nairn		*91.4*	*91.4*	*68.6*	*14.6*	
	Rhiedorrach,	G. T. Shoosmith	6 + 6 = 12	35	36	30	5¼	O.M.
	Perthshire			*88.9*	*91.4*	*76.2*	*13.3*	
	Glencally,	Major J. Gibb	5 + 5 = 10	35⅝	35⅝	25½	5	O.M.
	Angus			*90.4*	*90.4*	*64.7*	*12.7*	
1971	Monar,	Mrs C. Stroyan	7 + 6 = 13	37½	38	36½	5¼	O.M.
	Ross-shire			*95.3*	*96.5*	*92.7*	*13.3*	
	Dougarie,	S. C. Gibbs	5 + 4 = 9	36	34½	26½	4⅜	O.M.
	(Arran) Bute			*91.4*	*87.6*	*67.3*	*11.1*	
1972	West Argyllshire	Found dead	11	37	35¾	29¼	5	I.C.N.A
				94.0	*90.8*	*74.3*	*12.7*	
	Remony,	Dr C. Brown	5 + 4 = 9	35½	37	30¾	5¾	O.M.
	Perthshire			*90.2*	*94.0*	*78.1*	*14.6*	
	Glenkingie,	H. Wallace	4 + 4 = 8	36½ *av.*		26½	4¾	O.M.
	Inverness-shire			*92.7 av.*		*67.3*	*12.0*	

	West Argyllshire	?	6 + 6 = 12	36 *91.4*	35½ *90.2*	24¾ *62.9*	5 *12.7*	I.C.N.A.
1973	Private forestry, Ayrshire	Peter Forshaw	6 + 6 = 12	38¼ *97.2*	40¾ *103.5*	29⅝ *75.1*	5⅛ *13.0*	J.M.
	Cluanie, Ross-shire	Miss E. G. Robertson	6 + 6 = 12	38 *96.5*	37½ *95.3*	30½ *77.5*	5¼ *13.3*	O.M.
	Glenavon, Banffshire	D. S. Wills	5 + 4 = 9	37 *94.0*	36 *91.4*	27 *68.6*	5⅜ *13.6*	O.M.
	Badanloch, Sutherland	Captain Ritson	5 + 5 = 10	36½ *92.7*	36 *91.4*	31 *78.7*	4 *10.2*	O.M.
1974	Carrick (F.C.), Ayrshire	Lasse Sorensen	5 + 6 = 11	40⅛ *101.9*	36¾ *93.3*	36 *91.4*	5⅜ *13.6*	K.M.
	Kylestrome, Sutherland	Miss A. Broadhead	8 + 6 = 14	38 *96.5*	38½ *97.8*	31½ *80.0*	6 *15.2*	O.M.
	Garraries (F.C.), Kirkcudbrightshire	K. Macarthur	5 + 5 = 10	37½ *95.2*	36½ *92.7*	35 *89.0*	5¾ *13.2*	K.M.
	Garraries (F.C.) Kirkcudbrightshire	Henk Vlietman	6 + 6 = 12	37 *94.0*	36 *91.4*	26½ *67.3*	5½ *14.0*	K.M.
	Mar, Aberdeenshire	G. S. Panchaud	7 + 5 = 12	36 *91.4*	36 *91.4*	31½ *80.0*	4¾ *12.1*	W.F.
	Infield, Morayshire	Keeper	10 + 8 = 18	36 *91.4*	34 *86.4*	30½ *77.5*	6 *15.2*	W.F.
1976	Cairnsmore, Kirkcudbrightshire	Dr Sagel	4 + 4 = 8	37 *94.0*	38½ *97.8*	32 9/16 *82.6*	5 1/16 *12.8*	O.M.
	Sleat (Skye), Inverness-shire	N. Macpherson	4 + 4 = 8	37½ *95.3*	37 *94.0*	31¾ *80.6*	4¾ *12.1*	O.M.
	Hunthill, Angus	P. B. Hay	4 + 5 = 9	36 *91.4*	36¾ *93.3*	29¾ *75.6*	4 15/16 *12.6*	O.M.
	Glen Ey (Mar), Aberdeenshire	Sir W. Strang-Steel	5 + 5 = 10	34 *86.4*	36½ *92.7*	30 *76.2*	4¾ *12.1*	O.M.
	Fersit (Corrour), Inverness-shire	Captain Wallace	7 + 6 = 13	36 *91.4*	36 *91.4*	30½ *77.5*	6⅛ *15.6*	O.M.
1977	Ledgowan, Ross-shire	G. E. Ruggles-Brise	4 + 4 = 8	34 *86.4*	35 *88.9*	32½ *85.1*	4⅞ *12.3*	O.M.
1978	Fairburn, Ross-shire	Karl Frank	7 + 6 = 13	34¾ *88.3*	34¼ *87.0*	27¾ *70.5*	5½ *14.0*	O.M.
1979	Cluanie, Inverness-shire	Miss E. G. Robertson	6 + 7 = 13	38¼ *97.2*	38 *96.5*	31 *78.7*	5⅛ *13.0*	O.M.
	Strathconon, Ross-shire	A. J. Macdonald-Buchanan	7 + 5 = 12	37 *94.0*	36⅝ *93.0*	26¾ *68.0*	5½ *14.0*	O.M.
1980	Ardfin (Jura), Argyllshire	W. Macdonald	6 + 5 = 11	34 *86.4*	36 *91.4*	22 *55.9*	6 *15.2*	O.M.
1981	Ardtalla (Islay), Argyllshire	John MacTaggart	8 + 6 = 14	35 *88.7*	37⅞ *95.5*	30⅝ *78.0*	5⅞ *14.5*	A. de N.
	Dalclathic, Perthshire	Stalker	6 + 6 = 12	35¾ *90.8*	37½ *95.3*	23¼ *59.1*	5¼ *13.3*	O.M.
	Loch Choire, Sutherland	Lord Joicey	5 + 6 = 11	35 *88.9*	36½ *92.7*	28½ *72.4*	4⅞ *12.4*	O.M.

	Strathconon, Ross-shire	Mrs Philipson	6 + 5 = 11	36 *91.4*	35½ *90.2*	26¼ *66.7*	5⅜ *13.7*	O.M.
1982	Kinveachy, Perthshire	?	6 + 6 = 12	37½ *95.3*	34½ *87.6*	23½ *59.7*	4½ *11.4*	O.M.
	Glenartney, Perthshire	Lady Jane Willoughby	6 + 6 = 12	35½ *90.2*	36 *91.4*	26 *66.0*	5½ *14.0*	O.M.
1983	Glenavon, Banffshire	Sir Seton Wills	6 + 6 = 12	36½ *92.7*	36½ *92.7*	25½ *64.7*	6 *15.2*	O.M.
	Glenavon, Banffshire	C. Lloyd	6 + 6 = 12	36 *91.4*	36 *91.4*	26 *66.0*	7½ *19.0*	O.M.[1]
1984	Galloway, Kirkcudbrightshire	D. MacPhail	7 + 7 = 14	35⅞ *91.2*	37⅜ *95.0*	29½ *75.0*	5¼ *13.3*	G.K.W.[2]
	Sannox (*Arran*), Bute	H. Abram Sen.	6 + 6 = 12	35¾ *90.8*	37 3/16 *94.5*	27½ *69.8*	5⅜ *13.7*	G.K.W.[3]
	Strathconon, Ross-shire	J. I. H. Macdonald- Buchanan	6 + 6 = 12	36½ *92.7*	36¼ *92.1*	31¼ *79.4*	5⅛ *13.0*	O.M.
1985	Glenartney, Perthshire	Mrs Rotheschild	6 + 6 = 12	35¼ *89.5*	34½ *87.6*	29 *73.7*	4¾ *12.1*	O.M.
1986	Strathgrave, Ross-shire	S. A. C. Morgan	7 + 7 = 14	39 *99.0*	38½ *97.8*	?	5⅝ *14.0*	O.M.[4]
	Achnacarry North, Inverness-shire	?	4 + 4 = 8	36 *91.4*	35 *88.9*	27 *68.6*	4½ *11.4*	O.M.
1987	Mamore, Inverness-shire	H. G. Lange	7 + 6 = 13	36 *91.4*	36 *91.4*	23½ *59.7*	4¾ *12.1*	O.M.
1988	Kingairloch, Argyllshire	M. Thomson, (stalker)	5 + 6 = 11	37 *94.0*	36½ *92.7*	27 *68.6*	5¼ *13.3*	O.M.
	Arran, Isle of Bute	H. C. Abram	7 + 7 = 14	36 1/16 *92.0*	36 *91.4*	28 1/16 *71.3*	5⅛ *13.0*	G.K.W.
1989	Strathconon, Ross-shire	Mrs A. J. Macdonald- Buchanan	8 + 7 + 15	40½ *102.8*	41 *104.1*	27 *68.6*	5¼ *13.3*	O.M.[5]
	Glenartney, Perthshire	Mrs Rotheschild	6 + 6 = 12	35¾ *90.8*	36 *91.4*	29½ *74.5*	5 *12.7*	O.M.
1990	Ardfin (Jura), Argyllshire	H. Corbugy	8 + 7 = 15	37⅛ *95.0*	37⅛ *95.0*	31⅜ *79.7*	5 3/16 *13.3*	O.M.
	Langwell, Caithness	Mr Cameron-Rose	5 + 7 = 12	37½ *95.2*	36½ *92.7*	30 *76.2*	4⅜ *11.1*	O.M.
1991	Dunbeath, Caithness	L. Geddes (stalker)	4 + 4 = 8	38 *96.5*	38 *96.5*	32 *81.3*	5 *12.7*	O.M.
	Dunlossit (Islay), Argyllshire	Baron R. Schroder	6 + 7 = 13	36⅝ *93.0*	34⅝ *88.0*	32⅛ *81.7*	4⅞ *12.4*	O.M.
1992	Kinlochluichart, Ross-shire	J. Leslie Melville	6 + 5 = 11	34½ *87.6*	35 *88.9*	27 *68.6*	57 *12.7*	O.M.

1993	Ardnamurchan, Argyllshire	V. Becker	5 + 6 = 11	37½ / 95.3	37¾ / 95.9	32 / 81.3	5¼ / 13.3	O.M.
	Ardnamurchan, Argyllshire	W. Renidl	6 + 6 = 12	36¾ / 93.2	37 / 94.0	31⅛ / 79.0	5 / 12.5	O.M.
	Strathconon, Ross-shire	A. Branch	6 + 6 = 12	36½ / 92.7	35½ / 90.1	24 / 60.9	4¾ / 12.0	O.M.
	Glenisla, Angus	Roger Mitchell	6 + 6 = 12	36 / 91.4	35 / 88.9	26 / 66.0	5½ / 13.9	O.M.
1994	Kingairloch, Argyllshire	Mrs P. Strutt	6 + 6 = 12	36½ / 92.7	37½ / 95.3	30¼ / 76.8	5½ / 14.0	O.M.
	Kildermorie, Ross-shire	Found dead	7 + 7 = 14	36 / 91.4	35⅞ / 91.1	32½ / 82.5	4⅞ / 12.4	O.M.
	Caenlochan, Angus	Mr Patterson	6 + 6 = 12	35¼ / 89.5	36 / 91.4	23⅝ / 60.0	5⅞ / 14.9	O.M.
1995	Dunlossit, Islay Argyllshire	Baron August Finck	5 + 8 = 13	37⁷⁄₁₆ / 95.0	39 / 99.0	22⁷⁄₁₆ / 57.0	5⅝ / 14.3	O.M.
	Ardnamurchan, Argyllshire	K. Menz	6 + 6 = 12	35⅝ / 90.5	36¹⁄₁₆ / 91.7	34 / 86.4	5 / 12.8	O.M.
	Ardtalla (Islay) Argyllshire	David King	7 + 6 = 13	35⅜ / 90.0	35¾ / 91.0	28¾ / 73.0	4¾ / 12.0	O.M.

[1] Assuming that these measurements have been correctly taken, any circumference in excess of 6 in (15.2 cm) is unusual for a Scottish hill stag, and anything over 7 in (17.8 cm) quite exceptional.

[2] C.I.C. score 181.56 points.

[3] C.I.C. score 168.79 points.

[4] Forest enclosed – park blood.

[5] Feeder stag.

Table B – Inside Span

The inside span should be taken at the widest *inside* distance between the main beams. The spread is taken at the widest distance between the *outer* edge of the main beams or between tips of points, whichever is the greatest.

The widest recorded inside span came from an 11-pointer which was poached by Roualeyn Gordon-Cumming during the latter part of the last century in *Glenstrathfarrar* (Inverness-shire), with a measurement of 39½ in (*100.3* cm) – about 1½ in (3.8 cm) less than the spread. Its length was 35½ in (90.2 cm). Some damage to the right antler above the bay tine undoubtedly enlarged the spread (Millais 1897).

In 1959 an 8-pointer, with inside span measurement of 38 in (96.5 cm) was shot on *Glenkingie* (Inverness-shire) by Major A. Cameron, whilst a 10-pointer of similar span was obtained by the artist Brian Rawling, on *Ben Loyal* (Sutherland) in 1985. These two heads would appear to have the widest inside span of any stags shot in Scotland since the war.

Heads with an inside span measurement in excess of 33 in (84 cm) are not common in Scotland, and during the past forty-six years there were eleven in which no heads of this width were reported.

Table B lists the heads that have been shot in Scotland 1948–95 with an inside span measurement of 33 in (84 cm) or above.

TABLE B - INSIDE SPAN

Forest	Shot by	Date	No. of points L. R.	Inside span	Length L.	Length R.	Average beam
				Measurements (in/*cm*)			
Loyal,	B. Rawling	1985	5 + 5 = 10	38	31¼	34¾	$4\frac{15}{16}$
Sutherland				*96.5*	*79.4*	*88.3*	*12.4*
Glenkingie,	Major A. Cameron	1959	4 + 4 = 8	38	30½	27	4½
Inverness-shire				*96.5*	*77.5*	*68.6*	*11.4*
Badanloch,	Mrs G. Wood	1948	3 + 4 = 7	37½	35½	34½	?
Sutherland				*95.2*	*90.2*	*87.6*	
Talladh-a-Bheithe,	Capt R. Player	1969	5 + 5 = 10	36⅝	31½	31¾	4½
Perthshire				*93.0*	*80.0*	*80.6*	*11.4*
Monar,	Mrs C. Stroyan	1971	7 + 6 = 13	36½	37½	38	5¼
Ross-shire				*92.7*	*95.3*	*96.5*	*13.3*
Glutt,	Guest at Lochdhu	1962	5 + 5 = 10	36	35	*av.*	4¼
Caithness	Hotel			*91.4*	*89.0*		*10.8*
Affaric,	Major O.M. Gucst	1952	5 + 5 = 10	36	32½	*av.*	5½
Inverness-shire				*91.4*	*82.5*		*14.0*
Carrick,	Lasse Sorenson	1974	5 + 6 = 11	36	40⅛	36¾	5⅜
Ayrshire				*91.4*	*101.9*	*93.3*	*13.6*
Monar,	C. S. R. Stroyan	1969	5 + 5 + 10	36	31¾	31¾	5½
Ross-shire				*91.4*	*80.6*	*80.6*	*13.9*
Forsinard,	Herr Hinenberg	1976	5 + 4 = 9	36	31	31½	4⅛
Sutherland				*91.4*	*78.7*	*80.0*	*10.5*
Langwell,	Lady Anne Bentinck	1986	5 + 5 = 10	35½	35¼	34	4¾
Caithness				*90.2*	*89.5*	*86.4*	*12.1*
Meoble,	J. A. P. Charrington	1951	4 + 4 = 8	35½	36½	*av.*	4¾
Inverness-shire				*90.2*	*92.7*		*12.1*
Dalnessie,	I. S. Smillie	1965	5 + 5 = 10	35½	35½	35½	4½
Sutherland				*90.2*	*90.2*	*90.2*	*11.4*
Garraries (F.C.),	K. Macarthur	1971	6 + 5 = 11	35½	35½	34½	4¾
Kirkcudbright				*90.2*	*90.2*	*87.6*	*12.1*
Blackmount,	Mrs P. Fleming	1969	5 + 5 + 10	35½	35	34	5*
Argyllshire				*90.2*	*89.0*	*86.4*	*12.7*
W. Benula,	Mrs D. A. S. Bowlby	1957	6 + 6 = 12	35½	33½	*av.*	4½
Ross-shire				*90.2*	*85.1*		*11.4*
Arnisdale,	Col. C. L. Hanbury	1961	5 + 5 = 10	35½	36¾	38	5
Inverness-shire				*89.5*	*93.3*	*96.5*	*12.7*
Hunthill,	C. B. Amery	1976	5 + 5 = 10	35¼	32¾	31¾	4½
Angus				*89.5*	*83.2*	*80.6*	*11.4*
Garraries (F.C.),	K. Macarthur	1974	5 + 5 = 10	35	37½	36½	$5\frac{3}{16}$
Kirkcudbright				*89.0*	*95.2*	*92.7*	*13.2*
Garrygualach,	J. Gillespie	1964	5 + 5 = 10	35	34½	34½	4½
Inverness-shire				*89.0*	*87.6*	*87.6*	*11.4*
Killilan,	Mrs E. G. M. Douglas	1958	5 + 5 = 10	35	32	*av.*	5⅛
Ross-shire				*89.0*	*81.3*		*13.0*
Ben Armine,	M. R. M. Reed	1994	5 + 5 = 10	35	31½	31½	4¾
Sutherland				*89.0*	*80.0*	*80.0*	*12.0*
Wyvis,	Viscount	1972	5 + 5 = 10	35	30½	*av.*	4
Ross-shire	Mountgarret			*89.0*	*77.5*		*10.2*
Ben Loyal,	L. Foghseaard	1994	5 + 5 = 10	35	29¼	*av.*	4⅜
Sutherland				*89.0*	*74.3*		*11.0*

Location	Name	Year	Points			
Garraries (F.C.), Kirkcudbright	K. Macarthur	1963	6 + 5 = 11	34¾ / 88.3	37¼ / 94.6 av.	4⅞ / 12.4
Ardnamurchan, Argyllshire	E. Dass	1995	6 + 6 = 12	34⅝ / 88.0	35¾ / 91.0 · 35¹⁵⁄₁₆ / 91.3	4¾ / 12.1
Garraries (F.C.), Kirkcudbright	K. Macarthur	1970	4 + 4 = 8	34½ / 87.6	38 / 96.5 · 39 / 99.0	5⅛ / 13.0
Corrievarkie, Perthshire	J. Loder	1964	4 + 4 = 8	34½ / 87.6	33½ / 85.1 · 33½ / 85.1	?
Strone, Ross-shire	N. Jardine-Paterson	1974	2 + 2 = 4	34½ / 87.6	29½ / 74.9 · 29 / 73.7	3⅝ / 9.1
Badanloch, Sutherland	B. Lyall (understalker)	1987	4 + 4 = 8	34¼ / 87.0	27 / 68.6 · 27 / 68.6	4⅝ / 11.7
Ardnamurchan, Argyllshire	K. Menz	1995	6 + 6 = 12	34 / 86.4	35⅝ / 90.5 · 36¹⁄₁₆ / 91.7	5 / 12.8
Hunthill, Angus	J. Svensson	1960	5 + 5 = 10	34 / 86.4	35 / 89.0 · 36½ / 92.7	4¼ / 10.8
Strathconon, Ross-shire	Mr Wallace	1993	5 + 5 = 10	34 / 86.4	34 / 86.4 · 35 / 88.9	5 / 12.7
Glenquoich, Inverness-shire	W. G. Gordon	1967	5 + 5 = 10	34 / 86.4	35 / 89.0 · 35 / 89.0	4¾ / 12.1
Strathvaich, Ross-shire	J. N. M. Frame	1971	5 + 6 = 11	34 / 86.4	33 / 83.8 · 33½ / 85.1	5 / 12.7
Attadale, Ross-shire	A. D. P. Pearson	1965	5 + 5 = 10	34 / 86.4	33 / 83.8 · 32½ / 82.5	4½ / 11.4
Reay, Sutherland	?	1980	3 + 3 = 6	34 / 86.4	32½ / 82.5 · 32½ / 82.5	4½ / 11.4
Guisachan, Inverness-shire	Col. A. H. Wilkie	1954	6 + 6 = 12	34 / 86.4	32½ / 82.5 av.	4⅝ / 11.7
Glenquoich, Inverness-shire	C. R. V. Holt	1969	4 + 4 = 8	34 / 86.4	32 / 81.3 · 32 / 81.3	?
Torrish, Sutherland	R. Strutt	1960	6 + 5 = 11	34 / 86.4	29½ / 74.9 · 30½ / 77.5	4½ / 11.4
Strone, Ross-shire	J. H. Dewhurst	1976	3 + 3 = 6	34 / 86.4	30 / 76.2 · 29½ / 74.9	4½ / 11.4
Badanloch, Sutherland	D. Hodgekiss	1994	3 + 3 = 6	34 / 86.4	23½ / 59.7 · 25 / 63.5	4⅞ / 12.3
Caenlochan, Angus	John Leslie	1961	5 + 4 = 9	33¼ / 84.5	33 / 83.8 · 31½ / 80.0	4¾ / 12.1
Braelangwell, Ross-shire	B. C. Matthew	1957	5 + 6 = 11	33¾ / 85.7	31 / 78.7 av.	4¼ / 10.8
Glengarry (F.C.) Inverness-shire	Herr W. Fauper	1978	5 + 5 = 10	33½ / 85.1	30½ / 77.5 · 32 / 81.3	?
Duchally, Ross-shire	G. G. A. Gregson	1963	4 + 4 = 8	33½ / 85.1	30 / 76.2 · 31½ / 80.0	4¾ / 12.1
Ben Hee, Sutherland	C. H. S. Garton	1983	5 + 5 = 10	33½ / 85.1	30 / 76.2 · 29½ / 74.9	4½ / 11.4
Craig, Argyllshire	C. S. MacFarlane-Barlow	1979	4 + 4 = 8	33¼ / 84.4	31¼ / 79.4 · 31¼ / 79.4	3½ / 8.9
Gatehouse of Fleet, Kirkcudbright	I. Fowler	1969	7 + 5 = 12	33 / 83.8	38½ / 97.8 · 37¾ / 95.9	5½ / 14.0
Garraries (F.C.), Kirkcudbright	J. Good	1970	4 + 5 = 9	33 / 83.8	37½ / 95.2 · 36 / 91.4	4⁷⁄₁₆ / 11.2
Glenquoich, Inverness-shire	W. G. Gordon	1957	5 + 5 = 10	33 / 83.8	36 / 91.9 av.	4⅜ / 11.1

Affaric,	C. Singleton	1987	6 + 6 = 12	33	35	35½	5
Inverness-shire				*83.8*	*88.9*	*90.2*	*12.7*
Glenartney,	Baroness Willoughby	1990	6 + 6 = 12	33	33	33¼	5
Perthshire				*83.8*	*83.8*	*84.4*	*12.7*
Ben Armine,	Lt. Col. A. M. Lyle	1963	6 + 5 = 11	33	32	34	4½
Sutherland				*83.8*	*81.3*	*86.4*	*11.4*
Dalnaspidal,	Peter Kennedy	1994	6 + 6 = 12	33	32	32	5
Perthshire				*83.8*	*81.3*	*81.3*	*12.7*
Kinloch,	A. W. G. Sykes	1989	5 + 4 = 9	33	31½	31	4⅝
Sutherland				*83.8*	*80.0*	*78.7*	*11.7*
Dunlossit (Islay),	Dr M. von Clemm	1991	6 + 6 = 12	33	29¾	30⅛	4⅞
Argyll				*83.8*	*75.6*	*76.5*	*12.4*
Knoydart,	Mr Fairy	1993	6 + 5 = 11	33	28¾	29¾	3⅞
Inverness-shire				*83.8*	*73.0*	*75.6*	*9.8*
Langwell,	Michael Watt	1989	5 + 3 = 8	33	28½	29¾	5½
Caithness				*83.8*	*72.4*	*75.6*	*14.0*
Achnacarry S.,	Mrs D. Laird	1977	6 + 6 = 12	33	28	28	5 3/16
Inverness-shire				*83.8*	*71.1*	*71.1*	*13.1*

* Feeder stag.

TABLE C – SCOTTISH MULTI-POINTED ANTLERS

The ideal wild Scottish head should have twelve long evenly well-developed points with all its 'rights' (brows, bays and trays) and three on top in the form of a crown or cup. That is a true 'royal', as featured in Landseer's famous *Monarch of the Glen* (1851), the model being a royal shot on *Braemore* forest, Ross-shire.

A 14-pointer - similar to a royal but with one of the crown tines bifurcating - is sometimes referred to as an 'imperial', but there seems no justification in this description. More than fourteen points on a *wild* Scottish head detracts from its beauty, but can be admired on park, farmed and continental heads. A truly wild deer, unless extensively fed in winter, can only produce a certain amount of antler, and when extra points are produced the antler points tend to become palmated, and length is sacrificed.

In the last century a stag was shot in the Cromarty Woods, Ross-shire with 22 'somewhat malformed points' (Millais 1913). In 1893 a 20-pointer was shot on *Glenkingie* (Inverness-shire) by Lord Burton which was believed to be an ex-Stoke park stag (*see* page 116). These two would appear to be the highest number of points on a stag shot in Scotland outside a deer park or deer farm, where heads of over 34 points have been recorded.

During the inter-War period a 19-pointer was shot on *Strathconon* (Ross-shire) in 1939. It was a wild stag that was kept in an enclosure, and on the outbreak of War, Captain C. Combe, the owner, decided it should be shot.

16-pointers were shot in 1925 on *Caenlochan* (Angus) by Major General Sir Colin MacKenzie, in 1926 on *Coignafearn* (Inverness-shire) by Mrs Latilla, and in 1935 on *Fasnakyle* (Inverness-shire) by P. M. Stewart. None of these heads exceeded 33½ in (85 cm) in length.

During the 1966 season, however, a stag with 21 points was seen on *Glomach* (Ross-shire) on 14 October. It was observed for about twenty minutes at a range of only 40 yards (36 m). It would appear to have been a stranger to the ground, but what became of it or where it had come from, I never discovered.

The following is a list of multi-pointed heads from stags killed in Scotland since 1948 which are reported to have carried 15 or more points. Due to palmation some, however, cannot fulfill the correct description of a tine or point which should be a minimum length of ¾ in (2 cm).

TABLE C – SCOTTISH MULTI-POINTED ANTLERS

Forest	Shot by	Date	No. of points L. R.	Length L.	Length R.	Inside Span	Average beam
				Measurements (in/*cm*)			
18 points							
Infield, Morayshire*	Keeper	1974	10 + 8 = 18	36 *91.4*	34 *86.4*	30½ *77.5*	6 *15.2*
Inverbroom, Ross-shire	L. J. Haes	1955	10 + 8 = 18†	21¾ *55.2*	*av.*	23⅜ *59.3*	3¾ *9.5*
16 points							
Strone, Ross-shire	Found dead	1972	8 + 8 = 16	33⅛ *84.1*	32 1/16 *81.4*	23 1/16 *58.6*	4½ *11.4*
Tarbert, Jura, Argyllshire	P. D. Young	1965	8 + 8 = 16	33 *83.8*	33 *83.8*	24 *61.0*	5¼ *13.3*
Cluanie, Inverness-shire	Miss E. G. Robertson	1970	8 + 8 = 16	32½ *82.5*	33 *83.8*	27 *68.6*	5 *12.7*
Achdalieu, Inverness-shire	K. Ritchie	1981	8 + 8 = 16	31½ *80.0*	32½ *82.5*	?	4¾ *12.1*
Affaric, Inverness-shire	St John Hartnell	1985	8 + 8 = 16	25 *63.5*	25 *63.5*	27 *68.6*	4¾ *12.1*
15 points							
Strathconon, Ross-shire	Mrs A. J. Macdonald-Buchanan	1989	8 + 7 = 15	40½ *102.8*	41 *104.1*	27 *68.6*	5¼ *13.3*
Ardfin, Jura, Argyllshire	H. Corbugy	1990	8 + 7 = 15	37⅛ *95.0*	37⅛ *95.0*	31⅜ *79.5*	5¼ *13.3*
Strathconon, Ross-shire	A. J. Macdonald-Buchanan	1979	7 + 8 = 15	37 *94.0*	36⅝ *93.0*	26¾ *68.0*	5½ *14.0*
Langwell, Caithness	M. Watt	1972	15	35 *88.9*	35 *88.9*	29 *73.7*	5 *12.7*
Dunlossit, Islay, Argyllshire	Comm. M. Forsyth-Grant	1991	8 + 7 = 15	34⅝ *88.0*	33 *84.0*	27½ *70.0*	5 *12.7*
Glencarron, Ross-shire	A. I. Sladen	1957	7 + 8 = 15	34½ *87.6*	*av.*	30½ *77.5*	4⅜ *11.1*
Ederline, Argyllshire	E. Maclean	1970	6 + 9 = 15	32 *81.3*	34 *86.4*	18½ *47.0*	4⅞ *12.4*
W. Monar & Pait, Ross-shire	C. S. R. Stroyan	1992	8 + 7 = 15	33½ *85.0*	33¾ *83.8*	30.0 *76.2*	6½ *16.5*
Cairnsmore, Kirkcudbright	G. Kenneth Whitehead	1955	8 + 7 = 15	33⅞ *86.0*	32¾ *83.2*	26¾ *68.0*	5½ *13.8*
Glenmazeran, Inverness-shire	W. R. Benyon	1989	7 + 8 = 15	33 *83.8*	33¾ *85.7*	22⅜ *56.8*	5 *12.7*
Glenquoich, Inverness-shire	W. G. Gordon	1956	7 + 8 = 15	33 *83.8*	*av.*	27 *68.6*	4½ *11.4*
Glen Ey, Mar, Aberdeenshire	J. T. Gore	1967	8 + 7 = 15	32 *81.3*	32½ *82.5*	26 *66.0*	5 *12.7*
Wyvis, Ross-shire	Viscount Mountgarret	1976	8 + 7 = 15	32¼ *81.9*	31½ *80.0*	28½ *72.4*	4½ *11.4*
Killin, Perthshire	R. S. Stroyan	1950	15	31½ *80.0*	*av.*	28½ *72.4*	5 *12.7*
Achentoul, Sutherland	Lt.-Col. Sir H. Nutting	1950	8 + 7 = 15	30¾ *78.1*	*av.*	22½ *57.2*	4 *10.2*

Glenavon,	?	1974	15	29½	30	30	5
Banffshire				*74.9*	*76.2*	*76.2*	*12.7*
Inveraray,	Herr Helmut Sholten	1982	7 + 8 = 15	30½	29⅞	28	4¼
Argyllshire				*77.5*	*75.4*	*71.1*	*10.8*
Brodick, Arran,	C. Fforde	1967	8 + 7 = 15	30	29½	26	5¼
Bute				*76.2*	*74.9*	*66.0*	*13.3*
Garraries,	K. Macarthur	1966	8 + 7 = 15	29½	29½	22⅜	4¼
Kirkcudbright				*74.9*	*74.9*	*56.8*	*10.8*
Glenavon,	D. S. Wills	1978	8 + 7 = 15	29½	28½	21	5¼
Banffshire				*74.9*	*72.4*	*53.3*	*13.3*
Dalnaspidal,	?	1949	7 + 8 = 15	28¾ *av.*		23½	4¾
Perthshire				*73.0*		*59.7*	*12.1*
Ben Damph	Maj. C. A. H. M.	1948	8 + 7 = 15	28½	28¼	20	4¼
Ross-shire	Noble			*72.4*	*71.7*	*50.8*	*10.8*
Ben Loyal,	Count Adam W. J.	1992	8 + 7 = 15	28½	27⅛	25⅜	4⅝
Sutherland	Knuth			*72.4*	*69.0*	*64.5*	*11.7*
Inveraray,	H. H. Johnson	1959	7 + 8 = 15	?		29¼	?
Argyllshire						*74.3*	

* Probably descended from some Warnham park (Sussex) stags introduced to Pitgavenny in about 1940–43 (*see* page 115).

† Palmated tops, and could more correctly be described as a 16-pointer. Upper points ill defined.

Chapter 26

Weights of Scottish Red Deer

Stags – General

Generally speaking, reference to the average weight of stags killed on a Scottish deer forest during a season is not a very satisfactory statistic, for the weight of a stag will vary tremendously depending on whether shot before, during or after the rut. It is probable that a wild stag, weighing about 16 stone (100 kg) 'clean' before the commencement of the rut, could lose about 30 per cent of its weight if faced with a hard rut, and with many hinds to serve. Moreover, as one forest owner succinctly put it, there is a great temptation on the part of the stalker to 'forget', in the reckoning, one or two 'piners' so as to keep the average up.

Prior to the 1960s most carcases were butchered in the estate larder, where they were weighed immediately on arrival from the hill, and included the *complete* carcase along with the 'pluck' (heart, lungs and liver), the only absentee being the gralloch which had, of course, been removed immediately after the stag had been shot, and left on the hill. The majority of carcases today, along with the 'pluck', which is required for veterinary inspection, are collected daily from estate larders 'in the skin', with only head and feet removed. So, possibly, not so much attention is now paid to home weighings as formerly, for it is the game dealer's weight that brings in the revenue.

Some forests ignore the weight of 'piners' in their reports and record only the average weight for, perhaps, say twenty of the total number of twenty-five stags killed. This is probably the wisest course to take, and I entirely agree with Sir Peter Walker-Okeover, the owner of *Glenmuick* (Aberdeenshire), when he suggests that recording an average weight for *all* stags killed 'may give the wrong impression, for the aim should be to shoot *all* bad stags as early in life as possible – weight should, therefore, never be a consideration for selection, but rather the opposite'. A stag is seldom weighed before removal of the gralloch (stomach and entrails) as this has been removed before the carcase reaches the larder. Assuming the stag is not badly run, the gralloch of an early September stag weighing about 16 stone (100 kg), 'clean' will weigh about 40–50 lb (18–22kg), so this can be added to obtain an approximate live weight.

Formerly, it was universal practice to weigh the carcase 'clean' i.e. with gralloch removed, but including heart and liver which are both edible, and the lungs which could be used for the dog. If, therefore, heart, lungs and liver have been excluded from the weight, depending on the size of the beast, the difference would be up to about a stone (6.3 kg) as follows:

	lb	kg
Heart	2½–3	1.1–1.4
Liver	4–5	1.8–2.3
Lungs	5–6	2.3–2.7
	11½–14	5.2–6.4

It is evident that some of the reported 'average weights' cannot possibly be true average weights if all beasts shot have been taken into account. For instance, in 1965, one forest reported an average weight of 13 st 6 lb (85.3 kg) for 80 stags killed, yet the weight of the two heaviest for that season were only 16 st (101.6 kg) and 13 st 7 lb (85.7 kg).

During the 1948 season *Mar* (Aberdeenshire) had the remarkable average of 19 stone (120.6 kg) for the 16 stags killed on the Home beat, the heaviest being 21 st 7 lb (136.5 kg). On this particular beat, the deer were able to enjoy both good feed and shelter, but even so, it is a remarkably good average. Both *Knoydart* and

North Morar (Inverness-shire), which then belonged to Lord Brocket, also had exceptionally good weights that season, the overall average for the eighty stags shot being 16 st 2 lb (102.5 kg). The first forty stags of this total averaged out at 17 st 2 lb (108.8 kg), but the final lower figure was due to the loss in weight occurred by the rut.

During the 1955 stalking season weights were very disappointing, for those deer which had survived the harsh winter of 1954–55 were not helped by the dry summer that followed, and in consequence the average weight of stags from many forests was down by about a stone (6.3 kg). Although the first grass of 1955 came early, the summer that followed was one of the driest on record, and grass soon became so parched that it was surprising that the general condition of the deer was as good as it was. Nevertheless, some extremely low average weights were recorded that autumn, particularly from Aberdeenshire. On the *Derry* and *Home* beats of *Mar* forest, for instance, the average weight was only 11½ stone (73 kg) for 32 and 29 stags respectively. The 29 stags killed on *Glen Ey* beat of *Mar* weighed slightly better at 14 stone (88.9 kg), but even this was about 1½ stone (9.5 kg) lighter than normal for this ground. Whilst the method of weighing may have been different to that being practised in 1955, a difference of 7 st 6 lb (47.2 kg) between the average weight of stags coming off the Home beat of *Mar* seven years previously is remarkable (*see* above).

It would appear that fifty or more years ago the reported average weighs were slightly higher than they are today, but this is perhaps hardly surprising, for the average age of stag reaching the larder then was probably higher. This, unfortunately, is the result of commercial stalking which has developed throughout Scotland in recent years, allowing fewer stags now to reach maturity (*see* page 165).

Several owners have complained that their average weights have suffered owing to small beasts being shot in error. This, of course, can easily happen when mist and rain prevent a more careful study of the intended target, but the chief culprit must be the paying client who must shoot a stag regardless of quality on, perhaps, his only one or two days on the hill.

By 1966 a number of forest owners were expressing concern that, although they were trying to spare all good young and heavy stags, this class of beast had little chance of survival with so much 'butcher-shooting' taking place. Unfortunately, venison prices were improving and since there was also, at last, a sale for venison on the home market, it only encouraged the shooting of the biggest and best. Indeed, shooting to maintain a good average weight for the season, rather than to spoil it by killing off light-bodied beasts with miserable heads, is undoubtedly bad forest management, but the latter will generally not suit the butcher or trophy hunter.

During 1988 *Ben Loyal* (Sutherland) had the remarkable average weight of 17 st 4½ lb (110 kg) for 12 stags – a stone (6.3 kg) heavier than in 1987, and bettering the previous record for the forest in 1985 by 3½ lb (1.6 kg). The following season (1989) the average dropped to 14 st 12 lb (94.3 kg) for fourteen stags. In contrast, one of the lowest average weights in recent years came from *Kylestrome* (Sutherland), due to the fact that it was decided, in 1985, to shoot no stag with more than seven points, and concentrate only on animals of poor quality. As a consequence, the average weight for the thirty-five stags shot that year was 11 st 2 lb (70.7 kg) – about a stone (6.3 kg) lighter than the average for the previous season. Carcases on *Kylestrome* are weighed *without* heart and liver, which would account for a further three quarters of a stone (4.7 kg).

One of the best trophies shot in 1978 was an extremely heavy 13-pointer shot by Karl Frank on *Fairburn* (Ross-shire), the measurements of which were: length 34¾ in (88.3 cm) left; 34¼ in (87.6 cm) right; beams, left and right 5½ in (14 cm); inside span 27¾ in (70.5 cm). Even more impressive was the weight – 26 st 12 lb (170.5 kg) – which would appear to be the second heaviest stag shot in Ross-shire this century, one of 27 st 5 lb (173.7 kg) having been shot at *Kildermorie* in 1938. Roderick Stirling, the owner of *Fairburn*, assured me that it was 'a truly wild animal' and had been shot on the open hill where it had regularly been coming to the rut for the previous few years. It was not known where the stag had wintered, but it had not joined the feeders on neighbouring *Strathconon* (Ross-shire), so had not come from there. It was concluded, therefore, that it had probably spent most of the year in the woods along Strathglass on either *Erchless* or *Struy* estates (Inverness-shire). There is, of course, now a deer farm at *Struy*, which is situated 8 miles (12.8 km) to the south, with *Erchless* intervening, but deer farming only started there in 1980–81, so it could not have come from there. In my opinion it was probably an escapee from *Strathgarve* (Ross-shire) deer park which is situated only some 10 miles (16 km) to the north beyond the Conon river and Loch Garve (*see* page 166).

There are, of course, a number of reasons that can account for the sudden appearance of a weighty monarch. Stags that go 'crop-raiding' will generally weigh considerably more. A stag, which had been raiding *Foich* Lodge (Ross-shire) gardens in 1965, weighed 21 st 10 lb (137.9 kg) when shot, whilst a crop-raider from *Glenmuick* (Aberdeenshire) was only half a stone (3.2 kg) lighter.

A stag weighing 21 st 3 lb (134.7 kg) was shot on *Killiechonate* (Inverness-shire) during the 1965 season. It was believed that this beast 'could have been a semi-pet stag which grazed in a neighbouring crofting township with comparatively good feeding, for it hadn't returned to its base by end of November'.

The deer on the Island of Lewis (Ross-shire) are small compared to mainland deer, and there is no record of any stag having achieved a weight of 17 stone (108 kg). In 1923 a stag was shot on *Morsgail*, weighing 16 st 4 lb (103.4 kg) which would appear to be the heaviest on record for the island. The average weight during the past ten years on *Park*, the largest forest on the island, has been about 11½ stone (73 kg).

On the question of average weights, this of course depends very much on numbers being shot and the type of animal being culled. Some forests work to a policy of not shooting any 'master stag'. One of these is the R.S.P.B. property of *Abernethy* (Inverness-shire), and during 1992, out of a total cull of 82 stags (81 shot and 1 found dead), only 10 stags were estimated to be more than six years of age – the oldest being an eleven-year-old. The other age groups were divided up as follows: six-year-olds 9, five-year-olds 23, four-year-olds 10, three-year-olds 7, two-year-olds 12, one-year-olds 10.

Stags shot before the rut will obviously weigh their best, and on *Badanloch* (Sutherland), due to winter-feeding, many more stags than formerly, estimated to number around the 350 mark, are now wintering on the forest, and this has enabled the stalkers to kill about 50 per cent of the stag cull during September, thus enabling stalking to end by about 15 October before the stags are not much run.

Once past mid-September and the onset of the rut, average weights will generally start to tumble – some quite dramatically so – as the stags rapidly lose condition and become 'run'. Not so, however, on *Glenfeshie* (Inverness-shire) in 1993 – a season which followed an exceptional growth of grass on the hill during the summer and autumn months. During that autumn, not only was the average weight for the season up by half a stone (3.2 kg) on 1992, but there was a gradual *increase* in average weights throughout the season as follows:

Month	Number of stags shot	Average weight
July	22	13 st 2 lb (83.4 kg)
August	45	13 st 3 lb (83.9 kg)
September	44	13 st 10 lb (87.1 kg)
October	75	14 st 9 lb (92.9 kg)

Average weight for 186 stags – 13 st 12¾ lb   (88.3 kg)

Now that many forestry fences are rapidly falling into disrepair, an increasing number of stags weighing in excess of 18 stone (114 kg) are being shot on the open hill – the stags having vacated their woodland retreat to join the hinds for the rut – before returning, if not by then a statistic, to their 'costa foresta' for the winter months.

Islay (Argyllshire) has always produced some very heavy stags, and during the 1989 season at least eight stags came off this island with weights in excess of 20 stone (127 kg). These included five from *Dunlossit* – heaviest 22 st 8 lb (143.3 kg); 2 from *Ardtalla* – heaviest 21 st (133.4 kg); and one from *Sanaigmore* 23 st 4 lb (147.8 kg), which happened to be the heaviest stag of the year reported from Scotland.

At the lower end of the scale, during the same season two stags, each weighing only 8½ stone (53.9 kg) and both estimated to be about twenty years of age, were shot on *Loch Choire* (Sutherland).

Appearances can be deceptive, and often when a carcase reaches the larder the weight has been lower than anticipated. It is a case of plenty of fat around the kidneys etc., but little lean meat, and this, of course, cannot be seen until the beast is hanging in the larder. On the hill, however, one can generally distinguish youth from age, and a young beast, if outstanding, should always be given the chance to mature, and something less promising shot, even if its weight will be disappointing on the scales.

Variation in spleen weights during the rut

The spleen acts as a scavenger in removing old or damaged red blood cells, and other particles from the blood. It also plays an important part in fighting infection.

In human beings, an enlarged spleen is a typical symptom of a number of infectious diseases such as typhoid fever, malaria and syphilis.

In deer it would appear that during the rut there is also an enlargement of the spleen, but further research is required.

So far as I am aware no one has yet made a study of the relation between spleen weight and the rut. In Scotland it is seldon that the rut on the mainland starts in earnest before about the last week of September – in some seasons not until the first week of October.

During the 1975 season the spleen weights of eighteen Scottish red deer stags were taken just prior to and during the rut, the spleen being weighed with a spring balance immediately after the stag was shot. The results were as follows:

Period	No. of stags	Average spleen weight	Heaviest spleen weight
26 Sept-1 Oct	5	249.5 g (8 oz)	276 g (8⅞ oz)
1 Oct-10 Oct	8	367.2 g (11¾ oz)	500 g (1 lb)
11 Oct-20 Oct	5	416.0 g (13⅜ oz)	620 g (1¼ lb)

From the few weighings I have taken it would appear that there is a comparable increase in weight of spleen in roe and sika deer during the rut.

It will be appreciated that these weights cover only a very brief period and are, therefore, neither complete nor conclusive. For a more complete picture, spleen weights will have to be taken throughout the twelve months, and probably from animals of similar age. Furthermore, hinds are not normally shot during the rut, but doubtless a number shot in late October or early November will have been with a rutting stag. It is not known, therefore, if there is any change in the hinds' spleen weights during the period of the rut, but I would think probably not, for there is no comparable loss in condition of the hind at this period.

Hinds – General

The average weight of a wild Scottish hind will vary between 7 and 9 stone (44–57 kg), with an occasional beast that has had access to crops or woodland exceeding 10 stone (63 kg).

In 1982 a hind weighing 12 stone (76.2 kg) 'clean' was shot during the second week of November on *Ardtalnaig* (Perthshire) which, with head and feet removed, weighed out at 9½ stone (60.3 kg) dealers weight.

This is about 1½ stone (9.5 kg) more than the *average* 'clean' weight for an adult hind. 12 stone, however, is by no means the record weight for a *wild* hind in Scotland. In 1958 an old hind, weighing 13 st 2 lb (83.4 kg) 'clean' was shot on the Forestry Commission ground of *Glenhurich* (Argyllshire), whilst in the late 1970s an 18-stone (114.3 kg) hind was reported to have been killed on F.C. ground in *Galloway* (Kirkcudbrightshire) – an area where stags weighing 24 stone (153 kg) have been recorded.

Scotland's Heaviest Recorded Red Deer Stags

The heaviest ever recorded stag for Scotland appears to have been at *Glen More* (Inverness-shire) in 1877, with a weight of 33 stone (209.5 kg).

The heaviest recorded stag this century was one shot at *Balulive* (Isle of Islay) in 1940, with a weight of 32 st 8 lb (206.8 kg). However, its weight did not include the 'pluck' (heart, liver and lungs). This would have added another stone, thus making it heavier than the *Glen More* stag by a few pounds.

In 1932 a stag weighing 32 st 2 lb (204 kg) was shot at *Cumloden* park (Kirkcudbrightshire). There is little doubt that some of the large red deer stags which now frequent the Galloway forests owe their origin to escapees from both *Cumloden* and nearby *Cairnsmore* early in the century (see page 176).

The heaviest recorded stag shot in Scotland since the War was one shot on *Strathgarve* (Ross-shire) in 1979, but this was a park-bred animal in an enclosed area (*see* page 166). It weighed 31 stone (196.8 kg).

The heaviest *wild* stag shot in Scotland since the War was one shot on *Brodick* (Isle of Arran) in 1973 with a weight of 27 st 4 lb (173.2 kg).

Heavy stags with a weight in excess of 26 stone (165 kg) have included the following:

Weight	Locality	Date	Weight st	lb
33 stone (209.5 kg)	Glen More, Inverness-shire	1877	33	0
32 stone (203.2 kg)	Balulive, Isle of Islay	1940	32	8*
	Cumloden, Kirkcudbrightshire	1932	32	2†
31 stone (196.8 kg)	Strathgarve, Ross-shire	1979	31	0†
30 stone (190.5 kg)	Beaufort, Inverness	1876	30	2
	Dunkeld, Perthshire	pre-1839	30	0
29 stone (184.2 kg)	Brodick, Isle of Arran	c.1870	29	8
	Killiechonate, Inverness-shire	?	29	5
	Laggan, Isle of Islay	1937	29	1*
28 stone (177.8 kg)	Langwell, Caithness	1994	28	6
	Brodick, Isle of Arran	1872	28	6
	Killiechonate, Inverness-shire	?	28	2
	Glenfiddich, Banffshire	1831	28	0*
	Strathgarve, Ross-shire	1979	28	0†
27 stone (171.4 kg)	Brodick, Isle of Arran	1888	27	8
	Brodick, Isle of Arran	1973	27	4
	Kildermorie, Ross-shire	1938	27	6

* weighed without heart, liver and lungs.
† shot in enclosed area

Scottish Stags of 20 Stone (127 kg) plus, 1948–1994

* park stag
† wood stag
‡ estimated
§ hummel?

26 Stone (165 kg)

Forest	Date	Weight st	lb
Argyllshire			
Aros, Is. of Mull	1912	26	10
Kildalton	1936	26	7
Ardtornish	1923	26	6
Ardfin, Is. of Jura	1872	26	4
Ardfin, Is. of Jura	1978	26	2
Isle of Islay	1994	26	1
Ben More, Is. of Mull	?	26	0
Proaig, Is. of Islay	1929	26	0

Banffshire

Glenfiddich	1955	26	6
Glenfiddich	1954	26	0*

Buteshire (Isle of Arran)

Brodick	19th cent.	26	4

Inverness-shire

Glengarry	pre-1839	26	0

Morayshire

Binhill	1974	26	12

Perthshire

Tombuie (Bolfracks)	1931	26	10*
Tombuie (Bolfracks)	1936	26	10*
Tombuie (Bolfracks)	1934	26	6*

Ross-shire

Fairburn	1978	26	12
Applecross	1848	26	0

Sutherland

Glencanisp	1975	26	8

25 Stone (158.75 kg)

Forest	Date	Weight	
		st	lb

Aberdeenshire

Glen Clunie	1934	25	0

Argyllshire

Ardkinglass	1948	25	12
Ardfin, Is. of Jura	1990	25	10
Isle of Islay	?	25	2
Ardkinglass	1948	25	0
Ardmore, Is. of Islay	1965	25	0
Inveraray	?	25	0

Ayrshire

Merkland	1963	25	0

Banffshire

Glenfiddich	1953	25	4*

Bute (Isle of Arran)

Brodick	1973	25	13
Dougarie	1974	25	7

Caithness

Sandside	1910	25	10
Langwell	1969	25	8*
Braemore	1932	25	0

Inverness-shire

Dochfour	1958	25	2
Ranachan	?	25	0

Ross-shire

Ardross	1836	25	0

Sutherland

Dunrobin	1932	25	0

24 Stone (152.4 kg)

Forest	Date	Weight	
		st	lb

Argyllshire

Isle of Islay	1947	24	7
Isle of Islay	1949	24	7
Kingairloch	1985	24	6
Ben More, Is. of Mull	1966	24	4
Inveraray	1949	24	4
Ben More, Is. of Mull	1960	24	2
Isle of Islay	1995	24	1
Ardkinglas	1949	24	0
Ardlussa, Is. of Jura	1971	24	0
Aros, Is. of Mull	1959	24	0
Tarbert, Is. of Jura	1925	24	0

Bute (Isle of Arran)

Sannox	1983	24	12
Sannox	1982	24	9
Sannox	1977	24	8
Sannox	1981	24	4
Sannox	1992	24	4
Sannox	1975	24	2
Sannox	1982	24	2
Sannox	1984	24	2

Caithness

Langwell and Braemore	1929	24	10
Langwell and Braemore	1930	24	10

Inverness-shire

Ardverikie	1937	24	10
Glengarry	c. 1938	24	5

Perthshire

Dall	1923	24	12
Tombuie (Bolfracks)	?	24	8

Ross-shire

Braemore	1937	24	6*
Wyvis	1912	24	1
Benula	?	24	0
Kinlochluichart	1965	24	0

Sutherland

Kylestrome	1981	24	2

23 Stone (146 kg)

Forest	Date	Weight	
		st	lb
Aberdeenshire			
Mar	c. 1938	23	0
Argyllshire			
Inver, Is. of Jura	1927	23	10
Inveraray	1986	23	10
Kingairloch	1988	23	8
Kingairloch	1988	23	8
Kingairloch	1994	23	8
Auchnacraig	1995	23	7
Torosay, Is. of Mull	1994	23	7
Ardmore, Is. of Islay	1965	23	6
Ardfin, Is. of Jura	1979	23	2
Ardtalla, Is. of Islay	1992	23	2*
Craig	1937	23	0
Dunlossit, Is. of Islay	pre-1939	23	0
Isle of Islay	1958	23	0
Ayrshire			
Carrick	1964	23	0
Banffshire			
Blackwater	1955	23	12
Bute (Isle of Arran)			
Dougarie	1961	23	13
Dougarie	1977	23	0
Isle of Arran	1962	23	0
Dumbartonshire			
Ben Vorlich	pre-1939	23	0
Inverness-shire			
Strathaird, Is. of Skye	1971	23	7
Braulen	1928	23	4
Dochfour	1976	23	4
Knoydart	pre-1922	23	4
Alvie	1968	23	2
Kincardineshire			
Glen Dye	1932	23	8*
Glen Dye	1933	23	7*
Perthshire			
Boreland	1958	23	8
Auchnafree	1923	23	2
Suie	1984	23	2
Atholl, West Hand	1957	23	0
Atholl, West Hand	1977	23	0
Glenartney	1972	23	0
Tombuie (Bolfracks)	1985	23	0†

Forest	Date	Weight	
Ross-shire			
Wyvis	1976	23	6
Ledgowan	1970	23	3
Kinlochluichart	1965	23	1*
Coulin	1893	23	0
Kinlochewe Lodge	pre-1939	23	0‡
Sutherland			
Bowside	1974	23	11
Dunrobin	1975	23	5

22 Stone (139.7 kg)

Forest	Date	Weight	
		st	lb
Aberdeenshire			
Balmoral	pre-1939	22	12
Mar Lodge	1986	22	12
Glenmuick	1963	22	11
Glen Tanar	1958	22	6
Angus			
Caenlochan	1993	22	6
Invermark	pre-1939	22	0
Argyllshire			
Ardtalla, Is. of Islay	1995	22	12
Torosay, Is. of Mull	?	22	9
Ardfin. Is. of Jura	1983	22	8
Ardfin Is. of Jura	1994	22	8
Auchnacraig	1986	22	8
Dunlossit, Is. of Islay	1989	22	8
Isle of Islay	1995	22	8
Torosay, Is. of Mull	1968	22	8
Inveraray	1989	22	7*
Kingairloch	1994	22	7
Torosay, Is. of Mull	1970	22	7
Ardfin, Isle of Jura	1983	22	6
Ardnamurchan	1911	22	5
Ardtalla, Is. of Islay	1993	22	5
Ardfin, Is. of Jura	1964	22	4
Ardfin, Is. of Jura	1978	22	4
Ben More, Is. of Mull	1980	22	4
Dunlossit, Is. of Islay	1960	22	4
Kingairloch	1985	22	4
Inveraray	1979	22	7*
Inveraray	1990	22	3*
Ardfin, Is. of Jura	1986	22	2
Ardfin, Is. of Jura	1961	22	0
Ben More, Is. of Mull	1953	22	0
Dalness (Royal)	1886	22	0
Glenforsa, Is. of Mull	?	22	0
Banffshire			
Glenfiddich	1964	22	0

Bute (Isle of Arran)			
Sannox	1982	22	5
Sannox	1994	22	4
Dougarie	1971	22	2
Dougarie	1973	22	0

Caithness			
Langwell	1971	22	0

Inverness-shire			
Garrygualach	1922	22	12
Sconser, Is. of Skye	1929	22	12
Glenshero	1969	22	9
Achnacarry	1931	22	8
Abernethy	1931	22	7
Braulen	1975	22	7
Glenshero	1989	22	7
Langass, North Uist	1897	22	7
Balmacaan	c. 1870	22	6
Dochfour	1980	22	6
Kinveachy	1973	22	6
Aberchalder, Wester	?	22	4
Alvie	1969	22	4
Glenmazeran	1924	22	4
Glenmazeran	1957	22	3
Dochfour	1959	22	0
Glenmazeran	1986	22	0

Perthshire			
Rhiedorrach	1980	22	8
Camusericht	1993	22	7*
Remony	1972	22	3
Suie	1980	22	2
Atholl, Forest Lodge	1958	22	0
Atholl, West Hand	1977	22	0
Auchlyne & Suie	1995	22	0
Garrows	1933	22	0
Glenartney	c. 1882	22	0

Ross-shire			
Ben Damph and New Kelso	1989	22	7
Lochrosque	c. 1894	22	6
Corriemulzie	1977	22	4
Garbat	?	22	0
Glencarron	?	22	0

Stirlingshire			
Inversnaid	?	22	0

Sutherland			
Dalnessie	1981	22	12‡
Achentoul	1991	22	2
Ben Armine	1922	22	2
Ben Loyal	1992	22	1
Mudale	1965	22	0
Reay	1877	22	0

21 Stone (133.4 kg)

Forest	Date	Weight	
		st	lb
Aberdeenshire			
Corndavon	1992	21	7
Mar	1948	21	7
Invercauld	1936	21	4
Glenmuick	1965	21	3
Invercauld	1988	21	2
Angus			
Caenlochan	?	21	10
Hunthill	1923	21	1
Argyllshire			
Forest Lodge	1932	21	12
Kingairloch	1986	21	12
Blackmount	1984	21	11
Inveraray	1986	21	11
Kingairloch	1977	21	11
Ardfin, Is. of Jura	1988	21	10
Ardlussa, Is. of Jura	1927	21	10
Ardtalla, Is. of Islay	1995	21	10
Ederline	?	21	10
Torloisk, Is. of Mull	?	21	10
Torosay, Is. of Mull	1983	21	10
Ardtalla, Is. of Islay	1966	21	9
Gruline, Is. of Mull	1957	21	8
Inveraray	1980	21	8
Ardfin, Is. of Jura	1995	21	8
Ardfin, Is. of Jura	1995	21	8
Auchnacraig	1949	21	7
Conaglen	1949	21	7
Inveraray	1988	21	7
Ardfin, Is. of Jura	1990	21	6
Ben More, Is. of Mull	1957	21	6
Kingairloch	1986	21	6
Torosay, Is. of Mull	1974	21	6
Ederline	1965	21	5½
Inveraray	1980	21	4
Torosay, Is. of Mull	1988	21	4
Kingairloch and Glensanda	1973	21	3
Kingairloch and Glensanda	1974	21	3
Inveraray	1987	21	2
Inveraray	1988	21	2
Conaglen	1966	21	1
Inveraray	1983	21	1
Inveraray	1985	21	1
Torosay, Is. of Mull	1990	21	1
Ardfin, Is. of Mull	1978	21	0
Ardfin, Is. of Mull	1992	21	0
Ardfin, Is. of Mull	1992	21	0
Ardfin, Is. of Mull	1994	21	0
Ardlussa, Is. of Jura	?	21	0
Ardtalla, Is. of Islay	1972	21	0

Ardtalla, Is. of Islay	1985	21	0
Ardtalla, Is. of Islay	1986	21	0
Ardtalla, Is. of Islay	1989	21	0
Blackmount	1993	21	0
Dunlossit, Is. of Islay	1991	21	0
Eredine	?	21	0
Glen Etive	1952	21	0
Inveraray	1985	21	0
Inveraray	1989	21	0
Inveraray	1993	21	0
Inveraray	1995	21	0
Inveraray	1995	21	0
Torosay, Is. of Mull	1977	21	0

Banffshire

Glenavon	1968	21	8

Bute (Isle of Arran)

Dougarie	1993	21	12
Lochranza	1961	21	7
Dougarie	1975	21	4
Sannox	1980	21	1
Sannox	1990	21	1
Sannox	1985	21	0

Caithness

Rumsdale	1993	21	6
Langwell	1959	21	2
Langwell	1982	21	2
Langwell	1990	21	0
Langwell and Braemore	1968	21	0

Inverness-shire

Braulen	1980	21	11
Erchless	1995	21	10
Glenfeshie	1992	21	10
Guisachan	1880	21	9
Achnacarry N	1971	21	7
Braulen	1980	21	7
Kinlochmoidart	?	21	7
Rhum, Isle of	?	21	7
Ardverikie	1992	21	6
Glendessary	1955	21	6
Glendessary	1991	21	6
Glenfeshie	1937	21	6
Kinveachy	1972	21	6
Glenmazeran	1961	21	4
Kinveachy	1977	21	4
Levishie	1978	21	4
Killiechonate	1965	21	3
Mamore	1976	21	3*
Achdalieu	1986	21	1
Braulen	1973	21	1
Dochfour	1970	21	1
Kilchoan	1993	21	1

Braulen	1983	21	0
Coignafearn	1923	21	0
Dochfour	1958	21	0
Dochfour	1978	21	0
Glenkingie	1924	21	0
Strathmashie	?	21	0
Struy	pre-1939	21	0

Perthshire

Glenartney	1991	21	7
Remony	1932	21	7
Remony	1978	21	6
Camusericht	1975	21	4
Auchlyne	1990	21	1
Camusericht	1995	21	1

Ross-shire

Cluanie	?	21	12
Strathconon	1987	21	12
Foich	1965	21	10
Inverbroom	?	21	10
Cluanie	1973	21	6
Achnashellach	1987	21	5
Couldoran	1976	21	5
Strathconon	1932	21	5
Ledgowan	1993	21	4
Inverinate	1970	21	3
Kintail	1916	21	2
Ledgowan	1934	21	2
Kinlochluichart	1974	21	1
Inverinate	pre-1929	21	0
Inverlael	c. 1945	21	0
Leckmelm	1976	21	0
Strathconon	1994	21	0
Wyvis	1981	21	0

Sutherland

Achentoul	1990	21	11
Ben Loyal	1986	21	10
Kinloch	1959	21	8
Ben Loyal	1981	21	7
Mudale	1968	21	6
Inchnadamph	?	21	3
Strathmore	1995	21	3
Ben Loyal	1987	21	2
Badanloch	1974	21	1
Cambusmore	1992	21	0
Clebrig	1983	21	0
Dunrobin	1966	21	0
Dunrobin	1981	21	0
Loch Assynt	?	21	0
Uppat	1958	21	0

20 Stone (127 kg)

Forest	Date	Weight	
		st	lb
Aberdeenshire			
Corndavon	1993	20	7
Glenmuick	1971	20	5
Glen Ey, Mar	1968	20	4
Glen Ey, Mar	1987	20	1
Glen Clunie	1963	20	0
Glen Ey, Mar	1956	20	0
Glen Ey, Mar	1990	20	0
Invercauld	1976	20	0
Invercauld	1990	20	0
Mar Lodge	1989	20	0
Angus			
Caenlochan (Tulchan)	1973	20	10
Glencally	1995	20	10
Glenogil	1970	20	3
Glenmoy	1993	20	2
Caenlochan (Tulchan)	1985	20	1
Caenlochan (Tulchan)	1992	20	1
Argyllshire			
Kingairloch	1970	20	13
Kingairloch	1980	20	12*
Torosay, Is. of Mull	1975	20	12
Torosay, Is. of Mull	1990	20	12
Conaglen	1994	20	11
Auchnacraig	1995	20	10
Caolasnacoan and Kinlochbeg	?	20	10
Ardfin, Is. of Jura	1964	20	10
Ardfin, Is. of Jura	1982	20	10
Ardfin, Is. of Jura	1988	20	10
Ardtalla, Is. of Islay	1986	20	10
Blackmount	1977	20	10
Blackmount	1991	20	10
Inveraray	1992	20	10
Kingairloch	1987	20	10
Kingairloch	1992	20	10
Ardfin, Is. of Jura	1989	20	8
Auchnacraig, Is. of Mull	1986	20	8
Auchnacraig, Is. of Mull	1992	20	8
Auchnacraig, Is. of Mull	1994	20	8
Blackmount	1933	20	8
Kingairloch	1979	20	8
Strontian	1959	20	8
Carse	1964	20	7
Dalness	?	20	7
Glenkinglass	1991	20	7
Inveraray	1987	20	7
Ardfin, Is. of Jura	1989	20	6
Conaglen	1994	20	6
Kingairloch and Glensanda	1924	20	6
Ardkinglas	1960	20	5

Ardnamurchan	1963	20	5
Ardtalla, Is. of Islay	1989	20	5
Auchnacraig, Is. of Mull	1957	20	5
Dunlossit, Is. of Islay	1987	20	4
Dunlossit, Is. of Islay	1995	20	4
Kingairloch	1980	20	4*
Kingairloch	1987	20	4*
Pennyghail, Is. of Mull	1983	20	4
Ardfin, Is. of Jura	1980	20	3
Inveraray	1994	20	3
Ardfin, Is. of Jura	1991	20	2
Carse and Airidh	1974	20	2
Torosay, Is. of Mull	1975	20	2
Ardnamurchan	1993	20	1
Ardfin, Is. of Jura	1987	20	0
Ardfin, Is. of Jura	1993	20	0
Ardkinglas	1962	20	0
Ben More, Is. of Mull	1956	20	0
Ben More, Is. of Mull	1958	20	0
Ben More, Is. of Mull	1959	20	0
Ben More, Is. of Mull	1978	20	0
Ben More, Is. of Mull	1982	20	0
Carse	1962	20	0
Druimavuic	1962	20	0
Dunlossit, Is. of Islay	1959	20	0
Dunlossit, Is. of Islay	1987	20	0
Glenfyne	1961	20	0
Glenstrae	1991	20	0
Inveraray	1964	20	0
Inverinan	1959	20	0
Kilchoan	1959	20	0
Kilchoan	1994	20	0
Kingairloch	1982	20	0
Torosay, Is. of Mull	1960	20	0
Torosay, Is. of Mull	1974	20	0
Torosay, Is. of Mull	1978	20	0
Torosay, Is. of Mull	1984	20	0
Torosay, Is. of Mull	1988	20	0
Banffshire			
Glenavon (Inchory)	1993	20	11
Glenavon (Inchory)	1994	20	10
Glenavon (Inchory)	1986	20	8
Glenavon (Inchory)	1983	20	0
Glenfiddich	1962	20	0
Glenfiddich	1966	20	0
Bute (Isle of Arran)			
Sannox	1990	20	11
Sannox	1980	20	10
Dougarie	1989	20	8
Sannox	1995	20	4
Sannox	1977	20	0
Sannox	1989	20	8
Sannox	1989	20	8
Sannox	1995	20	2

Caithness

Langwell	1980	20	12
Langwell	1983	20	10
Langwell	1963	20	8
Langwell	1971	20	7
Langwell	1970	20	6
Langwell and Braemore	1968	20	6
Dunbeath	1991	20	6
Langwell	1985	20	4
Langwell	1994	20	4
Braemore	1991	20	2
Langwell	1970	20	2
Langwell	1987	20	2
Langwell	1990	20	0

Inverness-shire

Glendessary	1992	20	13
Kinrara	1959	20	13
Achnacarry S.	1988	20	12
Fasnakyle	1935	20	12
Gaick	1990	20	12
Achdalieu	1991	20	11
Achnacarry N.	1992	20	10
Affaric	1971	20	10
Arnisdale	1925	20	10
Braulen	1983	20	10
Erchless	1994	20	10
Eskadale	1964	20	10
Glenmazeran	1986	20	10
Kinrara	1979	20	10
Kinveachy	pre-1923	20	10
Knoydart	1994	20	10
Scalpay, Isle of	1895	20	10
Struy	1895	20	10
Achnacarry S.	1995	20	9
Glenfinnan	1993	20	9
Achnacarry S.	1988	20	8
Coignafearn	1963	20	8
Dochfour	1986	20	8
Dunmaglass	1935	20	8
Affaric	1922	20	7
Braeroy	1936	20	7
Kinloch Hourn	pre-1900	20	7
Knoydart	1982	20	7
Affaric	1980	20	6
Dochfour	1977	20	6
Glenfeshie	1991	20	6
Glenquoich, Easter	1969	20	6
Achnacarry N.	1924	20	5
Achnacarry S.	1994	20	5
Dochfour	?	20	5
Glenfeshie	1983	20	5
Glenmazeran	1987	20	5
Glenmoidart	1933	20	5
Glenshero (Corryarick)	1992	20	5

Kinrara	1978	20	5
Knoydart	1982	20	5
Achdalieu	1989	20	4
Achnacarry N.	1977	20	4
Ben Alder	1912	20	4
Struy	1964	20	4
Achnacarry S.	1929	20	3
Dundreggan N.	1923	20	3
Erchless	1973	20	3
Glendessary	1973	20	3
Glenshero (Corryarick)	1935	20	3
Achnacarry N.	1976	20	2
Achnacarry S.	1969	20	2
Affaric	1961	20	2
Inverailort	1993	20	2
Kinveachy	1961	20	2
Knoydart	1976	20	2
North Morar	1925	20	2
Achnacarry N.	1970	20	1
Achnacarry S.	1975	20	1
Achnacarry S.	1990	20	1
Glencannich	1971	20	1
Glendessary	1982	20	1
Knoydart	1953	20	1
Achdalieu	1976	20	0
Achnacarry N.	1986	20	0
Achnacarry N.	1988	20	0
Achnacarry S.	1961	20	0
Culachy	pre-1914	20	0
Dochfour	1978	20	0
Eilanreach	?	20	0
Gaick	1933	20	0
Glenaladale	?	20	0
Glenkingie	1956	20	0
Glenkyllachy	1962	20	0
Glenmazeran	1962	20	0
Glenmazeran	1966	20	0
Kinrara	1977	20	0
Kinveachy	1954	20	0
Kinveachy	1965	20	0
Kinveachy	1965	20	0
Struy	1956	20	0
Struy	1965	20	0
Struy	1970	20	0

Kirkcudbrightshire

Cairnsmore	1951	20	4

Perthshire

Remony	1990	20	12
Clunes	1973	20	11
Glenartney	1993	20	11
Suie	1982	20	11
Auchlyne	1992	20	8
Remony	1993	20	6

Auchlyne	1993	20	5	Kildermorie	1954	20	0
Remony	1988	20	5	Kinlochluichart	1968	20	0
Auchlyne and Suie	1988	20	2	Rhidorroch W.	1962	20	0§
Glenshee	1980	20	2	Scatwell	1957	20	0
Meggernie	1971	20	2	Wyvis	1982	20	0
Auchlyne and Suie	1990	20	1				
Forest Lodge	1994	20	1	*Sutherland*			
Stronvar	1949	20	½	Achentoul	1989	20	9
Auchleeks	1967	20	0	Ben Armine	1936	20	8
Bolfracks (Tombuie)	1961	20	0	Ben Armine	1980	20	8
Bolfracks (Tombuie)	1982	20	0	Dalreavoch	1985	20	8
				Dunrobin	1955	20	8
Ross-shire				Dunrobin	1992	20	8
Scatwell and Strathconon	1971	20	12	Kinloch	1959	20	8
Flowerdale	1934	20	10	Loch Choire	1984	20	8
Kildermorie	1989	20	10	Skelpick and Rhifael	1992	20	8
Strathconon	1978	20	10	Achentoul	1983	20	7
Glenshiel	1936	20	9	Ben Hee and Corriekinloch	1963	20	7
Killilan	1936	20	9	Achentoul	1985	20	6
Strathconon	1994	20	8	Badanloch	1992	20	6
Achnashellach	1971	20	7	Dalnessie	1983	20	5
Kinlochluichart	1972	20	7*	Kinloch	1959	20	5
Monar	1926	20	6	Kildonan	1993	20	4
Pait	1949	20	6	Ben Loyal	1985	20	3
Glomach	1936	20	5	Achentoul	1989	20	0
Kildermorie	1992	20	4	Badanloch	1950	20	0
Strathconon	1984	20	4	Ben Armine	1987	20	0
Coulin	1978	20	3	Corriemulzie	1984	20	0
Kildermorie	1986	20	2	Dalnessie	1953	20	0
Letterewe and Fisherfield	1989	20	2	Dalnessie	1909	20	0
Strathconon	1979	20	2	Dalnessie	1956	20	0
Strathconon	1981	20	2	Dalnessie	1961	20	0
Cluanie	1968	20	0	Invercassley	1969	20	0
Fairburn	1987	20	0	Kinloch	1958	20	0
Glencalvie and Dibbiedale	1936	20	0	Loch Choire	1994	20	0

CHAPTER 27
Venison

General

It is probably true to say that, over the years, the price of venison has been the controlling factor of Scotland's wild red deer population. When the price is favourable to laird, farmer marginal to a deer forest and poacher, the population, except in the most out-of-the-way places, will fall – not, unfortunately, among hinds, which most need reducing, but principally among stags, for not only will they weigh heavier, but after a hard rut they will be the most vulnerable. When the price is rock bottom, unless there is a national body like the Red Deer Commission (R.D.C.) to wield a big stick, both forest owner and poacher will probably be thinking alike – why kill if there is no financial gain from doing so?

During the War years there was relatively little stalking for sport, most of the deer being shot by stalkers and almost anyone who was clever enough to keep out of trouble with the police, who then had other matters to attend to. Moreover, at that period – and indeed until 21 October 1962 (The Deer (Scotland) Act 1959) there were no close-seasons for either sex, so shooting deer was a twelve-month, legal occupation for those who wished to do so and had no conscience.

During the immediate post-War years not only were some of the larger estates being broken up into smaller units which, as a consequence, gave the deer less protection, but their habitat in many areas was being disrupted and eroded by the spread of forestry and the development of various hydro-electric schemes (*see* page 65). During these formative years most of the venison was being sold on the home market, but tonnages were never large, for it is only comparatively recently that deer meat has been generally accepted by the British housewife.

During the past twenty-five years the price of red deer venison obtained from registered game dealers has ranged from a record low, in 1970-71 of 5-15p per pound for deer killed out of season to 90-95p per pound in 1988-89 for in-season venison.

Roe venison has always been a better seller, and in 1990, when red deer venison was fetching from about 50p to 60p per pound, the price for roe venison was about double, but in the following year had dropped to about £1, whilst red deer venison had increased to about 75p.

A Summary of Venison Prices for Scottish Red Deer for the 40 years 1954-95 appears on page 210. The following are some of the reasons to account for the widespread fluctuations.

1954-60

During 1954 there was a dramatic fall in venison prices which, in some areas, fell from around 3s 6d (17½p) to as low as 6d (2½p) per pound, though a deer's liver was still able to command a price of about 3s (15p) per pound. This fall in price obviously made deer poaching not quite so profitable an occupation as it had been in previous years, and during that winter there was a noticeable decrease in this obnoxious activity.

During 1956 the Scottish Landowners Federation (S.L.F.) received an enquiry from Germany, with a view to importing venison to that country. Accordingly, representatives of the Federation met the German importer, Herr Dietrich, at Inverness on 12 September, in order to discuss the possibility of arranging for the export of venison from Scotland to Germany. Lieutenant-Colonel Donald Cameron of Lochiel, the owner of a number of deer forests in Inverness-shire, presided at the meeting.

During the meeting, the Federation representative suggested that the minimum price

at which a majority of deer forest owners might be interested in selling venison for export would be 1s 6d (7½p) per pound, unskinned and delivered at the quayside, Leith. Herr Dietrich, however, explained that it would not be possible for him to offer such a price if venison purchased in Scotland was to compete with venison currently being imported from Poland and Hungary. Apparently, there was a considerable import of venison from these eastern bloc countries, but still not enough to satisfy Germany's demand.

In summing up the discussion, Lochiel said that, if Germany would consider paying the above mentioned sum of 1s 6d (7½p) per pound, unskinned at the quayside, Leith, he thought there would be a large tonnage available. Nevertheless, it would not be possible to ensure that all the venison had been well shot. Therefore no guarantee could be given to this effect.

Following the meeting the Federation sent out, on the 21 September, a circular to all those members who had shown an interest in the proposal, with a view to ascertaining from them what supplies might be available. By this date, of course, the season was already in its final stages, and the response was probably less than it might have been had the circular reached owners in August. However, two consignments, one of 5½ tons (5,588 kg) and another of 1½ tons (1,524 kg) were exported to Germany through the Federation, and it was planned to send a consignment of hinds later in the winter. The scheme was, of course, restricted to members of the S.L.F., although other exports of venison to Germany had also been arranged by some leading Scottish game dealers.

It would appear, however, that most deer forest owners found the proposition unattractive for, by the time the venison had reached Leith, the net financial return to the producers would only be about 9d (4p) per pound. On the other hand, game dealers in Perth and Inverness were able to collect venison from owners' larders at about 11d (4½p) per pound, and doubtless some of this was also reaching Germany.

Nevertheless, Germany continued to be a good outlet for venison and, out of the seventy-nine stags shot on *Affaric* (Inverness-shire) during the 1958 season, all but four were marketed in this way, the average price working out at about

£7 13s 0d (£7.65) per beast. The Lochiel forests also, among others, disposed of much of their venison to Germany, which resulted in a fair price to the proprietor. 'It is my opinion', commented Colonel D. H. Cameron of Lochiel, 'that this market arrangement has no effect at all on poaching of deer. No carcases can be sent to Germany by this channel except by members of the Scottish Landowners Federation. Moreover, it is known that poachers find a much easier and equally good market nearer at home.'

1961–70

By 1961 it had already become more profitable to dispose of venison to Germany than on the home market, for there was little difference between the export price and that obtained through most outlets in this country.

During 1967 an outbreak of foot and mouth disease which was reported in the R.D.C. *Annual Report*, occurred in England, and as a result Scotland was designated a *Controlled Area* for foot and mouth disease purposes. Although this restriction was removed with effect from 30 January 1968, the majority of E.E.C. countries maintained a ban on the import of venison for a further six months until 8 May 1968. In West Germany, however, the ban was not lifted until 1 June 1968.

Although during part of the *Controlled Area* period the shooting of deer was prohibited, 'the Commission obtained permission to authorise estates who wished to cull within the estate or named area on the estate under Article 2 of the *Animal (Miscellaneous Provisions) Order* 1927' (*in lit* 27 Jan '95). The Commission were also 'issued with a General Licence under the same Order to enable them to deal with marauding deer during the *Controlled Area* period.'

'While the ban on imports of venison to West Germany was in force, venison dealers continued to accept carcases from their customers until storage became a major problem.'

In the previous year an outbreak of foot and mouth disease had been confirmed in Cumberland on 21 July and as a result a number of areas in the county of Roxburgh were, on 22 July, declared *Infected Areas*, and this restriction remained in force in some areas until midnight 6 September, when all parts of Scotland were finally excluded from the *Infected Area*. Apart from the possibility of a stray fallow deer, the only resident wild deer in Roxburgh are roe.

During 1968 a substantial increase in the price of venison renewed fears that this would encourage more poaching, and there was increased pressure in some quarters for a complete ban on the sale of venison for any deer shot out of season. In their *Annual Report* for 1969, the Red Deer Commission, however, stated that they had 'no direct knowledge of the number of deer shot out of season, but examination by Commission staff of the records which venison merchants are now required to keep in terms of the Sale of Venison (Scotland) Act 1968, should show the extent of the trade.' It was very considerable in so far as the stags were concerned.

The Sale of Venison (Scotland) Act 1968 came into operation on 3 July 1969, and for the first time the R.D.C. had an opportunity to examine the record books of registered game dealers. According to these records, out of a total of 23,830 deer carcases received by the dealers, which consisted of 11,518 stag and 12,312 hind carcases, no less than 22 per cent of stags had been shot out of season, whilst hind out-of-season killings amounted to only 4 per cent.

As mentioned on page 149 one possible solution was to make their sale illegal. Had, however, such a regulation been in force in 1969 this would have resulted in about 3,000 carcases – or about 12½ per cent of total deer carcases sent to dealers in the autumn and winter of that season – being declared unsaleable. Certainly a situation of wanton waste and one that should never be considered.

During the following season, out-of-season killing of stags and hinds was slightly reduced, amounting to 19 per cent of stags and 3.7 per cent of hinds – an overall total of 11 per cent. Twenty years later, according to the 1992 Red Deer Commission's *Annual Report*, out-of-season killings had been reduced to 12¾ per cent for stags and 1¼ per cent for hinds – a total of 5.1 per cent for both sexes. Still a sizeable total, and one that should certainly not be declared unsaleable. Far better to have legalised their slaughter by the issue of official tags before their cull than have their sale afterwards condemned.

The high price of venison, which in 1969 was as much as 4s 11d to 5s (24½ to 25p) per pound in some areas, was double the price of a few years before, and this not only encouraged the deer poacher to become more active, but also increased out-of-season killing on the grounds of marauding. All venison, under the Sale of Venison (Scotland) Act 1968, had now to be disposed of through a licensed game dealer who was required to register all purchases and keep records available for inspection by the R.D.C.

Such a requirement may read well, but should a dealer fail to register any venison obtained from a doubtful source, how on earth could any such omission be detected? It would not take too much ingenuity to match up carcases in the larder with entries in the book and, unless each game dealer's premises were being *regularly* visited by inspectors, there was no guarantee that the entries were complete or that some carcases received from less reputable suppliers had not been omitted. As I have advocated on numerous occasions over the years, a system of carcase-tagging would prevent illegally taken carcases reaching game dealers' premises. An inspection of a game dealer's cold store – *not* his record book – would, by the presence of tags, show at a glance whether he was obtaining his carcases from a reliable source (*see* Carcase Tagging page 146).

1971–75

The high price for venison – which for an unskinned, in-season carcase varied between 15p and 21p per pound, and for an out-of-season carcase between 5p and 15p, which was about 2p per pound up on the previous year – remained a temptation to cash in on killing so-called marauders, which could be killed quite legitimately out of season if considered necessary. Moreover, in view of an increase in beef prices which, in consequence, made venison – price-wise if not taste-wise – an attractive alternative, the temptation to kill more out-of-season marauders was even greater. One advantage for the deer, however, was that more forest owners had resorted to winter feeding, and this had restricted the wandering tendency of many deer and kept them out of trouble.

Venison prices continued to rise, and at one period during 1972 a carcase 'in the skin' – but minus head and feet – was fetching as much as

53p per pound, which resulted in carcases of some of the larger stags being worth about £100 or more, with even an average beast having a price tag of around £70 to £80. Even a good, fat hind-carcase would fetch about £30, and a so-called marauding stag shot out of season considerably more, so the temptation to kill excessively or poach remained.

By 1973 the German market was being flooded with venison not only from the eastern bloc countries of Europe, but also from the import of some 500 tons (508 tonnes) of reindeer meat from Scandinavia. The net result was that game dealers in this country suddenly found that they were no longer able to dispose of their stag carcases to Europe except at a loss, and prices accordingly plummeted down. It is understood that a similar situation was affecting supplies of venison to Germany from New Zealand.

By the end of 1973 it was estimated that approximately 25,000 to 30,000 carcases of red deer, of which over 80 per cent would be exported to Europe, were being handled by game dealers in Scotland. By the end of that season, hind venison was fetching only about 30p per pound.

By September 1974 there was a further slump in the venison market, and, by Christmas the price for hind venison had fallen to about 11½p per pound, the reason being a change in regulations concerning the importation of venison to Germany which was to become effective as from 1 January 1975.

Among the proposed new regulations was a clause to the effect that each carcase, complete with head and feet, and accompanied by the 'pluck' – heart, lungs and liver – had to be in the hands of a game dealer *and* submitted for veterinary inspection *within* 24 hours of being shot. Each 'pluck' and carcase had to be easily identified, so that if any part was condemned there would be no doubt as to its origin.

Other requirements included that game for West Germany must be placed in a temperature of 7°C within ten hours of killing, and the export of cut-up venison would not be permitted unless the cutting had been done under veterinary supervision.

Clearly, a daily collection of carcases by a game dealer – particularly from some of the more remote deer forests in Scotland – was just not possible, and even if it were, the majority of deer larders in Scotland did not comply with some of the stringent requirements laid down by the new regulation. Furthermore, the existing resources of the veterinary service in Scotland were totally inadequate for undertaking such a detailed inspection of all deer carcases at game dealers' premises, quite apart from the extra work involved, and it was a process all game dealers would have preferred to avoid if an alternative market could be found. Until, therefore, there was some relaxation in these new regulations, or until an alternative market had been found, it was hardly surprising that prices in 1974 reached rock bottom.

The requirement that, under the new export regulations *each* "pluck" and carcase must be easily identifiable' would seem to emphasize my conviction that no carcase should be able to leave a deer forest larder without an official tag attached. It might be necessary to have tags in duplicate – one to attach to the carcase and the other to the 'pluck', in case the two become separated. Otherwise, for instance, should a consignment of, say, ten carcases be collected from one forest, and one of the 'plucks' – which could not be properly associated with an individual carcase – fail the veterinary inspection, then all ten carcases in that particular load would, automatically, have to be rejected for export.

In 1974, while the British veterinary authorities were trying to negotiate with Germany an easing of the new regulations, all exports were temporarily 'frozen'. However, a number of establishments, whose premises could not fully comply with the German requirements, but which otherwise were basically considered to be suitable, were granted permission to continue trading until 31 December 1975, after which date they would then have to meet the full requirements of the German regulations.

During the stag season of 1975, prices seem to have fluctuated between about 23p and 29p per pound, 'in the skin' – the latter price being paid to forests that had installed chilling facilities. A few forest owners, however, were able to dispose of their carcases locally to hotels etc., and up to 35p per pound was being obtained.

During that year, venison from deer farming in Scotland was very much in its infancy, but from a small herd of about fifty deer at his farm at

Reediehill, Auchtermuchty (Angus), John Fletcher was selling venison as a mail order service, at £1 per pound for frying steak, whilst for a roasting joint the price was about 80p per pound.

In November 1995 John Fletcher was charging £4.48 per pound (£9.8 per kilo) for a whole haunch (bone-in) and £5.25 per pound (£11.5 per kilo) for a saddle (bone-in), whilst a liver was priced at about £2.45 per pound (£5.4 per kilo).

The deer at Reediehill are slaughtered at about 18 months of age. Prior to starting his farm at Reediehill, John Fletcher, in association with the Cambridge University Veterinary School, was involved in a domesticated deer herd project on the Isle of Rhum, for research into their behaviour and physiology. From there, tame deer had been supplied, in 1970, in order to start the pilot deer farm unit at *Glensaugh*, which was being run jointly by the Rowett Research Institute and the Hill Farming Research Organisation, under the jurisdiction of Kenneth, – later Sir Kenneth – Blaxter.

Currently, there are about sixty deer farms operating in Scotland – probably some twenty less than three or four years ago, as a number have changed over to sheep farming which is heavily subsidised.

Although farmed venison is becoming increasingly available in the supermarkets of Britain, it would appear, ironically, that much of it is being imported from New Zealand deer farms, where, with grass growing all year round, venison can be provided more cheaply than on the deer farms of Britain.

1976-79

During the 1977 season, prices for stag venison remained around the 70 to 75 pence per pound mark, which meant that an average stag carcase was fetching around £100 and the larger ones considerably more. Small wonder, therefore, that poaching and the 'legal' shooting of alleged marauders out of season once more become a profitable business and, with the maximum poaching fine of only £20 under the Deer (Scotland) Act 1959, there was every encouragement to continue both practices.

It so happened that, during the 1977 season, I was out stalking when a local shepherd was caught red-handed poaching on *Dunbeath* forest (Caithness), having shot three hinds out of season. When taken to court at Wick, although he was fined £20 for poaching, no charge for shooting female deer out of season was preferred against him – nor was his rifle confiscated, which could have been done under the Deer (Scotland) Act 1959. It was unfortunate that the Criminal Law Act 1977 only applied to England, for under that law the maximum fine for poaching could have been £500 for a first offence.

At the end of 1979 two in-skin carcases consigned for export to the continent were stopped by Customs at Felixstowe because they did not comply with the terms of the Endangered Species (Import and Export) Act 1976, on the grounds that, since the Scottish red deer (*Cervus elaphus scoticus*) closely resembled the endangered red deer (*C.e. barbarus*) of North Africa, a special export licence would be required. The matter was referred to the Department of the Environment who were responsible for administering the Act, and after two days of bureaucratic haggling, an 'open general' licence was granted which would cover the future export of all in-skin carcases from Scotland.

A number of years ago I had a similar problem with Customs when bringing back a European fallow buck (*Dama dama dama*) head from Denmark, for the powers-that-be apparently considered that a deer from Europe might just be the endangered Mesopotamian fallow (*D. d. mesopotamica*). Such incidents only demonstrate how much time and trouble can be wasted by those in authority who have insufficient knowledge on which to base their decision.

1980–1994

Pre-war, many forests observed the unwritten law that the stag shooting season should terminate by 15 October at the latest – with some, even by 5 October – thus ensuring that most of the stag venison reached the larder before being 'run' and almost unfit for human consumption. Until 1985, purchasers in Europe appeared to be not too concerned about whether the venison had come from a rutting stag or not, but after the Chernobyl disaster of April 1986 any venison from Western Europe, which included Scotland, was looked upon with grave suspicion as having, perhaps, been contaminated by radio-active fall-out, and the venison market suffered considerably.

From then on, carcases were regularly monitored for radiation by the Red Deer Commission, which was also becoming increasingly concerned about the state of some carcases that were reaching the game dealers from Scottish estates. Quoting from their *Annual Report* of 1987, whilst the standard of carcases presented by the Forestry Commission was uniformly good,

> it was equally noticeable that some carcases from certain other estates and agencies were badly shot and/or sent to the venison game dealers in an appalling condition. Unfortunately the overall percentages of such instances was higher than expected.

And the R.D.C. concluded their censure by commenting

> At a time when venison prices are low, estates cannot afford to have revenues jeopardised by the loss of considerable income following veterinary condemnation as a result of careless handling of carcases.

This, moreover, was not the first occasion the R.D.C. had expressed concern over the quality of venison being supplied to licensed game dealers, and in particular they had already referred to 'the quality of out-of-season venison which was being exported to the continent, mainly West Germany, and the consequent bad name that the product might receive' (R.D.C. *Annual Report* 1980).

By 1990, prices for hind venison had slumped to around 30 pence per pound, compared to about 80 pence per pound twelve months previously. There was, however, by now quite a demand for the purchase of live hinds for the deer farming industry but, since the deer farmer is only interested in young animals, this market is limited.

Accordingly, in 1989 both *Glenmuick* (Aberdeenshire) and *Gaick* (Inverness-shire) had included a number of live hinds in their annual cull figures – the former with 60 and the latter 170.

There is little doubt that the quality of Scottish venison has benefited considerably as a result of the strict regulations imposed on importation of venison to the continent, for many deer larders in the 1950s and 1960s – and even beyond – could hardly have been described as hygienic. Isolated and seldom, if ever, visited by health authorities, it was clearly a case of being out of sight and out of mind. One of the worst larders I have ever visited was in Perthshire, when I took a German friend to go roe stalking on the low ground of a small deer forest. It was mid-July and, having got his buck, I took it along to the estate larder to skin and cape out. On reaching the larder, not only was there still dried blood on the floor, left over from the hind season which had terminated some five months previously, but the gauze netting which covered the windows was so perforated as to invite every hungry fly in Perthshire in for a meal. Had German health authorities visited similar larders in Scotland, it is hardly surprising that their import regulations were so strict.

Leaving a Carcase out Overnight

It is important that, whenever possible, a carcase should not be left out on the hill overnight, but occasionally, due to bad weather, lack of transport or a beast being shot too late for recovery that evening, it may be unavoidable. However, it should not be carried to extremes and extended beyond a night. Following the 1969 stalking season I received a letter from C. W. M Glover, who, during the third week of October, had been stalking along with his father, as tenants on *Benmore Assynt* (Sutherland). He expressed concern about the loss of carcase weight resulting from this practice. Apparently, 'for a variety of reasons – mainly staff and mechanical difficulties – a number of stag carcases were left out on the hill for as long as three nights in a row.' On a rain-free night it has been suggested that loss in weight might amount to about 7 lb (3.2 kg), but it could well be increased with a 'rain-sodden' coat should the night have been wet.

After a day or two on the hill, however, I have little doubt that, as a result of the raptor or vulpine attention so vividly described by Ian Alcock in his *Stalking Deer in Great Britain* (1993), the weight could well be less. On one particular occasion three small stags were left out overnight on his small forest of *Strathmore* (Sutherland), but when he returned the next day, 'four eagles lifted off the carcases . . . and we found that they had caused considerable damage to the carcases, both tearing large areas round the bullet holes and damaging other parts of the animals.' Subsequently, any carcase that had to be left out

overnight on the hill had plastic bags attached to an antler to scare away the birds, and this proved successful.

Venison Grading

Ever since 1951, when I first advocated a system of carcase tagging (*see* pages 146–149), I also proposed that there should be some form of venison *grading*, and these views were reiterated in more detail in an article to *The Field* (16/5/74), in which I suggested that the price a dealer should be expected to pay for his venison ought to be reduced progressively as the season advanced, until only perhaps about a quarter of the autumn figure would be paid for deer killed out-of-season.

Prices will obviously fluctuate from year to year, and even during the course of a season, so there would be no constraint upon a dealer having to pay up to the maximum price fixed – it would all depend on supply and demand – but he should not pay more. Badly shot carcases would be subject to deductions.

Prior to the stalking season, say during June, the maximum price for licensed game dealers to pay for their venison would be announced.

During the 1973-74 season, which coincided with the appearance of this article, venison prices to dealers ranged from 45p to 53p per pound and, using these as a basis for the following season, the following prices were suggested:

Stag carcase	1 July-30 September	- up to 50p/lb
(maximum	1-10 October	- up to 35p/lb
prices)	11-20 October	- up to 25p/lb
	out of season	
	21 October-30 June	- 10p/lb
Hind carcase	21 October-31 December	- up to 35p/lb
(maximum	1 January-15 February	- up to 30p/lb
prices)	out of season	
	16 February-20 October	- 10p/lb

Calves would be open to negotiation, but not less than 10p per pound. Such a price control system would encourage deer forest owners to kill their stags early in the season before they became 'run' during the rut. Hinds killed before Christmas are also better venison than those shot late in the season.

In order to reduce the number of deer being shot out of season, some have suggested that a complete ban on the sale of such carcases might be a solution but, as pointed out on page 205, this would be an unacceptable waste of meat and money. Many of these out-of-season stags are shot during the legitimate open-season for hinds, and in some cases, with a young stag, swopping of carcases would be possible.

Moreover, some deer have to be shot as genuine marauders, and the low price obtainable for such killings would provide some monetary compensation for the crofter or forester whose crops have suffered.

Scottish Highland Venison Marketing Limited adopted, a number of years ago, a tagging system whereby tags were issued to the estates from where their venison was being obtained, and by this means any venison in their warehouse could be identified to any particular estate. So far as I am aware this is the only company to have operated such a scheme. Such a tagging scheme has proved useful in associating individual 'plucks' with their respective carcases.

Hind venison after Christmas is priced down, not only because the quality is deteriorating, but in most cases the venison has to be frozen and kept in store for a long period. Scottish Highland Venison no longer do any processing and concentrate solely on the 'in-skin' market.

Etceteras and By-products

In my review of the 1975 stalking season (*The Field* 19/1/76) I mentioned that there was a ready market in the Far East for deer by-products which included testicles, leg sinews, tails etc., should anyone consider exploring this market. By 1978 a firm calling itself Deer By-Products Limited had set up business and was offering £3 each for red deer tails (£2 if small or damaged); up to £2.50 for a deer pizzle; £1 for a deer antler (hard) or £2 (in velvet); and 16 pence for the lower legs (set of four).

Some of the game dealers had also started to pay comparable prices, which was obviously a more convenient way of disposal as they could be collected along with the carcases. The etceteras, including the tushes, then amounted to about £10 to £12 per stag or about £4 per hind – so, on a forest culling around 100 stags and 100 hinds per season, this represented about £1,400 to £1,600 per season – or over the whole of Scotland, probably well over £250,000 – a source of revenue

which but a few years previously had been left on the hill to rot. By 1975 much of this was now finding its way into a stalker's purse as a perk (*see* page 23).

Recently, game dealers have developed a trade in the sale of deer skins, although at one time they were almost worthless on account of warble fly (*Hypoderma diana*) larvae damage. By 1995, however, a strong demand for skins had developed and game dealers were able to trade them at up to £5 each which was a great advantage to them (John Fletcher *in lit* 1995).

Apropos the value of these etceteras and by-products of deer, in February 1995 thieves stole more than 2,000 stags' tails and 300 pizzles – estimated to be worth about £10,000 – during a raid on Highland Venison Marketing in Grantown-on-Spey (*Daily Telegraph* 8/2/95).

Summary of Venison Prices for Scottish Red Deer 1950–95

1950   About 2/3 (11p) per pound.

1954-55   Varied from about 3s 6d (17½p) per pound in some areas to as low as 6d (2½p) per pound. A liver, however, could fetch about 3s 0d (15p) per pound.

1955-56   A figure of 1s 6d (7½p) per pound for export to Germany was under consideration (see page 204).

1958-59   An average of about £7 13s 0d (£7.65) per *beast* was being paid for carcases exported to Germany.

1968-69   Varied from about 4s 11d (24½p) to 5s 0d (25p) per pound.

1970-71   Varied between 15p and 20p for deer killed in season and, for deer killed out of season, from about 5p to 15p.

1971-72   From about 21p to 22½p per pound.

1972-73   Varied between about 45p and 53p per pound in the skin.

1973-74   Varied from about 75p per pound for stag venison at the beginning of the stag season, but prices fell to as low as 30p per pound for hind venison.

1974-75   Varied between 23p and 29p per pound in the skin to game dealers, but a few private sales to locals hotels were fetching up to 35p per pound.

1975-76   Varied between 50p and 60p per pound, with an additional 13p per pound being paid for all edible offal ('pluck').

1976-77 Apart from a short-term peak of about 90p per pound, prices generally remained at around 70-75p per pound.

1977-78 Price fluctuated between 55p and 65p per pound.

1978-79 Price fluctuated between 55p and 65p per pound.

1979-80 Price fluctuated between 65p and 75p per pound.

1980-81 A price of about 75p per pound was maintained until November, when it dropped to about 55p per pound for hind venison.

1982-83 Price remained low at about 55-65p per pound, depending on sex and whether killed in or out of season.

1983-84 A slight increase to about 68p per pound.

1984-85 Price fluctuated between about 68p and 83p per pound.

1985-86 Wide variation of prices, ranging from 90p per pound at the beginning of season in some areas to around 60p per pound after 21 October when the hind season commenced.

1986-87 During August 1986, prices had fallen to about 50-55p per pound.

1987-88 Prices remained low, roughly in line with previous season.

1988-89 At the start of the season, prices of around 90-95p per pound were being paid, but fell at the turn of the year.

1989-90 At the start of the season prices had slumped to about 55-65p per pound, and throughout the season continued to fall, finishing up at about 30-45p per pound.

1990-91 Prices throughout the season fluctuated between 45p and 60p per pound.

1991-92 Prices continued to improve slightly, and most estates were able to sell their carcases within a range of 50-75p per pound.

1992-93 Average price* for *in-season* venison ranged from 63p per pound (stag) and 65p per pound (hind) to 40p per pound for both sexes *out-of-season*.

1993-94 Average price* for *in-season* venison ranged from 60p per pound (stag) and 50p per pound (hind) to 35p per pound for both sexes *out of season*.

1994-95 Average price* for *in-season* venison ranged from 65p per pound (stag) and 70p per pound (hind) to 60p per pound for both sexes *out of season*.

During the period 1992-95 the price per pound for roe venison (buck and doe) increased from £1.00 in 1992 to £1.40 (1994-95).

* Prices quoted by Mitchell Game Limited (Dundee). All prices in skin, with head and feet off, and minus gralloch, heart, lung, liver etc.

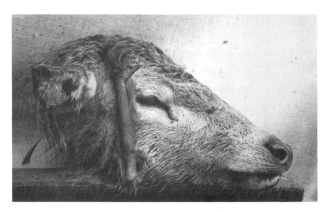 

Half hummel, with swinging right antler stump, shot on *Barrisdale* (Inverness) in 1953.

(Left) Malformed 'switch' head, with left antler sprouting from a damaged pedicle.

(Below left) Five pointer, with 'swinging' left antler still in velvet.

(Below right) 'Swinging' right antler as a result of a damaged pedicle, shot by author on *Ben Loyal* forest (Sutherland) in 1993.

 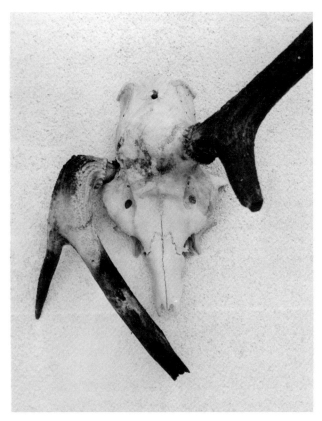

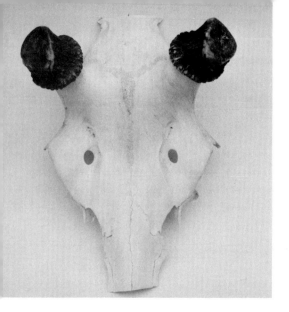

Stunted antler growth of Red deer stag –
stags with similar malformed antlers have
been shot on a number of other forests
including *Strathvaich* (Ross-shire) and
Glen Clunie (Aberdeenshire).

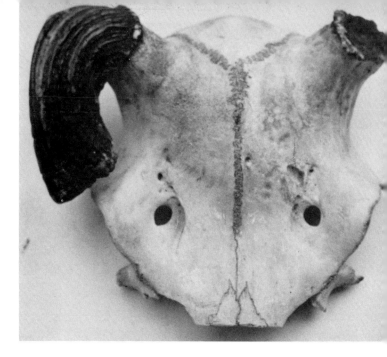

Down-bent right beam of stag with stunted antler growth.

Frontal bone of stag with stunted antler
growth, and with broken tine end of an
opponent penetrating its skull behind the
left pedicle.

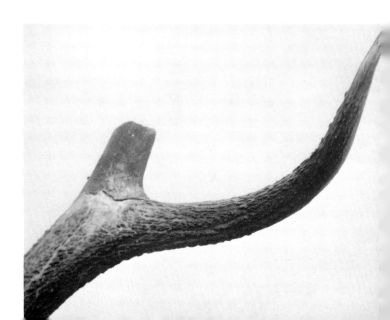

Tine end damaged by maggots whilst in velvet.

Peruke (Perruque) stag shot on *Leckmelm* (Ross-shire) in 1976. *(RDC)*

'Cromie' head.

Two one-antlered stags shot by author on *Inverbroom* (Ross-shire) in 1957 – one has six points and the other three points.

A fine three-antlered head of stag found dead near Fort Augustus (Inverness-shire) in 1959 – 6 + 2 + 3 = 11 points.

Three-antlered head from *Black Corries* (Argyllshire) shot in 1950 by David Whateley – 6 + 2 + 3 = 11 points.

Multi-antlered heads

Although having the appearance of possessing four antlers, this head has only two due to the fact that all three evenly matched stems on the right side share a common pedicle.

Three-antlered head from *Gaick* (Inverness-shire) shot in 1990 by A. Bezzola – 4 + 1 + 3 = 8 points.

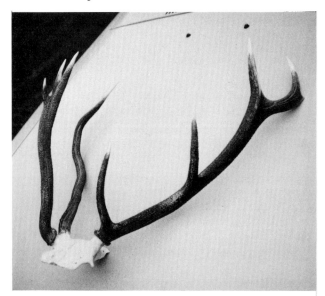

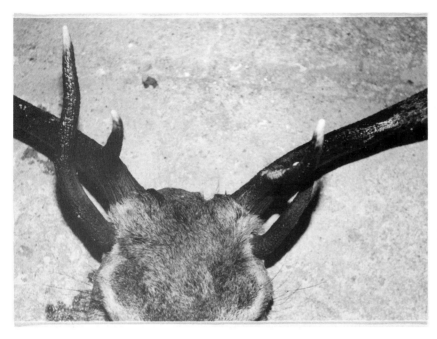

Four-antlered head from *Glenmazeran* (Inverness-shire) shot by Jan Huybs in 1994.
Number of points 10.
(Front pair 1 + 1; rear pair 4 + 4.)

Four-antlered head from *Ben Loyal* (Sutherland) shot by Angus MacKenzie in 1989.
3 + 1 + 3 + 4 = 11 points. Three of the beams, each with a separate coronet, emanate from a bifurcation of the left pedicle.

An impressive 8-pointer shot by R. Williams on *Strathvaich* (Ross-shire) in 1967.

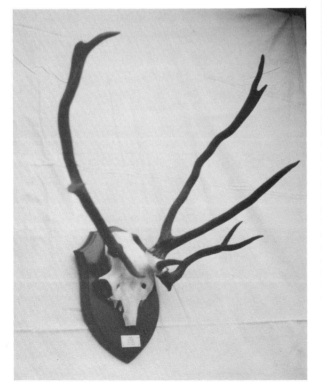

Palmated antlers

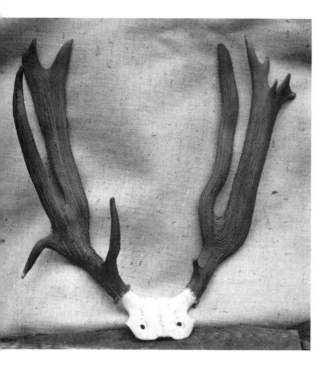

An unusual malform, with both main beams showing a tendency to palmate.

Double palmated tops of a stag shot on *Inverbroom* forest (Ross-shire) by L. J. Haes in 1955. *(D. Whyte's Studio)*

A strong pair of antlers, with a palmated left top, shot on *Glenavon* forest (Banffshire) in 1974. *(Anon)*

13-pointer shot by Captain C. E. Lucas on *Braulen* (Inverness-shire) in 1905 – the 'official' Scottish record head 180.73 CIC points.

14-pointer from *Sannox*, Isle of Arran, shot by H. C. Abram in 1988.

Peter Forshaw's royal from Ayrshire, shot in 1973.

19-pointer from *Strathconon* (Ross-shire) shot on outbreak of war in 1939.

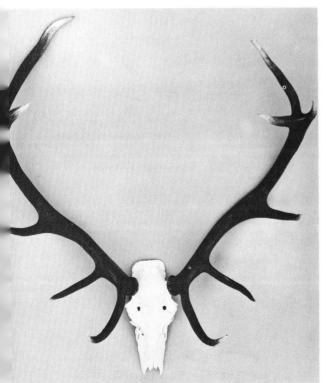

The last stag of the season.

PART V:

REVIEW OF SCOTTISH DEER STALKING SEASONS, 1948–1995

CHAPTER 28

Half a Century of Scottish Deer Stalking Weather

General

Weather plays a big part in every outdoor sport, not only for its enjoyment but also in the result, and in no outdoor activity is this more true that in deer stalking in the Scottish highlands.

Deer stalking in Scotland is an all-weather sport but, unfortunately, on average it has to be pursued on more wet than fine days.

There have been many stalking seasons in Scotland which have been described as 'the wettest ever', but generally this opinion has been based on a comparatively small area and not on Scotland as a whole.

In the last century the seasons of 1872, 1873 and 1874 each, in turn, earned this accolade whilst, in the early years of the present century, so did the seasons of 1922, 1923, 1924, 1934 and 1935.

Since the War, the following autumns certainly did their best to ensure that drying rooms in the numerous lodges situated around the Scottish highlands were well patronised each evening after a day on the hill: 1950, 1952, 1954, 1955, 1961, 1963, 1965, 1974, 1975, 1980, 1982 and 1985.

In most bad-weather seasons it is seldom that all forests throughout Scotland will have suffered equally. When the west-coast forests have been having their 'wettest-ever' season, those in the east may have been having an 'Indian summer', or vice versa. The above dates are, therefore, intended to refer to Scotland as a whole, and not to a district or region.

Not everyone will agree on what constitutes good weather for stalking. For instance, in 1965 a report received from a head stalker described the weather for the season as 'good', but his boss thought otherwise, and in his opinion it had been 'a very stormy season throughout'. A similarly contradictory report was received from another estate in 1967 which, according to the head stalker, had been 'ideal weather for the forest', but in the tenant's opinion it had been 'a cold and windy one, which was up to gale force at times'.

A report on the season's weather will most probably only refer to those weeks or months during which stalking has actually taken place and, so far as the smaller forests are concerned, this will very much depend on whether it is a 'stag forest' or 'hind forest'. If the former, then there is not much point in trailing to the 'high tops' in mid-October once the stags have broken out for the rut and joined the hinds elsewhere, so most of the stalking on such terrain will be from late August to the end of September. On the other hand, if it is 'hind ground' few stags will be shot before the rut, so any weather reports for these forests will normally refer only to late September and October.

It is not only rain and low cloud that causes poor visibility, for during a period of hot, sunny and sultry weather, a blue haze can make it extremely difficult to pick out deer with the telescope or binoculars unless the sun's rays have actually showed up their colour. Moreover, even when a stag has been discovered, it is never certain that other stags may not have been overlooked, subsequently to ruin the stalk.

Both rain and mist, if not actually ruling out any stalking for the day, do restrict the use of the telescope, for under such conditions it may soon become fogged up and will remain useless until a warm night in the drying room has dried it out. Under wet conditions, binoculars are far better than a telescope for they are less inclined to fog up. Nevertheless, on some occasions, even binoculars will become useless, and the stalker will then have to rely on hearing a roar or two in order to keep in contact with a rutting stag during a stalk.

Under such adverse conditions, fortunate are those whose eyesight enables them to use the 'open' or iron sight, but comparatively few rifles today are fitted with them. On those that are, unless the 'scope has a high shoulder-mount that will enable the open sight to be viewed underneath, the 'scope will have to be removed.

This will require re-zeroing when replaced before being taken to the hill again for stalking. Indeed, during the 1990 season the stalkers on *Rhiedorrach* (Perthshire) – and doubtless elsewhere – did, in fact, remove their 'scopes and, it was reported, shot with considerable success with the open-leaf sight. Under such weather conditions it is, of course, necessary to approach within about 90 yards (80 m) of a beast before attempting a shot.

In wet weather, when using a telescopic sight, it is essential that the 'scope should remain covered up until the *very last* moment before the shot is taken, for a few seconds exposure to heavy rain will soon render it useless. A good supply of absorbent 'loo' paper, therefore, already divided up into sheets and carried in roll form should be available for a last-minute mop-up – otherwise all your supply will be soaked through at the first application.

If all mopping up fails to leave a reasonably clear view through the 'scope, then one should not attempt a shot if only a blur of the target can be seen.

Incessant rain, as often as not accompanied by a gale-force wind, soon raises burns and rivers to flood level, or can make a loch too rough to venture out on a boat. During 1969 *Glencannich* (Inverness-shire) was one of the worst-affected areas, and on several occasions access to some of the best stalking areas by boat was quite impossible.

During 1974 the incessant rain not only kept the rivers and burns in constant spate, making it difficult, if not impossible, to gain access to some of the beats, but also turned any crawl over the sodden ground into a mud bath.

In that year there was a drowning tragedy on *Ben Alder* forest (Inverness-shire) when three men disappeared after their boat had overturned on Loch Ericht. Eventually two bodies were recovered by divers – one from a depth of about 35 feet (11 m) and the other from 130 feet (40 m), but it is not known when or where the third body was recovered.

Wind and Gales

Seldom does a season pass without one or more areas in the highlands having been affected by gale-force winds, and these can seriously disrupt the stalking on forests which have to rely on boat transport to reach some of the beats. During the 1978 season high winds made the lochs too rough, on both *West Benula* (Ross-shire) and *Kylestrome* (Sutherland), to venture out in a boat, so some of the best areas remained unstalked for several days.

In 1969 one of the worst affected areas was *Glenquoich* (Inverness-shire), where on one occasion the stalking party was literally blown flat down on their faces when only halfway up the hill. Nine years later the game dealer's van, while collecting carcases from *Glenavon* (Banffshire), was blown completely over.

During the 1961 season, on 16 September, a hurricane hit central Scotland, and Brigadier R. B. R. Colvin – the owner of *Corrievarkie* (Perthshire) – reported that forty-eight hours before its arrival, hundreds of hinds had started to come down to seek shelter in the birch woods along the north side of Loch Rannoch – an area in which they had never been seen before, even in a severe winter. The stags, however, sought shelter some 1,000 feet (300 m) higher up.

The winter of that year was one of the most severe and prolonged for many years, with deep snow on many forests from mid-November until March or April.

During 1978 *Coulin* (Ross-shire) recorded a September/October rainfall in excess of 50 in (1270 mm), whilst during the same season, in September alone, *Kingie* (Inverness-shire) recorded 23 in (584 mm).

In the following year, burns and rivers in spate made access to some of the best stalking areas on *Kinlochewe* (Ross-shire) an impossibility on a number of occasions, whilst in 1983, stalking on *Dalnessie* (Sutherland) had to be considerably restricted by swollen rivers. During the same season, on two separate occasions, torrential rain caused severe flooding at *Auchlyne* (Perthshire) – the first on 20 September and the second on 18 October.

More recently, on *Rumsdale* (Caithness) in 1993, a river in spate made it impossible to stalk on one particular beat on any occasion during the last two and a half weeks of the season.

During September 1982 the three rain gauges of the Institute of Hydrology installed on *Suie* (Perthshire) recorded an average of 18½ in

(470 mm) of rain – a figure that was exceeded on *Glenfinnan* (Inverness-shire) with a rainfall of 20 in (508 mm). *Dougarie* (Arran) experienced several days on which over 1 in (25.4 mm) of rain fell, whilst *Coulin* (Ross-shire) had a rainfall of 25 in (635 mm) during the months of August and September.

Mist

Mist is ever a problem with the deer stalker, for it can reduce visibility to nil and make a trip to the hill a pointless venture. For instance, on *Ben Alder* (Inverness-shire) during the 1982 season, all ground above 2,500 feet (760 m) was obliterated for three whole weeks, whilst on the same forest some seven years later G. K. Oswald, the stalker, reported that during his twenty-five years of stalking, he had never had to walk around in mist for so long as during that season.

For the same reason, during the 1982 season also, stalking on both *Ben Armine* and *Kinloch* (Sutherland) had to be confined to the low ground, whilst on *Letterewe* (Ross-shire) stalking had to be abandoned completely on eight days. Such events are, unfortunately, of regular occurrence in Scottish stalking when the *modus operandi* for each day has generally to be dictated by the weather.

Rain and stalking are synonymous, but although the former may perhaps be physically more unpleasant than mist, it is nothing like so disruptive, and more stags are probably shot on wet days than fine.

Fine Weather Seasons

Seasons in which the weather has been exceptionally fine over Scotland as a whole, and not in specific areas, have occurred during the following years: 1949, 1951, 1955, 1958, 1959, 1971, 1972, 1984, 1986, 1994 and 1995. Regarding the 1959 season, both August and September were extremely dry and windless over much of Scotland, and this kept many of the best stags to the highest parts of the forest, often out of range to all but the more active stalker. Here they remained until the oncoming rut forced them down to join the hinds at lower altitudes, but in many districts, owing to the mild weather, the break out did not occur until about 8 October.

Unfortunately for a number of forest owners and their guests - but perhaps more fortunately for some trophy stags - the autumn of 1959 coincided with the General Election, and by the time the rut had got under way, the more conscientious party supporters had already travelled south to help Harold Macmillan win his election. True, some did return north again for a further week or ten days, but by then many of the larger stags were so badly 'run' as to be unfit for venison.

Fine weather, apart from perhaps making a long crawl less arduous and being of considerable assistance when spying, does not necessarily make it any easier to kill stags - indeed the reverse may often be the case, for good weather can assist both sides. For instance, while good light will certainly assist the stalker in spotting and selecting his target, so too can the deer, unless looking directly into the sun, pick up the stalkers that much more easily - their presence, perhaps, being betrayed by a glint of sun on 'scope or spectacles.

I sometimes wonder, on a large forest, if the stalker is not too ready to blame lack of success on the wind instead of giving due credit to the stag for having selected an invulnerable position for itself. After all, the stag is as much concerned with its survival as the stalker is in its demise!

The exceptionally fine weather of 1972 kept the deer high up in order to take advantage of any light breeze which might help to keep the midges at bay. To reach the deer, therefore, meant more climbing than usual on some forests, and many a *Rifle* straight from his city desk soon discovered that he was not quite as fit as he had hoped! At times it was so hot that it was possible to walk around the high tops in shirt-sleeve order, and even normally wet areas were bone dry, revealing large cracks in the peat ground. Indeed, on some days it was quite a novelty to get one's knees wet whilst crawling!

A significant comment on Scottish weather came from Major Sir Gerard Fuller in his 1966 report for *Glencannich* (Inverness-shire), which stated, 'A splendid season only spoilt by the B.B.C. commentator telling us too often at 7.55 a.m. that the wind would be variable which thus ruined many a good day!'

Postscript

During 1983 the weather was so bad that one of the less-dedicated owners confessed that by mid-October they had decided to call it day, as by then they had all run out of dry clothes! I have no doubt that many other less courageous stalkers would have been on the same train south had they been given the choice!

Annual Summary – 1948–95

1948

Sunless, but highly satisfactory, would just about sum up the 1948 deer stalking season in Scotland. The west-coast forests, particularly *Rhum* and those in the *Kinlochewe* area, undoubtedly suffered the most from bad weather, especially during the latter part of September, but on the whole it cannot be said that many stalking days were lost on this account. Sutherland also had its share of rain, but the *Mar* and *Invercauld* forests in Aberdeenshire were favoured throughout most of the season with mild and dry weather - in fact the rainfall in the area throughout the year was remarkably low.

As a contrast to the prolonged blizzards of the 1946–47 winter, the winter of 1947–48 was mild and dry, with little or no snow to deprive the deer of their feed. The sharpest spell occurred during the last fortnight of November 1947, but thereafter the weather remained open, with February exceptionally mild. A few late frosts, however, did occur in May. Good feeding continued throughout the summer with the result that, by the time stalking commenced, beasts were extremely fat, and heads, on the whole, showed a great improvement on recent years.

1949

This season will be remembered for the exceptional weather which prevailed throughout Scotland. Day after day the temperature seldom fell below 60°F, although on some of the more western forests, such as *Affaric* (Inverness-shire) and *Strathconon* (Ross-shire), the weather did eventually break at the beginning of October to give a period of mist and rain. Elsewhere, however, the more fortunate forests were able to enjoy a continuation of the fine spell until stalking ceased.

1950

In contrast to the previous season, the weather of 1950 was probably one of the worst, and all forests throughout Scotland seem to have received their full quota of stormy weather. From *Kinloch* (Sutherland) in the extreme north to *Atholl* (Perthshire) in the south, and from *Mar* forest (Aberdeenshire) in the east to the island of *Rhum* (Inverness-shire) in the west, the story was the same – rain, hail and gales, with sleet and snow on the higher ground. Just how bad it generally was, and how sport suffered in consequence, can be gleaned from reports received from various parts of Scotland.

From *Badanloch* (Sutherland) George Wood reports that 'in about 20 years of stalking the past season has been quite the most appalling; it was so cold and wet, and the very few days that were at all decent were only half days!' Other Sutherland reports were similar. Throughout Ross-shire the weather was probably even worse. 'Only two fine days were experienced throughout September, and none in the first week of October' was Major J. L. Garton's report for *Kinlochewe*. 'Rain, hail and sleet, combined with north-westerly gales were practically incessant. In 20 years experience of stalking, I never remember anything to equal or even approach it.'

Reports from *Coulin*, *Inverbroom*, *Strathconon* and many other Ross-shire forests all reported similar conditions. At *Strathconon* the first snow fell on about 20 September and for the remainder of the season the tops remained covered. Here the prevailing east and south-east winds prevented some of the best beats being stalked at all, and on the few occasions when the wind had shifted to west or north-west, the river Orrin was generally so swollen by flood water that access to the ground with ponies was an impossibility.

Conditions in Inverness-shire were no better. 'It was the most disagreeable season I have ever spent on the hill', was Brigadier R. B. R. Colvin's comment from *Braeroy*, whilst the report from *Affaric* (Inverness-shire) described it 'as the worst on record'. During the three months of August to October 35½ in (900 mm) of rain were recorded, about half of which fell during September. Further west, on *Glenkingie* (Inverness-shire), September was even wetter, with no less than 25 in (635 mm) of rain being recorded. From Aberdeenshire, Angus, Argyllshire and Perthshire reports were all equally bad. The islands fared little better and on only one day did the stalking party enjoy fine weather.

1951

The stalking season of 1951 began under conditions which were far from satisfactory. Following one of the wettest seasons ever, the winter of 1950–51 was, in many areas, one of the longest and severest on record. On a number of forests there was continuous snow from October until April, and as late as May the high ground was still deep in frozen snow which, on some of the higher hills, had not disappeared until the 1951 stalking season had begun.

Following the hard winter there was a long spell of cold, dry weather in many parts of Scotland, with bitter east and north-east winds which prevented any growth of grass until June. The 1951 calves, therefore, arrived just when their dams, themselves, needed nourishment, and because of lack of it many calves died for want of milk. In July there was a high rainfall, particularly in the western forests, and elsewhere the summer was inclined to be cold and showery, with a fair amount of rain during the early part of August. From then onwards, however, the weather improved considerably.

Needless to say, after such a severe winter and spring, casualties among the deer of all ages were high, with thousands dying in many areas (*see* page 43).

1952

Highland weather is notably capricious, but seldon can it have served up a more mixed fare than during the 1952 stalking season. For instance, the forests in Caithness, Sutherland and northern Ross-shire, which had had a rather cold and sunless summer with high winds in many areas, had an even wetter and stormier stalking season, and particularly was this the case in the Ullapool area, where the weather was described as 'the worst ever experienced'. On many days it was so bad that it was an utter impossibility to use a telescope, even if it had been possible to go on to the hill at all. Yet only some 20 miles (32 km) south, in the Loch Maree district, the weather was tolerably good, and further south still it was variously described as being either 'too good', 'quite excellent' or 'the best for a number of years, with, apart from one week, perfect visibility'.

Although forests in western Inverness-shire enjoyed fairly good weather, it was very wet and stormy in the more central areas, and, during one week towards the end of September, stalking was almost impossible. In eastern Inverness-shire, however, and in Aberdeenshire, as well as in all the other more southerly areas of Scotland, the weather was generally favourable for stalking, but the persistent north or north-east wind did not suit many forests.

Some of the Ross-shire forests had their first fall of snow as early as 5 September, and on 15 September *Kinlochewe* forest had one of the heaviest falls ever experienced at that time of year, with snow lying down to about 1,000-foot (300 m) level. On *Braeroy* (Inverness-shire), there was snow on the high ground continuously from 15 September until the end of the season. Throughout Argyllshire, however, the weather could not have been more congenial for the hill, even though 'the wind was in the wrong airt!' But when can everything be just right?

1953

During the 1953 stalking season Scotland lived up to its usual reputation of serving up a mixed fare of weather, and while a few fortunate stalkers were able to report that it had been 'very good indeed – in fact better than average', the opinion of the majority was quite the opposite – 'it could not have been worse!'

The winter of 1952–53 had caused no great hardship for the deer, and the weather during the early spring had been reasonably open and mild. Seasonal casualties had, therefore, been light and by early summer the deer were in a forward

condition. Unfortunately, conditions deteriorated considerably during the summer months, and whilst wet and cold weather made June in many districts an extremely unpleasant month for the deer, this was followed by a period of midges which drove the deer right up to the tops and unfortunately took them away from the best grazing. This particularly applied to Perthshire and parts of Ross-shire, but west Inverness-shire enjoyed a good summer. Nevertheless, due almost solely to the excellent start the deer had received in the spring, the stalking season arrived with stags in all districts well forward and in good bodily condition.

1954

No one expected a great season, and it is certain that no one got one. Practically every sport in 1954, except possibly salmon fishing, suffered from the poor weather, and the deer stalkers certainly had their full quota of rain. The west-coast forests probably bore the full brunt of the rain and gales of autumn, and *Tarbert* (Isle of Jura), for instance, reported the wettest stalking season for over fifty years, with only five dry days in two months. At *Glenmoidart* (Inverness-shire) it was said to have been 'the worst within living memory, with many days on which it was quite impossible to use a telescope'. At *Craig* (Argyllshire) there were 7 in (177 mm) of rain in September, and over 12 in (305 mm) in October.

In central Ross-shire and Inverness-shire there was not much improvement, and some forests such as *Monar* and *Pait* lost a number of days due to mist. Very high winds added to the stalker's difficulties and discomfort.

Some of the more northerly forests, however, appear to have had more congenial conditions. At *Inverbroom* (Ross-shire), for instance, although the weather was uncomfortable at times, on only two occasions did it prevent the stalkers going to the hill. The weather at *Kinloch* (Sutherland) did not interfere much with the stalkers either, but further east still, at *Langwell* and *Braemore* (Caithness), it was described as 'the worst for many years'. *Mar* (Aberdeenshire) also had 'a very wet season', with a lot of low mist, but only two days stalking had to be abandoned. Yet on *Glen Tanar* (Aberdeenshire), only some 20 miles

(32 km) to the east, weather conditions were described as good for stalking.

The first snow fell in Ross-shire on 17 September, followed by another fall on the 20th, and an even heavier one on the 27th which, in the Loch Maree area, lay down to the 600-foot (183 m) level. The last-mentioned snow fall also affected some forests as far south as *Innerwick* and *Roro* in Perthshire.

Generally speaking it was the last week of the season that provided the best weather conditions for stalking. Had this not been the case, many forests would have experienced difficulty in killing their planned quota of stags.

1955

In many areas the stalking season followed one of the finest summers in living memory, with drought in many areas continuing well into the season. Furthermore, there was very little really cold weather until about 15 October when, with abrupt suddenness, the 'Indian summer' gave way to frost and snow. For several days in many areas there was then intermittent snow, sleet or rain until, on about 20 October, the sun returned to make the snow-capped mountains look even more beautiful. By this date, stalking on the majority of forests had already terminated, although a few estates did continue until the weekend of 22 October. At that period, however, no close season for deer operated in Scotland.

Not every forest, however, enjoyed such congenial stalking weather. Those forests in the extreme north and west suffered most. On the Isle of *Rhum*, for instance, the good weather broke on about 1 September, and from then on until the end of the month it rained more or less every day, with some mist. On *Ben More* (Isle of Mull) the weather was fair in September but very wet in October. On the mainland, the last fortnight of the season on *Kinloch* (Sutherland), where stalking finished on 8 October, was very bad, with many days of mist and driving rain.

Further west, on *Inverbroom* (Ross-shire), the drought ended on 10 September, and from then on many days were ruined either by mist, which made spying impossible, or by high winds, which made approach to the west beats by boat impracticable. The weather on *Inverinate* (Ross-shire) during the stalking season was described as

'vile', whilst *Monar* (Ross-shire) also lost a number of days on account of bad weather.

On the whole, however, the majority of stalkers were well satisfied with the weather, even if the wind, which was predominantly north and east, did not always blow from the best quarter for their forest. At *Talladh-a-Bheithe* (Perthshire), the thermometer during August and September was frequently over 80°F in the shade.

1956

Generally speaking, the 1956 season was a very good one for deer, and mortality during spring and early summer was the lowest for many years. The spring was a dry one, and in consequence the growth of grass, particularly on the higher ground, was rather late in coming. However, when the rain did arrive there was a wealth of grass throughout the summer months, which benefited the weights but not the antlers, which must have good feeding in the initial stages of growth.

For once the west-coast forests seem to have had the best of the weather during the stalking season, and very few days were lost due to mist or rain. In the east, however, bad weather at the beginning of the season did hamper the stalkers on *Mar* forest (Aberdeenshire), with the result that the majority of the stags had to be shot during the latter part of the season. Days of hill fog considerably interfered with stalking on *Langwell* and *Braemore* (Caithness).

Throughout most of September the prevailing east and south-east winds brought day after day of fine weather which, in some areas, became too hot for comfort when stalking. Needless to say, such conditions also kept the deer high up and there was a dearth of stags on the lower-lying forests until the stags had broken out for the rut. During the first week of October many forests had their first fall of snow and, even as far south as *Glenlyon* (Perthshire), on 4 October the snow was down to the 800-foot (240 m) level – about the lowest within living memory at this early date.

1957

The winter of 1956–57 was an exceptionally mild one in Scotland and, with little or no snow to contend with, the condition of the deer in early spring could seldom have been better. Weights, however, were not as good as might have been expected, for the exceptional mildness kept the deer to higher altitudes than customarily and in consequence they were forced to feed on sparser grazing. Paradoxically, therefore, they did not fare as well as they might have done had the weather been less mild!

Although the weather, particularly during the early part of September, was wet and cold in many parts of Scotland, stalking does not seem to have been much hampered by mist. The west coast and the islands fared the worst, and several stalkers described weather conditions during the first fortnight of September as 'appalling'.

On 15 September, and again on 29 September, there was a coating of snow on many of the hills in Inverness-shire and Ross-shire, lying as low as 1,000 feet (300 m) on *Affaric* (Inverness-shire) on the former date. During October the weather improved generally, and in many central forests conditions were ideal for stalking, with the result that by 10 October a number of forests had already reached their quota.

1958

The most memorable thing about the 1958 stalking season was the weather which, in many forests during September, was one of the hottest and finest experienced for many years.

Deer, on the whole, had come through the 1957–58 winter well, but then had to face a long, cold and dry spring with late frosts and prevailing east winds which considerably delayed the growth of grass. Such conditions are always damaging to stock, for this is the one period of the year when the deer require ample nourishment, not only to recover condition after the rigours of the winter, but also to assist the stags in the early development of antlers, as well as preparing the hinds for calf bearing. June – the month of calf bearing – was wet and cold, and although July became milder, the damp weather continued, with little or no sun until the start of the stalking. The weather then relented, and throughout practically all September it remained hot and dry almost everywhere, with conditions in parts of Inverness-shire and Perthshire described as being 'too hot for stalking'.

This 'Indian summer', however, seems to have eluded the more central forests of Perthshire, where conditions were variously described as 'appallingly wet' (*Talladh-a-Bheithe*), 'worst in memory' (*Boreland*) and 'many days of mist' (*Atholl* forests). Mist hampered sport during the first fortnight on *Langwell* and *Braemore* (Caithness), and wet conditions with mist interfered with stalking on some of the Aberdeenshire forests during the early part of October. Elsewhere, stalking conditions during October were described as normal – a few fine days interspersed with wet and cold ones – some of the latter being particularly so! There was little or no snow anywhere during the stalking season.

1959

If all else is forgotten, the weather during the 1959 stalking season will, in many districts, long be remembered as being one of the driest and warmest within most stalker's memories. From almost all quarters the story was the same – warm days with cloudless skies and little or no rain between the opening of the stalking season in mid-August and its closure in mid-October. *Affaric* (Inverness-shire) recorded only two wet days and both were on Sunday! Rainfall over much of Ross-shire was similar, with only about two days of rain between 25 August and 15 October. Hazy conditions, however, proved a handicap on some forests, and quite a number of stalkers complained that it was too hot for stalking.

1960

The best weather during the 1960 stalking season was in the west of Scotland, where the forests in the western half of Sutherland, Ross-shire, Inverness-shire and most of Argyllshire, enjoyed an unusually fine and mild spell of weather. Some of the forests in Ross-shire did have a certain amount of rain and mist to contend with during September, but October, when the majority of the stags were being killed, provided almost perfect conditions. One thing that seems to have been universal throughout the season was the wind, which remained in the east, with occasional variations of north-east and south-east, almost throughout the season. Stalking conditions in Angus, Aberdeenshire and Caithness, however, were poor, on account of persistent easterly winds which brought many days of mist and rain, resulting in poor spying conditions.

1961

To many the 1961 stalking season was one of the wettest on record, and it was not surprising to hear that some stalkers were more relieved than sorry when it was over. Stalking in such conditions is more of a business than a pleasure – a business that has to be done if the quota of stags can be in the larder before the rut has made the carcases too 'run'. The worst-affected forests were on the west coast, and these were, in fact, the very ones which, in 1960, had enjoyed such ideal stalking conditions. The most fortunate forests were those in northern Sutherland and Caithness – but even in these areas, several days of mist and rain made stalking difficult. The bad weather, however, did have its compensation, for it kept the hikers and climbers away. On 16 September a hurricane occurred, and some forty-eight hours before it arrived Brigadier R. B. R. Colvin, the owner of *Corrievarkie* (Perthshire), informed me that hundreds of hinds had already started to seek shelter in the birch woods along Loch Rannoch, where they had never previously been seen, even in severe winters. In contrast, the stags sought shelter some 1,000 feet (300 m) higher up.

1962

Whilst it is difficult to generalise for the whole of Scotland, it would appear that, throughout the two months or so of the 1962 stalking season, the weather was exceptionally mild, with the wind predominantly blowing from a southerly direction. This was often accompanied by hill fog on some of the higher-placed forests, whilst on a number of fine sunny days there was a blue haze which so often accompanies a high glass, and which frequently made spying extremely difficult.

The forests which enjoyed the best stalking weather were situated in eastern Sutherland; the worst, so far as rain and mist were concerned,

being those in the western part of that county and in Ross-shire.

1963

A season better to be endured than enjoyed – that about sums up the weather picture described in the majority of reports. *Reay* forest (Sutherland) reported an exceptionally wild and wet season, which lasted from the second week of September until the end of stalking. Similar conditions prevailed on *Kinloch* in the northern part of the county, but to the east there was a slight improvement until the Caithness border was crossed. But elsewhere it was predominantly wet, with the wind blowing consistently from the south or west.

A similar pattern was followed in most of the other counties, apart from some fair weather during the early part of the season. In October, however, when the majority of stags would be shot, it was atrocious, with much rain and incessant, stormy winds reaching gale force at times. Snow fell on the high ground in Inverness-shire and Ross-shire on about 25/26 September. Mist was also troublesome in southern Inverness-shire and in central Perthshire.

On forests such as *Glenkingie* (Inverness-shire), which have beats that can only be reached by boat, the high winds made the loch too rough to risk putting the boat out. The western islands, however, were more fortunate and the weather on both Jura and Harris was quite good. Angus, also, had fairly good weather.

1964

The weather plays a major part in the success and enjoyment of a day's stalking, and generally speaking on most of the forests in northern, central and eastern Scotland, it was better than it had been in recent years, particularly during October when there was a fair amount of sunshine. Rain and mist, however, considerably interfered with the sport on those forests situated near the western seaboard, and in particular Lady Mary Grosvenor described the weather at *Kylestrome* (Sutherland) as being about as bad as it could be with rain, gales or mist almost every day from the beginning of July until the end of October. Weather conditions were similar on *Knoydart* and *North Morar* (Inverness-shire) and on *Cluanie* (Ross-shire), whilst on the few days that the weather did break fair, hikers and climbers were attracted to the peaks, thus interfering with the stalking.

1965

Few stalkers were sorry when the 1965 stalking season ended, for days of continuous rain and peering through fogged-up telescopes – when the mist allowed a spy at all – do nothing to enhance the enjoyment of this sport. Throughout the whole of September and into early October there was hardly a day in Aberdeenshire, Banffshire, Inverness-shire, Perthshire and Ross-shire without rain or mist, but during the last ten days of the season, particularly in Sutherland and western Argyllshire, the weather relented and some forests enjoyed almost summer-like conditions to finish the season.

The weather can change enormously in districts separated by only a few miles. As a case in point, the weather on *Rhidorroch* (Ross-shire) was 'often fine with very few wet days', whilst only 12 miles (19 km) away to the south on *Strone* (Ross-shire) it was 'wet with very poor visibility and there were at least six days on which it was impossible to spy'. Some 7 miles (11 km) further south it was even worse.

It seems, however, that not everyone's idea of good or bad weather for stalking agrees, for from one forest the head stalker's weather report was 'good', but the tenant thought otherwise and said 'it had been stormy throughout'.

1966

Weatherwise, the 1966 stalking season was generally one of exceptional mildness, poor light and gentle, variable winds. Some forests fared better than others, and *Affaric* (Inverness-shire) reported the best stalking weather for seven years.

Further east the weather was not so good, and most of the Aberdeenshire forests had a fair amount of rain and a lot of mist which interfered with spying. Angus was not much better, with too much east wind and a considerable amount of hill fog during the latter part of September. Banffshire, however, was spared the latter and, although there were some very wet days, the weather, on the whole, was excellent.

Further north, the forests in the eastern half of Ross-shire seemed to have fared better than those in the Loch Maree area, where rain and persistent mist handicapped the stalkers.

Weather conditions in Sutherland were mixed, those forests in the south and east having a lot of rain and mist, whilst the forests in the extreme north and north-west had a comparatively dry season. The weather on *Langwell* and *Braemore* (Caithness) was described by M. Leslie, the Duke of Portland's factor, as being 'one of the wettest in memory'.

Conditions in Perthshire were patchy, those forests in the western part of the county having the best of the weather. At *Corrievarkie* the weather was almost too fine and still for stalking, yet at *Glenfernate* it was the other extreme, with 'very bad mist and rain every day making it the worst stalking season for a long time'.

1967

For many deer stalkers 1967 was an uncomfortable season, especially during the latter part, for with continuous rain and hail the ground soon became saturated and burns were in spate. Snow fell during the first week of October and again during the third week, with some particularly heavy falls in parts of Inverness-shire and Ross-shire. Gales – bitterly cold in some areas – were of frequent occurrence, but fortunately few forests had much trouble from mist or low cloud, and few days were lost on this account.

Swollen burns and lochs, lashed by gales, were a hazard on some forests, and rough water often prevented access by boat to those beats only accessible in this manner. On one occasion a beast was recovered on *Inversanda* (Argyllshire) by floating the carcase down a swollen river, tailed by two drag ropes for about a mile, before it could be transported to the lodge by pony.

In contrast to the general pattern of weather elsewhere, the Westminster forests of *Reay* and *Kylestrome* (Sutherland) were able to report that the weather had been the best for three or four seasons.

1968

The 1968 stalking season will be remembered by many stalkers as being the finest and mildest for years, for the good summer continued well into the stalking season before breaking in early October. Even then, in many parts of Scotland, it remained mild with little rain. In the western half of Scotland, and in particular on *Reay* forest, the weather was described as the best for years, with glorious, clear skies right up to the second week of October.

In the east, in both Aberdeenshire and Angus, the fine weather continued until early October, when it finally broke to be followed by periods of heavy rain. It remained mild, but a complete week's stalking was lost on *Hunthill* (Angus), due to low cloud. Snow fell in parts of Perthshire, Ross-shire and Inverness-shire about the middle of October.

1969

The eastern and central parts of Scotland enjoyed one of the finest and mildest autumns for many years. With the wind predominantly in the west and south-west, few forests in this half of Scotland were much troubled by the mist which so often accompanies a wind from a more easterly quarter. Mist and bad light did, however, make spying difficult on some of the Perthshire forests, but on the whole throughout this county, as well as in the central and eastern parts of Inverness-shire, Ross-shire and Sutherland, the weather was good for stalking.

The further west one went, however, so did the weather deteriorate, and many forests in Argyllshire, as well as those along the western seaboard in Inverness-shire, Ross-shire and Sutherland, suffered days of continuous rain and mist during the latter part of the season. At times, periods of tremendous gales did make walking on the high tops a near impossibility, and on one occasion the stalking party on *Glenquoich* (Inverness-shire) was literally blown flat when only halfway up the hill.

On *Arnisdale* (Inverness-shire) 20 in (508 mm) of rain fell during the first three weeks of October. *Kingairloch* (Argyllshire) also had about 11 in (280 mm) recorded for September. *Affaric* had one of the wettest seasons in memory.

On about 28 September, snow fell in a number of areas of Sutherland, Ross-shire and Inverness-shire, but it did not lie for long. Otherwise, temperatures throughout the season were mild.

1970

As in 1969, the forests in the eastern half of Scotland enjoyed the best weather, whilst in the west, with few exceptions, continuous rain and high gales were the order. Among the wettest areas were *Reay* forest (Sutherland), which recorded the heaviest rainfall for almost fifty years, and *Cluanie* (Ross-shire), where rain and gale-force winds made stalking impossible for days on end.

Kingairloch (Argyllshire) had over 25 in (635 mm) of rain between 1 September and 20 October, while *Gordonbush* (Sutherland) also had one of the worst seasons since early in the century. Otherwise the forests in the east had some pleasant stalking weather, particularly Angus, Banffshire and eastern Aberdeenshire.

With the exception of some of the higher-placed forests of Perthshire, mist did not interfere too much with stalking and, apart from a few light falls of snow on the high ground during October, the season was warm and mild.

1971

The autumn of 1971 provided some ideal stalking weather – dry, good light for spying and it was never really cold – indeed the only adverse comment came from one Aberdeenshire stalker who complained that it had perhaps been too fine and hot!

There were a few minor breaks in this 'Indian summer', but these occurred mainly around the 10 and 11 October as well as during the following week. Those counties most affected were Argyllshire, Ross-shire and the western part of Inverness-shire. At about this time, Perthshire was enjoying some superb weather, with hard frost at night and days of cloudless blue skies. October, however, was not a good month in south-west Scotland and several days of mist and rain interfered with stalking in Galloway.

Several days were lost through mist on *Kinlochewe* (Ross-shire), which also had some heavy snow showers on about 11 and 12 October.

Mist also proved troublesome on *Blackmount* (Argyllshire) during October. Apart from these few isolated areas, mist was not troublesome anywhere else in Scotland, and any early-morning low cloud had usually cleared by about midday.

1972

Weatherwise, the 1972 stalking season must be ranked as being one of the driest this century, and at no time did any forest have more than an odd day's rain during a nine-week season extending from mid-August to 20 October. Some forests escaped the rain altogether, whilst elsewhere the odd shower did little else than lay the dust. *Corrievarkie* (Perthshire) had a couple of wet days around 6 September, when there was a little sleet and snow on the high tops. About this period some forests, and also in Sutherland, had a day or two of frost with snow on the high ground. Otherwise the weather throughout most of northern Scotland remained hot, sunny and dry, even causing a water shortage in at least one area! With the variable, light winds, a heat haze, however, did prove troublesome at times in Angus.

1973

In like a lamb but out like a lion would just about summarise the weather pattern during the 1973 season, which until about mid-October had remained dry and warm over much of Scotland. It then suddenly changed, and over a wide area there was a heavy fall of snow which, on most of the higher forests, persisted until the end of the season, with the heaviest snow falling on 17 October. In many areas, the previous week had been quite the opposite – blue skies accompanied by light winds which had provided ideal stalking conditions.

1974

Many forests, particularly those in Sutherland and Caithness, as well as some inland forests in Ross-shire and Inverness-shire, had one of the wettest seasons on record, with rain almost daily and snow on the higher ground from about 23 September onwards, during which time the wind seldom shifted out of the north. The forests of Aberdeenshire, Banffshire and Perthshire did not fare much better and, although there was a lot of rain and low cloud during the early part of the season in Argyllshire, conditions from about 25 September onwards were described on *Blackmount* as being almost perfect, 'with marvellous cold, clear and sunny days, but with more snow than usual'.

After a wet September, stalking conditions in Galloway were described as near perfect by October, with frost at night and quite a lot of sunshine during the day. Similar weather was also experienced on some of the island forests off the west coast, as well as on some Inverness-shire forests that bordered the sea coast. Elsewhere, however, few stalkers were sorry to see the end of a season that had been described by one as 'the vilest and most depressing ever known'.

Despite the incessant rain, few days were lost due to mist.

1975

In many respects the poor weather experienced throughout most of Scotland during the 1975 stalking season was a repeat of the previous year, but with one big difference – for those sportsmen who were only able to stalk during the last three weeks of the season had, in some areas, been able to enjoy almost ideal conditions, with little rain or mist to contend with. Those, however, who had been on the hill in September could not have had worse conditions, for throughout most of the month, if it had not been heavy rain driven before gale-force winds, then low cloud and hill fog had made spying an impossibility.

September was described by Roderick Watt, the Head Stalker on *Knoydart*, (Inverness-shire) as 'one of the wettest and mistiest experienced for a great many years'. The forests in the extreme north-east of Scotland, however, seem to have fared the best, and *Langwell* (Caithness) had only about two or three really wet days throughout the whole season. In both Ross-shire and Sutherland, apart from the last week of the season, the weather during most of September and first ten days of October was extremely poor, with heavy rain, gales and a lot of mist.

1976

Weather – and wind in particular – plays an important role in deer stalking and undoubtedly the most important feature of the 1976 stalking season was the direction of the wind which, for almost two full months, never shifted out of the east.

Although an east wind is favourable on some forests, it is often accompanied by hill fog which can make stalking impossible. On account of hill fog, eight days had to be abandoned on *Langwell* (Caithness), resulting in the target cull of stags not being achieved. On *Huntbill* (Angus) even more days were lost on this account, and during the four weeks between 20 September and 20 October stalking was possible on only fifteen days. On *Glenavon* (Banffshire) the weather was described as the worst for twelve years.

Rain and mist also interfered with stalking on some forests in Perthshire, whilst at *Ben Alder* (Inverness-shire) 16 in (406 mm) of rain fell during October. Further west, however, the weather was more amenable and quite favourable conditions prevailed in parts of Argyllshire though, even here, mist was a major handicap during the last fortnight of September.

On the whole the weather was mild throughout the 1976 season, and although some snow did fall in the central Highlands around 9 and 10 September, it did not last long.

1977

Although throughout most of the season wind, rain or mist was the usual order of the day, those forests which were able to continue stalking until the last day of the season (20 October) did have quite a good week or so to finish up on. Even so, mist was ever a problem in some areas, and in particular on some of the forests in Angus, Perthshire and Ross-shire.

The first snow fell in the central Highlands on 8 September, with a heavier fall on 10 October, but on neither occasion did it lie for long, and temperatures, generally throughout the season, were on the mild side.

During September and continuing into the early part of October, Arran had a lot of rain, which was often accompanied by mist and some very high winds. Thereafter, however, the weather turned dry and mild, and produced a number of sunny days.

1978

There is no doubt that this season turned out to be an extremely wet one, and in most forests west of a line drawn from about Elgin in Morayshire to Perth it proved to be one of the wettest and wildest on record.

Just how wet it was is shown by the records of some rain-gauge figures. *Achnacarry* (Inverness-shire) recorded 17 in (432 mm) in September, which was an inch more than the figure for *Dougarie* (Isle of Arran). *Kingie* (Inverness-shire) had an even wetter September, with 23 in (584 mm) being recorded.

One of the wettest forests was probably *Coulin* (Ross-shire), where the September–October rainfall exceeded 50 in (1270 mm). On 6 October, and again on the 20th, there was a sprinkling of snow on some of the higher ground, but generally the weather remained mild throughout Scotland for the whole of the stalking season.

Another feature of the weather was the gale-force, westerly winds which blew almost continuously throughout the season. On forests such as *West Benula* (Ross-shire) and *Kylestrome* (Sutherland), where parts of the ground can only be reached by boat, it was often too rough to venture out on the loch. On *Affaric* (Inverness-shire) and *Strathvaich* (Ross-shire), to mention but two, burns and rivers in spate prevented access to some of the best stalking areas for days on end. Yet, in contrast to the soakings many stalkers had to endure, those fortunate enough to be stalking in Angus, Banffshire and the eastern part of Aberdeenshire enjoyed almost perfect conditions with little rain or mist and good visibility throughout.

1979

The 1979 deer stalking season was, with few exceptions, not only one of the mildest, but in many areas the wettest for a number of years, with the worst in the north-west and the best in the north-east. In north-west Sutherland the weather was so bad at *Kylestrome*, with rain and mist almost continuously from mid-August to mid-October, that Lady Mary Grosvenor confessed, '. . . the stalking became just a necessary chore – something which I should never have imagined I would ever have to say, but it really was unbelievable.'

All along the west coast it was much the same, described at *Eishken* (Isle of Lewis) as the 'worst in living memory', while on *Blackmount* (Argyllshire) and *Coulin* (Ross-shire), 12 in (305 mm) of rain fell during September. On *Kinlochewe* (Ross-shire), burns in spate often made access to some beats difficult. Fortunately October relented and there were a number of quite good stalking days in many areas.

The Isle of Arran had a particularly wet season, while the weather report from many forests in Perthshire was either 'appalling' or 'atrocious', with heavy rain, mist and gale-force winds much of the time. Further east, although there was less weight of rain, many days of mist and southerly winds hampered the stalking in both Aberdeenshire and Angus. Caithness, undoubtedly, had the best weather, being mild throughout with little rain, and westerly winds in September changing to an easterly one in October. The stalkers on *Loyal* (Sutherland) were particularly fortunate, for during the whole of three weeks stalking the weather was described as 'one of the driest for a number of years'.

1980

If the autumn weather had matched up to the spring, then the 1980 stalking season would have been an outstanding one. Unfortunately the ghastly weather, which prevailed in central, north and western Scotland throughout most of the season, made it memorable only for its unpleasantness. After a reasonably warm and dry spring the weather started to deteriorate, and by early autumn in many parts of Scotland, and particularly in the western half, it turned out to be one of the wettest on record. Heavy rain and mist in September, which was followed by more rain, accompanied by gale-force winds in October, brought flooding which made access to some beats impossible. There were 22 in (559 mm) of rain recorded on the island of Mull during September.

In contrast to the west, the weather in the eastern half of Scotland seems to have been more reasonable and, although wet and misty at times, the rain could be more aptly described as showery than prolonged. Angus probably fared the best, although the prevailing west wind did not suit some forests. However, much improved weather during the third week of October did provide some of the mainland forests of Argyllshire with a few days of 'ideal' stalking conditions – a period which coincided with a fairly heavy fall of snow over much of the country on some of the higher-placed forests.

1981

So far as the weather was concerned, the 1981 stalking season in parts of northern and western Scotland was a repeat of 1980, only worse, for in addition to heavy rain and gale-force winds, most forests had snow on the higher ground from early October onwards.

The worst-affected forests were those in north-west Scotland and Wester Ross, and on 13 October there was snow down to sea level on the *Reay* forest. In more than forty years stalking, I had never experienced such conditions in October.

Caithness escaped much of the snow, and the weather there, after a mild start, was generally wet accompanied by gale-force winds. Aberdeenshire and Angus probably fared the best for, apart from a few days of wintry weather during the first part of October, conditions were quite good for stalking. In Banffshire, however, the weather from late September onwards was described as 'dreadful'.

In the more central counties of Perthshire, Inverness-shire and Argyllshire, the early part of the season was extremely mild with a fair amount of sunshine in Perthshire but, from late September onwards, rain, accompanied by gale-force winds and snow on the tops, was the order of the day.

It is mist rather than rain which will prevent stalkers taking to the hill, and this year few days were lost on this account. On some forests, however, such as *Affaric* (Inverness-shire), rivers and burns in flood for weeks on end very much limited the stalking ground, and spying was impossible on some days.

1982

Few stalkers were sorry when the 1982 stalking season ended for, with few exceptions, it proved to be an extremely wet one throughout much of Scotland, September being particularly bad. *Glenavon* (Banffshire), for instance, reported only four dry days in almost fifteen weeks of stalking, while on *Kingairloch* (Argyllshire) it was one of the longest periods of appalling rain, mist and gales ever remembered.

During September the three rain gauges of the Institute of Hydrology installed on *Suie* (Perthshire) recorded an average of 18½ in (470 mm) rain – a figure that was exceeded on *Glenfinnan* (Inverness-shire) with a rainfall of 20 in (508 mm). *Dougarie* (Arran) experienced several days on which more than an inch (25.4 mm) of rain fell, while *Coulin* (Ross-shire) had a rainfall of 25 in (635 mm) during the months of August and September.

Even when it was not actually raining, mist on some of the higher-placed forests was a severe handicap to the stalkers, and for three weeks on end all ground above 2,500 feet (762 m) was obliterated on *Ben Alder* (Inverness-shire). For the same reason, stalking on both *Ben Armine* and *Kinloch* (Sutherland) had to be restricted to low ground. On *Letterewe* (Ross-shire) stalking had to be abandoned on eight days, while many days were lost due to mist and rain on *Achnacarry North* (Inverness-shire), *Strone* (Ross-shire) and *Tombuie* (Perthshire). On *Blackmount* (Argyllshire), however, although there were rain and gales most days, the actual rainfall during September and early October was less than in the previous two years, so stalking was little affected. Weather on some of the west-coast islands seems to have been more amenable and stalking was not unduly affected on either *Rhum* or *Jura*.

1983

A cold, wet winter was followed by one of the driest summers in recent years, and this fine weather continued well on into early September. Then, just as the stalking season was getting under way, it suddenly broke to give many forests in the western half of Scotland one of the wettest seasons ever recorded.

In many parts of Scotland it was a repetition of the previous season, only perhaps wetter, but mild with no frost and only a light scattering of snow on the high tops of some of the more central forests.

Blackmount and *Glen Etive* (Argyllshire), for instance, during the six weeks from the beginning of September to mid-October recorded 25½ in (648 mm) of rain. At *Auchlyne* (Perthshire) torrential rain caused flooding on 20 September and again a month later. At *Dalnessie* (Sutherland) stalking was at times considerably restricted because the stalkers were unable to cross swollen rivers.

On the eastern side of the country conditions were more amenable, and although the forests of Caithness and Aberdeenshire had a share of stormy days with rain and gale-force winds, weather conditions in these two counties were mixed. Angus seems to have fared best, with the prevailing south to south-west wind apparently suiting most forests.

1984

Apart from some wet days accompanied by gale-force winds during the latter part of the season, the weather over much of Scotland was an improvement on recent years, and many forests enjoyed almost ideal conditions for stalking. It was generally mild throughout and, until the rut had commenced, these conditions kept the deer well out on the high ground, which provided more challenging stalking for the young and active.

Some of the more central forests of Inverness-shire did have a fair amount of rain during late September and early October, and some forests in the north-west of Ross-shire were troubled during October with spells of heavy rain and hill fog, which was also troublesome on some forests in Sutherland. Apart from one or two rough days, the mild weather provided ideal stalking conditions in Caithness.

1985

Stalkers who were able to restrict their stalking to the last fortnight of the season (7–20 October) enjoyed, in many areas of Scotland, almost ideal conditions, the weather being mild with good light for spying. Prior to this, however, the season had been described by some as one of the wettest on record. The low ground became so sodden that it forced many deer to move out on to the more heathery and dry ground higher up the hill, but unfortunately these areas were frequently blanketed out with hill fog which made spying impossible. Winds too, predominantly from a south to south-westerly direction, often reached gale force, and loch surfaces were whipped up, making access to some beats impossible. There was, however, little frost and virtually no snow, even on the high tops. The rains of spring and early summer had, however, produced a luxuriant growth of grass, and in consequence the deer were in excellent condition.

1986

This season was probably one of the mildest and driest for many years. Taking Scotland as a whole, both east and west enjoyed fair weather for most of the time with the eastern forests scoring best.

There were of course a few exceptions, and included among the less fortunate forests were *Reay* and *Loch Choire* in Sutherland. *Reay* had a wet but not particularly cold September and October, whilst *Loch Choire* had 'an indescribably awful September', which was followed by 'a pleasant October'. The report from *Monar* and *Pait* (Ross-shire) was not much better, with a lot of mist and rain from mid-September to mid-October, which of course coincided with the height of the stalking season.

1987

The weather during the 1987 stalking season was probably one of the best for many years, particularly in Sutherland, northern Ross-shire and Angus. The forests of Argyllshire, Perthshire and much of Inverness-shire also all had reasonable spells of excellent stalking weather but, like 'the curate's egg', it was only good in parts.

On *Affaric*, for instance, out of a total of fifty-four stalking days, twenty were dry and thirty-four wet, of which fourteen were described as 'very wet indeed', which caused rivers and burns to flood. Around 9 October three days of sleet and snow gave a covering down to the 900-foot (274 m) level. The best spell was between 28 September and 3 October, but the warm and sunny weather, accompanied by a south-east wind, produced a blue heat haze which made spying difficult. Despite the wet conditions, only six of the fourteen blank days, reports Duncan MacLennan, the head stalker, were attributable to weather, the remainder being due to disturbance from hill-walkers.

1988

In contrast to the previous year, the 1988 season turned out to be an extremely wet one and, apart from some beautiful days in parts of the west during the second week of October, the general pattern was rain, mist and days of high wind. Snow fell in some of the northern forests during the latter part of September and first week of October, with a covering down to about the 2,000-foot (610 m) level, but it didn't remain long and for the most part the weather was mild with only the odd night of frost. Hill fog severely handicapped spying in some forests, and on 7 October *Affaric* (Inverness-shire) had 2½ in (63.5 mm) of rain, with an overall total of 16 in (406 mm) for the nine-week stalking season. A visitor to Perthshire for a week's stalking had to return south without firing a shot, five of the six days having been completely washed out with torrential rain, with a blank on the sixth day. On the *Lochiel* group of forests (Inverness-shire) it rained steadily from 1 July to early October.

1989

Highland weather is notably capricious, but seldom can there have been a milder season than this year. The north-eastern and eastern forests undoubtedly fared the best, particularly those in Angus, Aberdeenshire, Caithness and the eastern half of Sutherland, where conditions were exceptionally dry and ideal for stalking. In the west, particularly on the islands and forests of western Argyllshire and Inverness-shire, mist and gale-force winds did, on occasions, hamper stalking, but everywhere it remained mild.

Mist was also a problem on some of the more central forests, and G. K. Oswald, the head stalker on *Ben Alder* (Inverness-shire), reported that during his twenty-five years on the hill he had never had to walk around in mist so much as during this particular season.

At the beginning of October Perthshire was having a few nights of frost, and on the 14th of the month there was a sprinkling of snow on the high tops of *Glenfinnan* (Inverness-shire), but these first signs of approaching winter were of short duration and the mild and sometimes humid conditions soon returned.

1990

With few exceptions the stalking season this year was not only one of the mildest in recent years, but also, in many parts of the west, an extremely wet one. In contrast, conditions in Angus were almost ideal, being mainly dry with little or no mist to handicap spying.

So far as weather is concerned, it is almost impossible to generalise, for in the highlands of Scotland, even in a single county, conditions can change dramatically within the space of a few miles. At *Langwell* (Caithness), for instance, the weather was described as 'mild, but very wet', yet only a few miles to the east, on neighbouring *Dunbeath*, the report was 'very good'. Some 15 miles (24 km) or so to the west, however at *Dunrobin* (Sutherland), it was 'the wettest for 20 years'. Not everyone's opinion of a 'soaking' is quite the same, however!

Around 20 September some of the higher-placed forests had their first fall of snow, and on both *Affaric* (Inverness-shire) and *Mar* (Aberdeenshire) snow cover remained for a day or two down to the 1,500 foot (457 m) level. Combined with a gale-force wind, snow such as this made stalking on the high ground well-nigh impossible, but fortunately it did not remain for long, and milder conditions returned for the remainder of the season.

1991

Extreme weather conditions greatly affected the start of the 1991 stalking season. Following a spell of very warm and dry weather during late August and into the first fortnight of September, most forests experienced a period of heavy showers accompanied by high winds which continued until 7 October. Thereafter, conditions were almost ideal for stalking and many forests were able to catch up on their cull before blizzard conditions hit many of the higher forests during the last three days of the season.

From mid-September onwards, hill fog proved very troublesome on some forests in Angus, and on *Invermark* three full days had to be abandoned on this account.

1992

During this season many forests in the east had to endure endless days of easterly winds. Such winds are accompanied, as often as not, by mist or a frustrating blue haze, through which even the best 'glass' is hardly able to penetrate. Early October provided, in many areas, a period of dry weather, offering ideal days for the hill but, come the middle of the month, snow and blizzard conditions hit most of the higher-placed forests and left a snow cover down to about the 1,500-foot (457 m) level until the end of the season (20 October). In Inverness-shire, apart from some good stalking weather during the early part of October, the weather generally was very mixed, with a lot of rain from about mid-August to mid-September, during which period *Glendessary* recorded 9 in (229 mm) of rain during a forty-hour period. On Arran, October provided some ideal days for stalking, with excellent spying conditions.

1993

For many forests in central and western Scotland the stalking season will be remembered for being one of the driest on record, with days of brilliant sunshine and an ideal light for spying. Throughout much of the season the prevailing wind was from the east or north-east, and although this did prove to be troublesome on some forests, it was preferable to the soaking which often accompanies wind from the west.

The more northerly and eastern forests were not so fortunate, and forests in Caithness,

Aberdeenshire, Angus and Sutherland all had a considerable amount of rain and mist to contend with. In fact, on the large *Mar* Estate forest of Aberdeenshire, which had a cull of 186 stags, stalking conditions were described as 'the wettest for many years'. On *Rumsdale* (Caithness), a river in spate made it impossible to stalk one beat for the last two and half weeks of the season.

From mid-October onwards snow fell over the northern half of Scotland, and many of the higher-placed forests had a covering of snow for the latter part of the season.

1994

The 1994 stalking season can justifiably be described as one of the driest for very many years, and seldom since perhaps 1970 have the drying rooms in the numerous lodges situated around the Scottish highlands been less patronised.

There was a covering of snow on some of the higher-placed forests during the first week of October, as well as a few days of rain about that period in some other areas, but on the whole the weather was exceptionally mild, with some stalkers complaining that on occasions it was really too hot for comfortable stalking. On *Sannox* (Arran) the exceptionally warm weather also made the stags lazy, many of them preferring to lie about in the sun than court their hinds or fight rivals.

During early October there was a period of rain, sleet and snow on the high ground of Sutherland, whilst periods of low mist proved a handicap to spying on some forests of Ross-shire. Midges also, in some areas, enjoyed the warm weather but their presence was not welcomed by the stalkers.

1995

Following a long hot summer, the weather over much of Scotland continued good until mid-September, and the ground became hard and parched, with burns reduced to a trickle, or even disappearing altogether. A number of stalkers, therefore, complained that it had been too hot for comfortable stalking.

Show fell in some areas of Ross-shire about 27 September but it did not remain for long, and although in many areas, during October, there were some heavy showers accompanied by gale-force winds, stalking was not interfered with. Mist, however, did trouble some forests, particularly in Sutherland, and as a consequence a number of days had to be abandoned.

CHAPTER 29
Scottish Deer Stalking Seasons, 1959–1995

A summary of the annual cull of stags and hinds, with
reference to estate owners and head stalkers.

Annual Stag Cull

In some cases the number of stags listed against an
individual forest may only refer to those beasts
shot by the tenant and his guests, but may not
include some additional stags shot by the stalker
in order to complete his planned cull.
Furthermore, some additional deer of both sexes
may have been shot out of season for alleged
marauding, and these also may not have been
included. In 1978, for example, it was reported
that 263 stags had been shot on *Glenspean*
(Inverness-shire).

The tenant may be a sporting agency, who will
be sub-letting stalking by the day, week or month,
and on a number of estates it has become
increasingly common for the stag cull to have
been achieved by numerous tenants rather than
an individual, as was the norm in pre-War years.

In recent years, also, some of the larger estates
have been disposing of some peripheral areas,
with the result that the present-day cull for that
particular estate has probably been achieved on a
much reduced area, so true comparisons are not
really possible. On the other hand, if the areas
disposed of are also being regularly stalked by
new owners, then more stalkers will probably

have been out, thereby causing greater
disturbance to the deer.

The Annual Hind Cull

In order to reduce the hind population in Scotland
there has been a considerable increase, during
recent years, in their cull, and this was particularly
noticeable during the winter of 1992-93, when
the cull on many of the forests can be considered
a one-off 'crash' figure rather than one that could
be maintained annually in the foreseeable future.

For instance, on the combined Portland forests
of *Langwell* and *Braemore* (Caithness), the hind
cull in 1992, as compared to an average annual cull
of *c*.220 over the previous twenty-five years, was
1,040, whilst on *Invermark* (Angus) the hind cull
in 1992 was 880 compared to 261 during the
previous quarter century. Other spectacular
increases occurred on *Glenartney* (Perthshire),
where the 1992 cull was 420 compared to 255 over
the previous twenty-five years, and on *Strathconon*
(Ross-shire), where the 1992 hind cull of 680 was
about four times the average since 1966.

A notable exception, however, was on *Glenavon*
(Banffshire), where the 1992 hind cull of 110

was well below the average (154) for this forest.

The following table illustrates the manner in which the hind cull – including calves – on some of the major forests of Scotland has fluctuated during the past quarter century.

Calves

Whilst culling hinds, stalkers are encouraged to kill the attendant calf, and this, of course, will be easier to achieve early in the season, particularly with a late calf that may be reluctant to leave its parent that has just been shot.

In their annual report, a number of estates are now separating the number of calves shot from the total hind cull, and on some of the larger forests this would appear to average out at about 20–25 per cent. A much higher percentage than this, however, was achieved on *Glenmuick* (Aberdeenshire) during the winter of 1993–94 when about 32 per cent of the total hind cull of 352 were calves. On *Glenartney* (Perthshire), during the same winter, out of a total hind cull of 573, 102 were calves – or approximately 18 per cent. On *Strathconon* (Ross-shire), during the

1991–92 winter, out of a total cull of 289, 71 were calves – about 25 per cent. During the following winter, 22 per cent of the hind cull on *Achentoul* (Sutherland) were calves.

On *Fealar* (Perthshire), during the winter of 1991/92, out of a total cull of 200 hinds and calves, thirty were calves – a percentage of 15%. During the following winter, out of a total cull of 197, 22 percent were calves.

During the winter of 1994–95, out of a total hind calf cull of 165 on *Kilchoan (Knoydart)* fifty eight were calves – a percentage of 35%.

Annual cull data

The annual cull figures, for both stag and hind, in the following tables have been divided into three categories – *average, highest* and *lowest* – with the reported year of the *highest* and *lowest* being recorded, and the number of years over which the *average* has been calculated. Obviously the most reliable *average* will be one covering most years, whilst *highest* and *lowest* only fulfil that status among *reported* data.

Table A: Variation in hind culls 1966–1992

County	Forest	Average cull 1966–1991	Highest cull	Lowest cull	1992* Cull	1993* Cull
Aberdeenshire	Glenmuick	c. 111	275 (1991)	62 (1967)	431	352
Angus	Invermark	c. 261	609 (1991)	142 (1972)	880	810
Argyllshire	Blackmount	c.98	136 (1991)	63 (1984)	174	140
Banffshire	Glenavon	c.154	344 (1966)	76 (1967)	110	141
Bute (Arran)	Sannox	c.152	210 (1986)	55 (1973)	193	190
Caithness	Langwell and Braemore	c.220	562 (1990)	84 (1968)	1040	1022
Inverness-shire	Ardverikie	c.179	280 (1991)	90 (1967)	211	164
Perthshire	Glenartney	c.255	500 (1986)	106 (1978)	420	573
Ross-shire	Strathconon	c.155	356 (1967)	55 (1981)	680	550
Sutherland*	Achentoul	c.83	256 (1989)	43 (1985)	176	119

* Prior to 1993 the overall cull of hinds, including calves, for *Reay, Lochmore,* and *Gobernuisgach* (Sutherland) was generally included in the overall cull for *Reay* and has, therefore, been omitted from the Table.

In 1993 the overall cull of hinds, including calves, for these forests, was 284, divided up as follows: *Reay* (North) 206; *Reay* (South) 42; *Gobernuisgach* 36.

On some forests the annual 'cull' has included both hinds and calves which have been caught up for deer farming, and these include *Glenmuick* (Aberdeenshire), *Gaick* and *Glenbanchor* (Inverness-shire).

Table B   The annual stag and hind cull on some Scottish Deer Forests since 1959

ABERDEENSHIRE FOREST	Owner 1995 or at date of last report	Stalker 1995 or at date of last report	ANNUAL STAG CULL			ANNUAL HIND CULL		
			Average	Highest	Lowest	Average	Highest	Lowest
Ab.1 Corndavon	Invercauld Estates	Jim Davidson	19(12)	35(1995)	11(1982)	115(12)	206(1989)	80(1986)
Ab.2 Derry	– see Mar Forest Ab.11		—	—	—	—	—	—
Ab.3 Geldie								
Ab.4 Glenbuchat	Col. J. Barclay Milne (1965)	?	25	25	25	—	—	—
Ab.5 Glencallater	Invercauld Estates	M. Falconer	39(34)	67(1995)	35(1969)	82(34)	200(1991)	57(1978)
Ab.6 Glenclunie	Invercauld Estates	David Howe	21(36)	31(1960)	17(1978)	45(24)	107(1992)	20(1970)
Ab.7 Glen Ey	– see Mar Forest Ab.11		—	—	—	—	—	—
Ab.8 Glenmuick	Sir Peter Walker-Okeover	A. Taylor	45(32)	80(1986)	13(1960)	137(22)	431(1992)	61(1967)
Ab.9 Glen Tanar	Lord Glentanar (1963)	?	17(4)	24(1960)	7(1961)	?	?	?
Ab.10 Invercauld	Invercauld Estates	Peter Fraser	56(34)*	90(1965)	29(1988)	127(26)	230(1976)	48(1985)
Ab.11 Mar Forest Glen Ey Derry	M. M. Nicolson	Ian Campbell (1995)	66(26)	101(1978)	40(1977)	208(4)	283(1966)	25(1986)
Geldie			152(19)	210(1959) 329(1995)	98(1974)	325(22)	1000(1992)	100(1968)
Lodge	National Trust for Scotland.	S. W. Cumming						

Footnote Aberdeenshire * Prior to 1981, when the stag cull on *Invercauld* (Ab.10) included stags shot on *Corndavon* (Ab.1) the average was 64 per annum.

ANGUS FOREST	Owner 1995 or at date of last report	Stalker 1995 or at date of last report	ANNUAL STAG CULL			ANNUAL HIND CULL		
			Average	Highest	Lowest	Average	Highest	Lowest
An.1 Caenlochan (Tulchan)	Tulchan Estate Ltd	R. Smith	100(9)	169(1994)	38(1960)	150	287(1992)	149(1984)
An.2 Craig Lodge	see Glenprosen An. 8			—	—		—	—
An.3 Fern – see also Glenogil An. 7	The Earl of Woolton	Hamish Ferguson	28(5)	64(1982)	15(1991)	?	?	?
An.4 Glencally (Glenisla)	Major J. P. O. Gibb and A. J. Gibb	D. Sharp	27(14)	120(1994)	5(1962)	179(3)	200(1995)	148(1993)
An.5 Glendoll – see Rottal An. 13	The Earl of Airlie			—	—		—	—
An.6 Glenmoy	The Earl of Airlie	Michael Nisbet	53(16)	81(1993)	31(1986)	134(12)	255(1992)	43(1976)

ANGUS cont.

FOREST	Owner 1995 or at date of last report	Stalker 1995 or at date of last report	ANNUAL STAG CULL			ANNUAL HIND CULL		
			Average	Highest	Lowest	Average	Highest	Lowest
An.7 Glenogil – incl. Fern and Glenquiech	The Earl of Woolton	Hamish Ferguson	86(12)	121(1993)	86(1994)	146(7)	210(1990)[1]	61(1993)
An.8 Glenprosen	Glenprosen Sporting Ltd.	Alex Boath	63(17)	127(1994)	34(1986)	196(11)	462(1992)	59(1982)
An.9 Glenquiech	The Earl of Woolton	Hamish Ferguson	13(5)	29(1982)	5(1984)	included in Glenogil		
An.10 Hunthill	H. N. L. Keswick	D. Wilson	53(34)[1]	150(1993)	6(1969)	128(26)	328(1991)	19(1969)
An.11 Invermark	The Earl of Dalhousie	F Taylor	98(35)	163(1995)	70(1969)	310(28)	880(1992)	142(1972)
An.12 Millden	J. Stevens	Dennis Caithness	74(3)	108(1993)[2]	25(1990)	72(4)	120(1992)	44(1993)
An.13 Rottal & Glendoll	The Earl of Airlie	Alex Mearns	73(17)	103(1995)	71(1985)	167(14)	250(1976)	105(1981)
An.14 Tulchan	see Caenlochan	—	—	—	—	—	—	—

Footnote (Angus) [1] The hind cull was divided up as follows: *Glenogil* (An.7) 184, *Fern* (An.3) 24, *Glenquiech* (An.9) 2 = 210
[2] This total on Millden (An.12) includes 56 stags shot out of season. In the following year 70 stags had to be shot.

ARGYLLSHIRE

FOREST	Owner 1995 or at date of last report	Stalker 1995 or at date of last report	ANNUAL STAG CULL			ANNUAL HIND CULL		
			Average	Highest	Lowest	Average	Highest	Lowest
Ar.1 Accurach	Part of Inveraray (Ar.37)	—	—	—	—	—	—	—
Ar.2 Altchaorunn	- see Dalness (Ar.21)							
Ar.3 Ardfin (Jura)	A. W. A. Riley-Smith	William Macdonald	49(18)	60(1980)	30(1964)	71(16)	150(1992)	48(1978)
Ar.4 Ardgour	Robin Maclean of Ardgour	Allan Cameron	29(18)	40(1970)	12(1967)	66(4)	98(1991)	38(1987)
Ar.5 Ardkinglass	John and Michael Noble (1965)	?	21(4)	30(1960)	15(1965)	—	—	—
Ar.6 Ardlussa (Jura)	Mrs A. R. Nelson (1963)	?	88(5)	102(1963)	77(1960)	?	?	?
Ar.7 Ardmore (Islay)	Sir Ian Mactaggart (1966)	?	32(2)	45(1965)	18(1966)	?	?	?
Ar.8 Ardnamurchan	J. C. Grisewood	Rowantree, Niall A.	38(2)	42(1995)	38(1993)	68(1993)		
Ar.9 Ardtalla (Islay)	Sir John Mactaggart	Gillian Diviani (1990) Callum Sharp (1993)	45(12)	63(1987)	18(1963)	89(9)	135(1987)	70(1992)
Ar.10 Ardtornish	Ardtornish Estate Co. Ltd. (1979)	Ian Thornber	51(1)	51(1979)	51(1979)	82(6)	109(1976)	62(1978)
Ar.11 Auch and Invergaunan	N. W. Braid Aitken (1968)	?	25(5)	40(1965)	12(1959)	—	—	—
Ar.12 Auchnacraig (Mull)	Colonel M. P. de Klee	Owner	9(13)	11(1987)	5(1989)	23(5)	25(1991)	10(1989)

ARGYLLSHIRE cont. FOREST	Owner 1995 or at date of last report	Stalker 1995 or at date of last report	ANNUAL STAG CULL			ANNUAL HIND CULL		
			Average	Highest	Lowest	Average	Highest	Lowest
Ar.13 Barrs	Forestry Commission (1962)	?	5(3)	6(1960)	4(1962)	—	—	—
Ar.14 Ben More (Mull)	Viscount Massereene & Ferrard (dec'd)	A. Elwiss	22(32)	41(1968)	12(1989)	13(19)	27(1987)	5(1981)
Ar.15 Black Corries – see also Glencoe	Vicomte Adolphe de Spoelberch	Peter O'Connel	43(19)	64(1962)	28(1983)	53(15)	180(1976)	12(1987)
Ar.16 Blackmount[1]	Robin Fleming	Hamish Menzies	73	119(1970)	36(1988)	102(28)	167(1994)[5]	63(1984)
Ar.17 Caolasnacoan	British Aluminium Co. Ltd	?	10(1)	10(1973)	10(1973)	?	?	?
Ar.18 Carse	Ian P. Coats, D. L.	?	4(12)[2]	11(1972)[2]	1(1974)	?	?	?
Ar.19 Conaglen	F Guthrie	Donald Kennedy	58(31)	88(1967)[3]	30(1986)	88(26)	230(1994)	44(1985)
Ar.20 Craig and other F.C. property	Forestry Commission (1982)	?	17(4)	37(1981)	12(1979)	?	?	?
Ar.21 Dalness (Altachaoruan)	R. J. Fleming	A. Hunter	18(25)	34(1967)	9(1990)	15(17)	37(1992)	1(1980)
Ar.22 Druimavuic	Broadland Properties Ltd.		10(3)	14(1962)	7(1960)	—	—	—
Ar.23 Dunlossit (Islay)	Dunlossit Trustees Ltd	D. J. MacPhee	39(11)	63(1987)	2(1961)	77(6)	121(1985)	52(1991)
Ar.24 Ederline	Major W. Warde Aldam	E. Maclean	9(29)	16(1990)	3(1983)	2(16)	11(1993)	0(1991)
Ar.25 Eignaig (Ardtornish)	Ardtornish Estate	Ian Thornber	2(5)	3(1993)	1(1989)	13(3)	19(1994)	8(1987)
Ar.26 Forest Lodge (Jura)	G. R. Rickman and W. S. Wilson (1962)	?	15(3)	17(1962)	12(1961)	?	?	?
Ar.27 Glencoe – see also Kinlochberg Ar.42	Vicomte Adolphe de Spoelberch	?	23(9)	41(1976)[4]	12(1970)	?	?	?
Ar.28 Glencreran	Simon Fraser (1971)	?	21(1971)	?	?	?	?	?
Ar.29 Glenetive – see also Blackmount Ar.16	Robin Fleming	Hamish Menzies	14(14)	24(1975)	3(1986)	19(1994)	19(1994)	?
Ar.30 Glenfyne	J. and M. Noble (1969)	?	18(4)	29(1961)	12(1967)	?	?	?
Ar.31 Glenhurrich	see Conaglen Ar. 19		—	—	—	—	—	—
Ar.32 Glenkinglass	Hon. Mrs Schuster Hon. Mrs Fleming	Tim Healey	40(21)	60(1983)	27(1962)	80(15)	240(1992)	30(1994)
Ar.33 Glensanda, also Kingairloch Ar. 41	Foster Yeoman Ltd	Ian Thornber	4(1994)	?	?	*see* Kingairloch (Ar.41)		

237

ARGYLLSHIRE cont. FOREST	Owner 1995 or at date of last report	Stalker 1995 or at date of last report	ANNUAL STAG CULL			ANNUAL HIND CULL		
			Average	Highest	Lowest	Average	Highest	Lowest
Ar.34 Glenshira – see Inveraray Ar.37	—	—	—	—	—	—	—	—
Ar.35 Glenstrae	R. Schuster	Tim Healey	28(3)	30(1991)	26(1993)	23(3)	40(1992)	6(1994)
Ar.36 Inver (Jura)	Sir William J. Lithgow (1973)	?	21(11)	40(1973)	11(1960)	29(3)	37(1972)	21(1971)
Ar.37 Inveraray	Trustees of the 10th Duke of Argyll	J. Black	70(21)	150(1987)	20(1989)	151(10)	264(1993)	40(1990)
Ar.38 Inversanda	Miss Maclean of Ardgour (1969)	?	14(7)	15(1969)	11(1967)	7(3)	9(1968)	6(1966)
Ar.39 Islay Estate	Islay Estates Co.	Brian Wiles	105(2)	107(1994)	103(1995)	155(2)	170(1994)	14(1993)
Ar.40 Kilchoan (Ardnamurchan)	J. C. Grisewood	Drew Harris	13(10)	38(1994)	7(1959)	91(5)	140(1990)	0(1994)
Ar.41 Kingairloch see also Glensanda Ar.33	Foster Yeoman Ltd	Ewen Malcolm	32(34)	44(1960)	20(1989)	49(24)	70(1977)	23(1980)
Ar.42 Kinlochbeg – see also Glencoe Ar.27	Vicomte Adolphe de Spoelberch	?	10(3)	25(1965)	Few(1964)	—	—	—
Ar.43 Laudale	T. Abel-Smith (1963)	?	11(4)	26(1978)	4(1963)	?	?	?
Ar.44 Pennyghael (Mull)	Mr and Mrs J. D. Glaisher (1983)	?	19(5)	22(1983)	9(1965)	33(4)	60(1978)	9(1980)
Ar.45 Shielbridge	C. B. Holman (1971)	?	18(11)	23(1964)	10(1959)	15(4)	23(1967)	1(1966)
Ar.46 Torosay (Mull)	Christopher James	David Bennett	11(35)	19(1987)	6(1976)	21(25)	48(1985)	3(1979)

Footnote (Argyllshire) [1] Total cull on *Blackmount* (Ar.16) sometimes included whole or part of cull on *Dalness* (Ar.21) and/or *Glenkinglass* (Ar.32) but not always indicated in report.
[2] These totals include a few sika deer.
[3] This total includes some stags shot on *Glenburrich* (Ar.31).
[4] Includes some stags shot on *Black Corries* (Ar.15).
[5] Includes Glenetive

BANFFSHIRE FOREST	Owner 1995 or at date of last report	Stalker 1995 or at date of last report	ANNUAL STAG CULL			ANNUAL HIND CULL		
			Average	Highest	Lowest	Average	Highest	Lowest
Bn.1 Glenavon	Sir Seton and Lady Wills	John McDonald	91(29)	121(1980)	38(1991)	139(28)	344(1966)	76(1967)
Bn.2 Glenfiddich	Major H. T. Morton (1968)	?	45(10)	54(1968)	34(1959)	51(1967)	?	?

| BUTE | Owner 1995 or at date of last report | Stalker 1995 or at date of last report | ANNUAL STAG CULL | | | ANNUAL HIND CULL | | |
FOREST			Average	Highest	Lowest	Average	Highest	Lowest
Bu.1 Brodick	Arran Estate – Lady Jean Fforde	?	24(8)	48(1963)	8(1967)	[1]	[1]	[1]
Bu.2 Dougarie	S. G. Gibbs	David Wilcock	40(28)	68(1978)	17(1966)	38(26)	105(1979)	16(1974)
Bu.3 Sannox	C. J. G. Fforde	Alan S. Ross	58(27)	114(1977)	6(1961)	155(21)[1]	350(1979)[1]	55(1973)[1]

Footnote (Bute) [1] Figures for hind cull on *Sannox* (Bu.3) includes cull on *Brodick* (Bu.1).

| CAITHNESS | Owner 1995 or at date of last report | Stalker 1995 or at date of last report | ANNUAL STAG CULL | | | ANNUAL HIND CULL | | |
FOREST			Average	Highest	Lowest	Average	Highest	Lowest
Ca.1 Braemore	Welbeck Estates Co. Ltd	James Bain	85(36)[1]	123(1994)	39(1964)	278(28)	1040(1992)	92(1984)
Ca.2 Langwell								
Ca.3 Dunbeath	R. Stanton Avery	Lachlan Geddes	25(24)	60(1995)	16(1966)	63(19)	200(1990)	40(1980)
Ca.4 Glutt	Lord Thurso (1965)	?	26(3)	50(1965)	20(1960)	?	?	?
Ca.5 Lochdu	Lord Thurso (1963)	?	22(3)	50(1965)	19(1962)	?	?	?
Ca.6 Rumsdale	Hon. John Sinclair	G. Lathom	—	20(1993)	—	8(1992)	—	—
Ca.7 Sandside	Exors. of late H. B. Taylor (1963)	?	11(3)	15(1959)	3(1971)	—	—	—

Footnote (Caithness) [1] About 35% of the total cull on *Langwell* (Ca.2) and *Braemore* (Ca.1) will probably come off the later ground.

| INVERNESS-SHIRE | Owner 1995 or at date of last report | Stalker 1995 or at date of last report | ANNUAL STAG CULL | | | ANNUAL HIND CULL | | |
FOREST			Average	Highest	Lowest	Average	Highest	Lowest
In.1 Aberarder	Loch Laggan Estates	?	22(9)	32(1984)	13(1965)	38(3)	52(1966)	19(1984)
In.2 Aberchalder	Miss Jean Ellice (1988)	Alan Booth (1986)	13(22)	32(1981)	3(1961)	51(9)	70(1966)	16(1972)
In.3 Abernethy	Royal Society for Protection of Birds	David Lambie	29(33)	100(1993)	7(1966)	47(24)	238(1990)	1(1978)
In.4 Achdalieu	Donald Cameron of Lochiel Ygr	D. A. Lloyd	47(35)	62(1988)	30(1993)	70(26)	104(1988)	40(1983)
In.5 Achnacarry N.	Sir D. H. Cameron of Lochiel	Alex Macdonald	38(34)	59(1995)	20(1962)	60(26)	95(1992)	36(1983)
In.6 Achnacarry S.	Sir D. H. Cameron of Lochiel	Allister Morrice	51(30)	74(1962)	24(1965)	78(24)	98(1966)	47(1983)
In.7 Affaric	J. M. Wotherspoon (1993)	West beat: Duncan MacLennan (1987) East beat: John McLennan (1991)	73(31)[1]	92(1967)[1]	50(1984)[1]	103(25)[1]	175(1967)[1]	50(1984)[1]
In.8 Alvie	A. F. F. Williamson (1970)	?	30(10)[2]	36(1969)	27(1970)	39(4)	45(1969)	34(1968)

	INVERNESS-SHIRE cont. FOREST	Owner 1995 or at date of last report	Stalker 1995 or at date of last report	ANNUAL STAG CULL			ANNUAL HIND CULL		
				Average	Highest	Lowest	Average	Highest	Lowest
In.9	Amhuinnsuidh (Harris)	Major Miller Mundy (1964)	?	39(3)	63(1964)	18(1962)	?	?	?
In.10	Ardverikie	Ardverikie Estates Ltd	Gordon Duncan	102(23)	151(1980)	52(1965)	180(12)	280(1991)	90(1967)
In.11	Arnisdale	R. N. Richmond-Watson (1969)	?	29(10)	43(1969)	16(1963)	30(3)	46(1968)	18(1967)
In.12	Balmacaan	Balmac Forest Ltd R. MacLeod	Stuart MacNicol	21(19)	42(1992)	3(1964)	34(13)	62(1992)	10(1983)
In.13	Barrisdale	Major S. Gordon (1984)	?	18(3)	30(1965)	7(1984)	?	?	?
In.14	Ben Alder Ben à Bhric – see Corrour In.20	Agro Investment Overseas Ltd	Ian Crichton G. K. Oswald (1991)	61(35)	83(1979)	46(1992)	149(28)	201(1976)	56(1983)
In.15	Braeroy	B. K. D. and G. M. Buckle (1989)	Gordon I. Addison (1989)	64(24)	93(1977)	40(1971)	64(22)	105(1974)	25(1984)
In.16	Braulen[3]	Braulen Estate	James Phister	81(25)	102(1971)	57(1990)	138(19)	228(1976)	74(1983)
In.17	Camusrory (Knoydart)	Crosthwaite-Eyre family	W. G. Stalker	28(7)	36(1987)	19(1995)	74(9)	100(1992)	56(1994)
In.18	Coignafearn	Trustees of H. C. Whitbread (1969)	?	68(9)	93(1967)	50(1964)	152(2)	153(1966)	151(1967)
In.19	Corriegarth	D. Thomson (1976)	?	15(15)	40(1976)	6(1971)	21(7)	30(1975)	9(1966)
In.20	Corrour	Nether Pollock Ltd (1974)	?	114(6)[4]	138(1965)	40(1967)	53(6)	80(1967)	30(1966)
In.21	Corryarrick	British Aluminium Co. (1964)	?	74(5)	96(1962)	54(1963)	?	?	?
In.22	Cozac	see Glencannich In.42	—	—	—	—	—	—	—
In.23	Culachy	L. I. Biggs	Owner	18(35)	27(1973)	4(1989)	49(23)	90(1966)	24(1985)
In.24	Culligran (Part of Struy)	Frank Spencer-Nairn	?	21(3)	21(1970)	20(1968)	?	?	?
In.25	Dell	Earl of Bradford (1967)	?	12(8)	17(1964)	5(1967)	8(3)	12(1966)	3(1968)
In.26	Dochfour	Lord Burton	?	2(6)	4(1987)	1(1976)	14(1993)	?	?
In.27	Dorback	Lady Pauline Ogilvy-Grant	Brian Hamilton	26(11)	31(1993)	21(1981)	20(9)	29(1986)	10(1981)
In.28	Dorlin	Westminster (Liverpool) Trust Co. Ltd. (1971)	?	9(11)	13(1971)	6(1962)	8(5)	10(1969)	6(1968)
In.29	Drumochter	Brig. E. R. Kewley (1965)	?	22(1)	—	—	?	?	?
In.30	Dundreggan – see also Levishie In.71	Glenmoriston Estates Ltd. (1962)	?	5(2)	8(1960)	1(1962)	2(1971)	?	?

INVERNESS-SHIRE cont. FOREST	Owner 1995 or at date of last report	Stalker 1995 or at date of last report	ANNUAL STAG CULL			ANNUAL HIND CULL		
			Average	Highest	Lowest	Average	Highest	Lowest
In.31 Eilanreach	West Highlands Woodlands	?	25(14)	34(1972)	15(1965)	?	?	?
In.32 Erchless	E. M. W. Robson	G. Fraser	25(9)	32(1980)	25(1994)	31(13)	40(1987)	16(1970)
In.33 Eskadale	- see Braulen In.16	—	—	—	—	—	—	—
In.34 Farley	- see Braulen In.16	John Fraser (1991)	—	—	—	—	—	—
In.35 Fasnakyle	Mrs J. Grove	Billy MacLennan	34(25)	77(1995)	13(1969)	57(19)	109(1995)	21(1985)
In.36 Fersit (Corrour)	Forestry Commission (1968)	—	58(3)	70(1966)	43(1968)	?	?	?
In.37 Forest Lodge	- see Abernethy In.3	—	—	—	—	—	—	—
In.38 Gaick	Gaick Estates Ltd & Partners	Phil Cairney	84(24)	108(1984)	53(1960)	137(22)	217(1990)	32(1985)
In.39 Garryqualach - see Greenfield In.55	Forestry Commission	—	22(3)	25(1965)	21(1972)	30(2)	30(1971)	30(1970)
In.40 Glenaladale	Col. L. Gray-Cheape (1964)	?	12(1)	?	?	?	?	?
In.41 Glenbanchor	Avion Holding	C. Niven	20(35)	28(1983)	12(1960)	26(23)	68(1964)	3(1989)
In.42 Glen Cannich (Cozac)	Sir John Fuller Bart and A. Fuller (1989)	Donald Fraser (1989)	39(21)	60(1981)	19(1960)	62(12)	72(1971)	48(1972)
In.43 Glendessary	R. Schmitt	A. Walker	34(33)	41(1982)	18(1973)	38(22)	165(1988)	8(1986)
In.44 Glenfeshie	Bargeddie Ltd	A. Dempster	139(25)	214(1985)	95(1962)	145(15)	275(1969)	75(1967)
In.45 Glenfinnan	M. R. Warren	Duncan Stoddart	20(27)	33(1987)	6(1961)	36(20)	70(1992)	8(1978)
In.46 Glengarry North and South	British Aluminium Co. (1974) and Forestry Commission	?	38(6)	83(1972)	25(1966)	28(3)	35(1971)	20(1977)
In.47 Glenkingie	I. H. Brown Ltd	J. Cameron	44(20)	57(1977)	33(1959)	51(16)	109(1992)	30(1967)
In.48 Glenkyllachy	Major C. D. Mackenzie (1963)	?	7(2)	8(1963)	5(1961)	?	?	?
In.49 Glenmazeran	Glenmazeran Trust	James Irvine	24(31)	33(1993)	12(1965)	69(21)	120(1993)	22(1968)
In.50 Glenmoidart	J. Lees-Millais (1981)	?	19(18)	33(1981)	10(1969)	14(9)	30(1980)	5(1968)
In.51 Glenquoich	Major S. Gordon (1985)	?	45(11)	72(1960)	30(1984)	55(2)	60(1968)	50(1966)
In.52 Glenquoich East	Burton Property Trustees (1986)	Ian Campbell (1986)	11(20)	23(1974)	2(1970)	7(13)	20(1975)	1(1982)
In.53 Glenshero	Alcan Highland Estates	Alan McIntyre	76(19)[5]	100(1992)	64(1971)	114(18)[6]	160(1977)[6]	60(1987)[6]
In.54 Glenspean	E. Luxmore	Mr Strachan (1986)	13(13)	32(1976)	5(1987)	7(8)	13(1989)	2(1980)
In.55 Greenfield - see also Garryqualach In.39	Miss M. Ellice (1963)	?	17(5)	25(1963)	5(1962)	?	?	?
In.56 Insriach	J. R. F and S. R. F Drake (1970)	?	6(8)	8(1968)	2(1969)	10(4)	12(1969)	4(1967)

INVERNESS-SHIRE cont. FOREST	Owner 1995 or at date of last report	Stalker 1995 or at date of last report	ANNUAL STAG CULL			ANNUAL HIND CULL		
			Average	Highest	Lowest	Average	Highest	Lowest
In.57 Inverailort and Rannachan	Inverailort Estate	G. MacDougall	16(4)	22(1995)	10(1989)	45(2)	50(1988)	40(1987)
In.58 Invereshie	Forestry Commission (1970)	?	10(4)	15(1970)	6(1968)	13(2)	18(1967)	7(1966)
In.59 Invergarry N.	Russell Ellice	?	7(15)	24(1979)	2(1965)	29(4)	51(1981)	6(1969)
In.60 Invergarry Hotel Stalking	Capt. and Mrs L. Hunt (proprietors of hotel)	Various	81(5)	100(1961)	68(1967)	?	?	?
In.61 Kilchoan (Knoydart)	E. Delwart	Harris Drew	30(4)	40(1994)	35(1993)	118(3)	165(1994)	103(1992)
In.62 Killiechonate	Alcan Highland Estates	David Fraser	41(25)	69(1979)	8(1986)	52(16)	99(1979)	15(1988)
In.63 Killiehuntly	Bargeddie Ltd.	David Fraser	15(2)	15	15	17(2)	19(1992)	15(1993)
In.64 Kingie	– see Glenkingie In.47	—	—	—	—	—	—	—
In.65 Kinloch (Skye)	Forestry Commission (1977)	?	8(1)	?	?	?	?	?
In.66 Kinloch Hourn	H. C. Birkbeck	Donald A. Cameron	19(32)	26(1980)	12(1975)	—	—	—
In.67 Kinrara	Kinrara Estate Trustees (1978)	?	24(13)	40(1978)	9(1966)	56(8)	94(1976)	21(1968)
In.68 Kinveachy	Viscount Reidhaven	Frank Law	40(33)	75(1974)	22(1962)	79(19)	122(1976)	10(1981)
In.69 Knoydart – see also Kilchoan In.61	Titaghur	N. Morrison	81(30)	146(1981)	32(1986)	133(21)	265(1981)	42(1971)
In.70 Lettermorar	– see Meoble In.74	—	—	—	—	—	—	—
In.71 Levishie incl. N. Dundreggan	Glenmoriston Estates	?	21(14)	52(1978)	7(1960)	3(2)	4(1972)	3(1974)
In.72 Lochiel forests	– see In.4, In.5, In.6	Various	184(6)	221(1982)	102(1983)	*see* In.4; In.5; In.6.		
In.73 Mamore	Alcan Smelting & Power, Lochaber Works		45(20)[7]	71(1979)	27(1959)	79(18)	132(1976)	27(1985)
In.74 Meoble and Lettermorar	Feranti Farms Ltd. (1965)	?	37(2)	40(1963)	34(1965)	?	?	?
In.75 Moy	Loch Laggan Estates Ltd. (1965)	?	12(3)	16(1964)	6(1961)	?	?	?
In.76 Newtonmore	– see Glenbanchor In.41	—	—	—	—	—	—	—
In.77 North Morar	Sir O. E. Crosthwaite-Eyre (1967)	?	14(9)	27(1961)	3(1966)	17(1966)	?	?
In.78 Rannachan	– see Inverailort In.57	—	—	—	—	—	—	—
In.79 Rhum, Isle of	Nature Conservancy (1986)	L. Macrae (1986)	64(5)[8]	80(1981)[8]	50(1983)[8]	49(3)	61(1984)	35(1982)
In.80 Sherramore[9]	British Aluminium Co.	?	32(2)	33(1965)	31(1966)	[9]	[9]	[9]
In.81 Sleat (Skye)	Clan Donald Lands Trust (1976)	?	10(1)	?	?	?	?	?

INVERNESS-SHIRE cont. FOREST	Owner 1995 or at date of last report	Stalker 1995 or at date of last report	ANNUAL STAG CULL			ANNUAL HIND CULL		
			Average	Highest	Lowest	Average	Highest	Lowest
In.82 Straithard (Skye)	M. A., S. P. L., and W. M. Johnson (1973)	?	3(13)	6(1967)	1(1964)	?	?	?
Strathfarrar	– see Braulen In.16							
In.83 Struy	M. A. Spencer-Nairn (1994)	?	20(13)	38(1966)	11(1962)	28(5)	70(1966)	11(1967)
In.84 Torcastle	– see Achdalieu In.4		—	—	—	—	—	—

Footnote (Inverness-shire) [1] Omission of part of cull on *Affric* (In.7) during some seasons may have affected these figures (*see* page 239).
[2] No details supplied for *Altie* (In.8) after 1964.
[3] Prior to 1991 *Braulen* (In.16) known as the Lovat Estate.
[4] Average cull on *Corrour* (In.20) prior to 1965 when about two thirds of the forest were acquired by the Forestry Commission. For the next few years on the reduced area, the cull fell to about 50.
[5] Frequently combined with *Sberramore* (In.80) as a result of which the average cull of stags increased from about 76 to 123.
[6] The forests of *Glensbero* (In.53) and *Sberramore* (In.80) are often stalked as one unit.
[7] As from 1991 *Mamore* (In.73) and *Killiecbonate* (In.62) were combined and during the next four seasons had an average stag cull of 53.
[8] Only let part season – additional stags shot by stalkers, who also culled the hinds, but numbers not recorded.
[9] See also *Glensbero* (In.53).
Inverailort 17
Rannachan 5

PERTHSHIRE FOREST	Owner 1995 or at date of last report	Stalker 1995 or at date of last report	ANNUAL STAG CULL			ANNUAL HIND CULL		
			Average	Highest	Lowest	Average	Highest	Lowest
P.1 Atholl Forests – see P.2–P.6	Duke of Atholl	see below	318(36)	483(1994)	234(1965)	Apart from these two figures for hind culls in 1966 and 1967 no other information has been supplied		
P.2 Clunes	Duke of Atholl	C. Reid	44(28)	100(1992)	20(1959)			
P.3 Dalnamein	Duke of Atholl	G. Macleod	47(28)	107(1994)	24(1963)			
P.4 Forest Lodge	Duke of Atholl	Charlie Pirie	89(28)	120(1993)	52(1975)	160(2)		
P.5 Glenbruar	Duke of Atholl	I. MacCullough	47(28)	80(1987)	40(1995)			
P.6 West Hand	Duke of Atholl	Sandy Reid	76(28)	153(1994)	57(1970)	(74)1		
P.7 Auchleeks	I. J. Mackinlay (1972)	?	20(2)	26(1972)	15(1967)	?	?	?
P.8 Auchlyne	Mrs J. Bowser	G. D. Coyne	15(7)1	18(1987)1	9(1983)1	76	170(1992)	14(1983)
P.9 Auchnafree	Sir James Whittaker (1969)	?	22(2)	35(1962)	8(1969)	?	?	?
Bolfracks	– see Tombuie P.45	John Chalmers[2] (1988)	—	—	—	—	—	—
P.10 Boreland	Judge R. A. R. Stroyan Q.C.	T. Frost	35(15)	51(1994)	11(1966)	91(8)	114(1990)	65(1993)
P.11 Camusericht	Abacus Trust	George A. Macdonald	31(10)	43(1993)	22(1970)	61(8)	139(1992)	36(1974)
P.12 Cashlie – see Meggernie P.38	Lt.-Col. Sir Edward Wills	?	13(1)	—	—	—	—	—
P.13 Chesthill	Mrs D. J. Molteno (1973)	see Glenlyon P.32	41(5)3	60(1965)3	26(1960)3	?3	53(1970)3	—
Clunes	– see Atholl Forests P.2	C. Reid	—	—	—	—	—	—

	PERTHSHIRE cont. FOREST	Owner 1995 or at date of last report	Stalker 1995 or at date of last report	ANNUAL STAG CULL			ANNUAL HIND CULL		
				Average	Highest	Lowest	Average	Highest	Lowest
P.14	Corrievarkie	S. J. Loder (1975)	?	19(15)	28(1963)*	11(1969)	32(5)	43(1974)	28(1971)
P.15	Craiganour	Viscount Wimborne (1971)	?	51(8)	59(1970)	36(1959)	63(5)	73(1968)	31(1967)
P.16	Crossmount	- see Dunalastair P.22	—	6(1974)	—	—		—	—
P.17	Dall and East Black Corries	M. and D. Pearson (1977)	?	101(1)	101(1977)	?	?	200(1976)	?
P.18	Dalmunzie - see Glenlochsie P.31	D. Winton Estates Ltd (1963)	?	10(3)	15(1960)	5(1963)	23(5)	31(1971)	16(1968)
P.19	Dalnacardoch and Sronphadruig	Major R. Pilkington	?	102(15)	133(1971)	56(1961)	35(6)	111(1973)	10(1968)
	Dalnamein	- see Atholl Forest P.3	G. Macleod	—	—	—	76(5)	107(1966)	40(1971)
P.20	Dalnaspidal	Brian A. Adams	—	44(32)	62(1969)	24(1985)	42(24)	73(1977)	7(1967)
P.21	Drummond Hill	Forestry Commission	?	7(1)	7(1972)	?	?	?	?
P.22	Dunalastair (incl. Crossmount P.16)	Capt. I. C. de Sales le Terriere (1975)	?	24(8)	31(1963)	19(1971)	40(2)	49(1971)	?
P.23	Dunan	John Curzon (1959)	?	18(1959)	—	—	—	—	—
P.24	Edinchip	R. A. Dubery (1983)	?	15(3)	32(1982)	15(1981)	4(2)	5(1981)	3(1982)
P.25	Farlayer	N. F. Fane	J. Lambie	15(1986)	—	—	?	?	?
P.26	Fealar	Messrs. A. L. Spearman, H. Mellor, H. Teacher and J. Teacher (Managing Partner)	J. Lean (1982-94) M. Broad (1995)	75(22)	101(1991)	53(1984)	128(21)	200(1991)	699(1978)
	Forest Lodge	- see Atholl forest P.4	Charlie Pirie	—	—	—	—	—	—
P.27	Garrows	J. Kemp-Welch (1980)	?	10(4)	25(1980)	4(1960)	?	?	?
P.28	Glenartney	Baroness Willoughby	A. Work	112(35)	300(1986)	62(1974)	273(27)	573(1993)	106(1978)
	Glenbruar	- see Atholl forests P.5	I. MacCullough	—	—	—	—	—	—
P.29	Glenfernate	Sir John Heathcote Amory (1971)	?	46(12)	62(1972)	31(1959)	107(6)	140(1967)	100(1971)
P.30	Glenlochay	Ben Challum Ltd. (1979)	?	55(13)	100(1978)	6(1969)	4(9)	7(1974)	1(1975)
P.31	Glenlochsie	Dalmunzie Hotel & Estates Ltd (1979)	?	18(12)	40(1976)	10(1961)	17(3)	36(1975)	18(1977)
P.32	Glenlyon - see also P.13	Mrs D. J. Molteno (1973)	?	45(7)	60(1965)	25(1960)	37(3)	64(1968)	20(1969)
P.33	Glenshee	Capt. A. L. Farquharson	R. Hepburn (1993) Graham B. Kerr (1994)	18(32)	56(1995)	11(1965)	44(25)	164(1994)	27(1978)

PERTHSHIRE cont. FOREST	Owner 1995 or at date of last report	Stalker 1995 or at date of last report	ANNUAL STAG CULL			ANNUAL HIND CULL		
			Average	Highest	Lowest	Average	Highest	Lowest
P.34 Innerwick & Roro	J. A. Drysdale & Partners (1969)	?	45(4)	53(1969)	35(1966)	?	?	?
P.35 Invermearn[5]	Sir Edward Wills (1970)	?	33(2)	34(1970)	31(1964)	?	?	?
P.36 Lochs	Juliet, Lady Wills	W. Mason	37(16)	57(1991)	16(1964)	39(14)	65(1982)	17(1990)
P.37 Lude	Major S. Gordon (1985)	?	38(3)	c.50(1985)	20(1970)	?	?	?
P.38 Meggernie – see P.12, P.34, P.35	Lt.-Col. Sir E. Wills (1979)	?	134(17)	198(1965)[6]	97(1962)[6]	173(13)	290(1974)	20(1968)
P.39 Rannoch[7]	Forestry Commission	?	59(2)	84(1973)	35(1972)	?	?	?
P.40 Remony	A. and J. Duncan Miller	Angus Hogg	18(28)	35(1993)	10(1964)	53(20)	107(1989)	13(1969)
P.41 Rhiedorrach Roro – see Innerwick P.34	Capt. A. Farquharson	W. Bain	20(34)	66(1995)	12(1991)	89(25)	205(1992)	11(1981)
P.42 Strathardle	Forestry Commission	—	13(1)	—	—	—	—	—
Sronphadruig	– see Dalnacardoch P.19	—	—	—	—	—	—	—
P.43 Suie[8]	Mrs E. Patterson	G. D. Coyne	20(7)	26(1981)	16(1987)	31(6)	48(1986)	16(1981)
P.44 Talladh-a-Bheithe	Simon J. Loder (1970)	R. Robertson (1986)	28(21)	50(1985)	12(1960)	41(11)	70(1967)	25(1981)
P.45 Tombuie	J. D. Hutchison (1986)	?	10(17)	21(1964)	4(1968)	32(7)	40(1985)	?
P.46 Tummel	Forestry Commission	?	14(2)	14(1973)	14(1972)	?	?	?
West Hand	– see Atholl forests P.6	Sandy Reid	—	—	—	—	—	—

Footnote (Perthshire) [1] When combined with Suie (P.43) the average annual cull is about 51 stags and 136 hinds, including calves.
[2] Died on the hill 13 August 1988.
[3] Cull includes *Glenlyon* (P.32).
[4] When combined with *Talladh-a-Bheithe* (P.44) stag cull in 1967 was 37.
When combined with *Talladh-a-Bheithe* (P.44) hind cull in 1968 was 70.
[5] Part of *Meggernie Estate* (P.38).
[6] Includes whole or part cull on *Casbie* (P.12), *Innerwick* (P.34), *Invermearn* (P.35) and *Lochs* (P.36).
[7] *Rannoch* (P.39) Formerly included in Rannoch were *Corrievarkie* (P.14), *Craiganour* (P.15) and *Talladh-a-Bheithe* (P.44).
[8] After 1987 hind cull report combined with *Auchlyne* (P.8).

ROSS-SHIRE FOREST	Owner 1995 or at date of last report	Stalker 1995 or at date of last report	ANNUAL STAG CULL			ANNUAL HIND CULL		
			Average	Highest	Lowest	Average	Highest	Lowest
R.1 Achanalt and Strathbran	Marquess de Torrehermosa (1971)	?	16(9)	29(1971)	8(1962)	24(2)	30(1969)	18(1970)
R.2 Achnashellach	Major M. T. N. H. Wills	C. Mackenzie	24(28)	35(1961)	15(1986)	40(20)	75(1992)	26(1975)

ROSS-SHIRE cont. FOREST	Owner 1995 or at date of last report	Stalker 1995 or at date of last report	ANNUAL STAG CULL			ANNUAL HIND CULL		
			Average	Highest	Lowest	Average	Highest	Lowest
R.3 Alladale	Richard Macaire	R. Munro	24(8)[1] / 52(3)	67(1995)[1] / 56(1994)	20(1971)[1] / 46(1989)	168(6)[1] / 38(2)	261(1992)[1] / 46(1967)	117(1988)[1] / 30(1966)
R.4 Amat and Letters	P. J. F. Colvin (1965)	?	16(4)	19(1965)	10(1962)	?	?	?
R.5 Ben Damph[2]	T. D. Gray and D. N. Carr-Smith	Alistair Holmes	23(11)	29(1988)[3]	19(1995)	18(10)	30(1989)	6(1983)
R.6 Benula, East	Capt. G. M. Tennant (1961)	?	42(3)	44(1961)	40(1959)	?	?	?
R.7 Benula, West incl. Dorrisduan and Inverinate	Hon. Mrs David Bowlby (1979)	?	69(20)	102(1973)	32(1960)	59(4)	91(1974)	25(1976)
R.8 Braelangwell	D. F. S. Goodman (1971)	?	13(2)	14(1971)	12(1964)	5	?	?
R.9 Braemore	Miss Calder (1977)	?	22(15)	30(1976)	12(1968)	16(8)	28(1976)	8(1969)
R.10 Castleleod	The Earl of Cromartie, M.C. (1963) – see Garbat R.28		4(1)	?	?	?	?	?
R.11 Cluanie and Glenshiel	Burton Property Trust	Colin Campbell	43(23)	65(1994)[4]	26(1986)	31(9)	40(1974)	21(1993)
R.12 Corriehallie	– see Fairburn R.21		—	—	—	—	—	—
R.13 Corriemulzie inc. Letters	F. P. J. Colvin	Donald Snody	37(27)	67(1983)	15(1972)	109(17)	180(1986)	50(1967)
R.14 Couldoran	Miss S. Huntsman (1978)	?	4(18)	6(1978)	2(1973)	4(11)	7(1969)	1(1976)
R.15 Coulin	Philip Smith	Neil Morrison	29(34)	49(1981)	12(1960)	21(26)	33(1993)	14(1974)
R.16 Deanich	Richard Macaire	R. Munro	29(8)	37(1985)	25(1962)	see Alladale R.3		
R.17 Diabeg	Madame Mackenzie of Gairloch (1968)	?	10(1)	10(1968)	—	?	?	?
R.18 Dibbiedale	– see Glencalvie R.29		—	—	—	—	—	—
R.19 Dorisduan	– see Benula W. and Inverinate R.7		—	—	—	—	—	—
R.20 Eishken (Park) Is. of Lewis	N. Oppenheim	Chris Macrae	54(11)	89(1995)	28(1982)	47(5)	63(1987)	2(1994)
R.21 Fairburn and Corriehallie	R. W. K. Stirling of Fairburn	Keith Wilkinson	21(33)	31(1981)	5(1960)	50(27)	105(1990)	30(1967)
R.22 Fannich	T. W. Sandeman (1972)	?	51(8)	55(1968)	45(1970)	62(6)	72(1968)	50(1970)
R.23 Fisherfield	– see Letterewe R.46		—	—	—	—	—	—
R.24 Flowerdale	Madame Mackenzie of Gairloch (1968)	?	16(6)	17(1967)	15(1968)	3(1966)	—	—

ROSS-SHIRE cont. FOREST	Owner 1995 or at date of last report	Stalker 1995 or at date of last report	ANNUAL STAG CULL			ANNUAL HIND CULL		
			Average	Highest	Lowest	Average	Highest	Lowest
R.25 Foich	– see Strone R.67	—	—	—	—	—	—	—
R.26 Forest Farm	Benmore Estates Discretionary Trustees (1968)	?	12(2)	13(1968)	10(1967)	?	?	?
R.27 Forest Farm Corriemulzie Estate	P. F. J. Colvin (1967)	?	18(5)	26(1985)	10(1986)	?	?	?
R.28 Garbat and Castle Leod	Earl of Cromartie (1967)	?	15(9)	23(1959)	2(1966)	15(1967)	?	?
R.29 Glencalvie and Dibbiedale	A. N. Hickley (1966)	John Gordon (1986)	32(8)	51(1986)	26(1962)	?	?	?
R.30 Glencarron and Glenuig	Angus Sladen	Brian Watson	42(27)	52(1974)	25(1989)	56(25)	140(1988)	23(1973)
R.31 Glenshiel	Burton Property Trust	Ian Campbell	24(13)	48(1977)	9(1960)	29(12)	47(1969)	7(1966)
R.32 Glenuig	– see Glencarron R.30	—	—	—	—	—	—	—
R.33 Glomach and Killilan	Mrs E. G. M. Douglas (1979)	?	53(20)[5]	120(1977)	38(1968)[5]	89(16)	117(1969)	34(1980)
R.34 Grudie	Mrs Diana Grey (1961)	?	14(1961)	18(1961)	11(1959)	?	?	?
R.35 Gruinard	The Lady McCorquodale (1963)	?	18(4)	25(1961)	14(1963)	?	?	?
R.36 Inverbroom	L. W. Robson	?	24(10)	29(1972)	15(1961)	24(4)	32(1971)	12(1969)
R.37 Inverinate and Dorisduan	Hon. Mrs David Bowlby (1979) (dec'd) see also Benula West R.7	I. Smith (1976)	23(3)	25(1966)	20(1960)	59(9)	91(1974)	25(1976)
R.38 Inverlael	Dr S. M. Whitteridge (1991)	Allan MacGillivray	34(3)	50(1991)	12(1965)	57(2)	60(1993)	55(1990)
R.39 Inverpolly	The Polly Estate Ltd (1963)	?	12(3)	14(1962)	10(1961)	?	?	?
R.40 Kildermorie	Mr. and Mrs. I. Duncan	Andrew Russell	26(18)	34(1988)	17(1994)	47(18)	85(1992)	16(1989)
P.41 Killilan	see Glomach R.33	—	58(7)	75(1983)	29(1964)	—	—	—
P.42 Kinlochewe	H. W. Whitbread (1979)	—	38(17)	71(1978)	15(1966)	58(7)	68(1978)	25(1966)
R.43 Kinlochluichart	Lochluichart Estate, North	J. Logie	29(36)	50(1987)	18(1961)	38(20)	120(1986)	22(1972)
R.44 Leckmelm	C. N. Beattie	Alan Eltrincham	13(34)	28(1980)	5(1966)	24(24)	61(1992)	5(1970)
R.45 Ledgowan	J. Ruggles-Brise	T. Ross	26(34)	31(1994)	16(1989)	22(28)	30(1982)	12(1970)
R.46 Letterewe and Fisherfield	Col. W. H. Whitbread (1983)	?	75(14)[6]	106(1976)	62(1963)	48(12)	78(1966)	5(1980)
R.47 Letters	P. F. J. Colvin (1968)	?	19(4)	20(1968)	16(1964)			

ROSS-SHIRE cont. FOREST		Owner 1995 or at date of last report	Stalker 1995 or at date of last report	ANNUAL STAG CULL			ANNUAL HIND CULL		
				Average	Highest	Lowest	Average	Highest	Lowest
R.48	Loch-a-Bhraion	- see Inverbroom R.36	—	—	—	—	—	—	—
R.49	Lochluichart	- see Kinlochluichart R.43	—	—	—	—	—	—	—
R.50	Loubcroy	P. F. J. Colvin	—	20(12)	30(1989)	12(1991)	57(7)	78(1989)	20(1984)
R.51	Monar, W., incl. Pait R.54	C. S. R. Stroyan	D. Lippe	46(34)	71(1981)	19(1989)	70(20)	130(1977)	11(1982)
R.52	Morsgail (Is. of Lewis)	J. F. Robinson (1967)	?	4(9)	12(1967)	1(1965)	8(1968)	?	?
R.53	New Kelso	G. N., B. V. and R. M. Griffin	Alan Holmes (1986)	8(3)	10(1984)	6(1985)	4(2)	6(1984)	2(1985)
R.54	Pait	- see Monar R.51	D. Lippe	—	—	—	—	—	—
R.55	Park (Is. of Lewis)	N. Oppenheim	T. D. Macrae	see Eishken R.20					
R.56	Rhidorroch E.	G. and B. M. C. van Veen (1965)	?	18(5)	23(1965)	10(1962)	not recorded		
R.57	Rhidorroch W.	E. Scobie	Owner	19(28)	27(1995)	8(1970)	42(16)	67(1990)	21(1973)
R.58	Scardroy	Burnden Park Invest	Colin M. Hendry	28(21)	36(1994)	15(1983)	33(19)	52(1979)	11(1970)
R.59	Scatwell -	see Strathconon R.64	—	—	—	—	—	—	—
R.60	Shiel -	see Glenshiel R.31	—	—	—	—	—	—	—
R.61	Shieldaig	The Gairloch and Conon Estates (1962)	?	14(3)	18(1966)	7(1962)	7(1966)	—	—
R.62	South Eishken (Is. of Lewis)	N. Oppenheim	- see Eishken R.20 -						
R.63	Strathbran	- see Achanalt R.1	—	—	—	—	—	—	—
R.64	Strathconon[7]	Hugh J. Macdonald-Buchanan	Paul Smith	115(30)	178(1980)	52(1959)	219(21)	680(1992)	55(1981)
R.65	Strathrannoch	- see Strathvaich R.66	—	—	—	—	—	—	—
R.66	Strathvaich[8]	J. R. E. Smith, H. J. E. Smith and Countess of Verulam (1994)	Ian Bennett	75(6)	100(1977)	76(1980)	90(16)	169(1992)	60(1966)
R.67	Strone (Foich)	H. J. E. van Beuningen (1991)	A. M. Mackenzie	19(27)	24(1988)	10(1969)	36(19)	45(1987)	27(1968)
R.68	Torridon	The Earl of Lovelace (1970)	Lea MacNally (1993)	11(1959)	—	—	—	—	—
R.69	West Monar	- see Monar W. R. 51	—	—	—	—	—	—	—
R.70	Wyvis	Lars Gisselbach (1982)	W. Munro (1970)	39(16)	90(1981)	17(1971)	69(15)	85(1980)	51(1968)

Footnote (Ross-shire) [1] Includes *Deanich* (R.16).
[2] Includes *Torridon* (R.68) in some reports.
[3] Includes the *New Kelso* (R.53) beat.
[4] The 1994 cull divided as follows:
Cluanie (R.11) 27 } 65

[5] It is not certain if these figures refer to the combined forest areas or to only one part.
[6] *Fisherfield* (R.23) was sold in 1978, and for the following six years the stag cull on *Letterewe* (R.46) averaged 37, with the highest number (48) being shot in 1981.
[7] Reported cull figure generally includes *Scatwell* (R.59).
[8] After about 1977, the whole or part of *Strathbrannoch* (R.65) cull was included. Prior to that date an average of about 43 stags

SUTHERLAND	FOREST	Owner 1995 or at date of last report	Stalker 1995 or at date of last report	ANNUAL STAG CULL			ANNUAL HIND CULL		
				Average	Highest	Lowest	Average	Highest	Lowest
S.1	Achentoul	Sir Anthony Nutting	Angus Ross	57(26)	90(1994)	24(1969)	88(27)	256(1989)	43(1985)
S.2	Badanloch	The Viscount Leverhulme	Richard M. MacNicol	29(34)	53(1994)	20(1969)	70(27)	138(1992)	40(1967)
S.3	Balnacoil	Richard R. Tyser (1988)	David Whelan (1988)	37(8)	69(1978)	10(1966)	?	?	?
S.4	Ben Armine	Countess of Sutherland's Ben Armine Trust	Donald Ross	30(19)	47(1982)	13(1964)	39(8)	110(1989)	14(1988)
S.5	Ben Hee and Corriekinloch	Mrs S. M. G. Garton (1986)	Peter Ross (1986)	35(24)	47(1977)	20(1984)	45(11)	80(1974)	34(1979)
S.6	Ben Loyal	Count Adam Knuth	Jan Smart	15(21)	32(1995)	7(1974)	163(5)	217(1992)	91(1989)
S.7	Benklibreck	- see Clebrig S.14	—	—	—	—	—	—	—
S.8	Benmore Assynt	Benmore Estate (1971)	?	29(9)	35(1968)	21(1964)	?	?	?
S.9	Big House	W. W. MacFarlane (1964)	?	8(3)	10(1963)	7(1964)	?	?	?
S.10	Borgie	- see Syre – S.45	—	—	—	—	—	—	—
S.11	Borrobol and Skinsdale	M. Wigan (1980)	—	41(20)	70(1980)	22(1961)	64(12)	97(1966)	40(1979)
S.12	Caplich	- see Loubcroy R.50	—	—	—	—	—	—	—
S.13	Cashel Dhu	- see Strathmore S.42	—	—	—	—	—	—	—
S.14	Clebrig (Benklibreck)	Mrs P. Nicholson (1987)	D. G. Mackay (1987)	16(21)	23(1986)	10(1963)	27(16)	40(1982)	14(1986)
S.15	Corriekinloch	- see Ben Hee and Corriekinloch S.5	—	—	—	—	—	—	—
S.16	Dalnessie	Professor I. S. Smillie (1991)	I. Hepburn (1991)	19(22)	32(1991)	14(1962)	13(9)	50(1990)	1(1969)
S.17	Dalreavoch	Trustees – Countess of Sutherland's No.3 Settlement (1988)	E. Ballantyne (1988)	14(9)	25(1985)	4(1982)	62(8)	139(1988)	21(1982)
S.18	Dunrobin and Uppat	- ditto -	Ian Smith (1992)	26(19)	44(1977)	15(1963)	109(8)	205(1989)	23(1981)
S.19	Fiag	- see Mudale S.35	—	—	—	—	—	—	—
S.20	Forsinard	Brig. C. E. Tryon-Wilson	?	30(6)	40(1962)	31(1960)	14(3)	17(1971)	11(1972)
S.21	Glencanisp	E. H. Vestey (1971)	?	33(5)	34(1962)	30(1959)	38(1970)	?	?
S.22	Glencassely	Mrs David Lloyd (1965)	?	24(2)	25(1964)	22(1965)	?	?	?

| | Owner 1995 or at | Stalker 1995 or at | ANNUAL STAG CULL | | | ANNUAL HIND CULL | | |
FOREST	date of last report	date of last report	Average	Highest	Lowest	Average	Highest	Lowest
SUTHERLAND cont.								
S.23 Gobernuisgach	Anne, Duchess of Westminster	D. Campbell	28(11)	32(1994)	21(1960)	see Lochmore S.32		
S.24 Gordonbush	Richard J. Tyser (1988)	David Whelan	55(21)	101(1966)	20(1988)	76(14)[1]	152(1987)[1]	14(1979)
S.25 Inchnadamph	Lady Rootes (1964)	?	20(4)	23(1962)	17(1961)	?	?	?
S.26 Invercassley (Ben Eoin)	S. W. Urry	J. White	35(1995)	34(1994)	20(1962)	34(5)	50(1991)	8(1966)
S.27 Kildonan	Mrs M. E. A. Clay	Alastair Grant	36(20)	71(1995)	4(1977)	154(3)	168(1991)	87(1994)
S.28 Kinloch	A. W. G. Sykes	Adam Henderson	24(19)[2]	42(1990)	13(1974)	40(10)	100(1993)	33(1983)
S.29 Kintradwell	Richard J. Tyser (1977)	?	18(1977)	?	?	?	?	?
S.30 Kylestrome	Lady Mary Grosvenor	John Ross	39(34)	62(1961)	32(1986)	49(22)	136(1992)	25(1973)
S.31 Loch Choire	D. Knowles, Lord Joicey, Hon. A. H. Joicey, Duncan Leslie	Albert Grant	78(26)	105(1993)	12(1961)	131(12)	162(1990)	100(1983)
Lairg Estate*	Mrs P. A. Greenwood	David Allison	18(1995)	—	—	15(1995)	—	—
S.32 Lochmore, Reay	Anne, Duchess of Westminster	J. S. Morrison	89(5)	97(1994)	76(1960)	137(23)	315(1992)	100(1967)
Lochmore, Reay Gobernuisgach - *see* S.23	Anne, Duchess of Westminster	V. Anderson	115(26)	147(1980)	96(1970)			
S.33 Loyal	- *see* Ben Loyal S.6	Jan Smart	—	—	—	—	—	—
S.34 Merkland[3] - *see* also Ben Hee and Corriekinloch	R. B. Woods (1990) S.5	Mr Walker (1990)	22(1990)	—	—	50(1989)	?	?
S.35 Mudale and Fiag	Marcus Kimball	?	38(12)	45(1964)	27(1960)	35(4)	40(1968)	28(1966)
S.36 Polla	- *see* Rispond S.40		—	—	—	—	—	—
S.37 Reay (Kylestrome)	- *see* Kylestrome S.30		—	—	—	—	—	—
S.38 Reay (Lochmore)	- *see* Lochmore S.32		—	—	—	—	—	—
S.39 Rhifael	- *see* Skelpick S.41		—	—	—	—	—	—
S.40 Rispond and Polla	Mr and Mrs C. Marsham	John Morrison	10(5)	15(1991)	0(1995)	5(4)	6(1991)	2(1994)
S.41 Skelpick and Rhifael	Hon. G. E. Lopes	Bob McBain	26(7)	28(1993)	22(1995)	20(5)	35(1992)	10(1983)

250

SUTHERLAND cont. FOREST	Owner 1995 or at date of last report	Stalker 1995 or at date of last report	ANNUAL STAG CULL			ANNUAL HIND CULL		
			Average	Highest	Lowest	Average	Highest	Lowest
S.42 Strathmore (Cashel Dhu)	I. C. N. Alcock (1975)	Owner stalked	17(6)	23(1975)	11(1972)	7(3)	10(1975)	6(1972)
S.43 Strathmore incl. Cashel Dhu	Mrs D. J. H. Gow	Alasdair Sutherland	24(17)	37(1981)	24(1991)	35(16)	61(1991)	6(1980)
S.44 Suisgill	Lady Paynter (1970)	?	24(4)	30(1968)	11(1959)	19(2)	20(1969)	18(1967)
S.45 Syre and Borgie (S.10)	D. R. Midwood (1987)	Tommy Shaw (1987)	15(3)	19(1985)	9(1986)	8(3)	9(1986)	7(1984)
S.46 Uppat	– see Dunrobin S.18							

Footnote (Sutherland) [1] During some seasons Balnacoil (S.3) was included in the Gordonbush (S.24) total.
[2] Between 1968–73, when the cull on Ben Loyal (S.6) was included, about 24 would be shot each season.
[3] An alternative name for Ben Hee and Corriekinloch S.5.
* To the north-east lies Loch Choire forest (S.31).

251

APPENDIX AND INDEXES

APPENDIX

Stalkers and their Forests since 1986

Note: The years shown refer to the years in which reports were received and in no way indicate the duration of service with any individual forest.

Name	Forest	Year
Addison, Gordon I.	Braeroy, Inverness	1986-88
Aitken, Andy	Conaglen, Argyll	1987-89
Aitken, Andy	Ben Armine, Sutherland	1992
Allison, David	Lairg, Sutherland	1995
Anderson, V.	Lochmore, Reay, Sutherland	1987-94
Bain, James	Langwell, Caithness	1988-95
Bain, W.	Rhiedorrach, Perthshire	1986-94
Ballantyne, E.	Dalreavoch, Sutherland	1988
Bannochie, G.	Kildonan, Sutherland	1988-89
Bennett, David	Torosay (Mull), Argyll	1986-94
Bennett, Iain	Strathvaich, Ross	1993-95
Black, J.	Inveraray, Argyll	1987-95
Boath, Alex	Glenprosen, Angus	1986-95
Booth, Alan	Aberchalder, Inverness	1986
Broad, Mike	Fealar, Perthshire	1995
Buchan, Ronald	Ben Armine, Sutherland	1990
Cairney, Phil	Gaick, Inverness	1986-94
Caithness, Dennis	Millden, Angus	1990-95
Cameron, Allan	Glendessary, Inverness	1986-89
Cameron, Allan	Ardgour, Argyll	1990-92
Cameron, Donald A.	Kinloch Hourn, Inverness	1986-94
Cameron, Duncan	Kildermorie, Ross	1986
Cameron, John	Knoydart, Inverness	1989-90
Cameron, J.	Glenkingie, Inverness	1991-94
Campbell, Colin	Cluanie, Ross	1995

Name	Forest	Year
Campbell, D.	Gobernuisgach, Sutherland	1991-94
Campbell, Ian	Glenquoich, East, Inverness	1986
Campbell, Ian	Glenshiel and Cluanie, Ross	1986-95
Campbell, Ian	Glen Ey-Mar, Aberdeen	1987-95
Chalmers, John	Bolfracks, Perthshire	1986-88*
Coyne, G. D.	Auchlyne and Suie, Perthshire	1987-94
Crichton, Ian	Ben Alder, Inverness	1992-94
Cumming, S. W.	Mar Lodge, Aberdeen	1987-94
Davidson, J.	Glen Clunie, Aberdeen	1986-91
Davidson, Jimmie	Corndavon, Aberdeen	1993-94
Dempster, A.	Glenfeshie and Killiehuntly, Inverness	1986-94
Dey, George	Kinveachy Inverness	1992
Diviani, Gillian (Mrs G. Mitchell)	Ardtalla (Jura), Argyll	1988-90 1991
Donald Stuart	Glenmoy, Angus	1986-92
Duncan, Gordon	Ardverikie, Inverness	1986-95
Eltringham, Alan	Leckmelm, Ross	1986-94
Elwiss, A.	Benmore (Mull), Argyll	1989-90
Falconer, M.	Glencallater, Aberdeen	1994

Name	Forest	Year
Ferguson, Hamish	Glenogil, Angus	1986-94
Forbes, W.	Mar Lodge, Aberdeen	1986-93
Fraser, David	Killiechonate and Mamore, Inverness	1993-94
Fraser, Donald	Glencannich, Inverness	1988-89
Fraser, E. Lovat	Mar, Aberdeen	1986
Fraser, G.	Erchless, Inverness	1986-95
Fraser, John	Braulen, Inverness	1986-89
Fraser, John	Farley, Braulen, Inverness	1991
Fraser, Peter	Corndavon, Aberdeen	1992
Fraser, Peter	Glen Clunie, Aberdeen	1992
Fraser, Peter	Glencallater, Aberdeen	1993
Fraser, Peter	Invercauld, Aberdeen	1986-95
Frost, T.	Boreland, Perthshire	1989-95
Fyvie, R.	Glencallater, Aberdeen	1986-87
Geddes, Lachlan	Dunbeath, Caithness	1988-95
Gibson, Alistair	Glenfinnan, Inverness	1995
Gill, D.	Corndavon, Aberdeen	1986-91
Gillies, J.	Kinveachy, Inverness	1989-90
Gordon, John	Glencalvie, Ross	1986
Grant, Alistair	Kildonan, Sutherland	1990-95
Grant, Albert	Loch Choire, Sutherland	1986-95
Grant, W. G. G.	Dorback, Inverness	1986
Gunning, James	Benmore (Mull), Argyll	1986-8
Hamilton, Brian	Dorback, Inverness	1987-93
Harris, A. L. B.	Kilchoan, Knoydart, Inverness	1994-95
Harris, Drew	Kilchoan, Knoydart, Inverness	1994-95
Healey, Tim	Glenkinglass	1986-95
	Glenstrae, Argyll	1994-95
Henderson, Adam	Kinloch, Sutherland	1986-95
Hendry, Bruce	Glenshero, Inverness	1995
Hendry, Colin	Strathconon, Ross	1987-91
Hendry, Colin M.	Scardroy, Ross	1993-95
Hendry, Stephen	Glencallater, Aberdeen	1991-92
Hepburn, I.	Dalnessie, Sutherland	1986-91
Hepburn, J.	Glencallater, Aberdeen	1989
Hepburn, R.	Glenshee, Perthshire	1986-93
Hogg, Angus	Remony, Perthshire	1986-95
Holmes, Alan	New Kelso, Ross	1986
Holmes, Alistair	Ben Damph and Torridon, Ross	1986-95
Howe, D.	Glen Clunie, Aberdeen	1993-94
Hughes, Angus	Ben Armine, Sutherland	1987-88
Hunter, A.	Dalness, Argyll	1986-95
Irvine, James	Glenmazeran, Inverness	1991-95
Kennedy, Donald	Conaglen, Argyll	1989-95
Kennedy, John	Dalnaspidal, Perthshire	1986-95

Name	Forest	Year
Kerr, Graham B.	Glenshee, Perthshire	1994-95
Lambie, David	Abernethy, Inverness	1988-94
Lambie, James	Farleyer, Perthshire	1995
Lathom, G.	Rumsdale, Caithness	1993
Law, Frank	Kinveachy, Inverness	1991-94
Lean, J.	Fealar, Perthshire	1972-85
Lippe, D.	W. Monar and Pait, Ross	1986-95
Lloyd, D. A.	Achdalieu, Inverness	1990-95
Logie, A.	Achdalieu, Inverness	1988-89
Logie, J.	Achdalieu, Inverness	1986-87
Logie, J.	Kinlochluichart, Ross	1987-95
Loudon, George	Mamore and Killiechonate, Inverness	1986-95
Lyon, Alastair	Kinveachy, Inverness	1995
MacBain, Bob	Skelpick and Rhifael, Sutherland	1986-95
MacCullough, I.	Glenbruar, Atholl, Perthshire	1987-95
Macdonald, Alex	Achnacarry N., Inverness	1986-95
Macdonald, George A.	Camusericht, Perthshire	1994-95
Macdonald, William	Ardfin (Jura), Argyll	1986-95
McDonald, John	Glenavon, Banff	1986-95
MacDougall, G.	Inverailort, Inverness	1994-95
MacGillivray, Alan	Inverlael, Ross	1994
MacGregor, R.	Forest Lodge, Atholl, Perthshire	1987-91
McIntosh, G.	Glencallater, Angus	1988
McIntyre, Alan	Glenshero, Inverness	1986-94
Mackay, D. G.	Clebrig, Sutherland	1986-87
Mackenzie, A. M.	Strone, Ross	1986-94
Mackenzie, C.	Achnashellach, Ross	1989-95
MacKinnon, D.	Killiechonate, Inverness	1988-90
Maclean, E.	Ederline, Argyll	1986-95
Maclean, R.	Ardgour, Argyll	1988
MacLennan, Billy	Fasnakyle, Inverness	1994-95
MacLennan, Duncan	Affaric West, Inverness	1987
MacLennan, John	Affaric North, Inverness	1986-91
Macleod, G.	Dalnamein, Perthshire	1987-95
McLouchlin, Willie	Glenfinnan, Inverness	1988
McLugash, D.	Knoydart, Inverness	1988
MacNally, Lea	Culachy, Inverness	left 1969
MacNally, Lea	Torridon, Ross	1969-94
MacNally, Michael	Kinlochluichart, Ross	1986
MacNicol, Richard M.	Badanloch, Sutherland	1986-95
MacNicol, Stuart	Balmacaan, Inverness	1986-95
MacPhee, Donald J.	Dunlossit (Islay), Argyll	1990-95
Macrae, Christopher	S. Eishken, Ross-shire	1994-95
Macrae, Donald	Strathmore, Sutherland	1986-92
Macrae, L.	Rhum Island, Inverness	1986

Name	Forest	Year
Macrae, T.	Fairburn and Corriehallie, Ross	1986
Macrae, T. D.	Park (Lewis), Ross	1987-93
Malcolm, Ewen	Kingairloch, Argyll	1991-95
Mason, W.	Lochs, Perthshire	1986-94
Mearns, Alex	Rottall & Glendoll, Angus	1986-95
Meldrum, John	Scardroy, Ross	1986-88
Menzies, Hamish	Blackmount, Argyll	1986-95
Menzies, James	Blackmount, Argyll	retired 1967
Mercer, Jim	Ben Loyal, Sutherland	1986
Mitchell, Mrs	see Diviani, Gillian	
Morrice, Alister	Achnacarry S., Inverness	1986-95
Morrison, A. H.	Rispond, Sutherland	1989-92
Morrison, Duncan	Conaglen, Argyll	1986
Morrison, Ian	Reay, Sutherland	1986-95
Morrison, John	Rispond and Polla, Sutherland	1994
Morrison, J. M.	Kilchoan (Ardnamurchan), Argyll	1989-91
Morrison, J. S.	Lochmore, Sutherland	1994
Morrison, N. A. R.	Knoydart, Inverness	1991-93
Morrison, Neil	Knoydart, Inverness	1994
Morrison, Neil	Coulin, Ross	1995
Munro, Marcus	Alladale and Deanich, Ross	1994-95
Munro, Richard	Alladale and Deanich, Ross	1986-89
Nicol, George	Ballogie, Aberdeen	1995
Nicol, G.	Ardtalla (Jura), Argyll	1986-87
Nisbet, Michael	Glenmoy, Angus	1988-93
Niven, Colin	Glenbanchor, Inverness	1986-95
O'Connel, Peter	Black Corries, Argyll	1986-93
Ogston, J.	Ben Loyal, Sutherland	1987-88
Ogston, J.	Glencallater, Aberdeen	1989
Oswald, G. K.	Ben Alder, Inverness	1986-91
Phister, James	Strathfarrar, Inverness	1995
Pirie, Charlie	Forest Lodge, Atholl, Perthshire	1992-95
Purcell, M.	Achnashellach, Ross	1986-88
Reid, A.	Atholl, Perthshire	1986-90
Reid, A.	West Hand, Atholl, Perthshire	1995
Reid, C.	Clunes, Atholl, Perthshire	1987-95

Name	Forest	Year
Reid, Sandy	West Hand, Atholl, Perthshire	1991-95
Robertson, C.	Abernethy, Inverness	1986
Robertson, Percy	Glenmuick, Aberdeen	1987-88
Robertson, R.	Talladh-a-Bheithe, Perthshire	1986
Rogerson, Andy	Glenkingie, Inverness	1987
Ross, Alan	Sannox (Arran), Bute	1986-95
Ross, Angus	Achentoul, Sutherland	1986-95
Ross, Donald	Ben Armine, Sutherland	1994-95
Ross, John	Kylestrome, Sutherland	1986-95
Ross, Peter	Ben Hee and Corriekinloch, Sutherland	1986
Ross, Ronnie	Forest Farm, Sutherland	1986-87
Ross, T.	Ledgowan, Ross	1986-95
Rowantree, Niall A.	Knoydart, Inverness	1986
Rowantree, Niall A.	Camusrory, Inverness	1987-92
Rowantree, Niall A.	Ardnamurchan, Argyll	1993
Rowantree, Niall A.	Ardnamurchan, Argyll	1994-95
Russell, Andrew	Kildermorie, Ross	1986-94
Sharp, Callum	Ardtalla (Jura), Angus	1992-95
Sharp, D.	Glenisla and Glencally, Angus	1994-95
Shaw, Tommy	Syre and Borgie, Sutherland	1986-87
Shewan, Mr	Fasnakyle, Inverness	1986-92
Sinclair, Rod	Braeroy, Inverness	1989-95
Smart, Ian	Ben Loyal, Sutherland	1989-95
Smart, R.	Inverlael, Ross	1991
Smith, Ian	Dunrobin, Sutherland	1987-92
Smith, Paul	Strathconon, Ross	1992-95
Smith, R.	Caenlochan, Angus	1991-95
Snody, Donald	Corriemulzie, Ross	1986-95
Snody, Donald	Loubcroy and Caplich, Ross	1986-95
Stalker, W. G.	Camusrory, Inverness	1992-95
Stewart, D. M.	Dunlossit (Islay), Argyll	1987-89
Stewart, D.	Dougarie (Arran), Bute	1986-89
Stewart, S.	Coulin, Ross-shire	1986-94
Stoddart, Duncan	Glenfinnan, Inverness	1989-94
Strachan, Mr	Glenspean, Inverness	1986
Sutherland, A.	Langwell, Caithness	1986-87
Sutherland, Alasdair	Strathmore, Sutherland	1994-95
Taylor, A.	Glenmuick, Aberdeen	1989-95
Taylor, Fred	Invermark, Angus	1986-95
Thomson, M.	Kingairloch, Argyll	1988-90
Thornber, Ian	Eignaig, Ardtornish	1987-95
	Glensanda,	1987-95
	Kingairloch, Argyll	1987, 1992, 1995

Name	Forest	Year
Walker, A.	Inverailort, Inverness	1988-89
Walker, A.	Glendessary, Inverness	1990-95
Walker, Sandy	Glenfinnan, Inverness	1986-87
Walker, Mr	Merkland, Sutherland	1990
Watson, Brian	Glencarron, Ross	1986-95
Watson, J.	Glenmazeran, Inverness	1986-90
Wernham, W.	Aberchalder, Inverness	1988
Whelan, David	Balnacoil, Sutherland	1988

Name	Forest	Year
White, J.	Invercassley, Sutherland	1990-95
Wilcock, David	Dougarie (Arran), Bute	1990-95
Wiles, A. Brian	Islay Estate, Argyll	1994-95
Wilkinson, Keith	Fairburn, Ross-shire	1987-95
Wilson, D.	Hunthill, Angus	1986-95
Work, A.	Glenartney, Perthshire	1986-95

*died on hill 13 August 1988

Bibliography

In the following short bibliography only books and articles to which reference has been made in the text are included.

For a more complete Bibliography of books related to deer and stalking, reference should be made to the author's two books:
The Deer Stalking Grounds of Great Britain and Ireland (1960) and *The Whitehead Encyclopedia of Deer* (1993)

Breadalbane, Marchioness of (1935) *The High Tops of Blackmount* (2nd Edn), Edinburgh, Wm Blackwood & Sons

Cameron, A. Gordon (1923) *The Wild Red Deer of Scotland*, London, Wm Blackwood & Sons

Chalmers, Patrick R. (1935) *Deerstalking*, London, Philip Allan

Crealock, Lt.-General H. H. (1892) *Deer stalking in the Highlands of Scotland*, London, Longmans Green & Co.

Darling, F. Fraser (1937) *A Herd of Red Deer*, London, Oxford University Press

Evans, H. (1890) *Some Account of Jura Red Deer*, Derby, Francis Carter (privately printed)

Lincoln, G. and Fletcher, J. (1969-84) 'History of a Hummel in seven episodes', (1969) *Deer*, 1, (p.327); (1970) *Deer*, 2, (p.630); (1973) *Deer*, 3, (p.26); (1976) *Deer*, 3, (pp.552-5); (1977) *Deer*, 4, (pp.86-7); (1978) *Deer*, 4, (pp.274-5); (1984) *Deer*, 6, (pp.127-31)

MacNally, Lea (1993) *Torridon*, Shrewsbury, Swan Hill Press

McConnochie, A. I. (1923) *Deer and Deer Forests of Scotland*, London, H. F. & G. Witherby (1924) *Deerstalking in Scotland*, London, H. F. & G. Witherby

Millais, J. G. (1897) *British Deer and Their Horns*, London, Henry Southern & Co.

Red Deer Commission (R.D.C.) (1961 et seq.) *Annual Reports*, Edinburgh, H.M.S.O.

Scrope, W. (1839) *The Art of Deerstalking* London, John Murray

Whitehead, G. Kenneth (1960) *The Deer Stalking, Grounds of Great Britain and Ireland*, London, Hollis & Carter

(1964a) *Deer Stalking in Scotland*, London, Percival Marshall & Co.

(1964b) *The Deer of Great Britain and Ireland*, London, Routledge & Kegan Paul

(1980) *Hunting and Stalking Deer in Britain Through the Ages*, London, B. T. Batsford

(1986) *Practical Deer Stalking*, London, Constable & Co. (reprinted 1994)

(1972) *The Wild Goats of Great Britain and Ireland*, Newton Abbot, David & Charles.

Annual Reports

The annual reports of the Scottish deer stalking seasons by the author, which have been the basis of information for this book, have appeared in *The Field* (1948-86), the *Shooting Times and Country Magazine* (1958-96) and *Stalking Magazine* (1988-96) as follows:

The Field (1948-83)

Season 1948 *(12 Feb 1949)*	Season 1949 *(25 Feb 1950)*	Season 1950 *24 Feb 1951)*
1951 *(22 Mar 1952)*	1952 *(16 Apr 1953)*	1953 *(8 Apr 1954)*
1954 *(10 Mar 1955)*	1955 *(8 Mar 1956)*	1956 *(7 Feb 1957)*
1957 *(13 Feb 1958)*	1958 *(5 Mar 1959)*	1959 *(31 Mar 1960)*
1960 *(29 Dec 1960)*	1961 *(4 Jan 1962)*	1962 *(21 Feb 1963)*
1963 *(16 Jan 1964)*	1964 *(21 Jan 1965)*	1965 *(24 Feb 1966)*
1966 *(23 Feb 1967)*	1967 *(29 Feb 1968)*	1968 *(20 Feb 1969)*
1969 *(19 Feb 1970)*	1970 *(11 Feb 1971)*	1971 *(17 Feb 1972)*
1972 *(1 Mar 1973)*	1973 *(21 Feb 1974)*	1974 *(27 Feb 1975)*
1975 *(19 Feb 1976)*	1976 *(24 Feb 1977)*	1977 *(19 Jan 1978)*
1978 *(7 Feb 1979)*	1979 *(27 Feb 1980)*	1980 *(4 Feb 1981)*
1981 *(24 Feb 1982)*	1982 *(29 Jan 1983)*	1983 *(21 Jan 1984)*
1984 *(2 Feb 1985)*	1985 *(1 Feb 1986)*	

Shooting Times and Country Magazine (1958-96)

Season 1958 *(10 Apr 1959)*	
1959 (Pt.1 *8 Apr,*	Pt.2 *15 Apr. 1960)*
1960 (Pt.1 *20 Jan,*	Pt.II *27 Jan. 1961)*
1961 (Pt.1 *19 Jan,*	Pt.II *26 Jan. 1962)*
1962 (Pt.1 *15 Feb,*	Pt.II *22 Feb. 1963)*
1963 (Pt.1 *13 Feb,*	Pt.II *20 Feb. 1964)*
1964 (Pt.1 *11 Feb,*	Pt.II *18 Feb. 1965)*
1965 (Pt.1 *17 Feb,*	Pt.II *24 Feb. 1966)*
1966 (Pt.1 *23 Feb,*	Pt.II *11 Mar. 1967)*
1967 *(17 Feb. 1968)*	1968 *(22 Feb. 1969)*
1969 *(21 Feb. 1970)*	1970 *(20 Feb. 1971)*
1971 *(19 Feb. 1972)*	1972 *(3 Mar. 1973)*
1973 *(23 Feb. 1974)*	1974 *(13 Mar. 1975)*
1975 *(19 Feb. 1976)*	1976 *(17 Feb. 1977)*
1977 *(16 Feb. 1978)*	1978 *(15 Feb. 1979)*
1979 *(14 Feb. 1980)*	1980 *(5 Feb. 1981)*
1981 *(28 Feb. 1982)*	1982 *(20 Jan. 1983)*
1983 *(19 Jan. 1984)*	1984 *(24 Jan. 1985)*
1985 *(23 Jan. 1986)*	1986 *(29 Jan. 1987)*
1987 *(4 Feb. 1988)*	1988 *(2 Feb. 1989)*
1989 *(25 Jan. 1990)*	1990 *(24 Jan. 1991)*
1991 *(9 Jan. 1992)*	1992 *(28 Jan. 1993)*
1993 *(10 Feb. 1994)*	1994 *(2 Feb. 1995)*
1995 *(8 Feb. 1996)*	

Stalking Magazine (1987-96)

Season 1987 (*February 1988*)
        1988 (*February 1989*)
        1989 (*February 1990*)
        1990 (*February 1991*)
        1991 (*February 1992*)
        1992 (*February 1993*)
        1993 (*February 1994*)
        1994 (*February 1995*)
        1995 (*February 1996*)

Other articles

The Field

1944 – 'The story of a Hummel' – 12 August
1949 – 'Problems of a Deer Forest' – 23 July
1949 – 'Deer Forest Management' – 10 December
1951 – 'A Law to protect deer' – 8 September
1953 – 'Wild deer in Scotland'
        Part I – Their introduction and position today – 15 January
        Part II – Roe deer – 29 January
        Part III – Sika deer – 12 February
        Part IV – Red deer – 26 February
1954 – 'A Missing Law' – 22 July
1959 – 'Red Deer in Scotland' – 3 December
1964 – 'Three-antlered stags and hummels' – 5 March
1966 – 'Highland Deer out of bounds' – 10 February
1967 – 'Amendments to a Deer Bill' – 23 February
1971 – 'Counting the Red Deer in Scotland' – 16 September
1973 – 'New Factor in the Stalking Season' – 25 October
1974 – 'Tagging of Venison' – 16 May
1974 – 'The Law for a Poacher' – 30 May
1975 – 'Stalking Costs and Rents assessed' – 17 April
1975 – 'Venison Laws and Price' – 8 May
1976 – 'A Hummel, a Switch and a Thrill' – 2 December
1977 – 'Deer poached and a farce to follow' – 15 December
1979 – 'Red deer and the untried trial' – 14 November
1980 – 'Keeping tabs on the deer' – 20 August
1981 – 'Shuffling the stalkers' calendar' – 28 January
1981 – 'Support for Carcase tagging' – 1 April
1981 – 'Due protection for Scotland's Deer' – 17 June
1982 – 'Matters arising on deer – Snags and anomalies in the new laws for Scotland' – 18 August
1987 – 'Special case of woodland deer' – September

The Field Annual

1950 – 'Scotland's Red Deer'

Shooting Times and Country Magazine

1961 – 'The Shooting of Deer' – 26 May
1961 – 'Deer and the Law' – September 15
1962 – 'Deer stalking, prospects for 1962' – 10 August
1964 – 'A good deer deserves a good shot' – 6 August
1965 – 'Red deer Census work' – 12 August
1965 – 'When Red deer seek the low ground' – 19 May
1968 – 'Red deer stalking and the Future' – 27 July
1970 – 'Venison Control' – 31 January
1971 – 'Time for a Close Season' – 14 August
1972 – 'Stalking Perks or Carcase revenue?' – 7 October
1973 – 'Stalking in Britain' – 24 March
1973 – 'Deer stalking in Scotland' – 28 July
1981 – 'The Economics of Deer stalking in Scotland' – 10-16 September
1982 – 'Outstanding Red deer trophy' – 25 February-3 March
1984 – 'Zero that Rifle' – 20-26 September
1985 – 'Two more Galloway Beauties' – 27 December-2 January
1985 – 'Firearms and deer law in Scotland' – 27 June-3 July
1990 – 'The Elusive Hummel' – 10-16 May

Country Life

1946 – 'The Life Cycle of the Red Deer' – Part I – 11 October
1947 – 'The Life Cycle of the Red Deer' – Part II – 24 October

1950 – 'A Close-season for deer?' – 7 April

1952 – 'Deer need a close-season' – 14 March

1952 – 'Deer among trees' – 31 October

1952 – 'Taking Stock of Red deer' – 12 December

1953 – 'Revival of Red Deer in Morayshire' – 23 July

1954 – 'Why no close-season for deer' – 9 December

1961 – 'The Phantom Stag' – 24 August

1961 – 'Scotland's Red Deer Population' – 5 October

1962 – 'Future of Scotlands Wild Red deer' – 23 August

1964 – 'Shortcomings of the Deer Acts' – 26 March

1971 – 'Bambi – the Hind that went stalking' – 6 May

1974 – 'Red Deer at a Premium' – 25 July

Oryx (Journal of the Fauna Preservation Society)

1953 – 'The Problems of a Close-season for Deer' – Vol.2, No.3 – November 1953.

Index of Forests, Shootings and Sheepgrounds

Note: This list includes all properties in which reference has been made in the text. The number in brackets – i.e. Aberarder (In.1) – refers to the forest identification number in Chapter 29 Scottish Stalking Seasons (1959-1995) pages 233-251.

Index of Present or Former Forest Owners, Tenants and Stalking Guests etc. since 1959 mentioned in the text

Note: Dates given refer to the last year in which an annual report was received.

Identification of reference numbers appear in Table B pages 235-251

Column 1 Name of forest owner, tenant or guest.

Column 2 Reference number of forest. Unless stated otherwise, dates given refer to the last year in which a report was received.

When no date appears this will normally indicate that the ownership, in all probability, still remained in 1995

Column 3 Unless stated otherwise, dates given refer to the last year of notified tenancy.

When no dates occur in either columns 2 or 3, the person mentioned in Column 1 has, in all probability, been stalking as a guest on the forest indicated on the relevant page in Column 4.

Note In recent years ownership of an estate may have changed from an individual to a 'trust' or company, although the former owner has often remained as a partner or 'controlling member'.

1	2	3	4
Name	Ref. number of forest presently or formerly owned	Ref. number of forest presently or formerly leased	Page
Abacus Trust	P.11		243
Abel-Smith, Maj.		In.8 (1966), In.38 (1960), In.58 (1967–69), In.59 (1970)	
Abel-Smith, T.	Ar.43 (1963)		238
Abram, H.		Bu.1 (1973), Bu.3 (1973),	184

1	2	3	4
Name	Ref. number of forest presently or formerly owned	Ref. number of forest presently or formerly leased	Page
Abram, H. C.			184
Achentoul Estate Co.	S.1 (1969)		
Adams, B. R.	P.20		244
Agro Investment Overseas Ltd	In.14		240
Airlie, Earl of	An.2, An.5, An.6, An.8, An.13		235, 236
Alcan Highland Estates	In.53, In.62, In.73		241, 242
Alcan Smelting & Power Lochaber Works	In.73		242
Alcock, Ian C. N.	S.42 (1970-75)		179, 209, 250
Alder, Mrs	R.4 (1959)		
Alington, Nigel A.			181
Allan, Andrew			166, 176
Allerton, Lord		P.3 (1965-83)	26, 135, 140
Alvie Estates Ltd	In.8 (1960)		
Amery, C. B.			186
Amory, Sir John Heathcote	P.29 (1972)		244
Ancaster, Earl of		P.28 (1965-71)	
Ancaster, Lord			100
Anne, Duchess d'Uzès			15
Anne, Duchess of Westminster	S.23, S.32		20, 29, 131, 250
Ardtornish Estate Co. Ltd	Ar.10, Ar.25 (1979)		236, 237
Ardverikie Estates Ltd	In.10 (1953)		240
Argyll, Trustees of 10th Duke of	Ar.37		238
Armstrong, Lt-Col. G.		S.31 (1964-66)	
Arnim, Herr Harold von		Bu.1, (1967, 1969-70), Bu.2 (1969), Bu.3 (1966-67),	
Atholl, Duke of	P.1-P.6	P.2 (1970, 1972-73), P.4 (1969-80)	78, 124, 243
Avery, R. Stanton	Ca.3 (1977-93)		239
Avion-holding Spa.	In.41 (1994)		241
Baillie, Hon. Alexander		R.31 (1994)	
Bailey, Capt. E. A. S.		Ar.4 (1968), Ar.38 (1964-68)	173
Baillie, M. E. V. (Lord Burton)	In.26, In.52		32
Baillie Trust	R.31 (1959)		
Bainbridge E. de P.			15
Baird, Col. D. E.			54
Balder, Mrs.		P.31 (1969)	
Balmac Forest Ltd	In.12		240
Bannister Capt. G.		Ar.38 (1962)	
Barbier, Philippe		Ab.6 (1975)	
Barclay-Milne, Col. J.	Ab.4 (1965)		235

1	2	3	4
Name	Ref. number of forest presently or formerly owned	Ref. number of forest presently or formerly leased	Page
Braid Aitken, N. W.	Ar.11 (1968)		139, 236
Branch, A.			185
Brander-Dunbar, Capt. A.			115
Brassey, Hon. P. E.	R.56 (1959-60)		
Braulen Estate	In.16		240
Bray, H. M.		Ar.13 (1960-62)	
Breadalbane, Marquis of			93
Bridgeman, J.			181
British Aluminium Co. Ltd	Ar.17 (1959), In.21 (1959), In.46 (1959), In.62 (1959), In.73 (1959), In.80 (1959)		237, 240 241 242
Broadhead, Miss A.			183
Broadland Properties Ltd	Ar.22 (1963) Ar.19	Ar.19 (1962-1964)	237
Brookfield, J. C.		P.15 (1959)	
Brooks, H. and A.		In.73 (1966-69)	
Brown, Dr C.			183
Brown, I. & H. Ltd	In.47		241
Brundenell, E.		In.69 (1970), R.31 (1965)	
Bryans, D.		R.15 (1979-81)	
Buckle, B. K. D.	In.15		240
Buckle, G. M.	In.15 (1989)		240
Bullard, G. H.			181
Bullock, Mr			127
Burnden Park Investments	R.58		248
Burrell, H.		P.4 (1974-83)	
Burrell, Sir W.		P.4 (1962-65)	
Burrell, Mrs.		P.4 (1970-73)	
Burton, Lord (M. E. V. Baillie)	In.26, In.52	In.52 (1966, 1968-72, 1974, 1976-80), R.11 (1978, 1980), R.31 (1966, 1977, 1979)	61, 63, 110 182, 188 240
Burton Property Trust	In.52, R.11, R.31		241, 246, 247
Calder, J. J.	R.9 (1959)		
Calder, Miss	R.9 (1963)		246
Caldow, David	An.4 (1995)		
Calvert, Maj. E. A.	In.35 (1959)	In.35 (1970-72)	
Cameron, Col. A. E.		In.47 (1961, 1963-65, 1970-71),	
Cameron, Maj. A.		In.47 (1959-60)	181, 185, 186
Cameron, Allan			131
Cameron, D. A. of Lochiel	In.4		239
Cameron, Sir Donald H.	In.4, In.5, In.6, In.43 (1965)		47, 204, 205, 239
Cameron, F. M.			131
Cameron-Rose, Mr			184

1	2	3	4
Name	Ref. number of forest presently or formerly owned	Ref. number of forest presently or formerly leased	Page

1	2	3	4
Name	Ref. number of forest presently or formerly owned	Ref. number of forest presently or formerly leased	Page
Grant, Sir Arthur			116
Grant, Willie			103
Gray, T. D.	R.5		246
Gray & Son			179
Gray-Cheape, Col. L.	In.40 (1964)	In.62 (1963)	241
Green, Miss R. Lycette			
Greenwell, Sir Edward			
Greenwood, Mrs P. A.			250
Gregson, G. G. A.			187
Greig, Mrs D.	R.34 (1963)		
Grey, Capt. E. F.		R.17 (1968), In.55 (1961, 1963)	
Grey, Mrs Diana	R.34 (1961)		247
Griffin, B. V.	R.53 (1986)		248
Griffin, G. N.	R.53 (1986)		248
Griffin, R. M.	R.53 (1986)		248
Grisewood, J. C.	Ar.8, Ar.40		236, 238
Grosvenor, Lady Mary	S.30		81, 174, 223, 228, 250
Grove, Mrs J.	In.35		241
Guernsey, Lord		R.15 (1981)	
Guest, Maj. O. M.			186
Guthrie, F.	Ar.19		237
Guthrie, J. M.	Ar.19 (1959)		
Haes, L. J.		R.16 (1963)	176, 189
Haig, Col. Oliver, Executors of late	Ba.1 (1960)		
Hamiltons of Brodick			92
Hanbury, Col. C. L.			181, 186
Hardwick, V.	Ar.44 (1965)		
Hargreaves, Mrs D. W.	Ca.3 (1967)		
Hart, David		In.68 (1980–81)	
Hart, P.		In.68 (1983)	
Hart, T.		Ca.3 (1976), S.24 (1975)	
Hartley, Capt. John, H. B.		Ca.7 (1960)	
Hartnell, St John			189
Harvie-Watt, Mr			54
Hastings, Duke of Bedford			31, 128, 146, 154, 176
Hay, P. B.			183
Haywood, T. C. S.	In.41 (1959)	In.41 (1965–76), (1978–91)	
Healy, Tim			135
Hely Hutchinson, Hon, D. E.	An.10 (1960)		
Henderson, N. B.		Ab.5 (1965), Ab.6 (1959–74), Ab.11 (1959)	
Henderson, Mr			171
Henkel, Herr Otto		Bu.3 (1965)	

1	2	3	4
Name	Ref. number of forest presently or formerly owned	Ref. number of forest presently or formerly leased	Page
Moncrieff, Lt-Col. D. G.	S.28 (1959)		93
Moncrieff, Miss H.	*see* Gow, Mrs D. J. H.		
Moncrieff, Lt.-Col. J.	S.6 (1989)		
Morell, P.		R.21 (1983, 1986)	
Morgan, S. A. C.			176, 184
Morton, Maj. H. T.	Ba.2 (1968)		14, 238
Mountgarret, Viscount	R.70 (1970)	R.70 (1970-71, 1975-79)	54, 121 186, 189
Mountgarret, Exors of	R.70 (1971-)		
Munro, Jim			130
Munro, Sir Hector			22
Nairn, Michael		P.31 (1965)	
National Trust for Scotland	Ab.11		235
Nature Conservancy	In.79		32, 242
Naylor, C.		In.3 (1990-92)	
Naylor, H.		In.3 (1962, 1964-65)	
Naylor, R. C.			85
Naylor, Mrs T. H.		In.3 (1967-68)	
Nelson, Mrs A. R.	Ar.6 (1963)		236
Nether Pollok Ltd	In.20 (1974)		240
Nicholas, D.	Ar.22 (1963)	Ar.22 (1962)	
Nicholson, Maj. F. D.		In.18 (1967, 1969)	
Nicholson, James			176
Nicholson, Mrs J.	S.14 (1978)		
Nicholson, Capt. Mark	Ab.7 (1959)		
Nicholson, Mrs P.	S.14 (1987)		172, 249
Nicolson, M. M.	Ab.11 (1995)		235
Noble, Maj. C. A. H. M.			190
Noble, John	Ar.5, Ar.30 (1969)		236, 237
Noble, Michael	Ar.5, Ar.30 (1969)		236, 237
Norman, W. R.		Ar.40 (1963)	
Nutting, Sir Anthony	S.1	S.1 (1971)	249
Nutting, Lt.-Col. Sir H.			189
Ogilvy, Lord	An.1		
Ogilvy-Grant, Lady Pauline	In.27	In.27 (1985-89, 1993)	240
Oldham, Capt. R. A.	Ar.20 (1959)		
Onslow, N. Hughes		R.15 (1963)	
Oppenheim, N.	R.53, R.62		246, 248
Ormiston, C.			115, 180
Ormiston, E. C.		In.53 (1968)	
Ormiston, Ewan		In.80 (1965-66)	
Ormiston, J.		In.5 (1961), In.43 (1959, 1961), In.69 (1965), In.77	29

1	2	3	4
Name	Ref. number of forest presently or formerly owned	Ref. number of forest presently or formerly leased	Page
Rawling, Brian			185, 186
Reed, M. R. M.			186
Reid Walker, Capt. C. G.	In.14 (1959), In.17 (1959)		
Reid, Walker	In.14 (1963)		
Reidhaven, Lord			16
Reidhaven, Viscount	In.68		242
Renidl, W.			185
Rhodes, Hon. Mrs			180
Richmond-Watson, R. N.	In.11 (1959)		132, 240
Rickman, G. R.	Ar.26 (1962)		237
Rickman, Mrs M.	Ar.26 (1960)		
Ridley, Lord		P.2 (1963–68, 1970–80), P.3 (1961–64, 1982)	
Riley-Smith, A. W. A.	Ar.3		136
Riley-Smith, F. A.	Ar.3 (1964)		
Ritchie, K.			189
Ritson, Capt.			183
Roadnight, R.		In.15 (1968–73, 1976–77), In.21 (1963)	
Robertson, Miss A. H.		R.11 (1959–75, 1979)	182
Robertson, A. N.			182
Robertson, Miss E.		R.11 (1959–75, 1979)	29, 182, 183, 189
Robinson, J. F.	R.52 (1967)		248
Robson, E. M. W.	In.32		241
Robson, Admiral Sir G.		R.57 (1962–63), S.26 (1965)	
Robson, L. W.	R.36 (1973)		247
Robson, Hon. Maurice	In.32		
Rod & Gun Club		Ar.11 (1959)	
Rootes, Lady	S.25 (1964)		250
Rose, David			130
Rose, Hugh			86
Ross, Alan S.			56
Ross, M. G. A.		In.75 (1964)	
Rotheschild, Mrs			184
Rothwell, Dr W.		R.44 (1960)	
Royal Society for Protection of Birds	In.3		239
Ruggles-Brise, G. E.			22, 29, 132, 156, 183
Ruggles-Brise, J. R.	R.45		247
Russell, Sir John		R.42 (1968)	
Ryall, C.		In.23 (1964–66), P.18 (1962–63)	
Sandeman, T. W.	R.22 (1972)		183, 246
Sanderson, G. B.		In.28 (1961–62, 1966–71)	

1	2	3	4
Name	Ref. number of forest presently or formerly owned	Ref. number of forest presently or formerly leased	Page
Sopper, Miss J.		R.13 (1961, 1963)	
Sorenson, Lasse			183, 186
Southby, Richard			85
Spearman, A. L	P.26		244
Spearman, Sir A.	P.26 (1971)		
Spencer-Loch, Hon.	R.43 (1959)		45, 130, 165
Spencer-Nairn, Angus	In.83 (1971)		
Spencer-Nairn, Sir Douglas	In.24 (1970)		
Spencer-Nairn, F.	In.24 (1994)		103
Spencer-Nairn, M. A.	In.83	In.83 (1970–71), S.1 (1970)	182, 243
St George of Foich, Col. F.	R.67 (1963)		
Stackelberg, Baron	In.32 (1959)		
Sport in Scotland		In.15 (1987)	
Stainton, Hon. J.		R.57 (1960)	
Stevens, J.	An.12		236
Stewart, Col. D.		S.1 (1972–73)	
Stewart, Donald			43
Stewart, J. B.		S.23 (1991–94)	
Stewart, Louis			79
Stewart, P. M.			188
Stewart, T. P.			132
Stirling, Sir John	R.21 (1959)		
Stirling, Roderick, W. K.	R.21		106, 112, 246
Strang-Steel, Maj. F. W.		Ab.11 (1959–69, 1973–77)	88, 181
Strang-Steel, Sir W.			183
Strang-Steel, Lady			181
Strathnaver, Lord		S.4 (1990)	
Stroyan, C. S. R.	R.51, R.54	P.30 (1963–65)	181, 186, 189, 248
Stroyan, Mrs			182, 186
Stroyan, Judge R. A. R.	P.10		133, 243
Stroyan, R. S.			189
Strutt, Arthur	Ar.33 (1959)		
Strutt, Mrs Arthur		Ar.33 (1980)	15, 172
Strutt, Mrs P.		Ar.33 (1987, 1992, 1994), Ar.41 (1989, 1992–94)	185
Strutt, R.			187
Sturgis, Maj. Peter		S.18 (1960)	
Summers, Sir Spencer		P.12 (1964), P.35 (1964)	
Sutherland, Countess of	S.4, S.17, S.18, S.3 (1963)		249
Sutherland, Duke of			181
Svenssen, J.		An.10 (1962, 1965)	130, 181, 187
Sykes, A. W. G.	S.28		141, 188, 250
Sykes, Lady Pauline		In.27 (c.1980–84), In.68 (1977–81)	
Synott, P.		P.3 (1987), P.4 (1987), P.6 (1975–82, 1987),	

1	2	3	4
Name	Ref. number of forest presently or formerly owned	Ref. number of forest presently or formerly leased	Page
Van Beuningen, H. J. E.	R.67 (1991)		81, 248
Van der Straten Waillet, C. E.			126
Van Santen		In.68 (1983-84, 1988)	
Van Veen, B. M. C.	R.56 (1965)		248
Van Veen, G.	R.56 (1961)		248
Veco	In.41		
Verulam, Countess of	R.66 (1994)		248
Vestey, E. H.	S.21 (1971)		180, 249
Vestey, R. A.			154, 181
Vlietman, H.			183
von Clemm, Dr M.			188
Walker, A.		Ar.36 (1970)	
Walker, Howard			102
Walker-Okeover, Sir Ian	Ab.8 (1959-82)		
Walker-Okeover, Sir Peter	Ab.8		27, 192, 235
Wallace, Capt.			183
Wallace, Hamish		R.35 (1963)	183
Wallace, Mr			187
Warde-Aldham, Maj. W.	Ar.24		51, 140, 237
Warren, H. R.		S.3 (1965)	
Warren, M. R.	In.45	R.3 (1967)	131, 241
Wate, Sir C.		S.38	
Watret, I.			177
Watson, Brian			28
Watson, D.		In.6 (1965)	
Watson, Brig. Ian		R.57 (1963)	
Watson, I. S.		In.62 (1962)	
Watt, Michael			188, 189
Welbeck Estate Co. Ltd	Ca.1 (1959-95)		239
West Highlands Woodlands	In.31 (1976)		241
Westminster, Anne, Duchess of	S.23, S.32		
Westminster, 6th Duke of		S.32 (1987, 1990-94)	
Westminster (Liverpool) Trust Co. Ltd	In.28 (1971)		240
Whateley, David			174
Whitaker, Sir J.	P.9		243
Whitbread, H. C.	In.18 (1969)		240, 247
Whitbread, H. W.	R.42 (1979)		
Whitbread, Mrs Helen			27
Whitbread, M.		In.18 (1965, 1968)	
Whitbread, S. C.		In. 12 (1984-93)	

1	2	3	4
Name	Ref. number of forest presently or formerly owned	Ref. number of forest presently or formerly leased	Page
Whitbread, Col. W. H.	In.18 (1964), R.42 (1962), R.46 (1983)		247
Whitehead, G. Kenneth			179, 180, 189
Whitehead, R. B.			152
Whitehead, S. D.		R.36 (1959, 1960)	
Whitelaw, Maj. J.		R.21 (1986), R.28 (1963–65, 1967)	
Whitteridge, Dr S. M.	R.38 (1991)		247
Whyte, Sir Frederick			127
Wigan, Michael	S.11		156, 249
Wigan, Lady	S.11 (1965)		
Wilkie, Col. A. H.			187
Will Woodlands	In.44		
William, Prince, H. R. H. the Duke of Gloucester		In.69 (1965), In.77 (1965)	
Williams, Cdr A. M., C.B.E., D.S.C.	R.66 (1959)		
Williams, Charles	In.13 (1955)		15, 155
Williams, G.		R.40 (1993)	
Williams, Robert	R.65 (1959), R.66 (1963)		182
Williamson, A. F. F.	In.8 (1970)		239
Williamson, Hon. G. H. G.		In.8 (1960–64)	
Willoughby, Baroness	P.28		184, 188, 244
Wills, A. L.			180
Wills, D. S.			183, 190
Wills, Sir Edward	P.12 (1979), P.35 (1979), P.38 (1979)		243, 245
Wills, F. H. P. H.	R.15		
Wills, H. Murray		P.31 (1970)	
Wills, H. T.			31
Wills, I.		In.44 (1988, 1990)	
Wills, Lady Juliet	Ba.1		245
Wills, Lady	Ba.1		155, 182, 238
Wills, Maj. M. T. N. H.	R.2		245
Wills, Sir Seton	Ba.1		135, 184, 238
Wilmott-Sitwell, Maj.		R.44 (1966)	
Wilson, P.		R.9 (1962)	126
Wilson, W. S.	Ar.26 (1962)		237
Wimbourne, Viscount	P.15 (1971)		244
Windley, Sir Edward		R.26 (1967–68)	
Winstanley, J.		R.57 (1960)	
Winton, D. Estates Ltd	P.18 (1963)		244
Wolfkill, G. A.			180
Wood, George			219

1	2	3	4
Name	Ref. number of forest presently or formerly owned	Ref. number of forest presently or formerly leased	Page
Wood, Mrs G.			186
Wood, G. L.			180
Wood, M. and others		Ab.10 (1991)	
Woodhouse, G. W.		R.43 (1972)	
Woods, R. B.	S.34		250
Woolton, Earl of	An.3, An.7, An.9		235, 236
Wooters, Mr		In.68 (1985, 1988)	
Wotherspoon, Ian		In.7 (1970-72, 1975-84)	
Wotherspoon, J. M.	In.7 (1991)		239
Wyfold, Lady	Ar.32 (1959)		
Wyndham-Wright, M.			176, 179
Yeoman, Foster Ltd	Ar.33, Ar.41		
Young, P. D.			189
Younger, Col. Charles			132

Outline Maps Showing Location of Deer Stalking Grounds in Scotland

Estates, numbering 1-553, are listed numerically on each map, and refer to the main stalking grounds located in each county of Scotland. Not all these estates, however, have submitted an annual return, so the identification number of the reporting estate which appears in brackets - i.e. *Glenfeshie* (In.44) - refers to the identification number of *Glenfeshie* which appears in Chapter 29 (page 241). The location of this estate on Map 5 (p.309) is 264.

The shaded areas denote the principal habitat of red deer in the area.

F.C. = Forestry Commission.

MAP 1. Caithness
(page 239)

1(a). Langwell ⎫ Welbeck (Ca.1 & 2)
1(b). Braemore ⎭ Estate
2. Dunbeath (Ca.3)
3. Rumster (F.C.)
4. Dalnawillan

5. Glutt (inc. part Rumsdale) (Ca.4)
6. Lochdhu (inc. part Rumsdale) (Ca.5 & 6)
7. Altnabreac
8. Strathmore

9. Dorrery
10. Shurrery
11. Sandside (Ca.7)

The following estates in Sutherland are adjacent to the Caithness county boundary (Map 2) – page 303.

13. Big House (S.9)
14. Forsinard (S.20)

15. Grimachory
16. Suisgill (S.44)

17. Torrish

MAP 2. Sutherland
(pages 249–251)

12. Bowside
13. Big House (S.9)
14. Forsinard (S.20)
15. Grimachorry and
    Achentoul (S.1)
16. Suisgil (S.44)
17. Torrish
18. Helmsdale
19. Kintradwell (S.29)
20. Gordonbush (S.24)
21. Balnacoil (S.3)
22. Kildonan (S.27)
23. Borrobol (inc. Skinsdale) (S.11)
24. Badanloch (S.2)
25. Rhifael and Garvault (S.39)
26. Strathy (part F.C.)
27. Armadale
28. Skelpick (S.41)
29. Borgie (F.C.) (S.10)
30. Naver (F.C.)
31. Syre (S.45)
32. Ben Klibreck (S.7)

33. Loch Choire (S.31)
34. Ben Armine (S.4)
35. Scriberscross
36. Dalreavoch (S.17)
37. Dunrobin (S.18)
38. Uppat (S.18)
39. Morvich
40. Cambusmore
41. Skibo
42. Rovie
43. Tressady
44. Dalnessie (S.16)
45. Lairg
46. Shinness
47. Fiag (S.35)
48. Mudale (S.35)
49. Ben Loyal (inc. Ribigill) (S.6)
50. Kinloch (inc. Strathmore)
51. Hope (S.28)
52. Durness
53. Eriboll
54. Gobernuisgach (S.6)

55. Ben Hee (S.5)
56. Corriekinloch (S.5)
57(a). Crionach (Achany)
57(b). Sallachy (Achany)
58. Shin (F.C.)
59. Rosehall
60. Glenrossal
61. Invercassley (S.26)
62. Glencassley (S.22)
63. Duchally
64. Benmore Assynt (S.8)
65. Kylestrome (Reay) (S.30)
66. Lochmore (Reay) (S.32)
67. Gualin
68. Keoldale and Balnakill
69. Kinlochbervie
70. Loch Assynt
71. Inchnadamph (S.25)
72. Stronechrubie
73. Glencanisp (S.21)
74. Ledmore
85. Balblair (F.C.) part Ross

The following estates are beyond the Sutherland county boundary in Caithness and Ross-shire respectively:

IN CAITHNESS (Map 1) – page 297
1(a). Langwell ⎤ Welbeck Estate
1(b). Braemore ⎦ (Ca.1 & 2)
 5. Glutt (Ca.4)
 7. Altnabreac
10. Shurrery (Achvorasdale)
11. Sandside (C(a)7)

IN ROSS-SHIRE (Map 3) – page 301
75. Inverpolly (R.39)
76. Drumrunie
80. Loubcroy (R.50)
82. Langwell (Oykell)
83. Inveroykell
84. Braelangwell (R.8)

MAP 2: SUTHERLAND

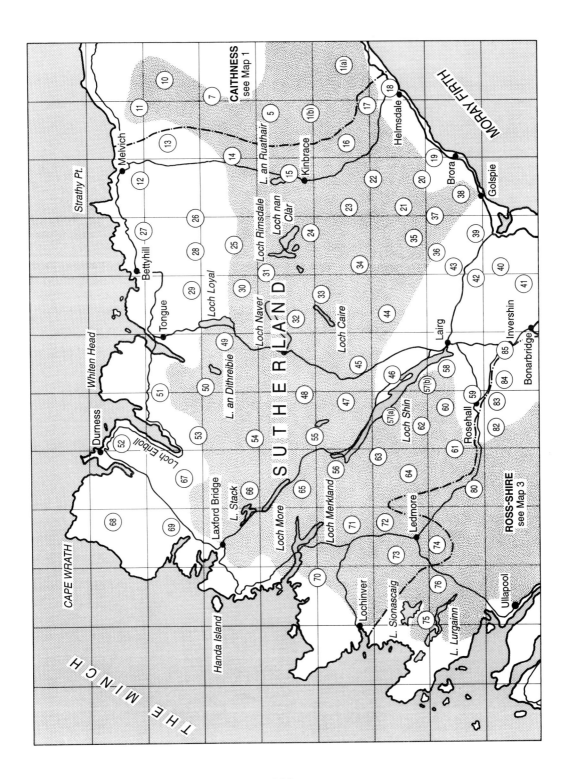

299

MAP 3. Ross-shire (excluding islands)
(pages 245–248)

75. Inverpolly (R.39)
76. Drumrunie
77. Ben More Coigach
78. Rhidorrach (West) (R.57)
79. Rhidorrach (East) (R.56)
80. Loubcroy (R.50)
81. Corriemulzie (R.13)
82. Langwell
83. Inveroykell (part F.C.)
84. Braelangwell (R.8)
85. Balblair (F.C.) (part Sutherland)
86. Craigs (F.C.)
87. Amat (R.4)
88. Alladale (R.3)
89. Glencalvie and (R.29) Dibbiedale (R.18)
90. Kildermorie (R.40)
91. Ardross (F.C.)
92. Novar
93. Kinloch
94. Swordale
95. Tulloch
96. Castle Leod (R.10)
97. Strathgarve
98. Garbat (R.28)
99. Wyvis (R.70)
100. Strathrannoch (R.65)

101. Inchbae (inc. Longart F.C.)
102. Strathvaich (R.66)
103. Deanich (R.16)
104. Braemore (R.9)
105. Lael (F.C.)

106. Inverlael (R.38)
107. Lechmelm (R.44)
108. Feighn (Dundonnell)
109. Strone (Foich) (R.67)
110. Inverbroom (R.36)
111. Dundonnell (Eilean Darach)
112. Dundonnell (Choire Moire)
113. Gruinard (inc. Achneigei) (R.35)
114. Letterewe and Fisherfield (R.46)
115. Inverewe and Kernsary
116. Ardlair
117. Kinlochewe Lodge (R.42)
    (a) Slioch beat
    (b) Glen Docherty and Glen Bruachaig beats
118. Kinlochewe (Incheril)
119. Fannich (R.22)
120. Cabuie (Fannich)
121. Lochrosque
122. Strathbran and Achanalt (R.63)
123. Kinlochluichart (R.43)
124. Corriemoille
125. Torrachilty (F.C.)
126. Coul
127. Little Scatwell
128. Scatwell and Cabaan (R.59)

129. Fairburn (R.21)
130. Corriehallie (R.12)
131. Strathconon (inc. part F.C.) (R.64)
132. Scardroy (Strathconon) (R.58)
133. Ledgowan (R.45)

134. Glencarron (R.30)
135. Coulin (R.15)
136. Beinn Eighe
137. Grudie (R.34)
138. Flowerdale (R.24)
139. Slattadale (F.C.)
140. Shieldaig (R.61)
141. Torridon (R.68)
142. Ben Damph (R.5)
143. Glenshieldaig
144. Hartfield
145. Applecross
146. Couldoran (R.14)
147. N. Strome (F.C.)
148. Tullich
149. New Kelso (R.53)
150. Achnashellach (F.C.) (R.2)
151. Monar (East and West) (R.51)
152. Attadale
153. Pait (inc. Rhiochan) (R.54)
154. Benula (East) (R.6)
155. Monaidh Mhor or Benula (West) (R.7)
156. Glomach (R.33)
157. Killilan (R.33)
158. S. Strome (F.C.)
159. Inverinate (R.37) and Dorisduan (R.7) and (R.19) (inc. part F.C.)
160. Kintail
161. Corrielair (North Cluanie)
162. Cluanie (R.11)
163. Glenshiel (R.31)
164. Ratagan (F.C.) (part Inverness)

The following estates are adjacent to Ross-shire in the counties of Inverness-shire and Sutherland respectively:

IN INVERNESS-SHIRE (Map 5)
(pages 303–305)
192. Eilanreach (In.31)
193. Arnisdale (In.11)
194. Kinloch Hourn (In.60)
195. Glenquoich (In.51)
196. Glenquoich Easter
197. Ardochy
198. Ceannacroc

202. Affric (In.7)
203. Fasnakyle (In.35)
206. Glencannich (In.42)
207. Braulen (In.16)
208. Struy (In.83)
209. Erchless (In.32)
210. Urchany and Farley (In.34)
237. Glaschoille

IN SUTHERLAND (Map 2)
(pages 298–299)
59. Rosehall
60. Glenrossal
61. Invercassley (S.26)
64. Benmore Assynt (S.8)
71. Inchnadamph (S.25)
72. Stronechrubie
73. Glencanisp (S.21)
74. Ledmore

For Ross-shire Islands, see Map 4 (page 303)

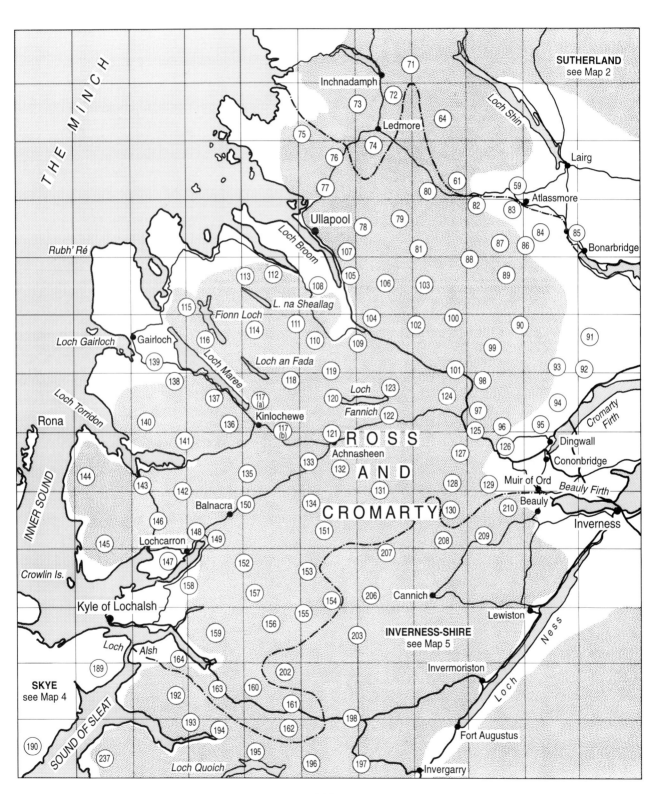

MAP 4. The Islands of Ross-shire and Inverness-shire

ROSS-SHIRE

165. Eishkin (Park), Isle of Lewis (R.20)
166. Soval, Isle of Lewis

167. Grimersta, Isle of Lewis
168. Scaliscro, Isle of Lewis
169. Uig, Isle of Lewis

170. Morsgail, Isle of Lewis (R.52)
171. Aline, Isle of Lewis

INVERNESS-SHIRE

172. Ardvourlie, Isle of North Harris
173. Amhuinnsuidh, Isle of North Harris (In.9)
174. Luskentyre, Isle of South Harris
175. Borve, Is. of Sth. Harris
176. Obbe, Is. of Sth. Harris
177. Rodel, Is. of Sth. Harris
178. Isle of Pabbay

179. Newton, Is. of North Uist
180. Langass and Sponish, Isle of North Uist
181. Isle of Raasay (part F.C.)
182. Isle of Scalpay
183. Skeabost, Isle of Skye
184. Glen Varragill (F.C.), Isle of Skye
185. Sconser (Macdonald's), Isle of Skye

186. Glen Brittle (F.C.), Isle of Skye
187. Strathaird (inc. Camasunary and Coruisk), Isle of Skye (In.82)
188. Strollamus, Isle of Skye
189. Kinloch, Isle of Skye (In.65)
190. Armadale, Isle of Skye
191. Isle of Rhum (In.79)

The following are adjacent to the above islands on the western mainland:

IN ROSS-SHIRE (Map 3) (page 301)
140. Shieldaig
144. Hartfield
145. Applecross
164. Ratagan

IN INVERNESS-SHIRE (Map 5) – (page 305)
192. Eilanreach (part F.C.)
236. Knoydart
237. Glaschoille

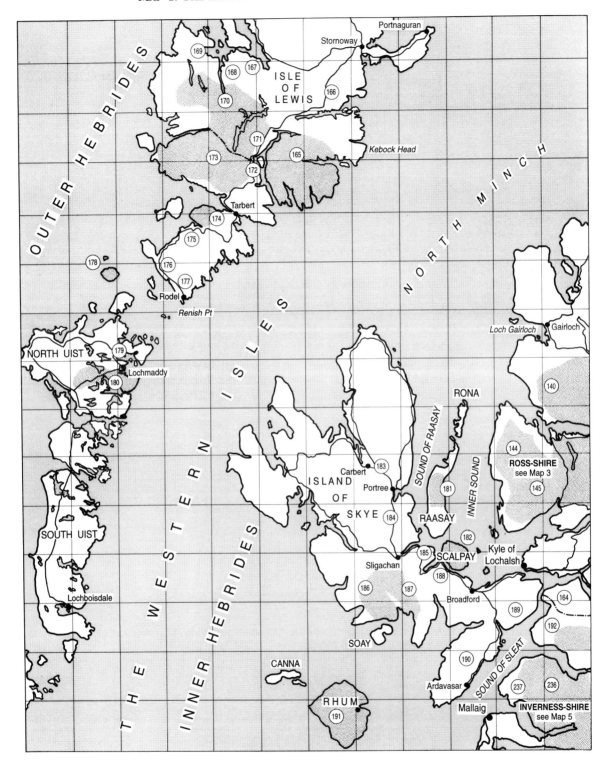

OUTER HEBRIDES

ISLE
OF
LEWIS

Stornoway

Portnaguran

Kebock Head

NORTH MINCH

Tarbert

Rodel

Renish Pt

THE WESTERN ISLES

INNER HEBRIDES

NORTH UIST

Lochmaddy

Loch Gairloch

Gairloch

RONA

SOUND OF RAASAY

INNER SOUND

ROSS-SHIRE
see Map 3

ISLAND
OF
SKYE

Carbert

Portree

RAASAY

SOUTH UIST

Lochboisdale

Sligachan

SCALPAY

Kyle of
Lochalsh

Broadford

SOAY

CANNA

Ardavasar

SOUND OF SLEAT

Mallaig

RHUM

INVERNESS-SHIRE
see Map 5

MAP 5. Inverness-shire (excluding islands)
(pages 239–243)

164. Ratagan (F.C.) part in Ross-shire
192. Eilanreach (part F.C.) (In.31)
193. Arnisdale (In.11)
194. Kinloch Hourn (In.66)
195. Glenquoich (In.51)
196. Glenquoich Easter
197. Ardochy
198. Ceannacroc (part F.C.)
199. Guisachan (Cougie) (part F.C.)
200. Hilton (Guisachan)
201. Knockfin
202. Affric (part F.C.) (In.7)
203. Fasnakyle (In.35)
204. Kerrow
205. Balmore and Craskie
206. Glencannich (or Cozac) (In.42)
207. Braulen (In.16)
208. Struy (In.83)
209. Erchless (In.32)
210. Farley and Urchany (In.34)
211. Beaufort
212. Eskadale (In.33)
213. Aigas (F.C.)
214. Boblainy (F.C.)
215. Dochfour (In.26)
216. Glen Urquhart (F.C.)
217. Buntait
218. Balmacaan (In.12)
219. Corrimony
220. Invermoriston
221. Creagnan Eun (F.C.)
222. Portclair (F.C.)
223. Levishie (In.71)
224. Inverwick
225. Dundreggan (In.30)
226. Inchnacardoch (F.C.)
227. Invergarry North (In.59)
228. Glengarry (F.C.) (In.46)
229. Clunes (F.C.)
230. Garrygualach (Greenfield) (In.39)
231. Achnacarry North (In.5)
232. Achnacarry South (In.6)

233. Glendessary (In.43)
234. Glenkingie (In.47)
235. Barisdale (Barrisdale) (In.13)
236. Knoydart (In.17)
237. Glaschoille
238. North Morar (In.77)
239. Meoble and Lettermorar (In.74)
240. Arisaig
241. Ranachan (In.78)
242. Inverailort (In.57)
243. Roshven
244. Kinlochmoidart
245. Dorlin (In.28)
246. Glenmoidart (In.50)
247. Glenaladale (In.40)
248. Glenfinnan (In.45)
249. Achdaliu (In.4)
250. Torcastle (In.84)
251. Glen Loy (F.C.)
252. Leanachan (F.C.)
253. Nevis (F.C.)
254. Killiechonate (In.62)
255. Glen Righ (F.C.)
256. Mamore (In.73)
257. Inverlair
258. Corrour (In.20)
259. Ben Alder (In.14)
260. Ardverikie (In.10)
261. Drumochter (In.29)
262. Phones
263. Gaick (inc. Glentromie) (In.38)
264. Glenfeshie (In.44)
265. Invereshie (In.58)
266. Inshriach (part F.C.) (In.56)
267. Rothiemurchus
268. Kinrara (In.67)
269. Alvie (In.8)
270. Dunachton
271. Balavil and Chapelpark
272. Pitmain
273. Newtonmore (Glenbanchor) (In.76)
274. Cluny Castle
275. Glentruim

276. Strathmashie (part F.C.)
277. Sherramore (In.80)
278. Glenshero (In.53)
279. Corryarick (In.21)
280. Aberarder (Kingussie) (In.1)
281. Moy (In.75)
282. Glenspean (In.54)
283. South Laggan (F.C.)
284. Braeroy (In.15)
285. Aberchalder (In.2)
286. Culachy (In.23)
287. Ardachie
288. Glendoe (inc. Borlum Grazing)
289. Knockie
290. Dell (In.25)
291. Garrogie
292. Killin
293. Stronelairg
294. Coignafearn (In.18)
295. Corriegarth (In.19)
296. Wester Aberchalder
297. Easter Aberchalder
298. Farigaig (F.C.)
299. Dunmaglass
300. Glenmazeran (In.49)
301. Aberarder (Strathnairn) (In.1)
302. Flichity
303. Farr
304. Aldourie
305. Strathnairn (F.C.)
306. Moy (Daviot) (In.75)
307. Glenkyllachy (In.48)
308. Strathdearn (F.C.)
309. Dalmigavie
310. Kinveachy (In.68)
311. Queen's, or Glen More (F.C.)
312. Abernethy (In.3)
313. Revack and Dorback (Seafield Estate) (In.27)
314. Carrbridge and Muckerach (Seafield Estate)

For Inverness-shire Islands, see Map 4 – page 303

The following estates are adjacent to Inverness-shire:

IN ROSS-SHIRE Map 3 – page 301
128. Scatwell and Cabaan (R.59)
129. Fairburn (R.21)
130. Corriehallie (R.12)
131. Strathconon (R.64)
151. Monar (R.51)
152. Attadale
153. Pait (R.54)
154. Benula (East) (R.6)
155. Monaidh Mhor or Benula (West) (R.7)
156. Glomach (R.33)
159. Inverinate and Dorisduan (R.37)
160. Kintail
161. Corrielair (North Cluanie)

162. Cluanie (R.11)
163. Glenshiel (R.31)
164. Ratagan

IN BANFFSHIRE Map 6 – page 307
321. Inchrory (Bn.1)

IN ABERDEENSHIRE Map 6 – page 307
335. Derry (Mar) (Ab.2)
336. Geldie (Mar.) (Ab.3)

IN PERTHSHIRE Map 7 – page 309
374. West Hand (Atholl) (P.6)
375. Glenbruar (Atholl) (P.5)
377. Dalnamein (Atholl) (P.3)

378. Dalnacardoch (P.19)
379. Dalnaspidal (P.20)
386. Corrievarkie (P.14)
387. Talladh-a-Bheithe (P.44)
388. Camusericht (P.11)
389. Dunan (P.23)

IN ARGYLLSHIRE Map 8 – page 311
450. Sheilbridge (Ar.45)
451. Achnanellan (Sunart)
455. Glenhurich F.C. (Ar.31)
456. Conaglen (Ar.19)
478. Kinlochbeg (Ar.42)
479. Black Corries (Ar.15)

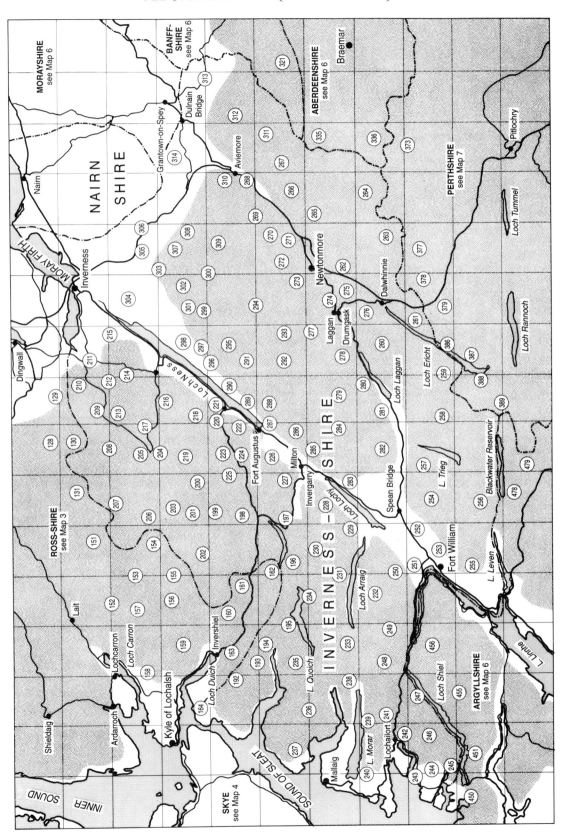

MAP 6. Aberdeenshire, Banffshire, Moray, Angus and Kincardineshire

ABERDEENSHIRE
(page 235)

322. Allargue
323. Glenbuchat (Ab.4)
324. Clova
325. Glenkindie
326. Tornasheen (F.C.)
327. Delnadamph
328. Corndavon (Ab.1)
329. Gairnshiel
330. Morven
331. Monaltrie

332. Micras
333. Invercauld (Ab.10)
334. ⎫
335. ⎬ Mar
336. ⎨ forest
337. ⎭ (Ab.11)
⎧ Home beat
⎨ Derry (Ab.2)
⎩ Geldie (Ab.3)
Glen Ey (Ab.7)
338. Glen Clunie and
       Baddoch (Ab.6)
339. Glencallater (Ab.5)
340(a). Balmoral*

340(b). Balmoral (Balloch-
          buie, or West beat)
340(c). Balmoral (White-
          mounth beat)
341. Spittal (Balmoral)
342. Birkhall (Balmoral)
343. Abergeldie
344. Alltcailleach (F.C.)
345. Glenmuick (Ab.8)
346. Glen Tanar (Ab.9)

* Balmoral forest also includes Bachnagairn (357) in Angus

The following estates are adjacent to Aberdeenshire in the counties of Inverness-shire and Perthshire respectively:

IN INVERNESS-SHIRE (Map 5) – page 305
264. Glenfeshie (In.44)
267. Rothiemurchus

IN PERTHSHIRE (Map 7) – page 309
363. Glenshee (P.33)
364. Rhiedorrach (P.41)
366. Fealar (P.26)

373. Forest Lodge (Atholl) (P.4)
374. West Hand (Atholl) (P.6)

BANFFSHIRE
(page 238)

316. Glenrinnes
317. Glenfiddich (Bn.2)

318. Blackwater
319. Glenlivet (F.C.)

320. Delnabo
321. Inchrory (Glenavon) (Bn.1)

The following estates are adjacent in Inverness-shire (Map 5) – page 305

267. Rothiemurchus
311. Queen's (Glen More)
312. Abernethy (In.3)

MORAYSHIRE

315. Pitgavenny   92

KINCARDINESHIRE

347. Blackhall (F.C.)

348. Glen Dye

349. Drumtochty (F.C.)

ANGUS
(pages 235–236)

350. Gannochy
351. Millden (An.12)
352. Invermark (An.11)
353. Hunthill (An.10)
354. Glenogil (An.7)

355. Rottal (An.13)
356. Clova
357. Bachnagairn*
358. Glendoll (part F.C.) (An.5)
359. Glenprosen (F.C.) (An.8)
   * Part of Balmoral (340)

360. Glenmarkie
361. Glencally (Glenisla) (An.4)
      (F.C.)
362. Caenlochan (Tulchan) (An.1)

The following estate is adjacent to Angus in Perthshire (Map 7) – page 309
363. Glenshee

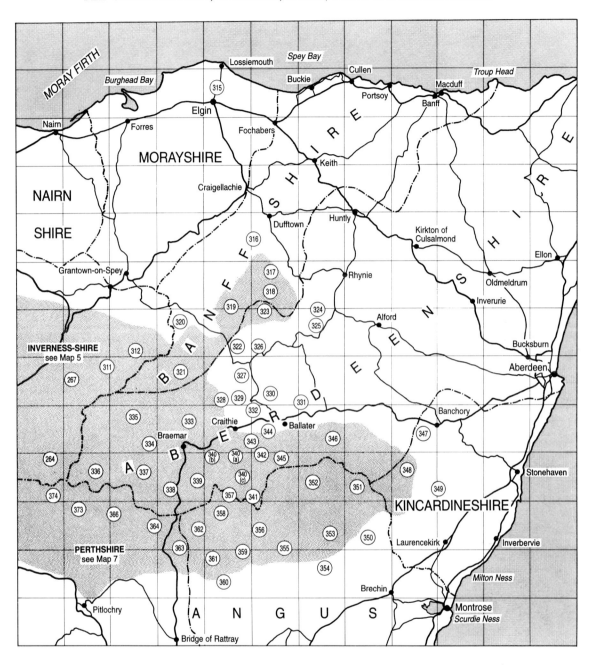

MAP 7. Perthshire, Stirlingshire and Dunbartonshire

PERTHSHIRE
(PAGES 243–245)

363. Glenshee (P.33)
364. Rhiedorrach (P.41)
365. Dalmunzie (Glenlochsie) (P.18)
366. Fealar (P.26)
367. Glenfernate (inc. Glenloch) (P.29)
368. Dirnanean
369. Ashintully
370. Tulliemet
371. Faskally (F.C.)
372. Lude (inc. Loch Vaaligan) (P.37)
373. Forest Lodge (Atholl) (P.4)
374. West Hand (Atholl) (P.6)
375. Glenbruar (Atholl) (P.5)
376. Clunes (Atholl) (P.2)
377. Dalnamein (Atholl) (P.3)
378. Dalnacardoch (inc. Sronphadruig) (P.19)
379. Dalnaspidal (P.20)
380. Auchleeks (P.7)
381. Glen Errochty (F.C.)
382. Allean (F.C.)
383. Loch Tummel
384. Dunalastair (P.22)
385. Craiganour (P.15)
386. Corrievarkie (P.14)
387. Talladh-a-bheithe (P.44)
388. Camuserricht (Rannoch) (P.11)

389. Dunan (P.23)
390. Barracks
391. Upper Finnart
392. Lower Finnart
393. Croscraig
394. Dall (inc. part F.C.) (P.17)
395. Innerhadden
396. West Tempar
397. Killiechassie
398. Moness
399. Dalguise
400. Dunkeld
401. Drumour
402. Kinloch (Amulree)
403. Glenquaich
404. Garrows (inc. Tirchardie and West Shian) (P.27)
405. Auchnafree (P.9)
406. Invergeldie
407. Dundurn
408. Torlum (Glenartney) (P.28)
409. Glenartney (P.28)
410. Ardvorlich
411. Glentarken (Glenartney) (P.28)
412. Graggan
413. Ardtalnaig
414. Remony (P.40)
415. Tombuie (Bolfracks) (P.45)

416. Drummond Hill (F.C.) (P.21)
417. Glenlyon (P.32)
418. Chesthill (P.13)
419. Innerwick and Roro (P.34)
420. Lawers
421. Morenish
422. Boreland (P.10)
423. Meggernie (P.38)
424. Lochs (P.36)
425. Cashlie (P.12)
426. Invermearn (P.35)
427. Glenlochay (P.30)
428. Auchlyne (P.8)
429. Inverhaggernie
430. Tyndrum
431. Cononish
432. Glenfalloch
433. Inverardran
434. Portnellan
435. Benmore
436. Edinchip (P.24)
437. Stronvar
438. Inverlochlarig
439. Loch Katrine
440. Strathyre (F.C.)
441(a). Achray-Loch Ard (F.C.) (See also Loch Ard, Stirling (441(b) and (c))
442. Kinlochard

The following estates are adjacent to Perthshire in the counties of Aberdeenshire, Inverness-shire, Argyllshire and Angus respectively:

IN ABERDEENSHIRE (Map 6) – page 307
336. Geldie (Mar) (Ab.3)
337. Glen Ey (Mar) (Ab.7)
338. Glen Clunie (Ab.6)
339. Glencallater (Ab.5)

IN INVERNESS-SHIRE (Map 5) – page 305
258. Corrour (In.20)
259. Ben Alder (In.14)
261. Drumochter (In.29)
263. Gaick (In.35)
264. Glenfeshie (In.44)

IN ARGYLLSHIRE (Map 8) – page 311
479. Black Corries (Ar.15)
480. Blackmount (Ar.16)
487. Auch (Ar.11)
488. Arrivain
489. Succoth
503. Glenfyne (Ar.30)

IN ANGUS (Map 6) – page 311
362. Caenlochan (Tulchan) (An.1)

441(b) and (c). Loch Ard

446. Ben Vorlich (Loch Sloy)

STIRLINGSHIRE (MAP 7) – page 319
443. Duchary

DUNBARTONSHIRE (MAP 7) – page 319
447. Glen Luss

445. Inversnaid

The following estates are adjacent to Dunbartonshire in Argyllshire (MAP 8) – page 311
503. Glenfyne (Ar.30)
504. Ardkinglas (Ar.5)
505. Ardgartan (F.C.)

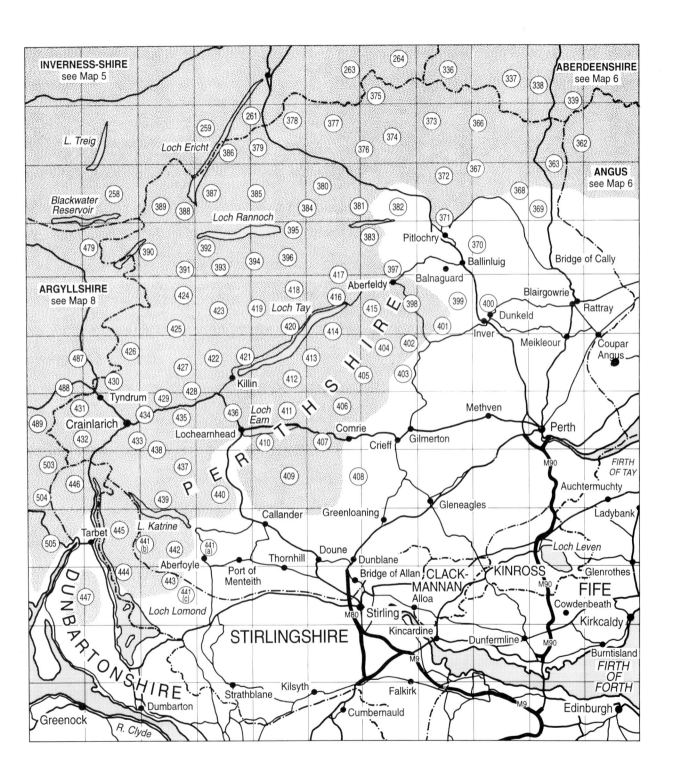

INVERNESS-SHIRE
see Map 5

ABERDEENSHIRE
see Map 6

ANGUS
see Map 6

L. Treig

Loch Ericht

Blackwater
Reservoir

Loch Rannoch

ARGYLLSHIRE
see Map 8

Loch Tay

Pitlochry
Ballinluig
Balnaguard
Aberfeldy

Bridge of Cally

Blairgowrie
Rattray

Dunkeld
Inver
Meikleour
Coupar
Angus

Killin

Methven

Perth

Tyndrum

Crainlarich

Loch
Earn

Comrie

Lochearnhead

Crieff

Gilmerton

M90

FIRTH
OF TAY

Auchtermuchty

Callander

Greenloaning

Gleneagles

Ladybank

Tarbet

L. Katrine

Doune

Loch Leven

Aberfoyle

Thornhill

Dunblane

Glenrothes

Port of
Menteith

Bridge of Allan

CLACK-
MANNAN

KINROSS

FIFE

Loch Lomond

Alloa

Cowdenbeath

M90

Kirkcaldy

STIRLINGSHIRE

M80

Stirling

Kincardine

Dunfermline

Burntisland

M9

FIRTH
OF
FORTH

Kilsyth

Strathblane

Falkirk

DUMBARTON

Cumbernauld

M9

Edinburgh

Greenock

R. Clyde

PERTHSHIRE

DUNBARTONSHIRE

MAP 8. Argyllshire
(pages 236–238)

448. Kilchoan
     (Ardnamurchan) (Ar.40)
449. Glenborrodale and
     Glenmore
     (Ardnamurchan)
450. Shielbridge (inc.
     Laga and Melbuie) (Ar.45)
451. Achnanellan (Sunart)
452. Resipol (Sunart)
453. Bellsgrove (Sunart)
454. Carnoch (Sunart)
455. Glenhurich (F.C.) (Ar.31)
456. Conaglen (inc. Craigag) (Ar.19)
457. Ardgour (Ar.4)
458. Inversanda (Ar.38)
459. Kilmalieu
460. Laudale (Glencripes-
     dale) (Ar.43)
461. Glencripesdale (F.C.)
462. Drimnin
463. Fiunary (F.C.)
464. Ardtornish (Ar.10)
465. Kingairloch and
     Glensanda (Ar.41)
466. Glenduror (F.C.)
467. Achnacone
468. Creran (F.C.)
469. Glenure
470. Druimavuic (Balli-
     veolian) (Ar.22)

471. Barcaldine (F.C.)
472. Inverawe
473. Dail
474. Barrs
475. Glenetive (Ar.29)
476. Strone
477. Dalness (Royal) (Ar.21)
478. Kinlochbeg (and
     Caolasnacoan) (Ar.42)
479. Black Corries (Ar.15)
480. Blackmount (Ar.16)
481. Dalness (Altchaorunn) (Ar.21)
482. Coileitir
483. Kinlochetive
484. Glenkinglass (Ar.32)
485. Glenoe and Inverliever
486. Craig (Ar.20)
487. Auch (Ar.11)
488. Arrivain
489. Succoth
490. Brackley
491. Cladich (inc. Sron Mor)
492. Upper Sonachan
493. Sonachan
494. Inverinan (F.C.)
495. Inverliever (F.C.)
496. Eredine
497. Ederline (Ar.24)
498. Craignure (Inveraray
     Estate)

499. Achnagoul (Inveraray
     Estate) (Ar.37)
500. Inveraray (Ar.37)
501. Accurrach (Inveraray
     Estate) (Ar.1)
502. Benbuy and Kilbaan
     (Inveraray Estate)
503. Glenfyne and Clachan (Ar.30)
504. Ardkinglas (Ar.5)
505. Ardgartan and Ardgoil
     (F.C.)
506. Glenfinart (F.C.)
507. Benmore (F.C.) and
     Inverchapel)
508. Corlarach (F.C.)
509. Lock Eck (F.C.)
510. Glenbranter (F.C.)
511. Strathlachan (F.C.)
512. Glendaruel (F.C.)
513. Minard (F.C.)
514. Lochgair and Asknish
     (F.C.)
515. Kilmartini and
     Kilmichael (F.C.)
516. Kilmory (F.C.)
517. Knapdale (F.C.)
518. Achanaglachach (F.C.)
519. Carse (inc. Airidh) (Ar.18)

ISLE OF MULL

520(a). Aros.
520(b). Ardnacross
521. Torloisk
522. Killiechronan
523. Salen (F.C.)

524. Gruline
525. Glenforsa
526. Tososay (Ar.46)
527. Auchnacraig (Ar.12)
528(a). Lochbuie

528(b). Laggan
529. Kinloch
530. Ben More (Ar.14)
531. Kilfinichen
532. Tiroran

ISLE OF SCARBA

533. Scarba

ISLE OF JURA

534. Ardlussa (inc. Barnhill
     and Kinuachdrach (Ar.6)

535. Tarbert (inc. Coriena-
     heira, Gatehouse and
     Scrinadle)
536. Inver (Ar.36)

537. Forest Lodge (Leargan
     Brach) (Ar.26)
538. Ardfin* and Jura
     House (Ar.3)

ISLE OF SCARBA

539. Dunlossit
540. Islay Estate

541. Proaig
542. Kildalton

543. Laggan
544. Callumkill

The following estates are adjacent to Argyllshire in the counties of Inverness-shire, Perthshire, Dunbartonshire and Buteshire (Isle of Arran):

IN INVERNESS-SHIRE (Map 5) –
page 305
245. Dorlin (In.28)
247. Glenaladale (In.40)
249. Achdalieu (In.4)
256. Mamore (In.73)
258. Corrour (In.20)

IN PERTHSHIRE (Map 7) –
page 309
390. Barracks
424. Lochs (P.36)
425. Cashlie (P.12)
426. Invermearn (P.35)
427. Glenlochay (P.30)
430. Tyndrum
431. Cononish
432. Glenfalloch

IN DUNBARTONSHIRE (Map 7) –
page 309
446. Ben Vorlich
447. Luss

BUTESHIRE (ISLE OF ARRAN) (Map 9)
page 313
545. Dougarie (Bu.2)
546. Brodick (Bu.1)

MAP 8: ARGYLLSHIRE

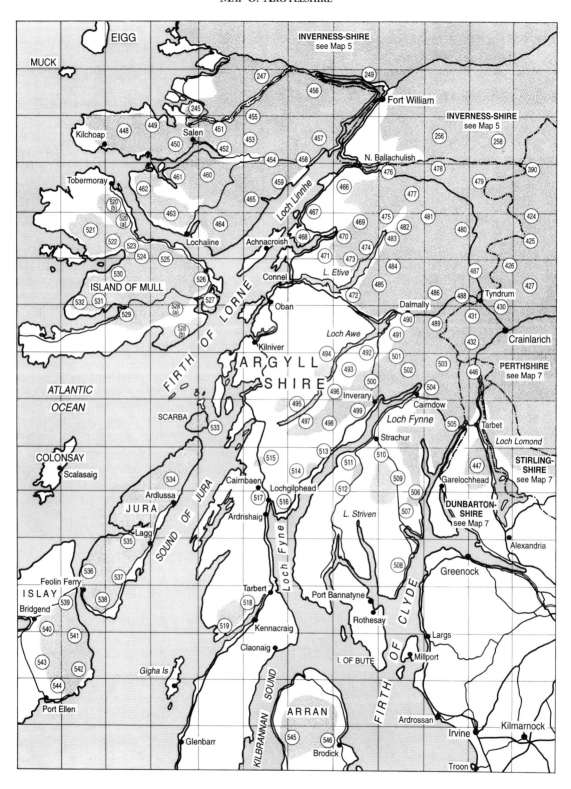

EIGG

MUCK

INVERNESS-SHIRE
see Map 5

247

456

249

Fort William

245

455

INVERNESS-SHIRE
see Map 5

Kilchoap

448

449

451

256

258

Salen

450

452

453

457

N. Ballachulish

454

458

476

478

390

Tobermoray

461

460

459

466

477

479

462

465

467

520
(b)

463

464

468

470

469

475

482

481

480

424

471

473

474

483

425

521

522

523

Lochaline

Achnacroish

L. Etive

484

487

426

524

525

485

486

427

530

526

Connel

472

488

Tyndrum

430

ISLAND OF MULL

Dalmally

532

531

527

489

431

Crainlarich

529

528
(a)

Kilniver

Loch Awe

490

491

432

528
(b)

ARGYLL

494

492

501

502

503

446

PERTHSHIRE
see Map 7

ATLANTIC

SHIRE

493

500

OCEAN

SCARBA

496

Inverary

504

533

495

499

Cairndow

505

Tarbet

COLONSAY

497

498

Loch Fynne

Loch Lomond

Scalasaig

513

Strachur

515

511

510

447

STIRLING-
SHIRE
see Map 7

534

514

509

Garelochhead

JURA

Cairnbaen

506

DUNBARTON-
SHIRE
see Map 7

517

Lochgilphead

512

507

Ardlussa

516

L. Striven

Alexandria

Lagg

535

Ardrishaig

508

Greenock

536

537

Tarbert

Port Bannatyne

ISLAY

538

518

Rothesay

Largs

Feolin Ferry

539

Bridgend

540

541

519

Kennacraig

Millport

543

542

Claonaig

I. OF BUTE

544

Gigha Is

ARRAN

Ardrossan

Kilmarnock

Port Ellen

Glenbarr

545

546

Irvine

Brodick

Troon

311

MAP 9. South-West Scotland (including Arran, Ayrshire and Kirkcudbrightshire)

ISLE OF ARRAN

545. Dougarie
     (Dubhgharadh) (Bu.2)

546. Brodick (Bu.1)

AYRSHIRE

547. Carrick (F.C.)

KIRKCUDBRIGHTSHIRE

548. Garraries (F.C.)
549. Glen Trool (F.C.)
550. Cumloden Park

551. Kirroughtree
552. Cairnsmore and
     Ketterick

553. Cairn Edward (F.C.)

General Index